INTER ALIA

INTER ALIA

by Ernest Kafka

International Psychoanalytic Books (IPBooks)
New York • http://www.IPBooks.net

Published by IPBooks, Queens, NY
Online at: www.IPBooks.net

Copyright © 2020 Ernest Kafka

All rights reserved. This book may not be reproduced, transmitted, or stored, in whole or in part by any means, including graphic, electronic, or mechanical without the express permission of the author and/or publisher, except in the case of brief quotations embodied in critical articles and reviews.

ISBN: 978-1-949093-60-5

CONTENTS

1. **Preface by Arlene Richards** xxi

2. **Introduction** 1
   a. Work and Love; Connection of Personal and Professional Life 1
   b. What is This Thing Called Psychoanalysis: The Easy Part of the Story, How it Evolved, Where I Am Now, Looking to the Near Past 3
   c. Homogenization of Psychiatric Writing; New Interests in Creativity 5
   d. Child Analysis 7
   e. Back to the Personal 8

3. **Childhood—Vienna** 11
   a. Vienna 1932–1938 11
   b. Family—The Family Background I Knew. 1932–1938 13
   c. Memories and Relics of Life in Austria—What I Remember of the Ambiance of My Habitat 17
   d. The Storm—More About the External World 21

v

e. Loss of People, Things, and the German Language When We Emigrated 25
f. International Politics in 1938; End of the Austrian State 26
g. A Few Words About Names 27
h. Our Vienna Apartment and Neighborhood 30
i. Perchtoldsdorf 31
j. Enthusiasms I Shared with My Family 32
k. Importance For Me of My Brother Fritz; Traditional Roles in My Family Structure, My Early and Abiding Resentment About Being Left Out of Things and Uninformed Because I Was "Too Young" 33
l. Wurstelprater and Grottenbahn 34
m. The First Big Trauma; Ether Anaesthesia 35
n. Envy of Fred; My Mother's Bicycle Accident 36
o. Emotions Aroused by Mother's Bicycle Accident 37
p. Psychological Connection Between My Head Injury & My Mother's Bicycle Accident. Reinterpretation of Events and Emotions in Psychoanalytic Hindsight 38
q. Safety; Fight or Flight; Resentment at Being Uninformed About Events, including My Mother's MS. Our Lack of Awareness as a Family About Her Illness 40
r. Again, Uninformed That and How We Were Going to Get Out of Austria. Fear of Being Trapped 42
s. Formation of the Dragon Phobia: Wagner's Siegfried and the Terror and Psychological Realism of Fairy Tales 42

CONTENTS

	t.	Freud's Abandonment of the Seduction Theory and Examination of His Own Dreams, Leading to Recognition of Rivalries 47
	u.	My Nanny: Another Oedipal Story—Betrayal of My Nanny 47
	v.	Discussing Politics in Vienna with My Brother 49
4.	**Emigration** 51	
	a.	Escaping Over the Border to Switzerland Just in Time 51
	b.	Paris, 1938; The Last Sunny Days of Relative Innocence 52
	c.	My Terror at the film *Snow White* in Paris; My Mother's Delight in it... 53
	d.	Paris and Pleasure; Nellie.. 53
	e.	The Day at Royaumont; Mary Wooster..................... 54
	f.	Riding the Tricycle at Royaumont 54
	g.	To the United States.. 58
5.	**New York** 59	
	a.	Arrival in New York, 1938.. 59
	a.	My "Anti-Ehrlich File"; Dislike of the Way He Practiced Medicine 60
	b.	Flushing, then Jackson Heights, Queens 61
	c.	Learning to Swim 62
	d.	Learning English; The Loss and Abiding Resonance of German Words.. 65
	e.	The Onomatopoeic Quality for Me of German Words... 67
	f.	He was Pathetic. He Embarrassed Me......................... 68
	g.	Further Notes on Language 72
	h.	The Unique Timelessness of Music 73

i. Communication Through Words and Non-Verbal Means 74
j. Wienerisch Jokes; Jokes are Funnier to People with Shared Backgrounds 75
k. The Meaning of Names 78
l. Pavlov's Dog; Behavior in Dogs and Humans That Goes Beyond Reflexive 79
m. Family and Other Stories Told to Me Before I Could Read and Write 80
n. Music, My Heart, and Heredity 81
o. Talents and Their Consequences–I Know I Am Talented; Also Greedy for Recognition and Belonging to a Group 82
p. My Tendency to "Digress"; In Fact, I Explore a Subject from Many Angles 84
q. What Makes You American? 85
r. Personal Identity and Governments 85
s. Adapting to America During WWII: My Initiation into a New Tribe at P.S. 149 86
t. My Childhood Strategies for Becoming an American 88
u. Defense Stamps and Victory Gardens 89
v. P.S. 149 and the Pledge of Allegiance Used to Create a Politico-Cultural Community 89
w. The Boon of the Opportunity Class 91
x. P.S. 148: Transfer to "Middle School" 91
y. My Bar Mitzvah 93
z. My Tonsillectomy; Revival of the Adenoidectomy Trauma 94
aa. Newtown High School; Some Things Hadn't Changed 95

	ab.	My Successes at Newtown High School 96
	ac.	My Mother's MS; Her Clinging to Me; Attraction to Girls; My Character 97
	ad.	Writing Reviews for the Newtown X-Ray 98
	ae.	Piano Lessons from Eduard Steuermann; Love of Vladimir Horowitz 98
	af.	My First Jobs 99
	ag.	Mon Amour Lodge 100
	ah.	Learning to Drive; My Father and Harry Freud 101
6.	**College** 103	
	a.	On to Harvard 103
	b.	Continuing Insomnia and Nightmares in the 1950s as a Result of 1938 104
	c.	The Harvard Crimson; My First Roommate at Harvard 104
	d.	Harvard in the 1950s: White and Smart 105
	e.	Demographics of Harvard Again; Encountering Students Better Educated Than I 107
	f.	My Controversial "Squib" 108
	g.	Second Year at Harvard 110
	h.	Social Life: Boston Bohemia 112
	i.	The Haunt of Beacon Hill; Contrast with Harvard ... 113
	j.	Gaynor Bradish and Success in My Major 114
	k.	Harvard Professors—the Study of History 114
	l.	Hyder Rollins; Bartlett Whiting–Literature 117
	m.	Warren Manshel 120
	n.	Revisiting Harvard in 1983 121
7.	**Barbara** 123	
	a.	Barbara's Posterior; First View 123
	b.	Barbara's Right-Left Confusions; My

	Tendency Towards Schiefsehen	124
c.	Her Parents' Apartment	125
d.	Westport, CT Weekend House	126
e.	Three "Jacks" in One Generation of Pesetski Siblings	127
f.	Jack's Success in the Perfume Business	128
g.	Barbara's Thwarted Ambition to Work for Her Father	129
h.	Barbara, a Natural Philanthropist	129
i.	A Memling; Jack and Lillian's Difficult Marriage	130
j.	Jack's Other Daughter, Barbara's Unexpected Half-Sister	131
k.	I Arm Wrestle Jack, and Lose	131
l.	Lillian's Law Career and Barbara's Companionship with Her Father	133
m.	Lillian's Family	134
n.	Jack's and Lillian's Different Sort of Jewishness	134
o.	Lillian's Admiration of Eleanor Roosevelt; Barbara's Ambivalence About Lillian	137
p.	Jewish Jokes Post-Emigration	138
q.	The Influence of German Sentence Structure on How I Write in English	139
r.	Opposites Attract; and Barbara and Jacques Guérin	141
s.	Europe With and Without Barbara; 1953	142
t.	Our Guide's War Stories	144
u.	The Political Acumen and Influence of the Springers During World War II	145
v.	My Competition with Debbie Stern for Barbara's Attention	148

CONTENTS

8. Finishing Up at Harvard 149
    a.   Senior Year at Harvard 149
    b.   Master Gordon Fair and the Crossword Clue 151

9. Medical School 153
    a.   St. Louis 153
    b.   Medical School, Mainly... 157
    c.   Carl V. Moore Radiated Dedication, Simplicity, Focus, and Honesty... 158
    d.   My Fascination with Anatomy Study 160
    e.   Carl and Gerty Cori, Professors of Biochemistry 161
    f.   Evolution of Pharmacology; Study of Physiology 162
    g.   Experiments on Live Animals; Killing Rats 162
    h.   More About What I Learned in Medical School and During My Later, Professional Career: Some Experiences and Some Generalizations 164
    i.   "First, Do No Harm." Sophie's Choices in Medicine.. 164
    j.   Making One Choice Eliminates Other Possibilities 165
    k.   Learning Tact and Kindness Towards Patients; "Medical Student's Disease"...................................... 166
    l.   Learning Patience in Diagnosis................................ 167
    m.   Frightening Medical School Experiences................. 168
    n.   My First Participation in an Autopsy 169
    o.   When Doctors Become Ill 173
    p.   History of My Motivation Toward Medicine............ 173
    q.   Childhood Medical Models 174
    r.   "Bauchreden" with Otto Gersuny; Anger at Incompetent or Dishonest Doctors........................... 175

INTER ALIA

10. Marriage 181
    a. Reuniting with Barbara 181
    b. The Wedding 186
    c. Happiness at the Wedding and Our Getaway Car 187
    d. Our Honeymoon; My Bout with Paratyphoid Fever.. 187
    e. Theft of Barbara's Engagement Ring 189
    f. Eden Roc and Hôtel du Cap d'Antibes 190
    g. Schoenbrunn, Private Theater; Performance of
       The Abduction from the Seraglio 190
    h. Vienna: So Familiar and Yet Very Strange 191
    i. Brigitte de Vallee and Cecil Altman 192
    j. Cecil's Story About His Onkel (Uncle) Fritz 192
    k. Barbara's Minor Car Accident; Gendarmerie
       in Passau 194
    l. Border Crossings Past and Present 195
    m. My Grudges and Guilt: Effect on Relationship
       with Barbara 197
    n. The Hotel Bisson in Paris 197
    o. Gershwin and Other American Composers;
       Visiting Mary Wooster in Paris 198
    p. The Honeymoon Ends–To St. Louis With Barbara.... 200
    q. Barbara's Cognitive Issues, Some Noted by Me;
       Others Not Diagnosed; Jack Taught Barbara to Drive 200
    r. Barbara's Need to Know 202
    s. Barbara's Uninteresting Ph.D. studies at
       Washington University 203
    t. Barbara's Childhood Amid Anti-Semitic
       Social Snobs 206
    u. Married Life in St. Louis: Our Landlords
       and Friends, the Landesmans 208
    v. The Crystal Palace on Olive Street 210

	w.	Chevy, Our Beloved Child Substitute 210
	x.	A History of Our Families' Love and Attitude Towards Dogs 213
	y.	St. Louis: Lessons from A Border City 214
	z.	Early Huge Global Migrations 216
11.	**Back to Medical School** 219	
	a.	Lessons from Hospital Life 219
	b.	Challenges to the Healthy in a Hospital Setting 220
	c.	The Meanings of "Provider" 220
	d.	Confronting and Learning About the Unknown; Health Workers Are Animals Too 222
	e.	Summer Work at NYU Lab with Jerry Lawrence 224
	f.	The Lessons of Queen Square, London: Social Life 225
	g.	Encounter Magazine, Edited by Spender and Kristol 226
	h.	Amusing Acquaintanceship with Elizabeth Hardwick 228
	i.	The Issues that Come with Knowing Powerful and/or Influential People 229
	j.	Queen Square, London (continued); Barbara at Encyclopedia Britannica 229
	k.	My Experience as a Student at Queen Square Was Not as I Had Expected, in Terms of Socializing, Manners, Behavior, or the Professional Approach 230
	l.	My Anger and Disapproval Towards Doctors Who Work Past Their Viable Years 232
	m.	Contrast Between Elkington and Cameron at Queen Square 234

xiii

	n.	Dr. Cameron's Empathy and Humanity Towards a Badly Damaged Patient 235
	o.	Artistry of Simple Procedures at Queen Square 236
	p.	Some Neurology Treatment at Queen Square Taken Over by Surgeons or Internists 236
	q.	After Queen Square: Travels to Austria, Greece 238
	r.	Graduation in St. Louis; My Father's Death 240

12. Return to New York — Internship and Residency 241

	a.	Return to New York; Warren Manshel; Artistic Circles in New York 241
	b.	Thiokol Makes Us Comfortably Well-Off 243
	c.	Warren Founds Foreign Policy 245
	d.	Art is Cool 246
	e.	Friendships with Motherwell, Noland, Kulicke, et al 246
	f.	Henry Geldzahler; Barbara Rose 251
	g.	Stella, Johns, Hockney; Castelli 252
	h.	Henry's Homosexuality; Mark Rothko 253
	i.	Rothko and Jack Get Along Like a House on Fire 254
	j.	Sir Anthony Caro 254
	k.	Leo Lerman, Jacques Guerin, Frank Stella, and Barbara Rose 255
	l.	The Downtown Poker Game 255
	m.	Our House on 92nd Street 257
	n.	Brigitte Altman and Barbara Compete at Cooking 257
	o.	Brigitte's Affair with Bertrand de Saussure and Later with Edward Sniders 296
	p.	Robert Haas; Oenophilia 297

q.	The Commanderie de Bordeaux	298
r.	Tablas Creek	299
s.	Barbara's Career at Conde Nast; Beginning of My Internship at Albert Einstein	300
t.	Life on the Wards	302
u.	My Home and Social Life with Barbara Suffers	304
v.	Perils of the Medical Profession	305
w.	Back to My Internship–The Effect of Chronic and Repetitive Health Problems in Patients	308
x.	Choosing Psychiatry as My Residency	310
y.	My Father–His Death	312
z.	The Moment of Decision: The Man in the Clean, White Coat	313
aa.	Milton Rosenbaum and His Influence at Albert Einstein—The Stagecoach Club. My Introduction to the Mind	316
ab.	My Introduction to Freud as a Resident; Maturation	320
ac.	Freud's Topographic Theory of Thinking	321
ad.	Freud's Later Structural Theory: Id, Ego, Superego	323
ae.	The Metapsychology of Anna Freud and Heinz Hartmann	324
af.	Brenner vs Hartmann	325
ag.	What Happened Next in Analysis—My Time	327
ah.	Mort Reiser During My Residency	330
ai.	The Pötzl Study	330
aj.	Reception of Our Work on the Pötzl Phenomenon	333

13. **Psychoanalysis** 335
    a. Why Psychoanalysis? Back to My Inner World 335

INTER ALIA

- b. The Unconscious Pilot.. 336
- c. My First Analysis: Milt Rosenbaum, Lou Robbins, & Edith Jacobson.. 337
- d. "Shrinkage".. 340
- e. My Second Analysis, With Martin Stein 341
- f. Psychoanalytic Studies and the Birth of Nicole 344
- g. The General Status of Psychoanalysis From 1962 and Later on the Conservative Side; the Confluence of European and American Thought; Development of the DSM 345
- h. Psychoanalysis as Valid Science; The Oedipus Complex 350
- i. More on the Oedipus Complex 351
- j. It's Not All About Me.. 354
- k. The Decision to Turn from Research to Interpersonal Psychiatric and Psychoanalytic Practice 355
- l. Psychoanalytic Training: Féria and Fafner, Among Others Empathy and Chemistry................... 357

14. **Central Europeans** 359
    - a. My Friendship with the Reisers and Its Deeper Implications; Our Shared Love of Wagner 359
    - b. Resemblance of Wotan to Milton Rosenbaum 360
    - c. More on My Central European Legacy and Its Present-Day Resonance... 365
    - d. History of Austria-Hungary...................................... 366
    - e. The Status of Jewish Analyst Emigres in America 367

15. **Adult Life-Passions and Challenges** 369
    - a. The Road Less Traveled? The Work of Writing; the Limits of Knowledge 369

CONTENTS

    b.   Beginning to Win at Poker–on Choice
and Chance 372
    c.   Betting on the Odds of a Winning Hand 372
    d.   1966 and Onward: Practicing Psychoanalysis
and Finding Avocations in the Arts 373
    e.   Psychoanalytic Studies at Aspen: Founders 374
    f.   I Reunite with Sam and Jeaneane and Take
Up Piano Again 376
    g.   Gerard Schwarz; YMHA 376
    h.   The Visual Arts: Forays into Museums 378
    i.   Art Collecting with Barbara 379
    j.   Collecting British Drawings and Watercolors 379
    k.   Photography 381
    l.   The Vermont and Garrison Houses–Vermont 382
    m.   Garrison 384
    n.   Lee Balter 385
    o.   Tom Pritchard 387
    p.   Barbara's freak accident; sale of the house in 2012 390
    q.   Oaxaca and Folk Art 390
    r.   Ongoing Evolution of My Family 395

16.   **Medical Miseries** 397
    a.   Barbara's Health: A Flashback to 1961 397
    b.   My Novel 398
    c.   Paul Desmond; Elaine's in the 1970s 399
    d.   My Heart Problems 401
    e.   Portuguese Water Dog, Stubbs, 1995 401
    f.   New Technology: The Indwelling Defibrillator 402
    g.   My First Episode of Endocarditis, Vermont 403
    h.   Two More Episodes of Endocarditis 404
    i.   Three Episodes of Renal Calculi 405

	j.	Major Depression	408
	k.	Two More Serious Medical Situations	409
	l.	My Strokes and Cardiac Events	413
	m.	The Rarity of Barbara's and My Ailments	414
	n.	My Denial of Illness	416
	o.	My Coma	416
	p.	Disgusting Soft Food; Unable to Speak; Post-Operative, Post-Traumatic State	418
	q.	My Delusional Roommate	419
17.	**Dreams**		421
	a.	Hallucinatory Dreams; Detailed Narratives	421
	b.	Dream of Benjamin Britten	422
	c.	Dream of My Hospital Ship	422
	d.	Railroad Dream	422
	e.	Coherent Plots and Sequences	423
	f.	The Dream-Subject of Captivity	424
	g.	The Purpose of Dreams	424
	h.	Return and Evolution of Post-Traumatic Dreams. Revelation: Intensity of My Irrational Guilt	427
	i.	Santa Claus	428
	j.	I Revisit My Theories About Life	429
18.	**The Beginning of the End**		431
	a.	Barbara's Decline	431
	b.	Barbara's Training Sessions with Susan Mask	433
	c.	Some Jewish Cultural Practices at Our New York Home	433
	d.	Memorial Service	434
	e.	My State of Mind; Barbara's Obituaries Bothered Me	434
	f.	My Anger and PTSD	435

g. June 19th, our 63rd Wedding Anniversary 436

19. **Part II—Further Psychoanalytic Reflections** 437
   a. Subjectivity: The Power of Bedside Manner; Another Example of Subjectivity: Freud's Mythical Analyst, the Objective Man....................... 437
   b. Training in Psychoanalysis... 439
   c. Introducing Transference... 445
   d. What Makes a Good Therapist and Teacher 447
   e. The Modification of Traumatic Effects 449
   f. Strain Trauma 450
   g. Cinematic and Other American Myths About Psychoanalysis; A Paean to Progress 451
   h. Exchange of Ideas and Theories Among Different Schools of Psychoanalytic Thought: A New Flexibility 455
   i. Evolution of Theories of Early Childhood Development From the 1950s to the Present............ 456
   j. How Does Thinking Become More Realistic?............ 461
   k. The Significance of REM Sleep 462
   l. My Writings on the Psychological Effects of Cognitive Weaknesses 463
   m. Aging and Ill Analysts 464
   n. The Freud Archives.. 465
   o. Clubs and Divisions in the Analytic Community...... 466
   p. Consciousness.. 472
   q. More Martin Stein; Unobjectionable Transference 476
   r. My Experiences as Analysand 478
   s. Examination Dreams.. 479
   t. "Honeymoon" Period of Analysis.............................. 481
   u. My Analysis with Edward Kronold 482

	v.	Robi Bak in My Analysis with Ed Kronold 485
	w.	Berta Bornstein and Child Analysis 487
	x.	"Basic Trust" and Evolution....................................... 489
	y.	How Far Can Analysis Take Us?................................ 493
	z.	The Biopsychosocial Approach, Intersubjectivity, and Creativity... 496
20.	**Index** 501

PREFACE BY ARLENE RICHARDS

Another memoir? Not only. Two things are promised the reader: First, a narrative showing how life experiences, connections with family, friendships with specific people, and a series of psychotherapies molded one psychoanalyst's analytic technique and theoretical choices. How his psychoanalytic thought community or collective shapes his thinking. By becoming part of the art world of New York in the 1960s and 70s, he tunes into the crucial problems of the day. By showing himself as brother, son, husband, son-in-law and father, he grounds his experience in his feelings.

Second, by returning recursively to pivotal events that are re-understood—as his experience expands his judgement—he combines his love of art and science to reveal the way a mind is developed and capable of touching the minds of others. Love for his wife, his children, and his patients, in that order, enlarge his capacity for forgiveness. Spiced with the pepper of his wit, enemies are skewered, and the balloon of pomposity is pricked with a long needle.

INTRODUCTION

Work and Love; Connection of Personal and Professional Life

Biography is reportage. The biographer writes about the life of some person. This may be based on personal knowledge and on information from contacts of the deceased, including friends, enemies, relatives, and more distant associates, and on mementoes, writings, published or not, letters and photos, and should be aimed at presenting an accurate, not an imagined, history. The author's purposes may be various: to amuse, teach, eulogize, propagandize or mythologize, but his opinions should be clearly related to facts. The reader should be able to understand what is editorializing and what are data. The connections between the two should be as explicit as possible. An author should be able to contest (prior) conclusions, supply new evidence, and apply new reasoning, just as hard science progresses. In my view, the main intention of biography is to present a "real" life in the "real" world for the pleasure and edification of "real" people.

Richard Henry Dana's *Two Years Before the Mast* is an example of a biography, to stretch the usual meaning of the word a bit, of life on a whaler. Dana, the reporter, is not the subject. The subject is the life of men in the world of the ship in the sea. Dana's genius was to give the reader a feeling of having experienced what it was like to hunt whales, without making himself an important figure in the description.

An autobiographer has himself as his subject. His descriptions and reports are necessarily subjective, as compared with someone like Dana, who probably took the point of view of a news reporter, able to be objective in describing his adventures. His history was based on observations that could have been corroborated for the most part by his sea-mates. Who can corroborate introspections? How can they best be expressed and assessed? Starting in the Romantic period, an interest developed in outing the inner life. Sigmund Freud then invented and developed a technique for working with introspection by concluding that through listening to unedited musings, thoughts, feelings, and memories of one person, another could help him find connections that would have been missed or discarded before as useless. That led to the psychoanalytic approach to the inner life. I am an autobiographer when I write about myself as if I were a long case history. I am able to incorporate my inner as well as my outer world.

As an example of what I mean by inner life, I gradually lost my wife who died, quite demented, after a long illness. I found a way to begin to reconcile myself to the loss by creating an object to relate to, this book. It is certainly a way to keep my sixty-three years with her alive in some sense. It is in large part a product of our lives together and is a tribute to her, even though it is about me. It seems to make my past more real. That part is for me. It may make a contribution to others. That comes from us.

I write, reasoning that, having spent much of my adult life in working together with my own analysts, with patients, with colleagues in discussion groups or privately, as a consultant, on panels at professional meetings, as an editor, a teacher, with students, I ought to share what I gained through it all.

INTRODUCTION

I want to report how I began and evolved into adulthood in interrelationship with people and the larger context of the social conditions as they impinged on me and I on them. I want to include the inner life; after all, I became a psychoanalyst. That means one who works with the hidden: the unconscious desires and the instinctual forces, the "Animal Spirits" and fears, the useful lessons and painful traumas as they influenced the creation of an observable character (by me as well as by other people). There is a fast pace to character formation, mainly up to the age of twenty or thirty, and then a slower time of gradual consolidation and revision. There is much that can be in a life: before birth—the influences of heritage and the early environment; after birth—love, traumas, migration, illnesses, changing physiology, school, choices about the future, and psychological treatments are all contributors. The great excitement occurs in rushes in youth; more sedately later, when revisions come more slowly.

Before going back to my own beginning and my evolution, maturation, and development, I wish to provide a bit of orientation as to what I am thinking as an observer of the profession over the course of the last 60 years, from when I entered medical school in 1954 until now. It should give the reader some explanation of the position from which I proceed in the present. I temporarily ensconce myself in the position of lecturer-historian to invite the reader to join me now as I write of the past from the present.

What is This Thing Called Psychoanalysis: The Easy Part of the Story, How it Evolved, Where I Am Now, Looking to the Near Past

In the nineteen-fifties, the medical model of diagnosis was exemplified by a story about how Dr. Loeb, the professor of medicine at Columbia-Presbyterian Hospital, led rounds. The professor and his entourage of aspirants were at the bedside of a patient. "Well, sir, how are you feeling?" Patient: "Man, I'm jiving!" Loeb: "Hyperthyroid. Next patient." The like is no more.

Now it is tests, rule out this and that, call in the sub-specialist.

In psychiatry, there were high hopes for talk therapy as a way of dealing with what were thought to be psychosomatic illnesses, and with depression and schizophrenia. Now we have come to realize that we need to adopt a more complex physiological as well as psychological orientation. The psychic conflict theory remains important, but the person-to-person therapeutic model is not the only way to think about what we deal with; biology, genetics, and physiology need to be taken into account, to a greater extent than in the forties and fifties, and the interpersonal relationship between doctor and patient is important in general medicine as well. The mind and body are not separate entities. Mentation is physiologic, too. We know so much more—and every discovery raises interesting questions whose answers we have yet to find.

We continue to learn about the placebo effect, suggestion, transference cure, therapeutic alliance, intersubjectivity—whatever the terminology, it all points to one important factor: what the interpersonal relation consists of, that is, the conscious and unconscious, verbal and nonverbal elements, that comprise it. It is a different way of thinking, from the transference/countertransference model (both being mildly pathological), and from the view that change occurs by way of the effects of verbal interpretation largely, or even alone. Besides, it also means that interpersonal factors always need to be considered in relation to teaching, nursing, judging, politicking, and, in general, carrying on domestic and societal life.

During my career, I became much more accustomed to working with people who made parallel use of modern drugs, psychological techniques for dealing with cognitive difficulties, twelve-step programs, exercise regimes, marital therapy, meditation in relation to mental life, and relationships with doctors. The approaches and their impacts usefully entered the analytic session. I ended a long way from the start of my career during my internship. The profession changed markedly in the talking part, in diagnostic approach (e.g., the reclassification of homosexuality as character trait rather than pathology), and in relation to partnership with other contributors, to psychological care (therapists, psychologists, social workers, et al). The pharmacological possibilities that came with the addition of mood stabilizers and SSRIs to the armamentarium, compared to what was available in those days, have made a big difference.

Homogenization of Psychiatric Writing; New Interests in Creativity

Meanwhile, as new approaches to psychotherapeutic possibilities were added, we also experienced losses in the psychoanalytic and psychotherapeutic areas. The literature became more boring. There was a certain homogenization; different schools of thought absorbed the ideas of other schools for themselves, so the differences between Sullivanian and neo-Freudian institutes became less, for instance. Lately, I have heard little about Orgone boxes and the use of mind-expanding drugs as ancillary to psychotherapy, though Jung still survives.

Perhaps studying the more mystical factors, especially in the nonverbal languages of the creative arts and sciences, will become more tempting now that the fears and curiosity about artificial intelligence and potential rivalry with robots have moved from the science-fiction realm to the laboratory and into study groups. Maybe machine-learning will contribute ideas or stimuli for ideas.

Psychoanalysis has become a larger part of the general culture. Even economists, who have been involved with historical and statistical models, have given in to the lure of the psychology of man. That mental problems stem from weak moral standards, laziness, or self-indulgence is a less prevalent view than it was; trauma is treated and viewed differently than it used to be. Hospitals have social workers and psychiatrists who visit post-operative patients, to ensure that these patients know that professionals are available to help those who are interested; schools are more sensitive to cognitive variations in children who might need specialized help. Psychotherapy and psychotherapy-based approaches have become less exotic.

On the other hand, nothing much new has been discovered as far as the psychotherapeutic approach is concerned. The excitement of a once-novel approach has diminished. Nothing as productive of information about the mind has appeared that approaches the power of interpersonal work; but, sadly, nothing has happened to lessen the disadvantages of that interpersonal method. Teaching psychotherapy in academically important medical centers has been recognized as a financial loss-making activity; staffing out-patient clinics for psychotherapy is expensive, and fees are low.

The same is true for private psychoanalysis; it is expensive and takes time. Reforming an already-formed mind goes slowly; I am still working on my own after years of variably halting progress. Insurance companies press for information from therapists and often don't understand privacy standards; difficulties in defining and measuring progress complicate the study of outcomes and cost-benefit valuation. Drug prescribing is encouraged, and often psychotherapy is seen as an alternative when a collaborative partnership seems more appropriate. Support for research and education goes to more fashionable modes of learning about the brain, such as making pictures to show when increased blood circulation and metabolic rates appear in which parts of the brain, which may or may not prove useful. In some areas, post-Freudian ideas have won; they have come to have a good deal of societal influence. On the other hand, the field is seen as passé in many quarters; there are fewer students and they get less support. Some of the fees, particularly for work with children and adolescents, seem onerous, even for prosperous families who pay tens of thousands for their children's educations.

Child Analysis

It is difficult to earn enough to raise a family in the metropolitan areas where there is a sufficiently interested clientele. If fees are too high for parents to pay for their young children while they still are receptive, we have little choice but to do what their parents ask and depend on having adults help orient them regarding health, education, and danger issues. Then, by the time those children have reached adolescence, they are often too inconsistent and obstreperous, as they struggle to separate from their parents, to accept help from adults in general. However, even brief treatment in adolescence can serve as a sample of something they might wish to take on sometime later. The best part of life for making use of prolonged treatment comes when things settle down; but by then minds have become less plastic.

New treatments, especially if they seem easy, simple, and quick to bring results, are enthusiastically oversold. As in politics, persuaders are more successful when the entrenched methods for dealing with a problem have had time to disappoint; this has been the case so far as over-sold psychoanalytic methods are concerned. Usually, bad experiences are remembered, and good experiences forgotten; bad encounters with doctors increase the likelihood of lawsuits and avoidance of future contacts, and they get more publicity than modest good results do. There seems to be little hope for the appearance of sensible, i.e., more modest and realistic, expectations on the parts of both patients and doctors.

We have been through cycles of hopefulness, disappointment, and frustration with schizophrenia, for example, where the hope for the discovery of a single genetic fault—as the pathogenic source of the condition—has dissolved into the conclusion (perhaps temporary) that there are a number of different diseases under the rubric of "schizophrenia," as well as a number of genetic and social factors. Simple solutions of such complicated problems are unlikely to be found; the same goes for cancer, and for social and economic problems as well. Nature does not soothe us with simple answers.

Back to the Personal

It was a long way from my beginning to the present situation. The "Ernest Kafka" person started in the usual way. There were the normal givens of family traditions, expectations, and a family history qua mythology that stretched back several centuries. Tales of past rabbis, teachers, doctors, and merchants (nobody talked of criminals) affect the styles of the caretakers, and, indirectly, the offspring. The direct influences have to do with contacts during development and maturation.

While there are prenatal influences, massive change begins at birth. Suddenly—plash, push, squeeze, shove, and out of the warm bath of the mother's womb—an infant appears in the outer world. The newborn must begin to breathe, though it is unclear how or how much this is experienced. Problems and conflicts then begin to appear. Chomsky deep language is predicated on a maturation which itself requires a caregiver who is just that. Imprinting in a duck and learning to walk in the trot-trot style of a French woman is probably dissimilar.

Now, it seems to me that, from birth on, I have been confronted by unexpected necessities; and I have still scarcely ingested them, let alone digested them. When have I ever had time to catch up with the effects of the most recent challenge, before the next one has overtaken me? Wounds do heal, but they leave scars, even if we often learn something from unpleasant events. It seems to me that birth initiates vast changes:

INTRODUCTION

of language, expression, custom, costume, anatomy, sexuality, and school; analogous to the cosmic process Jacques Monod described in *Chance and Necessity* in 1971, and to Darwin's view of the evolution of living things over eons of time. Chance and necessity were at work, but for the species. Others—from scientists to theologians—hope to find a Grand Universal Theory that might answer all questions and eliminate all uncertainties, that could account for the universe, a project that has already taken thousands of years. What does it all mean? Simply put, we are obviously both products of and subject to nature and nurture. What we know about these at present is perhaps little, but even that may be more than one mind can grasp. How many factors can one juggle at once? As for me, there was no preparation, certainly initially, and to my mind afterwards as well.

CHILDHOOD—VIENNA

Vienna 1932–1938

I was born on December 2, 1932, at the *Allgemeines Krankenhaus* in Vienna. I spent five and one-half years as a small child living in a city that, until fourteen years before my birth, had been the capital of a monarchy, a patched-together country made of disparate parts, the second most populous in Europe, held together by the rule of the Habsburg-Lothringen family for over a thousand years.

My life was profoundly changed in 1938. Kaiser Franz Josef, whose reign began in 1848, had died in 1916. Things in Austria had been in on-and-off states of crisis and near-crisis before and after the defeat of the Central Powers in 1918. Over the ensuing 20 years, conditions only became worse with the eventual progress toward Nazi rule. The old joke rings true: the situation in Germany is significant but not dire. In Austria, the situation is dire, but not significant. For my family and other Jews, the situation was both dire and significant. For me, personally, it was traumatic and fundamentally changed my life.

What occurred took place at a time in my mental development and physical maturation when some significant character organization had taken place. The events of March 1938 changed some things fundamentally, and, to a certain degree, ended my childhood. I was no longer a Viennese Austrian, but a refugee. Being Jewish went from being relatively unimportant in Vienna, to the reason why we came to live in New York. But through all this, one thing stayed the same: I was still a boy, living with my family. My parents tried to speak only English at home, and we all consciously tried to become American; but in some respects, we didn't know how to do this—it was a mistake, for example, for me to go to school carrying a rucksack. This still affects me—who am I, what categories apply to me, what niche do I belong in? Is this determined by other people? Or by my own history and demeanor? In one of Kafka's books, Gregor Samsa woke up one morning and discovered he had been transformed into an insect (*Ungeziefer*).

Everyone acquires one or more identities over the course of a life. One identity involves how you see yourself; others derive from what others see in you, from their own point of view. You are marked by qualities, appearance, and a set of ways of being, that identify you for others, and, to the degree that self-knowledge and memory allow, this forms a sense of self. We all gradually come to distinguish the "what" I am, the "who" I am, and the "who" I wish to become.

Some people become psychoanalysts. Certain of these are people become especially interested in introspection; how their inner lives form in the context of outside events, which may seem to produce a stressful, forced confrontation with unmanageable complexities, and threats to existence. The possibly unanswerable questions—"What happened?" and "How did this disaster come about?" "How could one have dealt with it?" and "How can the power of its effects be comprehended, not to say, understood and integrated into a life?"—become central issues. So does the fact that, with physiological maturation, the biological—what—and the psychological—who—a person is, cannot remain the same, even as they anchor one's view of the world and how it is possible to trust and function therein. Certainly, the confusions and disruptions of my first years stimulated my curiosity to the point of making it a need to understand outer and internal history. How else can one learn to manage an insufficiently reliable interrelationship?

Freud thought that we incorporate aspects of others, of our parents, for example. Perhaps a man shaves in the manner in which he saw his father shave—Freud used an analogy with eating: literally incorporation, a physical, sensory, neither verbal nor conscious act. The interest in how others came to be themselves, and influenced us, and vice versa, requires curiosity and self-discipline. It isn't conscious, but you are selecting and rejecting these influences, and altering them as well. Also, since the psychoanalyst wants to understand his client, but must use his own subjectivity as the instrument of contact with the other person, it is necessary that he have a strong interest in learning about himself. In addition to addressing the usual reasons that people have for seeking treatment (sufferings of various sorts and hopes for improvement by way of inner change), analysts seek to learn about themselves by way of their relationship with the analysand.

Family—The Family Background I Knew. 1932–1938

The family I knew included great-grandparents—Alexander and Clara Hecht, my grandmother (Mami) Stern's parents. Alexander was an engineer and teacher and regarded as something of a wise man among the Austrianized Jews of Vienna. I went on a trip to Europe in 1952. It included Vienna; I had a commission from Mami to go to the *Zentralfriedhof,* the cemetery, to inspect her Hecht parents' grave, and make sure it was well kept. Somehow, throughout the war, Mami had paid the upkeep: the money came by way of automatic deduction from her widow's pension.

I identified the grave, which was in good shape and quite large. I was also commissioned to retrieve a portrait of her father, Alexander Hecht, which had hung at the B'nai B'rith with portraits of all the other General Secretaries of that organization; but I could find neither the building nor the picture. "Opah" (Hecht), my great-grandfather, died in 1934, so I hardly knew him; "Omah," great-grandmother Hecht, died in the early 40s, having survived under Hitler under the protection of Marie Springer, (described below) who presumably paid a ransom, using money from somewhere outside the Reich.

I can hardly remember great-grandfather Hecht. He was a distant figure to me and died when I was not really aware of who or what he was, though I knew he was a person of obvious self-confidence and power. Later, I learned something of his significance in the Viennese-Jewish haute-bourgeoisie. He was for years the general secretary of the B'nai B'rith, the fellowship of the integrated Jews. There Freud played *Tarock* (Tarot) and gave seventeen lectures, including some about his dream theories. There were meetings and discussion groups, socializing and fellowship among the business and professional folk, contacts were formed, and business transacted. Alexander Hecht had the title of *Ingenieur* and was a teacher and a sage in the circle of Baron Gustav von Springer, who was an ennobled Jew of great wealth. Hecht, like Freud, Springer, and other Jews, admired Bismarck and his work in Prussia, where the schools were modernized, universal health insurance was instituted, Jews occupied significant positions in the government, the political role of the Churches was limited, justice was largely just, and the German states unified under the leadership of Prussia. Bismarck left office as chancellor with the accession of Wilhelm II in 1890.

As a philanthropy, Springer supported the Waisenhaus, an orphanage for Jewish boys founded by his father, who already had a German title, "Freiherr." Adolf, my father, lived there from the age of five, following his own father's death, until sometime before age sixteen, when he was conscripted. His mother earned only enough money to run a "notions" shop that supported his crippled elder sister. Hecht was the director of the Waisenhaus, running it for its seventy boys, whose prospects were heightened, not hindered, by their association with it. My father's social status was enhanced by having grown up there, and he impressed Hecht and through him, the B'nai B'rith and Springer, and my mother. My mother and father first met when she and her parents and brother visited her grandparents on weekends, and they became inseparable until my father's death. My father became a banker; Springer and his sole legitimate child, Marie, came to be his clients. The Springers, and my mother's family, were well-established and secure, so I was as well. My maternal grandmother, the Hechts' daughter ("Mami," to me) was married to Gottlieb Stern (Tatti). His father was the only one who never left Bohemia (and the only one who kept kosher).

My mother, ("Hanni"), was born in Vienna on April 18, 1903. She was the second of two children. A brother, Gustav ("Gusti" or "Gustl"), was three years older. The Hechts and the Sterns shared a large house in Perchtoldsdorf, a town at the edge of Vienna that was almost bucolic. My uncle Gusti's family lived nearby. Gusti was an obstetrician. His wife, Lise, had been an actress. They had a daughter, Evie, ten months my junior, who was one of my playmates and best friends. A Gothic-style church, with a fortified separate tower for the protection of the locals during the times of Ottoman invasions, stood nearby. Meadows and hills in the near distance made up the surrounding scene. One could picnic in the meadows, pick wildflowers, and go for hikes on paths through the woods, hunting for mushrooms.

Mami, a graduate of the Vienna Conservatory, was a first-rate pianist who played chamber music with Philharmonic players at home, not in public, and not professionally. Foreign players and conductors, in Vienna for a musical study *stage* (Viennese German was full of French words, e.g., *trottoir, vis à vis*), were sometimes housed with Mami, to benefit from the musical environment. My mother also played the piano; sadly, she lacked her mother's ability.

She practiced every day and did quite well at the Conservatory, but college was out of the question for a girl in her family. She was a mother and housewife who embroidered, cooked, baked, and entertained.

Mami also stayed home, took care of the house, and rescued stray dogs. During World War I, she nursed wounded soldiers and received a personal commendation from the Kaiser. The Kafkas took the two trolleys to Perchtoldsdorf on many weekends, and I was stabled there in the summer months, when my parents and brother Fritz were away on summer vacations. I heard a great deal of music.

Tatti practiced general medicine locally and at the *Allgemeines Krankenhaus* in Vienna. He also served as a doctor in the army, holding the rank of captain. Medical treatment was socialized in Austria at that time, following the Prussian-German example. Tatti was on a government payroll, as well as having private patients. As previously noted, during the entire period of World War II, Mami's widow's pension continued to be deposited into an account she had, until she withdrew the money at the end of the war. I wondered whether the Nazi state kept track of her, knew she was living, and in New York, and would have kept on until she died. Or, had she been sent to a death camp as my father's mother and sister and almost all his Czech relatives were, would it have stopped when she died, or when she arrived at the camp?

On the Kafka side, my grandmother, Sophie Dub, moved from Prague to Vienna with her daughter Camilla (born 1896), where my father was born (1898). His father, Max (born 1866), was never mentioned to me, but his name became my brother's middle name. His first name, Fritz. came from a great uncle, a brother of Omah Hecht. I neither learned who Ernst had been nor why I had no middle name. There was little contact with my grandmother, Sophie, or my aunt,

Camilla, even when I was a child, and I was astonished recently to learn that my father had another, older sister Elsa, unknown to me as well as to him. She died before he was born in Vienna, in Prague.

Memories and Relics of Life in Austria—What I Remember of the Ambiance of My Habitat

My parents had opera, theater, and Philharmonic subscriptions: it was a good, upper bourgeois house. There were pictures on the walls in the Vienna apartment where Fritzl, my eight-year older brother, and I each had our own rooms: a seashore scene by Isabey; an old man selling watermelons, a portrait of Tolstoy, a landscape by Austrian artist Felix Albrecht Harta, and another landscape by Alma Mahler's father, Emil Jakob Schindler. There was a photograph of my father's good friend, Alexander Freud, Sigmund's ten-year younger brother, and some family photographs. There was good contemporary, wood-upholstered furniture, a large Kermanshah rug, some smaller oriental ones, some Biedermeier pieces, Wiener Werkstätte silver, some pretty jewels, good Bohemian glass, and books, which included sets of Schiller, Lessing, Goethe, Heine, and Brehm's *Tierleben*. This last was a set of volumes with drawings and prints of, I was sure, all the animals the world contained, which had been given to my mother by her father or, maybe, her grandfather. Many of those made it to New York with us in 1938. When we emigrated, my mother also brought her Singer sewing machine, Turkish coffee grinder, chess books, recipes from her cooking classes and bakery lessons with Hirtz (a renowned baking savant), Philharmonic programs galore, some pieces of furniture, including the Bleuthner piano, and some silver linens and glassware arrived in New York, as well.

My parents were very attached to each other. They were not shy about kissing and holding hands, but sexual matters were never mentioned nor was gossip favored. They had a good number of friends who were invited for dinner parties. Naturally, I spied on these and tried to overhear the conversations, and I did sometimes understand a joke or a comment about the political situation (generally hazardous); but they seemed never to gossip about divorces, affairs, or scandals.

There were, though rarely, raised eyebrows about Gusti, who apparently had been a bit of a roué. He was supposed to have had an affair with the teen-aged Hedy Kiesler (later Lamarr).

Lise, his wife, came from a prosperous family, but was a bit suspect because she was an actress. Sometimes voices dropped to a whisper. Once I heard "Nellie" followed by whispering, and I later innocently asked, "Who is Nellie?" and got the fascinating answer, "A friend of your mother." (I later learned that she had run away scandalously with a man to Paris.) Nudity was mostly banned; "mostly," because at Gusti's house around the swimming pool, my cousin and I were usually nude, in the then modern way. My mother might wear low-cut blouses, but she always covered her cleavage with a piece of cloth or lace. A *Dirndl* was as close as she got to bare skin. It hinted at her shape. Her hair was always rolled up as quickly as possible after she washed it.

A door-to-door salesperson once rang the bell in Jackson Heights and offered to sell sanitary napkins to my mother; she was genuinely embarrassed and shocked. I was mystified. Especially as, because she suffered greatly from the humid New York summer heat, she walked about the house undressed except for a bra and a kerchief hanging over her pudendum, while wiping the perspiration away from her face.

My parents had grown up and lived in a political and social world that was the wider context in which their characters were formed. That had changed mightily by the time I was born. For one thing, they had experienced the 1914–1918 war. This left dark shadows I felt but could not fully comprehend.

Tati's brother, my grand uncle Rudolf, who lived in Vienna, came to visit, was playful with me, remembered my birthdays, and gave good presents. He was important to me. He was also associated with shadows. He had two children with his wife, Adi. The first was a son, Robert, whom I never met, and about whom I knew only that he had emigrated, married, and never returned. The younger, Ani, was about the same age as my mother. The two were good childhood friends, but Ani went to Sweden to escape the food shortages and other difficulties during the First World War, returning afterwards. These presented examples of gloomy possibilities. So did the stories of great-uncle Fritz, Oma's brother, whose exploits brought anti-Semitism to my awareness. He had been a hero, a captain in the army, in charge of a division of observation balloons, sometimes going up in the air to look down at enemy activity. He died in 1914 because he had one too many duels with anti-Semitic fellow officers and, as a consequence, was reassigned from a relatively safe command job to the front lines and, promptly thereafter, killed. There was plenty of scariness in the atmosphere. At the same time, the stories of Fritz were stirring for a little boy: flying balloons, duels, medals. Unfortunate to be killed, of course, but he might have been more careful. You only had to look at the photo—Fritz in army uniform, Gottlieb in soft hat and cape, Hanni as a five-year-old (just about my own age then), and Gusti, all standing on a cliff, with the spray of the sea flying from below, in Heeringsdorf on the North Sea. As I write, I am still amazed that what happened later—so unsuspectedly, so "you could have knocked me over with a feather," so sudden, so disastrous—could have been, retrospectively, so clearly possible. But life was so normal for me as a child, so pleasant, so welcoming, that I was utterly unprepared.

When Adi and Ani escaped to Stockholm it was painful for my mother. It also hurt me. I saw the two women only once more, on a visit to Sweden, where I accompanied my mother in 1961 or 1962, and we had a reunion in Salsjöbaden. For me, the central group was my mother's side of the family, the Perchtoldsdorf people. Lost to me were my favorite great-uncle, Rudolf, Tatti, and my only cousin (and first infatuation), Evi.

My father's mother and sister died in camps; my grandfather, Tatti, and great-grandmother, Clara, died natural deaths. My great-grandfather Hecht died in 1934, and my uncle Gusti's family vanished to Palestine while we moved to New York.

A note about my maternal great-uncle Emile (Gottlieb's brother), another 1914–1918 war related story. He was a Francophile who moved to Paris before 1914. He married twice—both women were Catholic Bretons. He had no children. He became more French than the French, including changing the spelling of his name to Emile. After the First World War, he contracted an illness and briefly became Austrian again. He cabled his brother, Gottlieb, and pleaded for him to come help him, as he didn't trust French doctors. Good Samaritan, brother, and doctor that he was, Gottlieb rushed to Paris, and knocked at Emil-Emile's door. When Emile opened the door, however, he took one look at his brother, shouted "*Va t'en, sâle Boche,*" and threw a dish at him. Evidently, the crisis had passed. They made up later. In 1952, Emile having died, I went to meet his widow. When she opened the door, she looked at me, threw her arms around me tearfully, and said, "*C'est Gottlieb!*" Naturally, I thought she was a fine woman. Gottlieb, Alexander, and my father were the great men in the family.

That, then, was the family ambience in which I lived until August 1938. There were a few other people I remember from that time. The barber who cut my hair was a friend, and so was a tailor who made a fine blue suit with short trousers for me. There was Terci Tzappert, whose prekindergarten I attended. I learned to play, to dance the waltz, and how to make a valentine for my mother. The heart-shaped card featured a compartment hidden by cutout folding doors which, when opened, revealed a photo of me, aged five, smiling happily, surrounded by squares of pasted-on colored paper. It expressed my love for my mother nicely, and hers for me, as she kept it for the rest of her life, in a box along with various awards and medals I later received—a Latin prize, my drama-group pin, and other relics, such as all my report cards.

Anyone I know now, shown that memento photo of me when I was with Terci Tzappert, would ask who is pictured, because only those who have known me continuously would know who that child was. People enjoy looking at baby pictures and speculating about which parent the subject favors. Only I, my brother, and Evi, the cousin who knew me before 1938, can recognize the subject of the photograph. We keep such things to remember ourselves as we were—the same impulse that leads us to write memoirs.

The Storm—More About the External World

On March 12, 1938, the Nazi invasion of Austria brought storm troopers, tanks, warplanes, the Gestapo, and Hitler himself to Vienna. Within weeks, thousands of the Austrian elite—professors, financiers, politicians, judges, unionists, journalists, and even Kurt von Schuschnigg, the Catholic nationalist right-wing Chancellor of Austria—were under arrest in a camp near Dachau. My father was among those picked up by the Gestapo in this early period of the *Anschluss*—the "attachment." One morning as he was crossing the Schottenring after eating his breakfast at Number 17, where my family lived, on his way to his office in the Börse, he, his newspaper, and his briefcase were put into a car. En route to the Imperial Hotel, where the Gestapo made its headquarters, he read that an employee of his at the bank which he and his partner, Adolf Weiss, Jr., owned had been made the economic chief of the new "Austrian Gau" of Germany.

On arrival at the Imperial, he was allowed a phone call, and so he called his office and spoke to his employee, telling the man that he had been arrested. "Oh, Adolf, don't worry, let me talk to someone in charge," said the staff member, in a tone reminding my father that the two had always taken to each other. "They'll let you go, come to the office, and I'll explain the whole thing." So, my father returned to his office and heard the explanation.

The fellow had only pretended to be taking time off around Christmas, rather than in the usual hot Vienna August. To arrange this departure from custom, he had claimed that Christmas was the sole time when he and his family could be together, because that was when school let out. In fact, during these holidays, he and his cohort of fellow secret Nazis were being tutored about the jobs they were destined to fill after the Anschluss that Hitler had been planning for years. This training had begun even before Hitler achieved power. Meanwhile, France was building the futile Maginot Line, which ended at the Belgian border, through which the Germans had invaded France in the war which began in 1914, and the route they were shortly to take again. The rest of Europe was passive.

Other aspects of the events of March 1938 remained unknown to me until years later. My father died in 1959, at the age of sixty. He had been able to amass enough money to allow my then wheelchair-bound mother, and a companion, to live reasonably comfortably in a Forest Hills two-bedroom apartment, until her own death fifteen years later. I had been resentful of my father throughout my adolescence and remained angry about what I deemed his feeble judgment—staying in Austria, despite all the information that was available about Hitler's treatment of the Jews in Germany and the Führer's rants about purifying Europe by eliminating the Jews. Not only had my father been incomprehensibly feckless; he was also unacceptably reticent. He shared little that was of importance with me—not his experience in World War I, not his thoughts and experiences after World War I, not even his attitude about my mother's multiple sclerosis. I had no information about what had moved, wounded, or emotionally affected my father.

When, in 1967, my wife, Barbara, gave a party for my mother's seventieth birthday, people from my Austrian period came, some of whom I knew, and some not. One, whom I met for the first time, was the son of Mr. Steinitz, who had been my father's partner in the bank. His father and mine had bought the name of a defunct banking company and built it back up to become a small private bank. I asked Steinitz, Jr., to sit next to me on a couch, and asked him about what he knew of the events of 1938. Why had his father sent him, his sister, and his mother out of Austria and stayed behind himself to face the hazards of the time, with the result that he disappeared and was presumed to have lost his life in a death camp? Why had my family remained until August, by which time the Nazis had managed to expropriate the family property? Our apartment and my grandfather's house in Perchtoldsdorf were "Aryanized," which meant forced sales to Aryans in which "transference," "license" charges, and legal fees ate up all the money. My brother, Fritz, and all the other Jewish boys at his Gymnasium were transferred to an inferior school in a nasty neighborhood. Jews were expelled from their teaching jobs and professions and humiliated and arrested. Bank Adolf Weiss, Jr., was closed.

At my mother's birthday party, Steinitz answered my question: "It was relatively straightforward. The Östereichische Credit-Anstalt failed in 1931, largely due to the worldwide depression. In 1934, Engelbert Dollfuss, the Nationalist-Royalist-Catholic-Conservative Chancellor, nationalized the banks. The government then made stiff regulations for banks, particularly with regard to foreign exchange arrangements. Only two Jewish banks had the right to do such deals, and, for whatever reason, Adolf Weiss, Jr. was one of them. In any event, Austria needed access to foreign currencies, as other countries and travelers needed Austrian schillings to be able to trade with Austria.

Steinitz continued, "When the Nazis took over in Austria, they were prepared to take over the Adolf Weiss, Jr. bank and the accounts. Our fathers must have had negotiations with the Nazis, probably to bring money in foreign accounts into Austria, in exchange for permitting the account owners to exit. It was a time when the Nazis were chiefly interested in stealing the Jews' assets, and getting rid of the Jews. That meant survival for those with money outside the country, and somewhere to go. The problem was that each of our fathers was taking care of his own clients, and your father finished with his people, before my father finished with his."

Had I known about the *Sophie's Choice* situation, I should have been a more serene and wiser person. My father had been exporting what money he could on behalf of his clients, not on his own behalf. Had my father trusted me to understand a bit more about the situation, I might have been better disposed toward him. (On the other hand, I might well have found some other justification for my hostility towards my father.) As it was, I lived in ignorance and suffered unnecessary antipathy to my father for many years, during which we two hardly had intimate contact.

The period between March 12th and the beginning of August 1938 left few memories. I visited the barber I had known for the whole of my young life for the last time. We said goodbye, and he gave me a comb to remember him by. I cried. My pre-kindergarten stopped, though I don't know whether the teacher/proprietor closed it down, or my parents removed me.

Walks with my tricycle ended. The maid vanished. Among my family, Lise, Gusti, and cousin Evi arranged to go to Palestine, presumably as more than ordinary refugees, since grandfather ("Tatti") had been a lifelong Zionist and friend of Herzl, and had his name inscribed in the Golden Book of Founders of Zionism. Lise's parents managed to get some money out, perhaps via my father, and transited to Hampstead, taking with them a few Kandinsky paintings and Riemenschneider carvings. My mother's cousin, Ani, went back to Stockholm with her parents, my mother's uncle Rudolf, and aunt Adi Stern. Ani's brother, cousin Robert, had married an English Lever Brothers relative, and they lived in Westport, Connecticut, mysteriously incommunicado. My grandmother Mami and grandfather Tatti stayed in Vienna, under the protection of an Austrian aristocrat married to a British aristocrat, Mary (Springer) Wooster, until Tatti died; and then my grandmother made the long trip across Siberia, Japan, the Pacific, and North America to New York.

Loss of People, Things, and the German Language When We Emigrated

I lost many people and many things. I lost the *Maronibrater*, the chestnut roaster, on the corner, and the *Schinkensemmel*, the ham roll, from another vendor. I lost the aroma of wet horse-chestnut trees along the streets in spring. I lost my tricycle, the pictures on the wall of my bedroom, and I lost the German language, with its *Wienerisch* jokes and word-play. I lost the meadow and the walks in Perchtoldsdorf. I lost my times with Fritz who, in Jackson Heights, would soon be too grown up to spend much time with me. He discovered girls, summer jobs, and, eventually, college, the army, and marriage. My father was off working, and I was now my mother's helper and companion.

I did not know how much I missed some things. Years later, soaking in the bathtub, and nursing a bad depression (supported tremendously by my wife, Barbara), I suddenly burst into tears with memories of my lost family, uncle Rudolf, aunt Adi, Evi, and the coal-fired toy train and swimming pool at Gusti's. Most of all I cried for the loss of Tatti, which was a great revelation to me. My grief made me feel more human, though less brave. It diminished my fear that I might be one of those persons who had little concern or affection for others.

My psychoanalytic experience, as patient and as professional, had helped by that time. Of course, whatever post-traumatic healing took place happened later than 1938. It was my fate to live a choppy, interrupted, distorted childhood, which never really became part of the gradual, general transformation which normally proceeds during early life. However, eventually, my self-protective distance from other people abated.

International Politics in 1938; End of the Austrian State

In 1938, the European international political arena included four totalitarian dictators, of whom three, Hitler, Stalin, and Mussolini presented a similar foreign policy. While Franco seems to have been content with ruling Spain and Yugoslavia, the policy of the others consisted of national aggrandizement by means of war—looting of victims' lands, properties and resources; enslavement, resettlement, or elimination of the victim populations; colonization of the newly won lands; and rule by the dictators. At that time, this was all Europeans knew. We were not paying much attention to what was taking place in North America, most of Africa or Asia, including to Hirohito, Chiang Kai-shek, and Gandhi, or the Dutch, French, Belgian, and Portuguese colonies.

The worldwide political storm generated by these dictators blew away what was merely a pause in a continuing world war, which had been interrupted by the Armistice of 1918, followed by the Treaty of Versailles, that ended the German, Austro-Hungarian, and Ottoman Empires. It ushered in a mass of chaos and misery for the losers and their colonies. It did not address the problems of the Levant. The Russian Empire had already disappeared, eliminated by revolution and civil war, leaving behind the Soviet empire of the proletariat and its dictator, Stalin.

Thus ended the Habsburg Austrian state. And with it ended a hundred years-plus of Kafkas, Sterns, Hechts, Taubers, Dubs, Stadlers and their colleagues, their relatives and friends, and their accomplishments, in Austro-Hungary. Their disappearance left tombs in the Jewish section of the *Zentralfriedhof* of Vienna, some stones in the Jewish cemetery of Prague, records of marriages, births, and deaths in the storage rooms at the *Israelitisches Kultusgemeinde* and the death records and remains of relatives from Bohemia, Prague, and Vienna who died at Theresienstadt.

And so, we left Austria. I, aged five years and eight months, was told nothing about what the future might hold, what the present meant, or why we were moving. I lost what remained of my feeling of security, which had already been damaged by the fears and anxieties that swirled around me in Vienna. I came to regard insomnia, bad dreams, and easy anger at the foolhardiness and incompetence of supposedly authoritative grown-ups as normal aspects of supposedly civilized life.

A Few Words About Names

The name "Kafka" often raises the question: are we related to Franz? My Kafkas were also from Prague, but there were not that many Jewish families in Austro-Hungary in the eighteenth and nineteenth century, and they seem to have intermarried to such a degree that their descendants, me included, are practically all connected, even if not by blood. My recent research shows that between the Stern side and the Kafka side, I am "connected" with practically every Jewish family who was Austro-Hungarian back to the time when Jews were required to have names. I am blood-related to hundreds. The connection to Franz is comical: Hermann Chaim Kafka (1854–1931), Franz's father, was my first cousin once-removed's ex-wife's sister's husband's wife's great-uncle's wife's aunt's husband's daughter's husband.

I was given the first name, Ernst (which means "earnest" in German), but never actually had the use of it. I was called Bubi (pronounced "Boobie"), Ernsti, Ernstl and then onto Ernie, but never Ernst. Also, I never became an earnest Ernst. Instead, I became provocative, frivolous, argumentative, flirtatious, and sometimes, in the view of others, charming. The charm was in evidence much less often between our settling in Jackson Heights and my marriage than it had been before.

Why name me Ernst and not have me grow up Ernst? Was it that my parents were ambivalent about me? My father strenuously objected to having a second child. My mother emphatically hoped for one, but she wanted a girl. When she first saw me, she reportedly said, "Go back, little stranger." My brother didn't particularly care one way or the other, although he supposedly said, "He's very ugly, isn't he?" on first seeing me. The name "Ernie" appeared sometime after I started school. Fritz became Frederick, and Adolf became Adolph, upon disembarking from the *Queen Mary* on Labor Day, 1938, at Ellis Island. The German first names were left behind with Austria.

My identities were complicated by more than just name changes. Hitler defined me as a Jew. Public School 149 defined me as a German American Jew refugee. Or, probably, as an unwelcome, transient, here-on-sufferance alien, not a native or even a citizen, a stranger, a foreigner, maybe an enemy, but clearly an alien. I became "Ernie" in an effort to become American. Nonetheless, though I had left Ernstl behind for many years, I was delighted when George Gero, an amiable Hungarian, welcomed me to a seminar he conducted on transference in the early 1960s, with a cigar, a glass of wine, and "Ah, Ernstl."

I lived with my parents until I left for college, where I shared a bedroom with my brother until he was drafted in 1943 and, briefly, my grandmother Stern, when she arrived from Vienna, after Tatti died. The persistence of something of the Austrian upper-bourgeois professional class around my small family group was later (1958 on) resurrected among the psychoanalysts, a larger group with whom I felt comfortable. That circle included the analysts with whom I studied and worked who themselves had studied, worked, and lived in Vienna in my time. To them, I was the familiar Ernstl, and they were familiar to me as well.

Names denote gender, rank, and achievements (*von*, *Doktor*, *Heimrat*, *Baron*, et al.), as well as nationality, religion, profession, and social status. In Vienna, German surnames, such as Stern and Hecht, indicated that the Jews bearing them were descended from people who lived in German-speaking Austria; Jews in Bohemia could have either German or Czech names.

Before emigrating to the U.S., we spoke Viennese German, not *Hochdeutsch*, and not *Wienerisch*—the local argot—and not Yiddish. We were a subcategory, assimilated Jews. "We" had been Austrian-German-Bohemian, minimally observant, Jewish-Austrians for two-hundred-fifty years.

Until Hitler informed us otherwise, we were Austrians. We had been from the time when Jewish men were allowed to vote and required by law to adopt surnames, at the end of the eighteenth century. Grandfather Gottlieb and great-uncle Fritz were army officers in the First World War, and my father, Adolf, was a decorated signal corps private who fought on the Italian Front, near Gorizia and Udine. My maternal grandmother, Margaret, was commended by the Kaiser for work with wounded soldiers. At the time of World War I, Uncle Rudolf ran a fez factory that exported to Ottoman Turkey. Everybody had at least one German name.

Vienna was a multilingual city that attracted people from all over the polyglot, un-unified Austro-conglomeration. It was similar to any modern cosmopolitan city. It was a place with a great deal of mingling, but with neighborhoods containing the homes of people of similar backgrounds. One could become Austrian, like Brahms (actually German), or Beethoven (also originally German), or be Austrian-born, like Mozart, Schubert, or Haydn. If you immigrated, you became Austrian and Viennese, more or less. More, if you were regarded as worth having. Less, if not. All were part of the extended family and had honorable burials in the Zentralfriedhof.

Our Vienna Apartment and Neighborhood

We lived at Schottenring 17, on the Ringstrasse, the broad avenue that circled the old inner city, taking the space where a defensive wall had stood in the time of the Turkish invasions. It was a project of Franz Josef in the nineteenth century. On it, across from us, were the *Börse* (Bourse or stock exchange) and, further away, Parliament, the *Votivskirche* (a Gothic church that Franz Josef had promised as an offering in behalf of the Kaiserin Elizabeth should she recover from an illness—which she did), the *Rathaus* (City Hall), parks, museums, apartment buildings built around interior courtyards, which housed the upper bourgeoisie, and the palaces of some of the rich and the titled.

Our corner apartment had three bedrooms. A large living room was on a rear corner of the building (away from the Ring), and we could look out on a small park, the Schlickplatz, and across that, we could see the *Rote Caserne*, the Red (for its brick construction) Armory. From two small balconies, later destroyed by the Russians, we overlooked the Ring, and the annual military parades of men on horses, caissons, and cannons. Many of the men wore gaudy uniforms. Every morning my father ate his breakfast, which included a soft-boiled egg, a habit I follow myself. Then he took his newspaper and briefcase, crossed the Ring, and went to his office in the *Börse* building. In the evening, unless he was out of town on business, he returned home. I had my dinner in the kitchen with the maid; my brother, with the privilege of eight years' seniority, had dinner with my parents. Sometimes my parents entertained, and these were treat days for me, because my mother loved baking and had even taken courses with a man named Hirtz, the proprietor of a famous baking school.

There was also a Zehn Uhr Jause (ten o'clock snack), and a Nachmittags Jause, with coffee for adults and chocolate with a bit of pastry for me. When I was courageous enough to be sneaky, I could get out of bed and listen to the conversation the adults were having with their coffee and dessert in the evening.

In good weather, the maid and I went for walks; I, at the usual age for such things, rode my tricycle. In the winter, once a month, the large Kermanshah in the living room was rolled up, the furniture moved aside, and I was allowed to zoom around the room on my tricycle.

Perchtoldsdorf

Often at weekends, we went to Perchtoldsdorf to spend time with our great-grandmother, Clara, and grandparents, Gottlieb and Margarethe, and to visit Uncle Gusti, Aunt Lise, and Evi. This involved a change of trams to reach the town at the edge of Vienna where city met the countryside. My ambition then was to become a trolley conductor, and my parents indulged me with the gift of a toy leather conductor pouch that I could hang around my neck, which contained "tickets" and a puncher.

At Perchtoldsdorf, in warm weather, we could play around Gusti's swimming pool. I had a rubber crocodile I could not stay atop, which made it of limited use; but there was also a garden hose, with which to spray cousin Evi, who likewise drenched me. We small children were nude.

My brother helped make Perchtoldsdorf exciting. We had the game of "Anschleichen." Parents, grandparents, and children and friends occasionally all went off to the Heide, a large, hilly meadow for a

Sunday picnic; the children, left to play, would all run away (under the supervision of Fritz, of course), and hide in the tall grass to sneak and slither, undetected, up close to the adults—not as in the city to spy, fearful of exposure—but to jump out to scare. The grownups jumped up in pretend-fear, and everyone laughed.

My uncle Gusti had installed a large toy train, which ran on steam, with real coal, on tracks around the pool and the lawn. He might fire up the train and let us watch. Gusti also had a Steyr convertible car at a time when traffic lights were rare. All this showed that he was modern.

We ate delicious bread copiously smeared with rendered goose fat. That was traditional.

Enthusiasms I Shared with My Family

Many things my mother enjoyed became enthusiasms of my own. These included photography, Alpine pursuits, mushroom foraging and identification, and oriental carpets. Also foods: *Tafelspitz (*boiled beef or veal in broth*)*, roast duck, *Palatschinken (*melted chocolate or jelly-filled sweet crèpes*)*, *Kaiserschmarn (*shredded, sugared pancakes*)*, chestnut cake; music and musicians: (Hubermann, de Sabata, Bruno Walter, Lotte Lehmann, Toscanini); and places: Maloja, Venice, St. Moritz, Salzburg and its festival. My father instilled in me an interest in politics and economics, word play (especially with funny rhyming riddles), and a regard for honorable behavior.

Trains and travel were of interest to everyone: first of all, to my mother, who enthused about Venice or Sils Maria; to Gusti, with his car and many trips throughout Europe and the Middle East, to my father who travelled on business, and to Fritz, who had his own toy electric train. Together, he and I would sit atop a culvert and watch the real trains, including the Orient Express, go by, and I could fantasize about being older and traveling myself. In the meantime, I had my trolley fantasies and my tricycle.

In the main, I had an easy life, with many foretastes of privileges and pleasures that would be available to me as I grew older. Still, there was an undertone of unease, of uncertainty about political and economic conditions and whether we might have to leave the country permanently. Fritzl maintained it would be soon. My parents' theories—with so many things being not-for-discussion in front of the children—were hard for me to guess.

Importance For Me of My Brother Fritz; Traditional Roles in My Family Structure, My Early and Abiding Resentment About Being Left Out of Things and Uninformed Because I Was "Too Young"

I envied and admired my big brother. He read to me about Indians and desert Arabs in books by Carl May; he could ride a real bicycle and go on school ski trips; he owned the Austrian wooden version of the Erector Set, Matador, with which he could construct cars, locomotives, and aerial tramways; and he could go on summer holidays with my parents, while I was left with our grandparents in Perchdoldsdorf.

The family structure, Gusti's ménage excepted, was largely traditional. Women were taught embroidery, sewing, cooking, and drawing and did not go to university. My mother and grandmother attended the Vienna Music Conservatory. Gusti, by contrast, became a physician, traveled far and wide independently, and led a free social life.

Small children were not deemed capable of understanding, or strong enough psychologically, to be able to participate in adult life. I had to be content with overheard scraps, or commentary from Fritzl. I was unprepared for shocks, which consequently came unexpectedly. I later realized that I resented the disrespectful and superior attitude toward me as a little boy, and the situation was aggravated by my being placed in the role of my mother's child, while Fritz was our father's.

I didn't get to take part in the family summer vacations until 1937, and then I had to suffer the humiliation of being unable to row a boat on the *Millstaetter See*, which Fritz could do. And when given the rudder, I steered in circles to much laughter and to my chagrin. These feelings I remember particularly well. Fritz also owned a costume Austrian Army hat, belt, and sword, which I envied. Fortunately, he was a self-confident, kindly, avuncular fellow, who could talk about all sorts of matters about which I was keenly curious. Clearly, his self-confidence had to do with his family role as a reliable, intelligent, mature person, while I was classed as the more artistic, immature, unfit-to-be-given-responsibility younger brother. Funnily enough, I hardly remember ever feeling more than envious about my brother's capacities.

Wurstelprater and Grottenbahn

Another thing Hanni loved was Vienna's Wurstelprater amusement park, and particularly the Grottenbahn. She liked to be a bit scared. The Grottenbahn was a train, shaped like a dragon, containing seats. One sat in the dragon-train, which entered a dark grotto-like tunnel, and there were screams, skeletons jumping out and falling down, and strange moans—all stirring, and a bit uncomfortable. She gladly took me along on Grottenbahn excursions, thereby adding another variant in the list of similar frights. Clearly, being an abducted child and becoming a prisoner was an example of what might happen to bad boys.

Strain trauma is a condition of life which persists and is a chronic stress; it is a condition accepted by the child as normal, relying upon his parents' example. You do not know what is going on, and nobody will, or wants, to tell you. An exception, within my own childhood, was my brother, Fritz, hinting to me, as we watched the railroad tracks together, that we might not be in Vienna very long.

Acute trauma, in contrast to strain trauma, is a significant experience, a blow to a person's sense of being in control: the knowledge that something terrible and unexpected has happened.

The First Big Trauma; Ether Anaesthesia

Some weeks before my fourth birthday I had an adenoidectomy. I had no memory of the induction of anaesthesia, or the operation itself, afterwards. Years later, at age thirteen, I had a tonsillectomy. The later experience, which I realized, at age 13, replicated the prior operation as to pain, hospitalization, and the first anesthesia, provided me with an understanding of the induction of, and recovery from, the ether in 1936. The ether anesthesia made me feel as though I were being smothered during induction; I could not escape, as I was being held down. The experience of not being able to breathe, the biting aroma of the ether, the pressure of the hands holding me still, the sense of falling, the sound of water flowing, gave me sensations such as you might feel while being swept down a dark tunnel, or caught in an eddy of rushing water. Still another fright to add to those aforementioned. I was accumulating material for bad dreams.

That I had not been prepared for this must have added to the traumatic effect. My reward from my parents, for being brave and uncomplaining, displayed an absence of empathy: the compensation was a marvelous toy dining car, containing tables and diners, visible through a removable roof, which could fit on Fritzl's tracks. It was just the sort of toy my mother relished, and even collected. It didn't escape my attention that this was a present *for* my mother as well as *from* her. It strongly resembled her toy funicular train, which she loved so much that it accompanied us to America, unlike most of my own toys. And, of course, I would have to wait until I was old enough to be entrusted to play with it without breaking it. The fact that they felt the need to reward me also showed that my parents had known what was going to happen and falsely told me it would be unimportant. No one troubled to indicate that the ether could be frightening. Instead, everybody ignored that part of the event. It never occurred to me until much later that my reaction was not strange or weak.

To this day, I remember nothing of the actual experience of the adenoidectomy. What I did, and do, remember, is envy of Fred, who was big enough to receive a present I craved and which was purportedly for me, but which was useless for me when I was undergoing a trauma. It only occurred to me years later that my life might have become much easier had my caretakers taken more care.

Envy of Fred; My Mother's Bicycle Accident

Another event of that autumn, one which provoked my incredulity, would feed into the constellation of thoughts I had formed following my adenoidectomy. My mother had decided to learn how to ride a bicycle, so that she could go cycling with Fritz. This offended me greatly because I was deemed to be too little; I had trouble dealing with the painful fact of being left out. Again, there was no external reassurance that my feelings were inevitable, and not reflective of bad character. One did not burden other people with complaints and suffering.

Then, as my mother tried to roll off and balance on the bicycle, she toppled over and fell to the ground. She lay, evidently dazed, for a brief time before she was picked up, crying and bloody-faced, to go to the hospital. She was then treated by the application of an ugly plaster mask. I couldn't understand how my mountain-climbing, athletic, brave mother could have fallen from a bicycle and really hurt herself. I didn't know about multiple sclerosis then, but her illness became evident not very many years later. I believe obvious deterioration of her walking ability and piano-playing might have begun around the time of the fall. In any event, the sight of her, unsteady on her feet and then bloody, frightened me. It is a curious thing that to see the fragility of one's parent is almost to experience it oneself. It seemed that I was aware of experiencing my own and my mother's vulnerability for the first time—and with an added sense of shock and surprise. The same feelings occurred again when I visited my mother eight years later and saw her looking small and frail in a hospital gown at the Neurological Institute, where she was to have her multiple sclerosis evaluated.

Emotions Aroused by Mother's Bicycle Accident

It now appears, in part, to have been poetic justice that in attempting to ride the bicycle, my mother fell and broke her nose, so close to the adenoids. I harbored a grudge towards her for falling, apparently revealing herself as too weak to protect me. Furthermore, I felt terrible, presumably because I wanted her to be there for me and not my brother. I had a longing for my mother to be all-protecting, and to know and anticipate my needs, including inchoate emotional needs. I remember well the fear my mother's bicycle accident caused me. Even parents could break things, which was not a reassuring discovery; if I had to wait for my dining-car until I was no longer likely to break it, I'd have to wait a very long time.

A second incident following the adenoidectomy occurred during a walk with my parents one day near our house in Vienna. During the walk, my parents talked animatedly with each other, paying no attention to me. I broke away from them and ran, colliding with a lamppost and hitting my head above my eye, where a faint scar remains as proof of my experience. Later on, I would see that I was angry at my parents, and that I was escaping from them, yet doing so in a way in which

I would be likely to be hurt, which would, in turn, be their fault. I punished them for the frustration I felt, which stemmed from their treating me as a small child, not old enough to enjoy my older brother's pleasures. It was only later, through retrospection, and precisely because I was no longer a child but possessed a more developed awareness, that I understood what had happened and why. I manufactured my own version of an accident analogous to my mother's. She frightened me. I frightened her. Now, I can theorize that hitting my head provoked disturbance and pain for my parents and probably even guilt.

Psychological Connection Between My Head Injury & My Mother's Bicycle Accident. Reinterpretation of Events and Emotions in Psychoanalytic Hindsight

The conclusion that I, as a four-year-old child, displayed motivated behavior in a seemingly impulsive act, inflicting, by way of damage to myself, a painful experience upon my parents, is a retrospective interpretation. I may speculate now that my parents' intent conversation, which drew their attention away from me, may have been about subjects which worried them. A less forgiving, more Oedipal interpretation of their behavior is that perhaps they were discussing their sexual pleasure from the night before.

In my world in Vienna, lots of things seemed to be fragile. I could see the effects of war; I noticed crippled people in the streets and signs for special reserved places for them on the trams, stories of the Dolfuss assassination, and of the country being saved when Mussolini, not yet a Hitler ally, mobilized on the border, forcing Hitler to withdraw. I asked my father how he would handle the Austrian situation *vis à vis* Hitler's attempted putsch of 1934. (I had only heard of it in early 1938, when the likelihood of another Hitler attempt to occupy Austria was strong, and a plebiscite was planned.) My father replied, "Stay away from politics."

And then there was my adenoidectomy and my dreams. I had nightmares of being buried alive, entombed, tied down unable to move, of drowning, unable to breathe. Apparently, early on after physical trauma, representations of the experiences are relatively straightforward.

Anesthesia = drowning—inability to breathe, sounds of water; being buried alive—immobility. Recovery = nausea, dizziness, whirlpools. These traumatic dreams eventually turned into more tolerable, if still frightening, examination dreams: dreams of being confronted by an important task assigned by a teacher, or the bill collector, or some other authority or disciplinary figure—the doctor, the anesthetist.

I can't say that traumatic events are beneficial, but my experience of these dreams at least had the effect of motivating a strong interest in these phenomena, an interest powerful enough to lead to one of my reasons for becoming a psychoanalyst. Moreover, it provided the material I used to write a well-received article, in which I could illustrate my theory of the origin and use of these dreams by calling on others' experience as well as my own. That patients who reported similar dreams most often, when asked, stated that they too had experienced ether anesthesia supported my theory of the traumatic "day residue" (so important in Freud's method of dream interpretation) of ether anesthesia in childhood.

Although my dreams were explained years later, the sense of imprisonment, claustrophobia, and fear of doctors derived from my adenoidectomy experience bothers me to this day. To be stopped for a traffic violation gives me a great fright. One day as I was seeing a patient, the doorbell rang, and an FBI agent tried to interview me about a patient who was being investigated for security clearance. I was scared, as I would have expected, but also became furious before I showed him the door. The police, the Nazis, and the doctors had fallen into the same symbolic basket.

Safety; Fight or Flight; Resentment at Being Uninformed About Events, including My Mother's MS. Our Lack of Awareness as a Family About Her Illness

It is highly likely that given the choice between dealing with danger and possible trauma actively or passively, the passive side was reinforced by my family's mores. Stay away from trouble, don't call attention to yourself, and don't be obviously ambitious. Survival in peace and the absence of pain is chancy, and this is the most likely road. An example of my training in this approach was the attitude toward my mother's multiple sclerosis. Presumably, her doctor father and her doctor brother knew about the disease, but they said nothing. Should my father not have been informed, for example, that while he was off in Udine in the war, his beloved future wife had endured a frightening period of partial paralysis? It took me years to realize that my mother's multiple sclerosis could not have been handled more constructively, even if we had all been more aware of the possibilities—after all, MS was untreatable.

The fact that I was a younger brother, babied by my mother, and somewhat overlooked when it came to the more overtly socially powerful activities, also tended to influence me toward the artistic, uncompetitive side. When it came to the oversimplified description of the "fight or flight" response, I tended towards flight; to be able to fight another day or, better yet, to be the Grand Vizier rather than the "Grand Turk." Being the power behind the throne, in my underlying theory, was safer than being king.

In addition to my family patterns, another support for my apparent conclusion that safety was to be found in control of competitive wishes and modest behavior was the class structure in Austria-Hungary. There were lines not to be crossed. One had a certain latitude, but many things were not permitted. My Austrian background encouraged me to remain unimpressive and undemanding, in my family as well as with respect to the state, as my father advised.

My size may have contributed to my reticence. I was always small, except for my brain, which was considerable. To sit behind a couch listening to someone else, expected to be mainly inactive, hearing secrets, but helping someone else toward greater confidence to act, was a position made to order for me. It took me a long time to get there. Other consequences of smallness were that I developed a socially unappealing, cynical, and fearful attitude about authority and a need to know, anticipate, and prepare, doubtless further prompted by my position in my family, where knowledge that would have helped me prepare was kept from me.

I wonder if I've failed to convey the importance of tribalism in social history. The family history of hundreds of years of living as Jews in Austria, through episodes of liberalization but with a continual tenuous, fraught relation to the polity at large, made an attack or "push" hazardous. Nationalism and populism were opposed to cosmopolitanism. German Austrians were a minority in the Empire; Jews were a minority in each of the Empire's constituents; not everyone was part of a minority.

Again, Uninformed That and How We Were Going to Get Out of Austria. Fear of Being Trapped

By the time we left, in 1938, there was a good deal of fear of being trapped and unable to get out of Austria. The exit papers, particularly, took a long time to arrive. The feeling of fear was there, but I wasn't made aware of the facts of what was dangerous. The protective influence of the Springer connection was also left out of my ken.

Gustav von Springer and Alexander Hecht were dead, but Gustav's only child, Marie Fould-Springer, married to her second husband, Frank Wooster, was alive and so our family's connections to the Springer contacts were still intact. After the Anschluss, the Sterns were protected until Gottlieb, banned from the U.S. because of rheumatic heart disease, died. That freed Margaret to leave Austria and go to New York, shortly before the Germans attacked Russia. She travelled through Siberia; how that came about, I still do not know.

There was talk about a place on the list for visas for the U.S, and about the need for an affidavit from an established American willing to assume responsibility for the needs of the applicant for immigration for a visa to be issued, but no word that a Kuhn Loeb partner was working on this for us. It would have been reassuring for me to know it, especially at age five.

Formation of the Dragon Phobia: Wagner's Siegfried and the Terror and Psychological Realism of Fairy Tales

During the frightening, pre-escape period, I developed a dragon phobia. The trigger that led to my construction of the phobia—clearly enabling me to avoid a stimulus that gave rise to fear—and which symbolically brought together hidden and unconscious guilt, anger, vengefulness, feelings of helplessness, sibling rivalry, a catalogue of consequences of the situation of the Oedipal child was the present Uncle Rudolf gave me for my fifth birthday. A book was the trigger, and "trigger" is an apt word, as it refers to a gun as a dangerous omen.

My great-uncle Rudolph (brother of my grandfather Stern) was an adorable man, one of my favorites, and came to visit around the time of my birthday. Thoughtful about bringing me presents, Uncle Rudi brought me my favorite sour candies on his occasional visits, and he had crafted a smashingly beautiful wagon, painted in bright colors, in which

I could be pulled along, for my fourth birthday. This time it was a book. The effect on me was an example of how exposure to something can provoke a powerful, unexpected response in a child; as it does, indeed, in adults. Things suddenly fall into place.

The book was an illustrated tale of the story of Richard Wagner's opera *Siegfried*, with the leitmotifs on music staves. The dragon form of the giant, Fafner, sat outside his cave, guarding the treasure trove of the Rheingold, emitting fire and smoke. The hero, Siegfried, appeared in the next frame, holding *Nothung*, the magical sword. Then followed a picture of the slain, bleeding dragon, lying dead, while Siegfried triumphantly waved the sword, gory with the blood of the suddenly dead Fafner. I felt terrified. My mother pasted tissue paper over these pictures so I could only barely make out what they showed; it was then possible for her to read the script to me, while I looked at the screened pictures. The pictures became part of a book—not a part of physical reality any longer. The representation was now categorized as "art" and became more like a dream. And, in dreams, one can recognize that one is dreaming and wake up. I sympathized with Fafner, greedy and undeserving dragon or not. I knew more about greedy and undeserving than I did about the greatness of the hero. I also had an unconscious identification with his lust for power and desire for revenge on the gods. Poor punished Fafner.

What would I have answered had I been asked what frightened me in these pages of text and pictures? I should have had to confess to bafflement. But now, the idea of punishment springs to mind. Fafner and his brother Fasolt are the two giants who built Valhalla for Wotan, the father of all the gods and the guarantor of contracts, law, and order. The builders/giants claim the Rheingold as payment, and kidnap the goddess Freia, whose golden apples keep the gods eternally young, meaning to trade her for the gold, when Wotan fails to pay for Valhalla. Fafner even claims the magic ring: when the gold piled up high enough to conceal Freia, standing behind it, it fails to conceal a gold shimmer from her hair. Wotan has to give up the ring. Greedy, fratricidal Fafner snatches it and kills his brother giant, Fasolt. Then he stores the gold in a cave and guards it, turning himself into a dragon.

Siegfried, Wotan's grandson, awakens the sleeping dragon-Fafner, and kills him with the sword, *Nothung*. Siegfried, bred to know no fear, takes the ring and passes through the wall of fire, with which Wotan has surrounded his daughter Brünnhilde, the Valkyrie, in order to preserve her until a hero who has no fear arrives to awaken her. Eventually, one opera later, everything—gods and Valhalla—are all destroyed.

For an adult, this tale may be treated as a Norse myth from the historic past—which it is—adapted by Wagner. For a five-year-old, it is close to the underlying human fantasy life, complete with lust, desire for power, a kidnapped woman, a nasty dragon, a killing, and dangerous magic. The piece of art makes everything fall into place, into a non-verbal aesthetic experience.

My mother read the story to me, as she read me other German "children's" stories. By the time we got to Fafner's death, I, presumably, knew about Wotan, his son and daughter, the twins Siegmund and Sieglinde, their son Siegfried, and the troubles that arose from the grandiosity of the gods, who wanted to have Valhalla built without paying for it and ran afoul of the builders. A smart little boy, I probably noticed that there was a fratricidal murder, (Fafner kills Fasolt), a series of thefts (Alberich steals the gold from the Rheinmaidens); the gods steal it (from Alberich); the giants kidnap Freia (to trade for it); Siegfried kills Fafner (to get it)—a collection of crime heaped on crime, ending in general ruin. The training of children, who are egotistic, intends to make them civilized, that is, to channel their needs and greed into social and culturally satisfactory behavior. The tools for doing this are the judicious employment of the carrot and stick.

Scary fairy tales are ubiquitous, and especially so in Germanic culture. Hanni liked to read me scary books. In one, a little boy is playing in a meadow on a walk with his mother. She tells him it is dangerous to separate from her. But the boy gets roused when he sees a pretty butterfly and runs after it with his net. Meanwhile, in the sky, dangling from a balloon, in a basket with a trapdoor in its floor, sits a Turk with a spyglass. He swoops down, captures the boy, and is on the way to whisking him to slavery in Turkey when—but I can't now remember what happened next. I do remember that the Perchdoldsdorf church had a separate tower, which was built to house the villagers, should the Turks attack, where they would be protected by that fortress-like structure. Looking down from balloons was what Uncle Fritz had done. Did I connect him with the Turkish kidnapper? Probably. Heide, anschleichen, Turk war all go well together in a child's basket of similar, exciting stories. Then there were the usual German children's books: *Der Struwwelpeter* and *Max und Moritz,* about bad boys and their eventual horrible punishments. I also knew about Richard Strauss's *Til Eulenspiegels Lustige Streiche,* in which the practical joker who mocks officialdom is eventually punished by being hanged.

In these, life is full of horrible punishments for misbehaving children who don't control their greedy impulses and need for power—the tragic flaw. That was bad enough, but if it could happen even to heroes, giants, and gods, it could certainly happen to me. Fafner should have stayed in his cave and given up his loot. He should not have slain his brother and made off with the gold, even if he did have a signed contract from Wotan, because he should have realized that Wotan (like all parents) had power and made the rules. I had been ordered to my room (my cave) many times, and sometimes been punished for sneaking out to listen to the grownups from behind a door. As my wise father summarized it, "Stay away from politics." Sadly, Hitler destroyed the myth that there was an option.

There were a number of other determinants that influenced my construction of my phobia. My mother loved trinkets, mechanical toys, and games. An example was her tin clockwork toy train. There was also the other toylike train, the Wurstel Prater riding through the Grottenbahn—the train with cars and engine, in the form of a wormlike dragon. Wagner used the German word "Wurm" for dragon, though the more usual Austrian word was "Drachen." I was never phobic about the Grottenbahn dragon as I was about the picture; but, of course, the picture was of a dyadic confrontation and a killing.

There was no smoke or blood in the case of the Grottenbahn ride; instead, there was a lot of pleasure and excitement. We were on a date, with no one else involved. However, I had another childhood contact with fire and death: I was walking with my parents, and we passed a burned-out house where, I heard them saying, two firemen had died in the blaze. This burned-out house would be symbolized and entwined with the dragon phobia in much later dreams occurring once we were in New York, the meaning of which I would decode only within my third analysis with Edward Kronold.

Freud's Abandonment of the Seduction Theory and Examination of His Own Dreams, Leading to Recognition of Rivalries

Freud thought, in the beginning, upon listening to his adult female patients, that seduction in childhood was responsible for their hysterical symptoms, including phobias. This changed later, as Freud went through his own dreams, attempting to understand what they meant. He decided he was thinking in his sleep, albeit in an unconscious state, different from waking. Freud observed that one of the features of his dreams was that they drew upon daytime "residues."

In the seduction theory, Freud had attributed symptoms of adult patients to childhood seduction by adults; he accepted patients' accounts of such seduction by an adult, particularly a father. Because of Freud's examination of his own dreams, he concluded that he had rivalrous feelings and hostile wishes towards his competitors and colleagues as an adult. He realized that this was similar to repressed childhood feelings about his father—that he wanted to attack and get rid of him, desirous of a sense of self-esteem tied to independence, self-reliance, and ownership of his mother: the Oedipus complex. Freud's emerging emphasis was that the notion of seduction was by and large, more or less, a fantasy of the child—the child's own creation, as, in my case, was the construction of the dragon phobia. He decided his own childhood fantasies about his father's purported weakness had influenced his adult attitudes and guilt feelings towards competitors whom he, often erroneously, believed he had mistreated.

My Nanny: Another Oedipal Story—Betrayal of My Nanny

Of course, Oedipal feelings are universal, and I was no exception, as can perhaps be inferred from some of the stories I have related. In yet another early experience of provocation and betrayal, we had a young maid, whom I adored. As my nanny, she used to take me on walks and tricycle rides and occasionally bought me some roasted chestnuts from a street vendor. One day my nanny and I went for a stroll and stopped at the *Votivskirche*. The nanny and I went into the church but she made me promise to wait, between the outer and inner doors. I waited, and I peeked through inner doors, which easily parted a crack.

I saw the maid with a young man talking and laughing, and they kissed goodbye. I felt furiously jealous, and when we returned home, I tattled to my mother that the nanny I loved had done something forbidden. She had taken me into a church and left me for a short time. I knew that church was taboo; I told my mother. The sexual aspect of the event, and my jealousy, went unmentioned. My mother fired her, and I still sometimes guiltily wonder what happened to her. I certainly wanted to punish her, which I achieved, but I didn't want to lose her. My response was to distance myself from my mother, but the incident supported my mistrustfulness, my need to provide for myself, and my guilt. I might have brought about a deserved punishment, but I loved the maid. So it also became, via my mother's unexpectedly stern response, a self-punishment.

Similarly, I wanted to punish my mother, of whom I was jealous when she tried to ride her bicycle to go with Fritzl. I certainly didn't want to lose my mother either, and her fall left me feeling responsible. I think I could tolerate seeing myself as Siegfried and the dragon as father, but not the dragon as mother—no matter how angry with her I might be. Insofar as the dragon was a loser, I didn't like seeing myself as him—and my mother had just demonstrated her fragility. I think this romantic, painful situation acted as a lesson about the hazard of expressing anger (the maid was not just injured, like my mother, but lost or destroyed, like Fafner), which I took with me into the future, limiting my tolerance for enacting aggressive wishes and disposing me toward depression.

Discussing Politics in Vienna with My Brother

By 1938 I knew that things had happened, and were happening, with regard to political events. Sitting by the railroad tracks, talking about future travels, Fritz made it plain that there was an expectation that we should be leaving home soon—when we had acquired some mysterious but necessary papers. I knew that Dolfuss, the Austrian Chancellor, had been killed by people called Nazis in 1934, and that, at some point,

Mussolini had mobilized his Italian army on the Austrian border, against the chief Nazi, who was called Hitler. I knew that Mussolini and Hitler were now allied, because I overheard discussions about how we could not hope for another rescue by Italy. I knew that a civil war had started in Spain in 1936, and still went on. I knew that Austria had a brief civil war after the world war, a war which had started with the assassination of the Austrian Grand Duke, Franz Ferdinand. This seemed a large disaster in response to a small event, but lèse-majesté was not, evidently, a small event. I knew I had gone on a family vacation in August of 1937, but that there was to be no vacation in 1938. In March, I knew the Nazis had invaded Austria, because I could hear and see the tanks on the Schottenring and the planes in the sky from our balcony.

I knew that the adults discussed these events and were concerned about the future. I knew that the world of our family had been, and was, well-to-do, but dangerous. Knowing that my parents had been hesitant to bring me into this world, I felt that I was fortunate to have been born and that I needed to be entertaining and easy to get along with to justify my presence, to be Ernstl, but not earnest.

Finally, I learned that Fritz had been moved from his Gymnasium together with his entire class shortly after the Nazis took over. I probably saw the triumphal parade the Nazis had on the Ringstrasse when they invaded. I certainly saw tanks, staff cars, and troops between March 12 and August when we decamped to France.

In addition, I had to be secretive about what I was not supposed to know, even while the adenoid-experience led to an enhanced interest in knowing on my part. The theory of spare-the-information and thereby spare-the-child, I was continuing to learn, was not a helpful attitude, though a consistent one. As these years progressed, "not for children" came to mirror "not for Jews." The adults, and above them, the rulers, were not to be challenged—and the not-knowing, not-challenging was perilous. The time between March 11 and the beginning of August was edgy.

EMIGRATION

Escaping Over the Border to Switzerland Just in Time

The necessary papers arrived, and the preparations for leaving began. Decisions were made about what could be taken. The Blüthner piano, of course. The silver. Fritz's bicycle could come, but there was no room for my tricycle or wagon. The Matador boxes; the parents' bedroom furniture; the children's beds; the piano scores; mother's collection of concert and opera programs; and, of course, clothing. What had to be left behind: grandparents and great-grandmother; my father's mother and sister; great-uncle Rudolf and Adi (who went to Sweden); my barber, Terci Tzappert; Gusti, Lise, and Evi. Not until, looking out of the window of the train to France after we crossed the border into Switzerland, did the four of us feel a sense of relief. Thus ended the first part of my life.

At about this time, Gusti, Lise, and Evi Stern migrated to Palestine. I don't know how they got out of Austria or into Palestine, but I imagine it had to do with Mary Wooster. Another possible way that the Sterns got to Palestine could have been Gottlieb and Herzl's connection; they had been close friends and allies in supporting Zionism. They wanted to help the Jews of Eastern Europe find a haven, and Gottlieb raised money and did whatever he could.

Gusti's family in Palestine was soon enlarged by the birth of a second daughter, Naomi. Of course, Jewish people are no different from Gentiles in the attitudes that they have about newcomers, non-Jews, or less-Jewish Jews. Gusti found Palestine unpleasant for several reasons. The Yekkes (German and Austrian Jews) were often regarded with hostile envy by the Eastern Ashkenazi and the Sephardim. Gusti could never accept the political influence of the Orthodox establishment who demanded that Evi adopt a Jewish name, a name that appeared in the Bible after the agreement between Abraham and God. They held that names, such as Eve, found before Abraham, were not Jewish. Further, Gusti had trouble finding three other congenial string players to form a quartet with him; he missed Vienna coffeehouse conversation and lacked other Central European Jewish intellectuals to talk to. Gusti (or, I imagined, perhaps ascribing my feelings to him) seemed to me to resent being defined as Jewish by the Nazis and, then again, by Jews who insisted on biblical Jewish names.

Paris, 1938; The Last Sunny Days of Relative Innocence

August, 1938, Paris. We spent a month in a third-floor walk-up apartment in Paris. I learned some French words. My mother sent me upstairs to ask the neighbors to lend us some *couteaux, fourchettes*, and *cuillières*. We went to the Eiffel Tower and sat at a café where I was allowed my first taste of coffee.

My Terror at the film *Snow White* in Paris; My Mother's Delight in it

In Paris, we also went to the movies to see *Snow White and the Seven Dwarfs*. My mother, still the intrepid walker through the mountains, and unsuccessful bicyclist, was responsible for this, being her usual curious self: very interested in Walt Disney, fairy tales, and the latest novelties for children. Of course, she loved it; and I was terrified, particularly when Snow White had to flee from the wicked stepmother, running through the forest, pursued by the woodsman who was to bring her heart back to the evil queen. Tree branches reached, clutched, and grasped to stop her—chilling for a child who was well aware that he and his family had just escaped from the wicked Nazis.

Paris and Pleasure; Nellie

There were many excellent aspects to Paris. The best was being out of danger, but eating in a restaurant (where I was introduced to the French fries that became a staple of my diet), trips to museums, walks through the beauties of Paris—all gave the family great joy. My mother had an old friend, Nellie Hammerschlag, who had taken up weaving, as my mother had taken up embroidery, baking, and piano playing, the acceptable pursuits for girls. It was Nellie who had made a scandal when she ran off to Paris with a man. I was intrigued by her loom. While the women were whispering—with some evil in my heart, annoyed at being neglected, as I had been with the maid at the *Votivskirche*, or during my ill-fated run into the lamppost, or at my mother's bicycle accident—I started to play with Nellie's loom, and made a mess of something she was working on. I was not conscious that meddling with her loom was in fact a hostile response to a recurrent sense of being neglected, for which I wanted to punish Nellie and my mother. No French Fries allowed for several days, but no serious punishment.

The Day at Royaumont; Mary Wooster

One morning a Peugeot arrived, the driver opened the doors, ushered us in, closed the doors. and drove us to the country—or so my brother recently told me. I had remembered the car as a large Daimler, and that creative exaggeration, in keeping with the grandeur of the original occasion, persisted as a certainty until Fritz proffered the Peugeot variant. We stopped at a gate, a man came and opened it, tipped his cap, and we drove up to a large, beautiful house. That is definitely correct, since the same person was still manning the big iron gates when I returned to the Palais Abbatiale de Royaumont on another visit in 1951.

We were greeted by the Baroness. She was friendly; my parents greeted her happily, though with obvious deference: this was an important person. Of course, I had heard of her, and of her father, Baron Gustav von Springer. (The Springer "von," meaning "from" is to be distinguished from the "von" of the true Germans, as defined by the Nazis, where the surname denoted the seat of the family.) "Springer" was supposed to have originated—von—describing jumping acrobats, who perhaps entertained the rich and powerful in the old days. Uncle Gusti was a borrowing of some royal Gustav's name—or maybe it was in homage to Gustav Springer?

Riding the Tricycle at Royaumont

The Frau Baronin, fifty-two years old, was not as interesting to me as the tricycle belonging to one of her children. I zoomed about on it, up and down the *allée* that led up a hill on the entrance side of the house. Fritz, meanwhile, had a much more exciting ride on a real bicycle. I felt cross about the tricycle, inferior to my own, which had a special transmission that worked using levers, unlike the usual mechanism with a chain. We rode about and, at some point, I was served tea and cookies. The grownups ate lunch; perhaps it was afternoon tea for them as well. There was a back stairway in a state of some disorder, with dolls, books, and toys strewn about. Later on, as an adult, I made up for my childhood feelings about driving—my lusts for trains, bikes, cars, boats and sense of deprivation, owning a succession of many cars, a sailboat, and having many travels.

Fritz's Vienna bicycle was packed up and on its way to America while we were at Royaumont, destined, in its very old and decrepit later life, to be passed along. By the time it came to me, the screw holding the handlebars to the front wheel had loosened somewhat, though gradually enough so that I could tighten it and not crash. For that, I carried a small pair of pliers in a little leather bag attached to a very uncomfortable saddle. It was passed on to me along with other hand-me-downs; and eventually I came to understand more about my negative response to what I perceived to be Fritz's relatively superior position. Eight years apart in age, we occupied different social and power strata of society. My brother enjoyed privileges I did not, symbolized by his model railroad, and other outward signs of superiority. I tended to think I was mistreated and deprived. Later, for instance, I had to wear his old, but still abrasive, Lederhosen to school. He argued, however, that in 1924, when he was born, our family was poorer than they were when I came along in 1932; he was therefore burdened, more than I, by the after effects of World War I; so, I was luckier than he. I greatly loved and admired Fritz, and still do; but it was hard for me to understand how he could have felt envious of me. He was so obviously preferred by our parents and generally better-off than I was. Yet he thought that our parents favored me, that he had burdens of responsibility, and a more deprived early life than I.

That day at Royaumont represented a significant introduction to a family with close ties to my own, further details of which I learned as time went on. Thinking about that situation now, I can see how I could have treated the sibling situation and the Kafka-Springer situation as analogues and felt that it was part of the natural order of life that being younger and weaker was like being of a lower class. Though not of the highest rank, the Springers represented a different class, and way of life, than the Kafkas, a desirable way of life that continued, as I learned years later, in the pre-World War II world, and even after. The Springers epitomized a class and a culture my parents grew up very near, but which was different from the restricted experience of my own childhood in Vienna, and very unlike what I subsequently encountered in America.

The Springers also embodied the possibility of upward mobility for pre-Nazi assimilated Jews, the Rothschilds being the chief example. Consequently, my life was influenced by close connection to differing worlds. In the background was the pre-World War I, Imperial Austro-Hungarian polyglot world of my professional class grandparents and great-grandparents; the world of my parents between the wars, prior to emigration; the new world to come in New York; and the world of wealthy, internationally connected semi-aristocratic Jews.

What I had not yet apprehended was that people living within different levels of power, influence, and wealth could view their situations as less desirable than someone else's, no matter that the general view is that greater power, influence, and wealth is better than less. In any comparison, in any disagreement, all the participants can, and often do, feel envious, worthier, but less advantaged than any other party. Fritz and I could disagree about who had or has a more difficult life, and whether greater wealth, influence, and power do or do not make a better life, or whether they are ancillary and permit contributions to social development. Is there something to be said for the inevitable—namely, hierarchies?

Royaumont was a lesson about envy, and it raised questions about what constituted the natural order. Yet Royaumont was beautiful and aspirational, not only in the aspiration for greatness, bigness, and power, but also in a desire for beauty. In Europe, perhaps creating beauty was a value more important than the material glory of the more commercial, mechanistic, post-industrial revolution value systems. The Springer family was significant to me and my family. Their philanthropy, consideration, and help for my family members, their involvements with the arts, their own style, and their posture as humane, cultured figures all represented to me a cultural spirit that I can admire, one that can bear comparison with elite culture in general, and American elite culture in particular.

As I will refer to them from time to time, I shall outline here some of the details. Our "Frau Baronin" was Baroness Marie-Cecile ("Mitzi" or "Mary") Fould-Springer, born May 23, 1886; she died December 9, 1978 at the Ritz Hotel, Paris. She was the daughter of Gustav von Springer (1842–1920) and Hélène Springer; she married, first, Baron Eugène Charles Joachim Fould-Springer, and, following his death, married, in 1929, Francis ("Frank") George Leyland Wooster (1890-1953). Mary was the mother by her first marriage of Baron Max Fould-Springer (1906-1999) and Hélène ("Bubbles," 1907–1997), who married Eduardo Propper de Callejón (1897–1972). They were the parents of Felipe (Phillipe) Propper de Callejón (born 1930), and of Helen (Elena, born 1934), who married Raymond Bonham Carter (1929–2004), Thérèse ("Poppy"), wife of Alan Pryce-Jones (1908–2000), and Liliane ("Lily") Elizabeth Victoria (1916–2003), wife of Elie de Rothschild (1917-2007). Among Mary's descendants are the actor, Helena Bonham Carter (born 1966), and the writer, David Pryce-Jones (born 1936), who has written about his family in *Fault Lines* (2015).

To the United States

August passed. We took another train, this time to Cherbourg, where we boarded the *Queen Mary*, were shown to our second-class cabins, and set off for America. I managed to stay up late, looking through the porthole, watching the lights in the harbor, the tugs, and the little lighthouses at the ends of the enclosing moles. I relished the reassuring sound of the rumbling engines and feeling the shiver of vibration. The five-day voyage was pleasant, a heavy cloud had lifted, the pain of loss had not yet come on, and the difficulties to be encountered had not yet appeared. On the ship, I was happy, by all reports charming and bright, and the Kafkas made friends with some other passengers, friendly and welcoming Americans returning from summer vacations. Among them were the family of the head of the University of Maine at Orono and the family of a DuPont engineer called Maurer who lived in Penns Grove, New Jersey, with whom we continued to have contact.

NEW YORK

Arrival in New York, 1938

We reached New York on Labor Day, 1938. I had my first experience of the Statue of Liberty and of being fingerprinted: the former produced a flush of American patriotism, the latter, a twinge of anxiety. We spent two weeks at a hotel on West 79th Street, and there met with friends of my parents, Edi and Reni Ehrlich, and their two sons, Karl, about nine years old, and Paul, my age. Edi was the ENT who had operated on my adenoids and had been a co-orphan with my father at the Waisenhaus, and he was also a medical colleague and friend of Gusti. The Ehrlichs soon established themselves in Newark. I felt guilty that I never came to like Edi much, as the couple were good friends of my parents. I didn't like feeling disloyal, but I found Edi to be one of those people who seemed always to be resentful about something, arrogant, in addition to demanding sympathy when he felt mistreated. Unfortunately, starting at about this time, I was beginning to feel that way myself. I was having more and more things to be dissatisfied and angry about.

My "Anti-Ehrlich File"; Dislike of the Way He Practiced Medicine

We visited the Ehrlichs in New Jersey frequently in the following years. Edi practiced at his house. He would take an otoscope to my ears, which he would wash out with gushes of water, muttering disgustedly about the quantity of dirty wax that he managed to flush out. Was I supposed to have clean wax or no wax? Another complaint I had was that on one of our visits, during a summer when the Ehrlichs had rented a house on some forlorn-looking lake, I was pressured into going swimming and came out of the water with a large number of leeches clinging to my body. I found this unpleasant and added it to my anti-Ehrlich file. Reni had a tendency to gush and to outtalk my mother. That, too, was added to my list of dislikes.

Later on, Paul Ehrlich and I were roommates at Harvard for our last three years and got along well, but he was another one who had a doubting, critical attitude. Maybe this was an example of the supposedly general, Middle European cynicism; probably it was occasioned by the fact that we Central European children between the two wars had more than the usual traumatizing experiences.

We did have additional sources of friction. I harbored resentment about the adenoid episode, though the significance of the ether did not become apparent until later. Paul annoyed me by assuring me that it was he who was responsible for my existence, as it had taken my mother seven years to persuade my father to allow her a second child. She had finally succeeded only when she used the argument that if Paul's mother, Reni, could have a second child, she, Hanni, was entitled to a second as well. By the time I heard this news, I was no longer a little boy but a young person with more complicated views, more or less reconciled to being a second-fiddle, somewhat deracinated, oddball, former Viennese-Austrian-Jewish-upper-bourgeois younger brother. It also seemed to me that beyond the obviously distressing intimation that my father didn't want another family member, which seemed to me to be all too true, I think that Paul really did feel that I owed him for his help in my coming into the world. We were never going to be best friends but, on both sides, having contact with some friends from the past was reassuring.

Flushing, then Jackson Heights, Queens

Our second New York address, for about two months, was Kissena Boulevard in Flushing, Queens, where we knew no one. I remember that my mother took me out for a walk, and her key did not fit into the lock when we returned. We took refuge with a neighbor; it turned out that the monthly rent, due that morning, had not been paid. The landlord had swiftly changed the lock while we were out. My father got home, paid the rent, and the lock was restored. Yet another addition to my list of exclusions/papers/passport problems.

Our third address was 34-58 90th Street in Jackson Heights. By this time, Fritz had become Frederick, Fred, or Freddie, and I became Ernest or Ernie. Two long blocks away was Roosevelt Avenue and the IRT line from Flushing to Manhattan and on to the Bronx. The building was pre-Depression, and already a little rundown. A school was in walking distance, and I was enrolled. The apartment had two bedrooms, one for Fred and me, with our beds from Vienna, of simple design with tubular frames, once clad in shiny 1930s chrome, now peeling. Originally, these had been installed in larger spaces with closets and bureaus in our separate Vienna rooms. A hallway led past the kitchen through the living room, which had space for the piano, chairs, end tables, and a bookcase, past the parental bedroom, to the bathroom. The small kitchen had a table, with an oilcloth cover; above it hung a grill-like frame with clothespins attached, and a rope and pulley to allow it to be lowered, loaded with wet laundry to dry, and then raised to make the table accessible for eating. Worn linoleum cove<u>r</u>ed the floor. Oilcloth, linoleum, shared bedroom and bathroom, and the laundry arrangements were all new to me. Windows faced east; the place was sunny and overlooked a little park, which belonged to the Open Stairs, a Queensboro Corporation Development, with open outside stairs and a tennis court.

In theory, the Queensboro Corporation accepted no Jews, though some bearing non-Jewish names were permitted to live there, but there was also a family named Mintz, whose son, Donald, became a friend. The El over Roosevelt was convenient. (The avenue was named for Teddy, not Franklin. Queens was Republican when it was developed in the 1920s. Consequently, it was anti-refugee, and America First, as I soon discovered at school.) We all quickly learned how to read and speak English, and my father learned how to fold the *New York Times* to make it possible to read on the subway while holding an overhead strap with one hand and the paper with the other.

Summers in Jackson Heights brought heat and humidity unrelieved by air-conditioning. Sometimes, even my mother agreed that piano practice while one's hands and body were moist was not feasible. This gave me a bit more freedom, in a time when boys of age eleven or twelve were able to travel on trolley cars.

Learning to Swim

My sense of independence was augmented by learning to swim. I would walk from 90th Street to Junction Boulevard, six blocks away, and board a trolley that stopped there. After a mile or two, I would transfer to a second, which dropped me at the Aquacade, a large public swimming pool in Flushing Meadow Park. The pool was left over from the 1939-1940 New York World's Fair, where it had been the site for a swimming extravaganza put on by the impresario Billy Rose, known for his chorus line of "Long Stemmed Roses." The fashion for swimming exhibitions by dozens of women led to stardom for Esther Williams, who carried on with such routines for years in the movies. I was old enough to use the men's changing room by myself (unlike the embarrassing necessity to change with my mother on Sundays in the ladies' room at Jack Riis Park beach).

Admission to the Aquacade was free, and swimming classes for children were conducted for a small fee. I had no money for these, but I could crouch next to the place where the lessons were held, and that was how I learned to swim. I enlarged my repertoire of strokes later on; I became an adept imitator of my grandmother and mother's leisurely head-above-the-water, looking-around-at- the-scenery style breaststroke, and its backstroke, frog kick version; I never conquered the breathing, and the flutter-kick, arm churning of the crawl, whether face down or up. The deep end of the pool was sixteen-feet; it was vacuumed by a man with a diving helmet, who walked on the bottom, with an air hose attached to his helmet and a vacuum hose in his hand. There was a high platform for diving, and one day someone jumped off and hit something on the way down; he needed to be rescued. The sight of this person, unconscious and a bit bloody, made me feel queasy, and so I learned that diving could be dangerous.

Our financial situation was poor. The small amount of cash the Nazis had allowed us to take out with us in 193839 was becoming depleted, and some Dutch bonds my father had secreted in his shoes could not be cashed. My mother gave piano lessons. She also tried baking and selling her creations to neighbors. They didn't sell well: "too rich" was the complaint. I thought whatever my mother baked was excellent, and never too rich—the neighbors didn't get it, and I didn't get them. I folded boxes for my mother's baked goods; Fred delivered and sold them.

She tried to conserve money in buying food for our own table. We had lots of offal: beuschl (minced lungs) and liver, which I didn't like, and brains, kidneys, and thymus sweetbreads, which I did. In the past I had envied my big brother's clothes. Now I was "privileged" to wear Fred's old school attire, the Lederhosen (hardly fashionable in Queens) and leather backpack (of an obviously Germanic style, never in vogue), high stockings, held up by visible garters, and (all too-Germanic) sandals. The long stockings which, my mother assured me, meant that I would never develop varicose veins, a malady I had never heard of, were especially galling. My mother imparted other old wives' tales as well, such as, "Eat lots of bread after swallowing a peach pit, or even a cherry stone, because otherwise a tree will grow in your stomach." This tall tale might be followed, in an offhand way, by "Look at my stomach," followed by showing her abdominal stretch marks, "which you gave me." The juxtaposition stumped me; in an early psychoanalytic symbolic insight, I realized that my mother had, unwittingly, told a joke about insemination and pregnancy. Eating cherries could cause trees to grow, at least in boys. Though I didn't know much sexual anatomy, I didn't believe eating a cherry stone could cause pregnancy.

My father was a first-rate salesman and found a job with something called "The American Globe Trotter Travel Agency;" but even his salesmanship could not overcome the difficulty of marketing tours to Central Europe in 1939. There was talk about selling the piano, and even the living-room rug, the Kermanshah that was my mother's most prized possession. One of the potential buyers, from a richer Jewish family, was the father of a girl in my class, Libby Goldstein. Walking to school with her, I often teased her, occasionally pushing her into the bushes in a way that was both flirtatious and, I now feel, nasty.

My father then found a more appropriate job, with an earlier immigrant from Germany, F. M. Mayer, who established a banking business at 30 Broad Street in Manhattan. The rug and piano both remained, so my mother happily went on practicing her Chopin, and I eventually inherited the carpet, which now lies in splendid, but thinning, decrepitude on the New York apartment floor. At F.M. Mayer, Adolf (né Adolph), bought and sold real estate, managed the properties ("Omnia Properties"), and did the same for other non-Omnia owners, plus currency arbitrage and investment management. He sold life insurance for the New York Life Insurance Company and, with an old friend from the bank in Vienna, organized a General Insurance business as well (WiKa, Inc., from the surnames Winter and Kafka). He joined the New York lodge of the B'nai B'rith, of which he had been a member in Vienna, where he found clients and broadened his narrow circle. Once again, he was *tüchtig* (able, diligent, reliable, hard-working), to sum up his most useful qualities in one word.

My mother's cake-baking enterprise did not prosper, but, fortunately, it did not have to. She enjoyed her piano teaching, though it rapidly faded as well, largely because her neurological disorder, now diagnosed as multiple sclerosis, was progressing, and gradually limited her walking and piano playing. Meanwhile, Fred was doing well in high school, and I was trying my best to be socially accepted in kindergarten.

Learning English; The Loss and Abiding Resonance of German Words

It might first have been as an adolescent with a command of English that I noticed my nostalgia for the experiences connected to certain German words that were potent in my early life. I became aware of a sense of loss elicited by particular sensory experiences—picking flowers, particular odors, giving my mother a smile, making a joke, and having someone laugh—that were indissolubly linked to German words. I felt grief at what seemed to be lost in translation.

At first, when I didn't speak much English, I took home the humiliating grade of "unsatisfactory" in the space for "dresses himself." In fact, when the teacher told the class to get their coats from the coat closet, I failed to understand the order. My language deficiency, combined with anti-immigrant sentiment, also brought about the result that, between semesters, when the smart kids were skipped into second grade, I was left to continue with the more challenged ones. I missed understanding a few "Why-don't-you-people-go-back-to-where-you-came-froms" but not many and not this one. "*Le ton fait la musique,*" as my mother used to say—in that case, quite accurately. I didn't need to be told in words that I wasn't skipped like the others simply because I didn't know English and, in any case, when this happened, I did. By the second half of the first grade I could read English and hear the tone in my head. By first grade, I could also hear music and could make it run through my fingers to the piano. As it eventually turned out, I was too gifted. My parents enjoyed showing off my musical prowess to visiting friends. but I suffered from stage fright, which conflicted with my enjoyment of the praise my performances brought. A sorry dilemma. A character expression offshoot of my phobic tendencies. The spotlight was dangerous. Zu viel ist ungesundt. Keep a low profile. Don't be too smart for your own good.

    I needed to learn English rapidly. This motivated me to examine words and their meanings before most other children did. My acquisition of the German language was automatic and followed the usual course of maturation. Learning English was different, and the process wasn't entirely automatic, as I remember a period of consciously translating German into English. Later, I simply spoke in English.

    Once in a while, a word might come to me in German, and I'd have to search for a translation. I became critical about grammar and vocabulary, and finicky about the correct use and pronunciation of words. When someone says "diddent," I shudder. Or, "I saw that before." Before what? I shiver. I have an almost obsessive attitude about the use of words. Misuse or mispronunciation is, if not quite sinful, embarrassing—the residue of my humiliation at my poor grade for not getting my coat when told, and my frustration when failing to understand.

The Onomatopoeic Quality for Me of German Words

Certain words still come to mind in German, together with the feeling that there is no satisfactory English word to replace the German one. There are English words aplenty, including exact synonyms for the German ones. Still, I feel the English ones do not quite match the German because they do not elicit the same old emotions, sensations, and associations. Examples of German words that still give me this feeling are "*Heide,*" "*Dickerle,*" and "*Schmetterling.*" The English words are "meadow," or alternatively, "moorland," "Fatso," and "butterfly."

Literally, *Dickerle* means "little fatty," or "fatso." It was my mother's pet name for Adolf. It has an affectionate, as well as deprecatory, sense. My mother continued to use it in America despite the fact that doing so negated my parents' objective: to become American, to live in a mixed, not refugee neighborhood, and, if possible, to adopt American table manners, forms of dress, and to speak only English. *Dickerle* was a word of intimacy that had many meanings that the words "Adolf," or "father," or "*Vater,*" could not convey.

For me, the word was as rotund as my father. It said a great deal about him. *Dickerle* was the fellow who disappeared behind closed doors with my mother for the night, and it is replete with other childhood associations. Our *Dickerle* was the unfortunate orphan who hadn't had enough to eat as a child and so was fat because he finished everyone's leftovers. His hungry soldiering in war didn't help either. My ambivalent feelings about my father, then and long after, included many that could be stuffed into the word *Dickerle*, which thereby became as fat as my father. As I outlined previously, as a child I resented my father and felt he was weak.

He was Pathetic. He Embarrassed Me.

Later, in adolescence, my childhood disdain for my father evolved. He didn't pay attention to me. He didn't even talk to me in a serious way. He had an appeal for my mother that I couldn't understand and resented. His face was prickly even after he had just shaved; how could my mother put up with that? Fred was little help. With respect to family participation, Fred was otherwise engaged—at school and after-school activities, away working in the summers, then at college, and then in the army.

Dickerle came to encompass all of this. It is a word that reaches back to the Old World, a part of Austria and of childhood, whose persistence gives me the knowledge that I am a creature of other worlds. It brings back the aroma of the Schottenring and the image of my father in underpants, shaving with his straight razor.

"*Schmetterling*" and "*Heide*" are two other such words, evoking nostalgia, with visual and olfactory sensations. They each evoke another, past world. They are paired as well as separate. "*Heide*" evokes the "*Schmetterling*" constellation of sensations and vice versa. Closely associated with all this is picnic nostalgia. "*Heide*" and "*Schmetterling*" both call up the nostalgic feeling of picnics on the *Heide*, including the picnickers, the food, and, if my reverie is not interrupted, a panoply of life in Perchtoldsdorf and ultimately in Vienna. It is like a movie close-up that enlarges and enlarges until a wide aerial-view comes up. *Schmetterling* is an excellent example of a word that I felt was untranslatable. It is tied to Perchtelsdorf. As a matter of fact, when "butterfly" came to me as a possible *Schmetterling*, I rejected it, because it didn't, in my mind, express *Schmetterling*-ness. When I told others about my translation problem, they would inevitably give me a strange look, and say, "Of course, it's a butterfly." Then I'd grimace in frustration and say, "Of course I thought of that, but it's just not right." "Butterfly" might bring up images of Monarchs fluttering in my milkweed-filled meadow in Vermont. I identify with the Monarchs because of the idea that they fly there all the way from Mexico, as I flew from Perchtoldsdorf, i.e., they are migrants and therefore variants of me. Still, they found their way to this strange place, but not to the *Heide* at Perchtoldsdorf. The word "Monarch" doesn't bring up *Schmetterling* or Perchtoldsdorf.

If the touch sensation, the proprioceptive sensation, and the visual aspect of the childhood *Schmetterling* are subtracted from the impression the word makes, then "butterfly" becomes just a word, a thing, subject to scientific examination, to reduction by classification. Literal translation of *Schmetterling* as just a word leaves out the rich tissue of meanings it connotes for me. Beauty lies in the complexity, whether it can be defined or not. *"Heide"* also leads to a bevy of visions of Perchtoldsdorf. *"Röslein"* (the diminutive of "rose") starts another path of associations starting with *"Röslein auf der Heide,"* the Schubert song from a poem by Goethe.

Then too *Heide* brings up the taste of the goose fat-covered bread we ate on the *Heide,* and at Gusti's swimming pool. The word carries my experience of the multisensory essence of butterfly-ness.

"Papillon" almost conveys the motion, delicacy, beauty, and evanescence of the *Schmetterling,* but also has another connection to a revivified past. It is Herr Wolteger's bow tie. The Woltegers, Oscar and Fritzi (née Kafka, but no relation), were close family friends in Vienna and later in New York. Wolteger was called just "Wolteger," as if he were an English schoolboy, and he always wore a bow tie, which, in our Vienna Austrian German circle was the French *"Papillon"* (In standard Austrian it was *"Fliege,"* fly). The Woltegers often came to dinner with us in Jackson Heights, as they had in Vienna, and I had to perform for them on the piano.

I think *"Papillon"* has weak *Schmetterling*-evoking power because it connotes Woltegerness, via the bow tie, a confusing second meaning of "butterfly." The fugitive essence of changes in childhood, with the intensity of feelings that were localizable but not describable, merged in the word. It goes with other French words used in Austrian-German, like *trottoir* (I cannot resist the feeling of trotting when that word is used, nor the memory of "Trot-Trot" the horse, nor the clang association to the word *Trottle*, meaning "idiot") for sidewalk or pavement (preferable to me, to the ugly German *Gehbahnsteige*) and "*vis à vis*," (which is clearly better than "two people, one across from the other" or "across from each other" or "one to one"; "eye-to-eye" is probably the best alternative and most literal translation of *vis à vis*), and other words that evoke sensations strongly. Even among the words of my childhood, certain ones evoke stronger sensations. The German "*Gesundheit*" sounds like a "sneeze," whereas the word Zumwohlsein" (both presenting a wish for good health) is blander for me, even though more Austrian; a form of defiance—I speak Austrian, not German.

Perhaps these experiences introduced me to the understanding that words and sensations overlap, flow together, and merge. The genre name "coming of age novel" can never carry the poetry and music of even the ugly word *Bildungsroman*, nor does "culture" convey what *Kultur* or *Bildung* conveys to me. Woe to the poor translator. Woe to the poor lexicographer. Woe for the loss of the mysteries of complexity, woe to the quest for simplification. I will get to psychoanalysis later, but it seems appropriate here to mention that Freud's way of listening is also the way of a curious traveler in foreign places with foreign languages, who is able to extract meaning from strange perceptions.

The main point, a*propos* mother tongues and languages that are acquired later, is that changelings like me need to remember that words in the original language become memorials. They have nostalgic, emotional, poetic, and sensual meanings attached to them. Translation into languages acquired later provides words that are literal, dictionary versions of the original, to-be- translated words. But they don't look like they sound, *and* don't carry the meanings of the untranslated, original-language word. The originals arose together with the child culture. They are words that evoke sensory experience, so much stronger in children than in adults, abutting on sensuality, and close to emotional life. They encompass context and history.

Even in ostensibly shared languages, there are differences in word definitions. In British English the word, "homely" translates as "cozy, comfortable." It is not used relating to a female person's looks, as in American usage. "Homely" has different contexts experienced in childhood, even though they are found in a mostly-shared language. The American "homely" means someone towards the ugly side of the "ugly-pretty" scale. The Brit expresses the American meaning of "homely" with the word "plain." Shared experiences have a greater likelihood of allowing bonds between people to come about than do unshared experiences. One Brit will know that another Brit will not need an explanation of what is meant by saying "homely," and Americans will not need an explanation about how to use "homely" with each other. The American and the Brit will both have to be informed, however, that they do not use this word in the same way.

I feel at home in Britain, but not as at home as I do in New York or Palm Beach and, certainly, not in the way I do in Vienna, though I have not had a home there for eighty years. This has to do with emotionally important and connected experiences. Twelve-step programs, to make an analogy, depend on the accepting attitudes of the participants, and the sharing of burdensome similar experiences of alcoholism. My father rarely shared his experiences in the *Waisenhaus*, or the army, but he kept up with some of the boys with whom he had shared his childhood, even with some he never liked. Though Viennese German has changed since my time there, and even though my vocabulary is limited, I'm still relaxed there in a way I am not in other places. The chestnut trees smell the same, and the *Schnitzel* and *Tafelspitz* taste much as they did when I was little. The center of the city, the light, the jokes, are familiar and homey. When in Vienna as an adult, Viennese and other Austrians sometimes ask me where in Austria I come from. They can't place me. I can give a simple explanation, but I lack the vocabulary for a more complicated one. It seems that "*sympatico*," "identity," "electricity," "*Gemütlichkeit*" often require only slight signs, smells, and sound.

English words sound quite different in different parts of the world. Cognoscenti can make much of how expressive sounds and accents communicate class and geography—and lots of other things about the background of the speaker. Works of art communicate nuances to the art historian, as do bones to the anthropologist—meanings, clues not accessible to the non-expert. John Pope-Hennessy wrote that he could tell by whom and when a portrait was made by the position of an arm or the tension of a leg. When people migrate, they have to overcome the strangeness of the new environment, and the natives have to cope with their own fear and suspicion of the strangers. For me, emigration, immigration, and the replacement of Austrian-German by English as the main vehicle of conscious communication began when I landed in New York on Labor Day 1938; as did my awareness that I would never be able, or wish to, separate myself from the childhoodness of childhood words, sensations, and emotional experiences. If my past makes me other, so be it. I am myself. My name has changed, but the remnants of my early years, modulated but active, remain.

Further Notes on Language

Items I've collected—paintings, photographs, watches, English drawings, pieces of Maiolica, piano pieces I've worked on, books on subjects I've studied—become mementos.

They help to connect parts of my life. Nonetheless, there has never been a home that was not also a not-home for me since leaving Vienna. I have a constant feeling that I have to find a way to fit in, to justify my presence to other people who are natives, while I am an alien. This is my other-world identity. A great deal of resentment follows from this condition—and drives it as well.

Music brings a partial relief. Music, painting, sculpture, and the other arts are universal and timeless, as are the affects, such as sadness, grief, and longing. I am on the fence about esthetic pleasure being a necessary condition of high art. No translation is required for high art, and so no loss is occasioned by the Babel-type situation that accompanies migration. The timeless, that which does not require translation into words is, for me, what distinguishes high art from propaganda, topical comedy, fashion, design, and so on. As you play or listen to a piece of music, or listen to or read poetry, or see a play or opera, apprehending the work itself involves the passage of time, but these works, if high art, are timeless in the sense of imperishable. While understanding the words can modify the experience, the art can be experienced without them. Painting and sculpture do not structurally involve the passage of time in this way, but they also provide a connection with the ages and are evidence that all mankind shares something. Music for me not only brings up a childhood world separated from the later world; it encompasses all possible worlds. Music moves and is moving.

The Unique Timelessness of Music

Music, being timeless and wordless, is an art whose materials are sounds and spaces, and my familiarity expanded as my repertoire of musical experiences expanded over time. I have mild synesthesia: music can evoke sensory associations, as in the experience of beeness via Rimsky-Korsakoff's "Flight of the Bumble Bee." Dance and music come together by the use of position, physical movement, and rhythm. Art song is an attempt to entangle the poetry of words with the poetry of music, to fuse two routes for the stimulation of experience. To the extent that the translation of the words omits the associations present for me in the original language, the effect of translation is diminution. Those who do not speak the original language may appreciate the translation, but still get less than they would if they heard and understood the original. The syntax and grammar of music is made up of the interrelation of theme, variation, reversal, inversion, harmony, dissonance, atonality, the interplay of instruments and are, therefore, never dependent on words for effect (which is not to claim that words have no part to play); it loses nothing in translation. That means that a Korean violinist can be taught German music by a Russian teacher in South America and can play freely around the world from Siberia to the Transvaal. However, I will probably never believe that German music is not better played by a German, French by a Frenchman, and so forth—the sensory experiences and culture of childhood affect interpretation.

Communication Through Words and Non-Verbal Means

Among the first things I learned at school was that there were many ways of feeling and communicating with others, through words, movements, and art. I discovered tropes, symbolism, musical and dream language, mathematical language, mysticism, art, poetry, and many other synesthetic and near-synesthetic stimuli. Unfortunately, childhood openness to vivacity of feeling, with its capacity to mix and meld, usually flattens with physical and psychological development. But less in my case, I suppose, than occurs in others who have a single home language. I never lost the sense of the complexity of personality, of interrelationships, of possibilities. In fact, that sense has increased over time, as has my pleasure in it. I have often experienced the annoyance of other people when I said, "Yes, but there's another way of looking at this." There is always, for me, the present, together with the not-present. I was an annoying child, a Donald Rumsfeld without the arrogance and peculiar orientation of the man, with my sense of "known, known-unknown, and unknown-unknown."

I have found other oddballs (like myself) among artists. It seems self-evident to me that two people, alike with respect to the sensation-feast I describe, will feel more in tune with each other than two people who are unlike. I had a friend, Kermit Lansner, who was editor of *Newsweek*. His LP record critic used to pass on the review discs to Kermit. He had no turntable for a time, but we could sit on the floor together, hearing the music in our heads, and would often smile at the same passages.

Wienerisch Jokes; Jokes are Funnier to People with Shared Backgrounds

There are jokes that are funnier to people with shared backgrounds and experiences. Graf Bobby and Baron Rudi jokes were part of pre-1938, Austrian pre-Hitler life. They are funnier to the Austrians who tell and hear them, because they arouse the sensations of the *Wienerisch* argot, as well as the sense of presence of the locations referred to. They turn on the interaction between Rudi, a sharp, clever, iconoclastic street person who speaks in *Wienerisch*, and his chum, Graf Bobby, a literal-minded and, therefore, easily-mocked young aristocrat. These jokes also serve as examples of people who use two first-languages, the formal German and the informal street language, *Wienerisch*.

An example: Bobby encounters Rudi on the Ringstrasse. (He who knows the Ringstrasse can call up the sensations of being on the Ringstrasse). Graf Bobby is riding a horse, and pulling another horse along, behind. Rudi greets Bobby and asks why he is on a horse. Bobby says he has a lunch date, and the trolley drivers are on strike. "But why the second horse?" "*No ja,* (*Wienerisch; bei,* or *an der* in standard German) *Mariahilfer Strasse mus I' (ich) doch umsteigen!*"

("I need to change [trolleys] at Mariahilfer Street.") Good mimicry helps the joke.

One effect is sensory. (Ringstrasse, riding the horse and pulling along another, the reins, the sound of the hooves etc., a piece of horseplay as wordplay—the German *"umsteigen"* is a word with sensory connotation. The literal meaning is not "change" but stepping from one place to another.) Is the story as funny for a non-Viennese as for a Viennese? Probably not. Its essence is mockery of rigidity and obsessional thinking (as of the storied Austrian bureaucracy à la Franz Kafka or *The Good Soldier Schweik*), as a way of avoiding the truth of human limitations. At the same time, it mocks the hopelessness that recognizes those limitations.

The need to understand both what words mean, literally, and what they can imply, figuratively, but cannot communicate in the absence of "*ton*," has been very important in my life, and so has my interest in the non-verbal "languages" that convey nonverbal meanings and interrelationships. I learned this lesson in German and I retained it after childhood. It doesn't happen as tellingly for me in English. It is a source of intimacy with the relatively rare person who shares a distinctive but indefinable sensibility, as I did with Kermit Lansner, and later, Paul Desmond. Desmond, the alto-saxophonist, once came back from a Brubeck Quartet tour and told a story about attending a party in Germany. Somebody came up to him and said, "What sort of name is Desmond?" and Paul replied, "It used to be Breitenfeld (the name of a town that passed back and forth, held sometimes by Germany, or Sweden, France, or Prussia)—and you had it last."

The connections between Paul Desmond and me included having roots in a heritage of change. Perhaps this contributed to our shared love of puns. Paul and I were both enthusiastic punsters who indulged in juggling meanings by moving sounds around and thereby taking words from one category and putting them into another. Punning echoes the horse-tram joke. That makes fun of the reductionist, Bobby, to whom the tram and horse are classified simply as carriers, whereas Rudy (and the audience of the jokester) know the crucial differences between animate and inanimate. In both, as elsewhere, creativity involves finding unexpected similarities between elements in some established category and thrusting them, unexpectedly, somewhere else. That creates a mingling of meanings and creates a new order. This is also found in the development of new words to go with new developments and technologies—"automobile," "email," and "snail mail," for example.

Desmond, a friend in the heyday of *Playboy*, jazz, The Half Note, and Gloria Steinem, took LSD before going to MOMA to look at pictures; the Tchelitchew painting of children's heads merging with and arising out of a tree was particularly stimulating, he averred. Paul used to keep his LSD in liquid form, dripped into an Animal Cracker cookie box; one day he came home from a road trip to find the Animal Cracker box gone, and was worried that his housekeeper might have taken it and given the cookies to her small children. She claimed she had merely thrown the box away; but still, Paul changed the hiding place. I always assumed that *Take Five*, Paul's most famous and profitable composition (still played in elevators and restaurants all over the world), which Paul claimed paid out enough in royalties to pay for all Dave's kids' college fees, was inspired by Paul plus LSD. Its formal novelty was the time signature; the word play of the title was pure Desmond—he was a consummate word manipulator. No jazz (or classical music I ever heard) had used that 5/4 time signature, and the name of the record carried on the wordplay that described the music-play: *Time Out*. Time Out for reconsidering jazz time, a pause for catching on to the catchiness. Of course, that was only a part of the story: Paul would ask me what tunes I'd like him to weave into a solo, and I'd ask for something like the opening of a Schubert piece, say, *Death and the Maiden*, and he'd mix it in with original ideas and variations.

Cultivating deliria has been a practice in all known times; Greek festivals, oracular musings stoked by magical substances, Roman Saturnalia, medieval fasting, Mesoamerican peyote use, Coleridge's opium, Freud's cocaine, Timothy Leary's LSD and Paul's are examples of practices that go back to the dim past. I don't think hallucinogens were too important to Paul; he favored Pall Mall cigarettes and good wine; we had many late meals at Elaine's when he was tipsy but not drugged. Many other musicians, then and presumably now, used and use drugs in the belief that music will come out. Paul made up new musical things. He was part of a band.

They had to create—in each set, each player improvised a solo. Notes were bounced around.

The Meaning of Names

I ask myself again about "Ernst." Why did my parents name me "Ernst," a name and a word meaning "serious, earnest, or grave"? From early childhood, pre-1938, I knew that my parents thought of me as the frivolous, humorous, unpredictable one. They liked me to be entertaining, to lighten the atmosphere. My mother liked games, tricks, and clever toys. I tried to satisfy her. My father was witty; we two shared wordplay. Maybe, like the joke, my parents hoped I'd be paradoxical. "Frivolous, humorous, unpredictable," and "Ernst" at the same time isn't possible. Though I try to be both, I don't succeed completely at either. "Present" and "not present" equals me, not quite here or there, this or that.

My parents thought of my brother, Fritz, (and treated him) as the earnest one. I remember Fritz, wearing an army hat and sword, sitting with me in his Indian tent, in Tatti and Mami's Perchdoldsdorf garden, reading Karl May, while I enviously admired his ability to read. Or me, with Fritz, the "not me," watching him playing with his electric trains, or thinking about him being away on a school ski trip, or him rowing a boat, of which I was incapable at age four. I always envied my older brother. He seemed free and to have a sense of himself as a consistent entity. I felt divided in myself; I wanted to be like him, but to be unlike him. Ergo, we never hummed the same tune for long.

Fred thinks in straight lines; his concepts are concrete and material and as simple as possible—he became an engineer. I, by contrast, see everything as being complicated, allusive, and very seldom straightforward enough to capture what I want to say in a single sentence.

My brother Fritz, conscripted as "Fred" in 1942, became a "Fritz," a warrior like the man after whom he was named. My brother Fritz's namesake, our great-uncle, was the Austrian army air officer whose story I told earlier. An Infantryman, my brother could have found work as an interpreter and used his German. Instead, he refused to speak German, carried a Browning Automatic Rifle, a semi-machine gun, and had a partner to help carry the ammunition. He was more liable to be sought out for destruction by the other side than your usual rifle-armed infantryman. It would never occur to him that he was doing it to live up to his name. Certainly, he wanted to fight the Germans, though he would never have said that: he wanted to be like his American comrades. Of course, he also had an army outfit as a child.

Pavlov's Dog; Behavior in Dogs and Humans That Goes Beyond Reflexive

When Pavlov's dog hears the bell, she is given food. When conditioned, she salivates when the bell rings, because she connects the sound with incipient food. Is this a simple reflex? Does the process involve ideation? Or does Noam Chomsky's "deep grammar" also work like this with canines? Dog hears bell, remembers food, constructs theory: bell leads to appearance of food. Or, perhaps, if a human subject were to replace the dog, (1) Experimenter rings bell, (2) presents "reward." Baby cries, mother appears and feeds it. When does memory enter? Human babies are conditioned by their mothers' stimulation of their reflexes; but also, at some point, when the brain and mentation develop, are influenced by stories from the past. You can teach and interact with a human—or a dog—rather than merely train them. For, just as the nervous system develops partially in response to sensory experiences, so the mind develops ideas and memories in response to far more immaterial stimuli. It is hard to claim that all behavior—human or canine—is purely reflexive: a ghost in the machine, *ein Geist in der Naturwissenschaft*. The brain develops; the mind appears.

Family and Other Stories Told to Me Before I Could Read and Write

Stories from the past were told before I learned to read and write. Of course, there were the usual family stories, but there were also books. Children's books have a special power—they are often illustrated, and this means that the stories they tell are perceived by more than one sense. Someone is reading them to you, so that you are hearing the voice and emotional tone of the reader, but you also understand the stories visually, by looking at the pictures. In the child's imagination what he gathers from hearing and from seeing amalgamate to make a richer experience, and this prepares him for the more complicated ways he will experience life as he matures physically and develops mentally and emotionally.

Music, My Heart, and Heredity

Music was ubiquitous, as my mother practiced her piano pieces every day. I spent summers with Mami and Tatti in Perchtoldsdorf. The house was awash with piano playing and chamber music. I write "awash" because music has a waterlike quality for me, the notes lap, and crash and always move. When I heard music, did I have thoughts? I know I had feelings. When I heard my brother practicing, I know I yelled from the next room when I heard wrong notes.

When I cried, "E, not E-flat," mother heard, rushed into my room, and exultantly cried out, "Absolute pitch!"

Little did I realize what that was to mean, but it changed my life. My yell was of pain at the wrong note, and also directed to my brother, with glee at my accomplishment. I had heard the false note, and he had not. I usually wanted intimacy with him. But I was also competitive. Had I hoped my mother would hear? Did I hope it might lead to promotion to Knight in my mother's chess game with her mother? And perhaps eclipse my brother's favor with her? Yes. Did I imagine that my musicality would strengthen her possessive attitude toward me and make me feel more suffocated by her? Less like *a* boy, more like *her* boy? Not likely. All of the above happened.

My mother's competitive relation with her own mother, as to who was the better musician, led her to want me to play better than Mami. Her desire was to sit next to me on the piano bench, correcting my errors and telling me what to do, which also had the effect of preventing me from doing other things I'd have preferred to practicing the piano—such as playing with the other kids on the street. It was many years later that I realized that this situation had fed my ambivalence about musicianship and further complicated my relationship with my father. He was a poor violinist, and the women were quietly mocking about his musicality (which could hardly have been developed in the conditions in which he lived as child). They also mocked his inability (which they—and he—did not know was the result of an anatomical anomaly) to climb heights in the Alps, or to run any distance. This in a family where

Gottlieb, my mother, and Gusti were great alpinists and admired for their climbing.

I have a similar physical constraining condition, which limited and embarrassed me. My father never knew about it, and I learned I had it only recently. It turns out to be caused by a limitation of cardiac output, resulting from an inherited cardiac structural defect, hypertrophic cardiomyopathy. Getting out of breath easily limits one's athletic career, as well as one's ability to mount mountains, and when the kids choose up sides or teams, one's popularity. Much later, my recognition of this complex relationship—the interrelation of physiology and reality, and of both with psychology—made me more aware of physiologic impacts in the character formation of patients. It enabled me to write and lecture about deficits and their later consequences.

In any case, as a boy, piano playing seemed girlish; it made me mother-bound and "weak" like my father. On the other hand, it was also unpleasant to be envied by my brother and my father (who was acquiescent about my being my mother's child), but I'm sure it made him draw away from me in favor of Fritz. That's the usual story about talent. It alters relationships.

Talents and Their Consequences—I Know I Am Talented; Also Greedy for Recognition and Belonging to a Group

Absolute or perfect pitch is one thing; a sensitive sensorium is another, and these things set me apart. Talents create unexpected connections that sometimes make new ideas available, but it can be hard for other people to follow the out-of-left-field lines of thought, which lead to the resulting ideas. This works both ways: one member of a group doesn't work on the same wavelength as another, so each experiences a sense of alienation and solitude. Things that are possible, and often easy, but that set one apart, are isolating. The strange and sometimes seemingly artificially-connected route (taking the road not taken), as pointed out by the gifted, annoys other people whose sensoria do more filtering, and who don't "get" the more intuitive, apparently unconnected thoughts. This breeds feelings of being unappreciated and isolated—in both parties who don't connect. One doesn't "get" the other, who doesn't "get" why the other hasn't "gotten" it, and wonders what's wrong with the way he presented what he said or did. There may be compensation in the richness of the mental activity of the more creative mind; however, the cost of being apart, given the reliance people have on their connections with other people, is serious. It takes time to accommodate. Talent makes one an outsider.

I write from the position of one who feels himself to be talented but is as greedy for recognition as anyone and resents being an outsider. There are more "normal" thinking people than there are those who question norms; questions are often taken as challenges. The gifted child stands out, not always positively. I could know the syllabus without having to work; I could see possibilities when others couldn't. These others held me back; they irritated me; how stupid they were, even the teachers. Being an angry young boy, I couldn't conceal what I felt, and I had a bad time at elementary school, until the upper grades. At bottom, I wondered how I had failed to communicate something that presented itself to me as clearly connected to the previous matter in my train of thought. There is of course the fact that giftedness may be treated as nerdiness sometimes is. Not all nerds are talented, nor are all talented people nerds. Still, the neglected genius may just be an untalented nerd, and I sometimes thought that that was me. Certainly, it is how I was treated.

My Tendency to "Digress"; In Fact, I Explore a Subject from Many Angles

As a teacher, I was subject to the opinions formed by students, who wrote assessments of my teaching. There were, broadly, two groups of responses. One was, "Kafka comes up with ideas that have nothing to do with the subject under discussion. He doesn't give straightforward answers to questions." The other group responded: "Kafka is a stimulating and thoughtful teacher. He often comes up with provocative ideas that make you think through the question under discussion from a new angle."

Deficits may coexist along with talents. Dyslexia, and various other cognitive deficiencies, as well as mood disorders, seem often to be present together with unusual capacities. Those with these disabilities find themselves doubly challenged: first, to seem odd to others; and second, to appear to have defects, which anger and frighten others. Meanwhile, it is hard to feel both envied and disliked, as well as poorly understood and not appreciated.

Montessori's educational theories, and other psychological work in early learning difficulties, such as that of Katrina de Hirsch and Jeanette Jansky, have shown that communicating what cannot be learned or expressed in a particular sensory modality can be delivered via other modalities. One can, for example, use vision with pictures and proprioception (the sense that allows you to tell you're holding your arm over your head, even if you're blindfolded) by moving parts of the body. Tutoring using sounds can be helpful for dyslexia. These discoveries have helped many children. Alternatives to standard approaches were not available to me. Recognition of differences was not emphasized or encouraged. My intellectual explorations were received as digressions. Not only was I not at home with them, as an immigrant, but I wasn't in tune with the other tribalistic inhabitants of the primary school classroom. I didn't "get" them and they didn't "get" me.

What Makes You American?

"Sticks and stones will break your bones, but words will never hurt you" was the teachers' anodyne in Jackson Heights Kindergarten, and in elementary school as well. That is a useless comment, like "Wait, you'll grow up," or "Others have it worse," or "It happens to everybody." These clichés hurt when they disrespect painful experiences. Since words will never hurt you, don't complain; but words do hurt. In Vienna, I had a kindly and friendly barber, who gave me a comb as a parting gift. In Jackson Heights, the barber yanked on my hair with unsharpened scissors, and told me that my favorite baseball team, the Brooklyn Dodgers, were known as "the Bums" because they had foreigners like Dolph Camilli on their team. (Camilli was an excellent first-baseman on the 1941 World Series Dodger team; he was no foreigner.) It didn't help that Dolph was a lot like Adolph, my father's name which, a touch pathetically, he had altered from Adolf with an "f" to make himself more American. That was done from love for America, and probably also from fear; he completed the transformation by adding a middle name, "John." The words hurt; so did the hair-pulling.

Personal Identity and Governments

During the earlier war years, the government classified and reclassified us, sometimes as "enemy aliens" and, at other times, as "friendly aliens." These were sources of anxiety or relief, depending on the classification. My father never criticized America openly, though he did sometimes indicate that he was less than fully trusting. The government was, after all, a *government*. In his younger days, following the First World War, Adolf had been a Social Democrat; the brief civil war from February 1216, 1934, went badly for the parties of the left, which led to my father's advice: "Never get involved in politics." (Much later, I claimed

Austrian citizenship, attended the Salzburg music festival, and wore *Tracht*, Austrian folk dress, to express my feelings of equal entitlement with the *Volk* that had persecuted me.)

When the Second World War ended (which now seems to me more a second act than a second war), Harry Freud—our family friend, the son of Sigmund's favorite younger brother, Alexander—was a colonel in U.S. Army intelligence. He was sent to Berchtesgaden, where he went through Hitler's papers. Among them were some documents awarding decorations (no actual medals were included), honoring faithful Nazis, signed and addressed by Hitler himself, as well as some Hitler book plates, which had not made it into Hitler's books. Harry sent a package of these memorabilia to my father, who hid them, fearing that the FBI would discover them, and think he was a Nazi. Later on, I bought some recordings of songs of the Lincoln Brigade, the Spanish Civil War foreign volunteers' corps. He insisted on hiding these too, "for the time being," because of Joe McCarthy, and the possibility that the FBI would think him a Communist. I regarded both ideas as far-fetched. However, I am also, I hope reasonably, not too much or too little, mistrustful of authority.

Adapting to America During WWII: My Initiation into a New Tribe at P.S. 149

The advantages of being a member of a tribe can hardly be overestimated. Tribalism expresses itself as nationalism, religiosity, and being clubbable. Clubs include people who have been accepted by the other members, and, equally essentially, they have non-members who are excluded. "No Irish need apply" doesn't work unless some Irish might like to join. Some Jews probably wished to join the aristocracy, but the aristocrats didn't often want them. On the other hand, these Jews weren't looking for converts (Judaism is not a proselytizing religion), and, as a matter of fact, Jews frequently shunned their co-religionists.

There is a joke about two Jews, marooned on an island after a shipwreck. Seeing a ship in the distance, they made a smoky fire that attracted it. Rescuers landed on the island and were given a tour; they were led to the gardens where the castaways had planted root vegetables and banana plants, the huts where they lived, and three larger structures. These were three Shuls (synagogues), one for each castaway, plus a third; necessary, as they explained to their rescuers, because "That's the one we don't go to." This is my extra world, the world of those with whom I don't associate myself, who aren't included in my personal club, and whose clubs I don't wish to join.

Victory—and safety—comes to the strong. Strength comes from size and a cohesive social community. It also comes from individual and communal permission to question traditional ways with a view to improving one's knowledge of reality, allowing evolution. Austria failed in these ways. As a kind of nineteenth-century League of Nations, Austria had conservative policies that aimed to change traditional institutions after the Napoleonic wars, but only gradually. These did not succeed in dealing with the effects of an Austrian Industrial Revolution, which turned isolated areas into large conglomerations of people, who found community in nationalism. There were too many groups made up of other groups. Austria had succeeded, with partners, in repelling the Turks and the Napoleonic French. However, the glue—provided by past intermarriages of the Habsburgs, which had brought German Austrians, Magyars, Bosnians, Croatians, Poles, Bohemians, Slovenians, Ukrainians, Serbs, and Eastern Orthodox, Catholics, Lutherans and Jews together over many centuries—dissolved. New material conditions brought by industrial developments, such as steam, electricity, railroads, and easier movement of peoples and armies, brought new social conditions, with harsher inter-and intra-national rivalries.

I was an Austrian; being a refugee made me a member of no nation; now perhaps I could become an American. When I started Grade 1A at

Public School 149 in the winter of 1939, the United States needed to become more cohesive. Regional difficulties needed to be put aside or overcome and the external enemy needed to be defeated. About a year later, the federal government began to issue Defense Stamps, intended to help the nation prepare for war. When the war actually broke out, they were renamed War Stamps.

If people come to fit their names, Mary E. Steel, the principal, was one who lived up to hers.

She was far from being a Stalin (meaning "steel" in Russian), but was pretty strong. She started a War Stamp contest between classes in our school, and between our school and others. Weekly solicitations in class sought to sell the stamps. The biggest stamp-collecting classes were the winners. The model for these arrangements seemed to be a baseball league, teams (classes and schools) all playing the same game, but each team hoping to win.

My Childhood Strategies for Becoming an American

When I was eight or nine years old and had a chance to speak to my father, I asked for money to buy stamps. My father asked me some questions. "What is the purpose of these stamps?" "To buy bullets to fight Hitler, and to earn money. When the book is filled with stamps, $18.75 worth, in ten years I'll get back $25." My father, the banker, then gave me a lesson. "If the government needs money, it can raise it through taxes. Or, it can issue bonds that people will buy with their savings to collect interest. It can print money that people will accept, though doing this will increase, and thus dilute the money already in circulation, and make it less valuable. In case of war, lots of people will be involved in factories and the army. The war will cost lots of money; the government will borrow, tax, and probably print money. They will introduce rationing: civilians will not get much gasoline or rubber.

Prices will be controlled. The war will end. In three years? Four years? Let's say four. Soldiers will come home. They will have accumulated money and want to buy things. The same for civilians. Prices will go up; and the value of the dollar will go down. If you're lucky, in ten years your $18.75 will be worth ten dollars. Or less. The government is lying to you. They're promoting patriotism. I'm not giving you money for defense stamps." This was certainly an unusual way of seeing the situation.

I was disappointed not to help win the contest and the war, but my father's way of seeing things made a profound impression on me. Our government was promulgating a fairy tale and taking advantage of the gullibility of that part of the adult population who were childlike enough to believe it.

Defense Stamps and Victory Gardens

I had to content myself, when I was ten and eleven years old, with helping the war effort by trying to grow vegetables in a small plot, in an empty lot that had been divided up into Victory gardens. This scheme, as far as I was concerned, was a failure; but I felt guilty about it. Another activity I took on was training myself to be an airplane-spotter. There were many air raid drills; all the lights went out, wardens patrolled the streets, and I peered through the window on the chance that the drill might be for real. I learned the shapes of all the invading airplane types in order to be able to report them to the authorities later.

P.S. 149 and the Pledge of Allegiance Used to Create a Politico-Cultural Community

I didn't realize that one of the functions of P.S. 149 was to promote the cohesiveness of society. The Pledge of Allegiance, Christmas plays, outings, PTA meetings, holidays, and stamp competitions all contributed to a sense of belonging to a politico-cultural community. At the time this was quite successful, certainly with me, an aspirant to the "I am an American" club. The school provided all sorts of communal activities, and the curriculum contributed other bits of historical interpretation. *The Star-Spangled Banner*, though prompted by the War of 1812, clearly pointed to the heroism of the Civil War, and to the struggle to achieve unity. I didn't notice then, but now I find it striking that the school's songs, holidays, social gatherings, and religious celebrations mirrored the institutions that gave the Jews cohesion, with rituals, holidays and liturgy, all combining to create the feeling that this didn't just happen to your ancestors—it is happening to you, now.

The Office of Price Administration was established in August, 1941, to set prices and oversee rationing, allowing goods to be distributed fairly, and to control inflationary price rises. It was headed by Ken Galbraith, who became a good friend later on, when we were neighbors in Vermont. When the war ended, inflation appeared; by 1949, a 1940 dollar was worth about 50 cents. My father had given me a valuable demonstration of hypocrisy in government, and the gullibility of parts of the population. It illustrated the wishful credulity of ill-informed people, when approached with a seeming bargain. Mary E. Steel was not giving good financial advice, whether she was aware of that or not, but she supported unity. The underlying lesson for me, about the war and its effects, was that the war brought about cohesiveness.

In fourth grade, I made a pest of myself. I was angry; I waved my hand to answer questions and interrupted the teacher by throwing spitballs. I read a book a day and also practiced the piano. I stole money from my mother's pocketbook, and she caught me, screaming at me "*Du bist ein Dieb!*" "You are a thief!" This scared me but didn't end my rebellious behavior; my self-confidence had improved, to the extent that I was able to be obnoxious. The outcome: my parents were summoned to a meeting with my teacher and principal. These authorities had decided that there were two choices for dealing with me: ejection from P.S. 149, or skipping me into the Opportunity Class, which was where my Grade One bright coevals were being taught.

The Boon of the Opportunity Class

Now ten years old, I escaped from the profound boredom and resentment of my first four years of school. I found the Opportunity Class congenial; the whole class was obstreperous and full of pranks. The girls had a club to mock the boys, the boys had two clubs, hard to tell apart, for creating various competitions, such as who could throw paper airplanes at Miss Cudner, the teacher, and bully the girls, without being caught. To be caught by Miss Cudner was to be placed on the floor under her desk between her legs, which was considered to be hilarious. I felt no religious prejudice at school. I felt no racial prejudice, either, but the only blacks I knew were our building superintendent, Gary, and Mr. Washington, a carpenter.

P.S. 148: Transfer to "Middle School"

P.S. 149 and its war bond competitions went only as far as sixth grade. For seventh and eighth grade we were transferred to nearby P.S. 148. Some influential events occurred during the time when I was eleven to thirteen, from 1942 to 1944. Fred was drafted from Columbia College, where he was majoring in chemical engineering. I had no clue about what might have led him to make that choice, but was still enamored of him and decided I could be a chemist too. I didn't know what engineering might be, but I did have a chemistry set that introduced me to some basic concepts, such as acidity and alkalinity. Fred was sent to Fort Bragg for basic training, and then into a program that trained engineers for the Army at Manhattan College. That didn't last long, and after a few months, he was moved to an infantry division from Idaho, and then to Italy. My mother's multiple sclerosis had advanced so that walking was quite difficult for her. Her ability to play the piano was gone.

Music remained central for me. Listening to Bach, I had a gut feeling that I could experience what the parishioners in Brandenburg had experienced in their Baroque city, and this gave me the feeling that I was one with humanity throughout time, or at least with those who responded to Bach as I did. Technical training in harmony and counterpoint, which I had, didn't seem to add much to the musical experience. Anybody, of any time, could respond to music. I'm sure there is a neurological basis for this.

There is no such thing as progress in this sphere: Beethoven was not an improvement over Bach. For me, Arnold Schoenberg was no improvement on any composer, though I could appreciate his zeal to destroy harmony and counterpoint, among other things, sadly including melody.

I was sent to a piano teacher who had an apartment in the West Eighties off Central Park West. Paul Aron had been a voice instructor at a conservatory in Brno in Czechoslovakia. His fees were low and affordable, and he was another refugee who needed help, but he was a terrible teacher. I needed technical help—playing an instrument is a physical, athletic activity; a pianist needs to learn how to sit, whether high or low, how to use the body, the shoulders and arms, and how to hold the hands. He could not address these. Aron could play accompaniments for singers and knew something about voice training.

He also knew about some contemporary and near-contemporary composers whose work he assigned me, and I played some Prokofiev, some Ernst Toch, Milhaud, and Ravel; but basically, each week when I took the subway to West 84th Street for an hour's lesson, I was wasting my time.

My Bar Mitzvah

In my twelfth year, I had lessons to prepare me for my Bar Mitzvah—"just for business and tradition," said my father. This took place in the basement of a synagogue, where none of us had attended services, though apparently my father went to meetings there to meet potential clients. I learned how to sound the Hebrew letters, but not to understand the meaning of the words. As with Paul Aron, this was wasted time.

I had no problem travelling around New York. As a small, immature preadolescent, I could walk to the subway station, go under the turnstile, and get to Manhattan in half an hour. When, later, it became more difficult to slip by, I paid a nickel. I went to the Museum of Science and Industry, the Metropolitan, and the Natural History Museum, but I liked the Modern best, because of the movies. The theater in the basement was usually fairly empty and showed extraordinary films. I think *Tol'able David* was my first there. Of course, I was particularly affected by World War I pictures. Especially moving were *The Big Parade*, a marvelous 1925 King Vidor opus, which showed the horrors of the trenches, and the later film it inspired, *All Quiet on the Western Front*. These last two films showed the patriotic hysteria, and loss of reason and thinking, that one could also see in "The March of Time" wartime newsreels. The vulgar, bombastic Hitler, screaming and shrieking, and the *Heil*-ing crowds made me wonder how you could possibly account for such a thing—this violent us-against-themness and dwelling on injuries, real or imagined, and long past. That question popped into my mind years later when I listened to a third-generation American of Irish descent, a bright and sensitive man who felt vengeful about iniquities inflicted on long dead ancestors. And then there is the wish of the orphan to find the biological parents, with the idea of finding out why that (being abandoned) was done to, or happened to, her or him when "it" was an infant—not a "her" or a "him." An answer—this is how people try to alleviate their vulnerability to physical pain and the pain of loss—hasn't satisfied me yet. I understand that belonging to a group brings a feeling of safety, but including the dead in one's social and societal alliances seems highly unrealistic.

In Middle School, I was one of a trio of friends, with Ronnie Friedrich and Nicholas Papayanis. Nicholas was very unusual; he was a mathematical prodigy. He told me he was corresponding with Alfred North Whitehead about mathematical questions arising from his readings of *Principia Mathematica*. He also told me his father owned a well-known restaurant called Sea Fare. It turned out later he was a head waiter. Nicholas may have been subject to a tendency to exaggerate. However, we did fiddle around with making crystal radio receivers and talking about Plato. At the time we reached the middle of high school, Nicholas was gone. an early admission to the University of Chicago.

My Tonsillectomy; Revival of the Adenoidectomy Trauma

After Middle School I revisited the trauma of my adenoidectomy. I underwent a tonsillectomy - at the hands of the same doctor, Edi Ehrlich. The information that ether anesthesia had been administered for the adenoidectomy at age three surfaced then, when I was thirteen and Edi Ehrlich did my tonsillectomy, and again used ether. Asked why, he explained that ether is a good thing, quite safe, and also, by causing vomiting, it provides a bath of acid gastric juices that help sterilize the wound. His Germanic authoritarian attitude distanced him from whatever empathy he might have felt about his patients. Once again, I felt isolated, frightened, and misunderstood, not only by him but my parents who had put me in his hands.

Newtown High School; Some Things Hadn't Changed

Thirteen-years-old, and it was time to go on to high school. Mother went to Columbia Neurological Institute for a "work-up": investigations in hope of a diagnosis. I lost my tonsils but gained a few scraggly pubic hairs. I went through the hypocritical Bar Mitzvah. Two atomic bombs were dropped on Hiroshima and Nagasaki to end the war.

On VJ Day I was at Lake Placid, and the northern lights appeared, together with fireworks, in celebration. Fred came home, was discharged, and this ended the worries that he might be sent to Asia to fight against the Japanese. He bought a fantastic red convertible Buick Super with electric windows, went back to Columbia, and met his soon-to-be wife, a seventeen-year-old Barnard girl, Mildred Joachim. I was overjoyed when Fred came home. Years later, I realized that unconsciously I had felt guilty at Fred's, and thereby my own, good fortune which could be construed as a) undeserved; and b) having occurred at the expense of others, for example, the estimated 225,000 Japanese who died at Hiroshima and Nagasaki. Survivor guilt, it would turn out, was an important burden to me.

I was not allowed to compete to be accepted for the elite schools, Stuyvesant or Brooklyn Tech, to which I longed to apply; my parents argued they were too far away. Mom told me she would wait for a brilliant doctor to find a cure for multiple sclerosis, while looking at me meaningfully. I did not wish to be my mother's companion. I wanted independence. At the same time, I was still physically small and sexually undeveloped, lagging behind the others. Running made me out of breath and nauseous after a hundred yards, which was difficult to conceal, and made me feel embarrassed.

My Successes at Newtown High School

At Newtown High School, classes numbered 1,400 to 1,200; there were 1,400 at the beginning of freshman year, 1,200 at graduation. The size of the entering class was larger than the space available for the students in the high school building, so a group of a few hundred, including me, was relegated to an annex in nearby PS 89. That meant missing various activities and extracurricular activities available at the high school building and its gyms. Without access to the gyms, physical training meant running around the block, and being eyed disapprovingly if you were unable to keep up, as I was. Newtown High had several distinctions; in my time it ran many programs, academic (for the college-bound), general (not college-bound), commercial (office workers, et al.), technical (potential engineers), industrial arts (factory workers and mechanics), and agricultural (with the only farming program in New York—Newtown had a farm in Flushing). It was white and mixed working-class and middle-class kids. It had good teachers and was a different world from elementary school, but it was not academically challenging for me and, in that regard, did not prepare me for college.

On the other hand, it was easy for me to get good grades; I had plenty of time to act in plays, work on the newspaper, represent the school in city-wide competitions of one sort or another, run one of the student political parties (quite successfully—we enlisted good candidates), play in the band and the orchestra. (An oboist was needed and with financial help from my father, I bought an oboe and found an instructor to teach me how to whittle reeds and to play it.) I got along with teachers and students. I ended up as the class valedictorian.

My Mother's MS; Her Clinging to Me; Attraction to Girls; My Character

No longer a confused and immature child, during high school I was a confused and immature adolescent. I was inhibited, pretend-modest, un-insightful, self-centered, unempathetic, wanting my own way, not knowing what I might come to be and little aware of what I was. My mother had become cloying. Her diagnosis was an ailment for which there was not a treatment, but, instead, the expectation of continuing deterioration. She wanted too much for me to remain her companion. I was desperate to be independent, and, of course, could not be a little boy forever.

About one thing at least, I never had to wonder, as I later understood some others did, about my gender or sexuality. I was a boy who was interested in girls. The first experienced ejaculation is sound evidence that a transition has occurred. In my case, this significant event occurred while I was reading a book about South Sea Island puberty rituals. Pictures and word by various anthropologists, including one by the never-to-be-forgotten name of Maclucho-Maclay, described infibulation, ampallangs, defloration of girls by appointed uncles or guardians; and I was astounded by the magical experience emanating from my genitalia, along with the first semen I had seen or smelled.

At the age of fourteen and fifteen, though doing well in school, I was too frightened to exercise intellectual freedom. I went to parties and drank too much. Two or three attractive girls liked me. One liked me a lot. I remember crawling under a piano groping Frances Fox, who was a Communist (I hated communism, but not Frances Fox). I still have a good friend from that time, Diane Kelder, a prominent art historian and curator, who is in my present life. Most of the time, I felt content. I was almost always happily busy. But when not actively occupied, I would get depressed.

Writing Reviews for the *Newtown X-Ray*

The Newtown X-ray student newspaper received a pair of free tickets from a theater group of young people led by Erwin Piscator, who had been a famous director in Vienna. As editor, I assigned myself the task of reviewing a performance of *Twelfth Night*. It was a revelatory experience to see real people, warty and piebald, on stage cavorting, funny and sad, in a story without bombast, without pomposity, without hyperbole but with simple poetic exaggeration, put on in an old theater on Second Avenue, with an appreciative audience of local people, including some Bowery homeless. Around that time, I had seen the Olivier film of *Henry V*. I took it as it was doubtless meant to be seen—as a wartime film to encourage the heroism and broadcast the beauty in the humanity of the common man. I can't pretend I put away my elitist attitudes about talent and intelligence; but I became a democrat, in having respect for practically every quirk and quiddity or eccentricity, save destructive zeal and self-destructive stupidity. I thought *Twelfth Night* was more profound and meaningful than *Henry V*, as I have never become able to think of myself as a part of a narrow category—as a patriot, as a Jew, as a white person, or even as a Freudian—except insofar as Freudianism is for humans. I wanted to become humane, liberal, and useful. Such was my adolescent, utopian thinking—too abstract and absent concrete choices. Also, absent passions.

Piano Lessons from Eduard Steuermann; Love of Vladimir Horowitz

Theater had its own magic, yes, but I was repeatedly astounded by the power of music, and of musicians to make music. My reaction to visual art was tepid: I saw, and I felt, but not much. Music, however, was intense. Horowitz was a musician, and I was humbled by his performances as I was whenever I was faced with someone of seriously brilliant capacities. His playing had an unparalleled effect, tender, dramatic, powerful, and his contact with the audience was astonishing. Like an extraordinary politician, it felt as though he was playing directly to me. My own work at the piano, then, was with Eduard Steuermann, a fine musician, if somewhat lacking in confidence and technique, who educated my ear. The point came when I could hear the interpretation of a piece that was being performed, as though inner music was playing in my head as I wanted to hear it, and I noted the difference. I could revel in Toscanini, but I would have liked some tempi a bit slower. I could appreciate the honesty of Serkin or Schnabel but wish for more warmth. I never had such critical feelings about Horowitz. And after an extraordinary evening of Scarlatti, Mozart, and Liszt, his patriotic I-am-an-American-too *Stars and Stripes Forever* transcription encore never failed to be the fitting, patriotic end, always leaving the audience weary from applauding. For that little while I could almost believe that America was the land of the free and the home of the brave.

My First Jobs

Naturally, I needed to earn some money. In grade school, I was the dog walker for the ancient wirehaired terrier belonging to an equally ancient woman who lived in our apartment house in Jackson Heights. In high school, I worked as an office boy in my father's office at 30 Broad Street, at the firm of F.M. Mayer, a Berlin banker who had emigrated early, with sufficient funds to start a banking business, similar to the one my father had in Vienna. There, my father found friends from Vienna, including Oscar Wolteger, he of the *Papillon* bow tie, and some other refugees. I carried packages, ran errands, stamped envelopes, and filed papers; but my chief ego gratification was to be entrusted with large amounts of currency to exchange at the nearby foreign exchange concern of Perrera & Co in 1946 and 1947.

There was then a brisk trade in French francs, which were rapidly depreciating in value as France had been devastated in the war and needed to borrow large sums to rebuild. The French were prohibiting the export of their currency in an effort to keep its exchange value up (as Austria, and other countries, had done in similar circumstances). At the same time, they were printing currency, and increasing the quantity of the currency available, decreasing the value of each unit. The result was the creation of a large arbitrage business, in which French people smuggled their cash out of the country to customers, who then paid what it was worth in the uncontrolled public market. At least that was my father's response when I castigated him for being dishonest. "Oh no," he insisted, "It's the governments who debase their currency and steal the savings of their citizens who are the criminals." It was an echo of our War Stamps discussion.

Mon Amour Lodge

In August 1944 and August 1945 my mother, father, and I went to a modest lakeside Lake Placid hotel, the Mon Amour Lodge for three-week vacations. Lake Placid is near the magnificent, enormous Adirondack Park, the largest park in the United States, with many trails. The nearest trails began at Heart Lake. They wind through forests, past lakes, across streams and log lean-tos that hikers use to pass nights. My mother was still able to walk, and the hills were not too high for my father and his compromised heart to manage.

My father was outgoing as usual and so we met many co-vacationers, including a few refugees who found that the Adirondacks were good reminders of the foothills of the Alps near Vienna. He made friends with the managing owner, Dr. Graves, a dentist, and sold him life insurance.

He sold him me as well, and Graves hired me for the summers of 1949 and 1950. I travelled to the Mon Amour Lodge on a Pullman, spending a night in an upper berth by myself. I was on my own—I was free. I was an adolescent. Lake Placid was a genuine job and then some. My work involved long hours, because I functioned as bellboy, boat-boy, busboy, coffee maker, and everything-boy. I received tips and made over five hundred dollars in the season, which was real money then (worth about ten times as much in 2018, at least $5,000.)

On my days off, I could hire a horse and ride through the woods. I had never had riding lessons, but that did not stop me or the livery. They assigned me an elderly and docile horse. Sometimes I would hitch a lift to the park, and I climbed Mount Marcy, New York's highest peak at 5300 feet, and Mount Algonquin, the second highest.

Learning to Drive; My Father and Harry Freud

The Graves family included his sister and a daughter, whom I found completely attractive. Unfortunately, she was in love with Gil MacDougald, a future New York Yankee baseball star, and, besides, she was two years older than I. The owner's sister offered to lend me her new car, a Kaiser, the first truly post-war new model car. I tooled ten miles to Saranac to visit an acquaintance, gloriously ignoring the speed limit, feeling like Danny Kaye in *The Secret Life of Walter Mitty* (which came out in August of 1947, when I was not quite fifteen). Of course, I was not yet licensed to drive; and my knowledge of how to drive came from watching my father having lessons from Harry Freud. My father had to learn how to stay in his lane. Freud counseled him to focus on a line over the hood ornament to the edge of the road, and he would always be able to find the middle of the lane. Harry also knew how to make good time in Manhattan, by making a turn crosstown to the next avenue, followed by another turn onto that avenue, going to the next cross street, to make yet another turn onto the next avenue, and so on—the two short blocks would allow missing the red lights. Of course, the avenues were all two-way at the time, and the traffic was sparse.

COLLEGE

On to Harvard

Finally, I was off to Harvard, the fourth consecutive Newtown Valedictorian in four years to be the single Newtowner admitted. Harvard allowed me to escape from my guilty dislike of living with my parents. They let me go because they knew Harvard's reputation for selecting the best, so how, in good conscience, could they keep me in New York any longer? I gave up a small scholarship which would have helped me at Columbia, where I would have saved my parents more money by living at home and commuting as Fred had done.

As the end of the summer of 1950 drew on, I returned to New York from my job at Lake Placid, little realizing how unprepared for college I was. I was seventeen. On to Harvard I went, equipped with the clothes I thought appropriate: two pairs of chinos, a tweed suit from Brooks Brothers, a couple of pairs of penny loafers with their pennies, some button-down shirts and ties, a bottle of aspirin, and a meager allowance. No uncomfortable, inappropriate hand-me-downs from my brother.

Continuing Insomnia and Nightmares in the 1950s as a Result of 1938

I had not yet recovered from 1938. Indeed, I am still unable to go on a trip, move to a new place, lose a friend, have a bad experience with a doctor, be stopped by a traffic cop, or accommodate to anything that seems related to Nazis, without having insomnia, bad dreams, and depressions of varying degrees. SSRI's have mercifully made a huge difference. However, 1950 was a long time before Lexapro. Fortunately, my symptoms at that time were mostly insomnia and nightmares. Falling asleep had been a problem from age six or so, more severe after my tonsil operation at age thirteen, and variable thereafter. My method of treating it had been to keep quiet and make a lantern using C-Cell batteries and my blanket to construct a hideout, concealing from my parents the fact that I was awake and reading till the early morning. I read *War and Peace* from beginning to end without sleeping, in my longest continuous book stint. Books saved me; at different times, I favored crime fiction, science fiction, Trollope, Galsworthy, James, Conrad, Twain, and Verne. From time to time, I would catch up on sleep. Naturally enough, loneliness after starting college led to episodes of insomnia; "heeling" (local argot for competing) for the daily, student-run college newspaper the *Crimson* served me well, since it necessitated late nights followed by early breakfasts, followed by missed classes. Poker, bridge, and movies were also useful.

The Harvard Crimson; My First Roommate at Harvard

On arriving, I made my way to my assigned quarters in Harvard Yard at Matthews South, a dark pile of mid-Victoriana. A stairway led to a dark wood-lined hall on the second floor, where the rooms I was sharing with Joseph Carter Oakley were. His embossed letter paper was present though Oakley was not; it indicated that he came from Bardstown, Kentucky, home of *My Old Kentucky Home*. We had previously filled out a form that, among other things, indicated our preferences in roommates, and we had each asked for someone from a different background in a different part of the country. Oakley turned out to be lanky, with a definite drawl and pride in Kentucky, Bardstown, and bourbon. As time went on, we found that the differences between us were more important than any common interests, so we never became fast friends. We got along reasonably well, given that we hardly saw each other, partly because we had different sleep schedules and social habits. Oakley once opined that we could have saved money if we had only one bedroom for the two of us.

Harvard in the 1950s: White and Smart

Others on my floor represented a good cross-section of the Harvard of that time. All were white and smart. We had a Dutch future banker-baron, who had a single, quickly joined the international social set, and had his rooms redone by a tony decorator. We had a Boston-Irish, florid faced, working-class fellow; he roomed with a gay, timid, odd-looking youth, who walked and looked a bit like a penguin, with his head tilted curiously, and a rotund and birdlike body. He later became the money-giver-away to needy artists for the Pollock-Krasner Foundation.

Next was a sweet, shy young man from Wyoming, where his family owned a ranch near Sheridan. He wore cowboy boots; eventually, we learned that his grandfather had been a Senator, and that his family were among the first settlers. His roommate was from Brooklyn, where his father was a well-known neurosurgeon. Oakley, Brophy (the Irishman), and I represented public school education. The others had been educated at boarding schools.

We had a good-looking tutor, ostensibly responsible for enforcing the parietal rules—keeping the place quiet, watching out for drinking, barring women, and so on. He soon revealed a collection of six-foot-long woolen scarves, which were fashionable, worn wrapped around his neck while strolling on cold but overcoat-free days, or at football games with the good-looking knitter on his arm. Our tutor didn't use the number of stripes on each scarf to show rank; instead, he used the number of scarves in his collection to demonstrate his prowess with ladies who knitted. Admired by the callow freshman Matthews South residents, he enhanced his stipend by running pyramid clubs that helped us learn to look out for cads, and for his own profit and amusement. After a few months, he disappeared from our view. His extra-curricular activities had probably been uncovered.

Prior to choosing the courses in which I was to enroll, I met my advisor, a young graduate student working for his Ph.D. in psychology under B.F. Skinner. He was training pigeons. I later learned that during World War II, before the invention and distribution of the Norden bombsight, pigeons were trained to watch the passing landscape from transparent cones on bombers, for the purpose of navigation, having been trained to locate themselves by walking over aerial photographs of the terrain below. When they positioned themselves to the right, that meant navigate to the right, or if left to bear left. I initially took this as myth. A friend who was a fan of Skinner, assured me that this scheme had actually been tried. At any rate, the advisor was no more helpful than the dormitory tutor. He interviewed me, discovered that I had placed out of all the introductory requirements freshmen had to meet—English, foreign language, math, chemistry, and physics—and that, therefore, I could register for any courses I wanted. Thinking quickly about my mother and her wish for a doctor son to help with her illness and knowing that one grandfather and uncle had followed this path, it occurred to me that if I got all the premedical school requirements out of the way early, I could then happily scout around in other areas at my leisure. Face the boring task first and save dessert for later.

Smart I might have been, but neither my naïveté nor my mental state helped me to make realistic choices. I elected to concentrate in chemistry, incidentally following in my brother's footsteps. My lizard-brain, unconscious pilot, was setting me up for problems as a medical school applicant. That primitive motivator knew better what was good for me than I did, and it craftily allied with my depression center to make certain avenues to future careers unlikely. I would never become a chemist, journalist, or attend an Ivy League medical school.

Demographics of Harvard Again; Encountering Students Better Educated Than I

Half the Harvard class had graduated from the elite boarding schools of the Northeast. Another large group came from the best high schools in the country, such as Boston Latin, Shaker Heights near Cleveland, and New Trier near Chicago. Others came from selective day schools. This large majority had benefited from the high level of teaching they received, and from being with others who could pick up ideas swiftly. One result was that they had learned much more than I. A second was that there were people from each of those schools at Harvard, and the newcomers entered a place about which they knew a lot. "Legacies," members of ancestral Harvard families were also common. Our class included a John Harvard, as well as a John Paul Jones, the crown prince of Afghanistan, Ted Kennedy, and three people—who became roommates—the grandsons of James Joyce, Henri Matisse, and the Aga Khan. A friend of mine, Clarence Chang, who later had a brilliant scientific career, was the grandson of Chang Tso Lin, the last significant warlord and anti-Japanese nationalist of Manchuria, who was blown up in his armored train by the Japanese. On the other hand, there was also a Candy Cohen and a Hershey Rosen; the place was both a meritocracy and an Old Boys' club. As being shown to a good table, rather than being seated in Siberia in a popular restaurant depends on how well-known one is, so the Harvard experience was affected by whether one was a legacy or came from a place where the admissions advisors had a relationship with the college deans and one had a circle of old boys to join. Harvard was a privilege to attend, even for the already privileged, and I am grateful for it.

Despite the differences in the scholastic and competitive environment between Newtown and Harvard, I tried to do what I had done with great success in high school, where I breezed through the academic requirements. Unfortunately, I also tried to do things that I didn't like and I took the most compressed, speeded-up courses. More sensible pre-med students knew they needed to give these their full concentration; I just wanted to get these courses over with, so that I could get to study the things that really interested me—literature, the arts, and history. At the same time, heeling for the *Crimson*—writing articles, proofing, writing headlines, and putting the paper to bed—took up varying amounts of time every day, but usually ten or twelve hours. I dated, went to football games, and sang with the glee club. I also slept through classes, especially differential calculus, and studied through the nights before finals. For that I got a C-. I switched majors from chemistry to English History and Literature,

My Controversial "Squib"

Another example of my naïve intemperance: I wrote a "squib," in which I quoted the dean of freshmen as telling a group of students that no Harvard men were likely to be drafted. This was during the Korean War, when college boys who performed well academically were likely to be exempt; practically all Harvard people would be among those. This was picked up by the Associated Press and spread to the nation. I was summoned to the dean's office and berated for not having known that what I had heard was meant to be off the record. I didn't think I had fatally wounded the regard the country felt for Harvard, but the people in the dean's office were angry.

I was happy to make the news board of the *Crimson*, to survive the forced drunkenness that was the traditional initiation rite, and was immediately promoted to the job of Telegraph Editor, responsible for keeping up with stories that appeared in the newspapers of Yale, Princeton, and the other Ivies. I sang with the Harvard Glee Club, with Charles Munch conducting the Boston Symphony Orchestra. That year we performed Stravinsky's *Oedipus Rex*, and the following year the Berlioz *Requiem*, dressed in white tie and tails rented from Max Keezer on Mass Avenue. Still feckless academically, I decided to take the next level of calculus in the spring term, assuming that, having finished with my extensive hours at the *Crimson*, and having gotten a passing grade without attending class in the first semester, I'd make up for my low mark by getting a good mark in the higher course. But it turned out that if you hadn't learned Math 1A, you wouldn't understand 1B. I failed, which led to being put on academic probation, which in turn prohibited extra-curricular activities. Competing to become editor-in-chief or president of the *Crimson* was no longer an option. My career as a journalist was at an end, but the *Crimson* had provided me with a few wonderful friends, like Michael and David Halberstam, Swidge (later Bill) Green—who became my Congressman in New York but was redistricted out of office and died young, Rudy Kass, an appeals court judge, Bill Simmons, who became a prominent politico, George "Digger" Abrams, who became a super-successful lawyer, and Milt Gwirtzman, who became Ted Kennedy's speech writer and died young. I did not go into politics or journalism like them. My inner lizard decreed I should not be a public person. It kept me out of politics and combined the hidden inner arrangements designed to preserve my safety, with my rash anger, need for attention, and self-punishment tendencies in creating a run-in with the dean, as analogy with my childhood lamppost. An ingenious construction of a character trait designed to manage a variety of requirements. It took a long time to realize that success meant danger from competitors as well as guilt over surviving better than others.

Second Year at Harvard

In my second winter in Cambridge, I thought that I'd like to learn how to ski, having been enthused by conversations I had had with Uncle Gusti and my mother about the beauties of snow and mountains. Besides, I had inherited my grandfather Gottlieb's alpine walking stick, with a metal point, its shaft festooned with badges of climbs he had made. As I didn't have money for skiing lessons or equipment, I found an army surplus store on the wrong side of Beacon Hill and got outfitted with skis (7'3" inches long and significantly warped). The salesman advised me that being 5'8" didn't matter, and, anyhow, my weight would flatten the skis; I also bought ill-fitting leather army boots and the least costly bindings, which lacked an automatic release.

Off I went to a weekend at North Conway, New Hampshire, and to the top of the mountain, where I stood watching groups of ski classes as they passed and listening to the instructions they were offered for a half-hour or so (similar to the way I learned from eavesdropping on my parents how to swim at the Aquacade). Then I set off downhill, until it became necessary to make a turn, which I didn't know how to do. So I fell down, and got up to try again, and fell again. The third time I landed, my left arm was thrown flailing into the air, my left shoulder gave a popping sound, and a pain revealed that something was wrong;

with a "thunk," my arm went back into the socket, and I made it to the bottom.

Some days later, I woke up one morning in my bed at Dunster House (my residence for the last three years at Harvard) on my stomach, raising myself as though to turn, when I heard "pop," again. This time my humerus didn't reset itself. I had to wake up my roommate, John Hirsch, who was sleeping in the other bed in our little room. "John, John," I said, "my arm's dislocated. Would you call Stillman Infirmary?" He phoned, announcing that his roommate, Ernie Kafka, had a dislocated arm. The response from the other end of the line was, to my surprise, to come in immediately.

We rushed to Stillman Infirmary, and, in a few minutes arrived there, dressed in pajamas under an overcoat, and a man announced he was Doctor Quigley, the football team orthopedist. Looking at me, obviously disappointed, he said, "You're not *Bernie* Kafka." (Apparently there was a Bernie on the Junior Varsity team.) Grumbling, the doctor reduced the dislocation, by grabbing my arm and twisting it in a certain clever way, inducing the now familiar "thunk." Now that I knew what to do the next time, and there were many next times over the years, I could do it myself. At least it was reassuring to know that football players at Harvard could expect quick responses to injuries.

I had one more contact with the health authorities at college. They required me to undertake a fitness program, when I became short of breath during a swimming test. I felt humiliated, as at P.S. 149, when a teacher discovered I was lisping and sent me to speech therapy; and at Newtown, when the running was too much for me. Self-esteem is so important, yet so easily deflated. Physical disability (which we did not know I had) is more tolerated, societally, than psychological. It is much better to have a deformity than to be regarded as a "wuss," or even an oddity. A defect is one thing. To be an oddball is another. I took refuge in being accepted by (hopefully worthwhile) oddballs.

Social Life: Boston Bohemia

In my second year, I renewed a friendship with Morty Schiff, who lived in my Jackson Heights neighborhood. He was then a senior at Tufts, about to continue his study of physics. At the time we met again, he was installing an apparatus on the roof of a building in Medford and some machinery in a lab below, which he had designed to catch and record cosmic rays. What he wanted to do with them, I never understood. He lived in an apartment not too far from the army surplus store where I had bought the equipment that I used for my ill-fated ski trip. It was also quite near the Old Howard and the Casino burlesque theaters, where I spent some happy hours watching the strippers and laughing with the comics.

Morty had met his roommate, Klaus Heimann, along with Severn (Sevvy) Teakle Darden III, and Guido Guidotti, another physicist, at the Woodstock Country School, at that time a progressive Eden for somewhat mad adolescent (good oddball) geniuses, unable to survive in normal school environments. Klaus went to Harvard, where a medical excuse allowed him to live off campus, the other two to Bard College. Supposedly Guido alarmed the deans when he consulted them to learn which were the approved whorehouses. He was surprised to hear that, contrary to the situation at his earlier college in Mexico, the deans were not in a position to satisfy his curiosity. Sevvy had already established a reputation for eccentricity at Bard, and then at the University of Chicago. At Bard, stopped by a guard while returning late at night, he challenged a man to a duel with pistols, which he had inherited from his father's family. His father was

District Attorney in New Orleans at the time. Sevvy wore a cape and drove a Springfield Rolls Royce (Rolls made upwards of 3000 cars in Springfield, Massachusetts. in the 20s), which he used to stage mock kidnappings; when pursued by the Chicago police, he made his way to the altar of Rockefeller Chapel, on the University of Chicago campus, where he claimed sanctuary. When he later joined the Compass Players and the Second City troupe, he toured with these groups of improvisational actors, including Mike Nichols, Elaine May, Del Close (all of whom figured in my later life), and Alan Arkin. Sevvy also had a Hollywood career; he played the president's analyst in the movie of the same name, and the chief ape in *Planet of the Apes*, among other roles. He died at age 66 in 1995.

The Haunt of Beacon Hill; Contrast with Harvard

These people drifted in and out of Boston and of my social life (then and later). The Morty Klaus apartment on the gritty, rundown back of Beacon Hill near Scollay Square was a permanent temporary haunt for me. It was there that my virginity ended; and where another girl, who briefly thought I might have impregnated her, gave birth not to a baby, but to a huge fright for us both. There were also hours of classical records, drinking and smoking, discussion of philosophical problems, great books, and political and economic issues. It was another world among my many worlds. Or maybe it was adolescence.

At the same time, there was the world of Harvard. Beginning in my sophomore year, I had two roommates, John Hirsch and Paul Ehrlich. John was the younger of two children of a Philadelphia lawyer who died years before John reached college. His mother remarried, and John's stepfather was a Chicago mail-order catalog scion (Spiegel). They lived a Glencoe country club life; John was sent to Andover, and then to Harvard. Paul was the second of two boys who were the children of my father's orphanage contemporary, Edi Ehrlich, the evil surgeon of my traumatic ether dreams. John and I still stay in touch.

Gaynor Bradish and Success in My Major

Gaynor Bradish was an exceptional English major; even in his junior year, he seemed destined for a professorship. Gaynor taught me a simple lesson in how to get As: prepare for exams, which consisted mainly of essay writing, by learning a modest number of lines of some poems in the assigned readings, and some prose lines for the exam essay questions that had to do with prose. A similar process was useful when writing lengthier essays, as called for during the class year. The method not only demonstrated that one had done the readings, but it also motivated one to think about the most interesting, telling, and central points in the work: I proceeded to receive lots of As and nothing lower than an A- until I graduated. I was flattered, and also tempted, when Herschel Baker, the chair of the English Department, offered me a place at the Harvard graduate school. But I thought that I wanted and needed to make something more of a contribution to both Harvard and my new country. In retrospect, as was often the case, I needed to choose the more difficult path, as I had done with my excessive demands on myself before. The later diagnosis was "*Minderwartiges Neurose*"—translation: "unworthiness." As for Gaynor, he became a well-known professor, as well as the man who discovered and encouraged Arthur Kopit and produced his play, *Oh Dad, Poor Dad, Mama's Hung You in the Closet and I'm Feeling So Sad*. Gaynor was—unfortunately—conflicted about being both a devout Catholic and gay, and never got tenure at Harvard during the course of his short life. (He died in 1989.)

Harvard Professors—the Study of History

The teachers at Harvard who affected my outlook included Helen Maud Cam, who taught the course on British constitutional law. I was then, and remain, an ardent Anglophile. The British and the Americans formed the modern, liberal, democratic, Western world, the first having evolved the Common Law and democratic institutions, the second republican ones, over hundreds of years. In the First and Second World Wars, they preserved the possibilities of continuing these arrangements. I give the Greeks and Romans credit for our institutions, and Napoleon as well, but we live by virtue of the development of the Common Law and the U.S, Constitution. Cam's course covered the development of laws, beginning with the earliest attempts to construct ways for populations to resolve problems of minor disagreements about ownership to major crimes, causing injury and death. It is a long road from the *Wergild*—the penalty assessed based on an assigned "value" for every being and piece of property—to the demarcations a society constructs between acceptable dispute and punishable behavior, which appeared in Britain in early times, and further to the complicated and often tedious way in which advanced communities deal with the problems associated with the adjudication, compensation, and punishments of wrongs.

Professor Cam meant a great deal to me. The European turmoil that went on in my parents' time, and so influenced my early life, was crucial in my personal history, and fed my interest in learning about how societies constructed conditions and structures to make it possible for communities to live together within organized groups and together with foreign communities. British history is steeped in Church study and preservation of the classics of Roman and Greek times; these represented the background of Western cultural developments, which created structures to support cultural and political life. The British islanders mingled and melded with the rough practices and pagan mythologies of north European and Germanic pre-Christian peoples. In my own time, the British became the savior society who successfully resisted the barbarism which, it seemed to me, had flowed from the foolish efforts of so-called civilized nations to resume an interrupted history after World War I.

I am a grandchild of the First World War. I had relatives who died in that war, and others who were traumatized. I knew that my mother's favorite cousin and her aunt had to move to Sweden to escape the trials of hunger and dangers of loss that would have threatened them in Vienna. I had grown up with tales of Ferdinand of Belgium and his looting and killing in the Congo, the poison gas use in the war, the depression and inflation in Europe after the war, the betrayal of the Balfour declaration, the rise of Hitler and Mussolini, the ridiculousness of the Powers' competition over colonies before the war, and the bickerings over who would get what part of the defeated empires after it. This fed my interest in the development of law and the conflicts over the centuries which related to my interests in how things come about, a fundamental issue in medicine and psychology.

I think that Arthur Maas, a conservationist political scientist, showed me what an intelligent gradualism in government could accomplish, in terms of long-range planning. A chief illustrative example of successful government planning was the Tennessee Valley Authority, which, it soon seemed to me, might have been the mother of federal, regional, and state governmental collaboration in the creation of major material structure, socially and physically. I had never come across a massive governmental project which had the beneficial effects the TVA did. It provided water power, electricity, fertilizer, water transport, flood control, employment, and industrial development across the southeastern states, setting the stage for long-term growth. It was the New Deal's most successful program. Gradualism shows governments can accomplish things over time—another leg in the path to progress and another support for a certain optimism and a greater admiration for the nurturing of patience.

David Owen taught a course in nineteenth-century English history. Each week, seats were filled by students, and learned visitors and colleagues, interested in hearing lectures delivered by a modest man who worked over his lectures from year to year. He had to cope with a hideous stammer in normal conversation, but rehearsing his lectures over and over made it possible for him to discourse smoothly. A lecture about the Crystal Palace exhibition of mechanical, architectural, and agricultural developments of the nineteenth century drew annual standing room only audiences, in the larger-than-usual room, the New Lecture Hall.

There are other important examples of the power of gradualism. Alexander the Great's invention of coinage, his road construction, and his insistence that his generals, whom he appointed to be rulers of his captured domains, were to intermarry with the indigenous leaders' families, changed the economic and political course of world history. The Marshall Plan was largely responsible for giving us an unprecedented seventy-plus years of peace among the major nations.

Hyder Rollins; Bartlett Whiting–Literature

Hyder Rollins, who taught the Romantic Poets, was inspiring. He breathed the lives and works of Keats, Coleridge, Wordsworth, Shelley, Byron, and some less august figures with a passion that one would not have expected could burn in such a small, spare person. He showed what love and devotion a teacher might experience and communicate through the medium of language. The Romantics amalgamated the emotional, the spiritual, and the humane aspects of the inner life for English speakers. The sincerity and humanity that characterized the poesy of the Romantic period, the introspection and psychological refinement that we learned to appreciate was stunning. The volumes of Goethe, Heine, and Schiller that my parents had brought from Vienna led me to read those masters, too, though sadly not in German, where my vocabulary was too slight. Later on, I realized the debt Freud and psychoanalysis—and I—owed to the Romantics.

Bartlett Whiting was another stammerer, who was devoted to his subject, Chaucer, and made it a joy. We read everything Chaucer wrote in the Middle English in which it had been written, going line by line, translating what needed to be translated as we went along. Chaucer is, of course, a delicious feast of stories, full of movement, written in a simple and clear language conveying color and sound, physical appearance, and bodily sensations—sensations acquired through exercise of all the major senses—and never omitting the complicated play of emotions and colors which characterize the musical movement of life. The love of mankind the author conveys to the reader is never absent. Humor, pride, valor, so many good and uplifting things are so simply put. The knight, who "gladly would he learn and gladly teach," served me as an exemplar of the morality of the university, of its hopes for the beneficial effects of teaching and learning as well as purposeful cultivation of the mind, generosity, honor, and pleasure and pride in accomplishment, and significantly, also in sensuality.

Albert Barron Friedman, who died at the age of 86 in 2006, was another English professor. His field was medieval balladry; he was a gay Jew from Missouri, with a private income. His value to me came from his interest in finding and nurturing talents, and in his projecting a diffident and timid personality, mixed with heroism about which he was reticent. He had an outstanding collection of drawings but he was not showy; few knew of his connoisseurship as he kept his collection in boxes stashed in closets in his rooms at Dunster House. He liked my brilliant Barbara—the woman with whom I would spend my life—and showed his drawings to us one day. He had to move a smallish box out of the way to get at something he wanted to show, and it fell open—it contained medals from Greece, Yugoslavia, and Italy. This large, soft man, too anxious to drive a car, had been parachuted into those countries, whose languages he spoke, to help set up underground organizations, which was why he had been invested with the Greek Order of This and the British and Yugoslav Orders of That.

When I won the Detur Prize for academic standing, Al Friedman's gift to me was to volunteer to find a proper award, which turned out to be *The Dunciad*, the great satire by Alexander Pope, a first edition in a fine Riviere binding. Al, like Gaynor Bradish (I was on first name terms with both of them), was a man who, I thought, deserved to be a tenured professor, and I suspect his homosexuality prevented that. There certainly were gays on the faculty, but perhaps there was a quota, as there was said to be for Jews.

Were I writing a Dunciad, due to my dislike of rote learning, for first dunce I'd nominate Louis Fieser, author of the *Textbook of Organic Chemistry* by Fieser and Fieser. His course was a full year, with a twenty-hour-a-week laboratory, during which the students were required to manufacture a variety of chemicals. Your grade depended on the quantity you produced; this was exceptionally boring and I got a B. Somehow, for no reason that I could imagine, the Ivies wanted medical school applicants to have at least an A- from Professor Fieser. Perhaps those medical schools were correct in thinking that cookbook-following, obsessional characters make more thorough, hence better, physicians.

I was also privileged to experience a political event that took place during my time in Cambridge, a lesson about democracy and free speech in a democracy. James Bryant Conant, an esteemed chemist and educator, and one of the scientists who led the work at Oak Ridge, left the office of president of the university. The overseers selected a quiet, religious man, Nathan Marsh Pusey, of Lawrence College, from the same Appleton, Wisconsin, whence had come Senator Joseph McCarthy. Pusey was a gentleman and provided a wild contrast to Joe McCarthy and his vulgar, rabble-rousing and red-baiting, which Pusey criticized vigorously. Pusey was not intimidated by McCarthy, and he protected the university as he reflected its values.

Warren Manshel

Warren Manshel came into my life in my sophomore year, and gradually we became close. He was a tutor in Leverett House and a cousin of my roommate, Paul. Warren was finishing his work for a Ph.D. in government. His subject was European integration, a timely subject in the period of Robert Schuman, Konrad Adenauer, and their associates, whose successful rearranging of European international affairs was so different from the hypocrisy and destructiveness of the Versailles settlement (just to mention one example of the hapless behavior of elites). Warren had been a refugee from Berlin, where his family had been well-to-do and was a younger brother, as I was. In my search for a Fritzl/Uncle Rudolf substitute, I regarded Warren as an older sibling, while he, in some ways, did the same by elevating me. We shared interests in political and economic European history and always had something to talk about.

Warren was a person who could be easy with practically anyone, of whatever socioeconomic class, and I think he rarely made an enemy. Not that he was incapable of rage; he could tear a telephone off an airline agent's desk when he found that his reservation was missing and berate his wife or children when he felt frustrated by them, but, generally, he was tactful and diplomatic. He could even be kindly and tolerant with his older brother, who was envious, grouchy, unsuccessfully competitive, and self-pitying. His name, incredibly enough, was Ernest. As might be expected, he needed lots of practical help. I could not have put up with him.

Warren was shy, and diffident with women, embarrassed about his height, which was six feet seven inches, and about supernumerary nipples on his chest. He was finicky about dress, manners, and being on time. Like Al Friedman, he was uncomfortable in cars, especially with someone else at the wheel, but had been decorated and wounded in his service during the D-Day landings. He was another bashful hero.

Revisiting Harvard in 1983

One further reassuring example from my Harvard experience happened in 1983, at my daughter Nicole's commencement from what by then had become Harvard-Radcliffe. An honorary degree was awarded to a man who, by name and manner, was a member of the Massachusetts Brahmin class. He had been a student at about the same time as I, then spent the intervening years collecting funds that helped support changes in the structure of Harvard's student body. In a touching speech, he described some things that had taken place. In my class, 1954, about 60% of the students came from private preparatory schools, 15% from New England, 10% from the rest of the U.S, and the rest from other countries, and other states. A majority were "legacies." I knew only two blacks and no Native Americans. The *Crimson* had only two women editors, Rita Labenow, who had come from my own public high school, Newtown, and Margaret Fechheimer, with whom Barbara and I were friends until Maggie's untimely death. A light black, Bill Simmons, was president of the *Crimson* as a senior, when I was a freshman reporter. In my daughter's class, 1983, by contrast, there were about 35% prep school people, 10-15% blacks, probably 20% Asians, as well as Native Americans, and essentially equal numbers of women and men, the women receiving joint Harvard and Radcliffe degrees. Tears came to my eyes as I realized that, in my time, the descendants of the founders and their families were continuing to support the institution, while offering members of the larger community places that would otherwise have gone to their own children.

BARBARA

Barbara's Posterior; First View

Every Christmas, Dunster House put on a theatrical evening. In my junior year, 1952–53, the producers decided on two one-act plays, the opener by Lady Gregory, and the second, by Synge. I went to the senior common room to watch, as I knew that notices had been put up at Radcliffe to invite women to audition. When I opened the door, I saw a woman facing away on hands and knees on the floor, butt in the air, reading a script. This was my first sight of the love of my life, a perfect use of that cliché, my wife-to-be, Barbara Poses. Though never a believer in love at first sight, I suppose what happened to my parents, when my father was aged eight or nine and my mother four, would rank as no more amazing than what happened to Barbara and me.

Barbara's posterior was never her most beautiful physical attribute, being somewhat spare; but now I think it was her position that stunned me. It was unladylike, yet comfortable; she was absorbed in what she was reading, and unaware of how contented she seemed, facing away from the entrance to the room, and the people in it, her face hidden. Her posture seemed to express an unconcern about what was going on around and behind her, as well as concentration on the text. That made her appealing, but also intimidating. Had I been functioning more rationally and less instinctually, I should have been more consciously aware of how this exemplified the way the creature on the floor herself operated: how she was, in part, reluctant and negative about new things, whether a house to live in, a dress to wear, a friend to make, or a child to bear. She always felt a resistance to accepting what would eventually become an attachment that would be hard to give up. She got the part she read for, and I offered her a ride home to Barnard Hall at Radcliffe, which she accepted with the proviso that she had a 10:30 date with a law student. To me this felt off-putting and unnecessary. I accepted with the condition that we should see each other again. We did, and soon after we sat together in Professor Whiting's Chaucer course. I met her friends, and she met mine; I met her parents and she met mine.

Barbara's Right-Left Confusions; My Tendency Towards *Schiefsehen*

Barbara knew how to help others better than how to take care of herself. I was a bit more competent than she at that. My mind did not work in the straight-line, categorizing way; Barbara was similar. I had a perverse tendency towards "*schiefsehen*," seeing things from an unusual angle—lots of word play, taking advantage of ambiguity, constructing alternative possibilities, and receiving unexpected ideas unexpectedly. Until her death in 2018, Barbara had right-left confusions, as her father did; she could never do serial sevens, a common test, which requires subtracting seven from a hundred, to ninety-three, eighty-six, and so on. I have always been absentminded and I misplace things. Both of us have had difficulty writing long pieces. Oddities such as these give me pleasure, especially when I come up with a peculiar thought, or someone else surprises me with an unanticipated idea. I find interest and amusement in eccentricity in others. Barbara liked all that.

Her Parents' Apartment

Barbara's parents, Lillian and Jack Poses, lived in an apartment on Fifth Avenue, at the corner of Ninety-Second Street, in Manhattan. The building replaced a mansion that had belonged to Marjorie Merriweather Post, in which, I was told, she took over the top three floors.

Now, in 1951, Ms. Post was no longer there, and her three floors had been converted into cooperative apartments, like the rest of the building. There were two apartments on every floor, each with an elevator. Six North was the Poses apartment, and it was larger than the South apartment.

You alighted from the elevator to be met in the foyer by Henry, the white-gloved, formally dressed butler, aged about sixty years, with a German accent. His wife, Hedwig, cooked, baked, and cleaned while Henry took the coats, poured drinks, passed hors d'oeuvres, and served at table. From the foyer you came into an entrance hall, about twenty by twenty-two feet, a space that could accommodate a four or five member dance band, and a modest number of dancers, which was how it was used at parties. Off to the right was a bar, decorated with wallpaper designed by Saul Steinberg (who had also created packaging for Jack's D'Orsay perfume company), showing a charming park scene with horses and riders, carriages, strollers, and dogs on leashes.

A long hall at right angles to the entrance connected with a library at its west end and led past Lillian's bedroom, Barbara's bedroom, and another used by Lillian's mother. At its east end, the hall terminated at the kitchen, dining room, servants' quarters, storage, and laundry rooms. When you passed through Lillian's bedroom and turned left, you went through a shorter hall; this connected two bathroom-dressing rooms and ended in Jack's bedroom. To the left of the area used for dancing was the living room, which must have been thirty-five by forty feet. Jack's bedroom, the library, and the living room overlooked Central Park, and provided a fine view of the sunsets in the evening. The apartment was furnished in good taste, with English eighteenth-century tables and chairs, stuffed modern couches and chairs, and walls hung with moderately important paintings, mainly French. A Picasso, a Braque, a de Staël, and other works were added to Soutines, Utrillos, a small Renoir, and a Modigliani. It was opulent, comfortable, and staffed, not intimidating, despite the luxury, and useful from the standpoint of entertaining, of which the Poseses did a lot.

Westport, CT Weekend House

On weekends everyone decamped to Westport, Connecticut, an hour and ten minutes away from 1107 Fifth Avenue, to an eighteenth-century farmhouse on Coleytown Road. Coleys had lived in that house and farmed the forty-plus acres that abutted. One of them, a doctor, made his name by using bee venom to treat cancer. John D. Rockefeller was a friend of Coley, and Rockefeller had another friend whose late teenage daughter developed a virulent bone cancer. Coley injected her with bee venom, and the cancer went into temporary remission; this success pointed to a pathway for research into the use of the immune system in treating cancer, currently an active and promising field. Rockefeller was moved by this experience to found the predecessor of the Rockefeller Institute, where further research could take place.

The sellers of the farmhouse to Jack and Lillian in the nineteen-forties were named Fraser. They had preserved the eighteenth-century house and barn, planted a beautiful English garden, planted trees, and dammed the Aspetuck River, which flowed through the property, creating an island and a swimming hole. In the water were some wise trout who were hard to catch; on the island was a wooden house with large glass windows, radiant heat, one large living room, and two little bedrooms and two bathrooms. Mrs. Fraser had also transplanted there a wooden shack with bedroom and bath, a sentimental memento of a property her family had owned in Canada. The Frasers also left some good colonial furniture, a barn, and a hen house.

Lillian had the old beams "pickled" with bleach, ripped out some of the trees and made other changes which, to Barbara's mind, were sacrilegious, typical of her mother's sometimes poor taste, and, on a deeper level, of her uncultured origins. Jack proudly called their lifestyle "gracious living," with a feeling of great accomplishment.

Three "Jacks" in One Generation of Pesetski Siblings

There were many Pesetskis, as Jack's family was originally called. We can only guess their ages at the dates of their emigration to the U.S.; one of the chief spurs to leaving Russia was the threat that the boys would be conscripted, so there was reason to be cagey about their ages. The mother, ten or eleven brothers, and one of their sisters, arrived in New York (I think) in 1912. On disembarking, some were renamed by the Immigration Service, as was not unusual in the case of non-English speakers. Thus, names were created for Barbara's father, Jack Poses, his brothers, Jack Perry, Herman Perry, Sam Poses, and sister Gertrude (originally Grunya). There was also a brother named Jack Posetski, so there were three "Jacks" in the same generation of siblings. Sonia, the oldest sibling, remained behind; she had married a Russian, and so became able to leave the family home, in the Pale of Settlement, to live in Moscow, at a time when Jews were banned from living in most of the country. Barbara loved to say her people had come "from Slutsk, near Pinsk, near Minsk, in Minski Gubernya."

Pushed by their mother, all the emigrants went to university, and some to graduate school. Their early lives were difficult. They lived in Washington Heights, and Jack Poses never forgot the struggles of his youth: the people on his newspaper route who didn't pay their bills, the flights of stairs he climbed, or the fights with the local Irish. Though he retained an attachment to Russia, he was a proud American. He never lost his gratitude for his education at City College of New York, and the opportunities the United States offered. Education was his enthusiasm and his main philanthropic interest. After college, he attended courses at night to study accounting, and got a job at Macy's where he soon became a glass buyer. Later he was able to buy a semi-defunct cosmetics line; he then obtained the license to distribute D'Orsay perfumes, a French luxury product.

Jack's Success in the Perfume Business

Jack displayed an extraordinary gift for negotiating for space in department stores, for coining slogans, advertising, and marketing. He was a good judge of ancillary staff who didn't threaten his authority; one of his finds was Jane Trahey, who became extremely successful with advertising and marketing, and Saul Steinberg did advertisements. Jack had an eye for packaging. He saw the trouble brewing in Europe before it was generally recognized, and organized a factory, hired a "nose," and imported essences and chemicals that allowed him to manufacture his perfumes in New York during World War II, giving him the advantage of being able to produce perfumes indistinguishable from the imported product, because made to the original formulae. He found Brad Storey, a conservative, ethical, and patient financial advisor, and did well with his investments. In his career, he benefited from the circumstances of his age: too young for World War I and too old for World War Two.

Barbara's Thwarted Ambition to Work for Her Father

Jack did not share responsibility, which avoided risks that might have caused big losses but also prevented him from enlarging the business appreciably. It precluded involving Barbara in the business. She was eager to work with him, but he always postponed the day, ultimately putting it off until she had children, by which time he had sold it. She was the beneficiary of a trust her parents set up when she was tiny; it had grown to the value of around a million dollars, a nice sum at the time, but she was given no authority over the money until both parents died. She never needed to learn how to manage things; what she did learn was that someone else would take care of the necessaries.

At brunch one day, Jack announced that he intended to leave an amount of money that would allow Barbara to lead a better-than-modest life, and that he was giving away the rest. The better-than-modest life envisaged would be less agreeable than the life she and her parents lived in her childhood, and less agreeable than Jack and Lillian lived until their deaths. Jack had an older brother, Herman, a roué in youth, who later had a handicapped wife, and Jack endowed them with a small trust of enough money for them to lead a modest life. That was a modesty too modest for me or for Barbara; but it was the model of what might have been, had we relied solely on Jack's generosity.

Barbara, a Natural Philanthropist

Barbara would work hard and be generous to her employees, whom she trained and encouraged to learn and move on to more responsible positions. At college, she gladly helped other students write papers, one of her forms of philanthropy. At her elementary school—the Lincoln School for gifted children, associated with Columbia University and partly funded by Rockefeller grants—Barbara's small allowance was ample enough for her to lend carfare to Roddy Rockefeller, a classmate who was being educated to mind his money. She was good at giving, but she largely left it to me to earn and manage our money. I depended on friends for advice to help me, and, as they knew more about markets than most people, things worked out well. However, I had chronic concerns about being able to provide what I felt were her necessities.

A Memling; Jack and Lillian's Difficult Marriage

Jack had overcome disadvantages. This impacted his behavior around money, with particular regard to generosity and control. His family was large, fatherless, and at first, poor; several of the children had to share beds. He was his mother's favorite and lived with her into his middle thirties. There was little cultural food; only Grunya, the second oldest child, had time and the wherewithal to read the Russian classics. Barbara and a framer/dealer friend, Bob Kulicke, once wanted to buy (for $500) a small painting of Christ that they thought was School of Memling.

Barbara appealed to Jack to advance money from her trust to buy it. Jack refused incredulously: "You want to buy a Jesus for this family?" It went to the Boston Museum of Fine Arts, who declared it a genuine Memling.

Jack and Lillian's marriage was difficult, with frequent arguments, sometimes about which one had introduced some important person to the other or who knew some piece of information first; at other times it was hard to tell what was going on. I assumed that Lillian's apparent lack of sexual interest in him and flirtations, and Jack's presumable liaisons with other women, contributed to the domestic problems. He had a rough masculinity and gave off an aura of power that was quite attractive to certain women. It is probable that personality problems came first. In any case, they slept in separate bedrooms, and I never, in the many years that I knew them, saw them show physical affection to each other.

Jack's Other Daughter, Barbara's Unexpected Half-Sister

My suspicions about Jack's extramarital relations proved to be correct. One day many years after our marriage, our doorbell rang and I opened it to a good-looking young woman of mixed-race. "Is this the residence of Barbara Kafka, formerly Poses?" she asked. "Yes," I said. "I want to meet her," she said. "Might I ask why?" "She's my sister." The personable young woman explained that she had been to university and had become a social worker; she was about to move to Atlanta with her husband but felt strongly that she should take this last chance of finding the sister with whom she shared a father.

Jack was a drinker who made advances, both seductive and hostile, to women. I sometimes cringed a bit at the Poses's parties, as Jack seemed misogynistic to me. But, at the same time that he was disparaging, he was seductive, and he was clearly attracted to accomplished, successful women, such as his wife. He might follow a "Not bad for a girl, eh?" with a wink and a too energetic backslap, a laugh, or a wave of a cigar, when he appreciated a woman's comment. Yet it was typical to have an argument at a meal, with Lillian bursting into tears and running from the table. After her parents saw *Who's Afraid of Virginia Woolf*, and Barbara asked how they had liked it; her father said, perfectly seriously, "Well, we never used foul language." That Barbara had to live with her parents after graduating from Radcliffe, or else test the threat of losing their support, probably hastened her marriage to me.

I Arm Wrestle Jack, and Lose

My initial contacts with Jack were tentative; he immediately challenged me to an arm-wrestling competition, which he easily won—a strong man, he had been a wrestler at college. Giving me a peculiar glance, he pointedly informed me that he had been the first Russian Jew to become a member of the Harmonie Club (the second oldest social club in New York, designed by Stanford White), a bastion of the German Jews of previous immigrant generations. I later realized that to him, I was one of the *Yekkes*, the German Jews who had excluded the later

Russians. I also eventually learned that A.A. Brill, a founder of the New York Psychoanalytic Society, was also an eastern Jew and also a member of the Harmonie Club, who had become a member before Jack. This knowledge would have annoyed Jack, if he had lived to hear of it. Jack would have had to contest the title of being the First Galicianer.

Initially, Jack wondered how he should introduce me to people. "What am I to say? This is my son-in-law, the doctor?" I used to joke that that was my first intimate experience with anti-Semitism. But I also realized, with guilt, that I felt a bit superior towards the Yiddish-speaking, *Kultur*-deficient Galicianer Ashkenazis, from the East. Clearly, Jack and Lillian were pleased that Barbara was making a good marriage, while resenting my more elevated status, which they disliked not having been born to. On the other hand, I was very aware of being less well off. We soon became comfortable with each other; when we were in New York, we saw a lot of the parents. We spent time in Westport, went to 1107 Fifth Avenue for brunches frequently, and for parties several times a year; and I went for walks around the reservoir with Jack, took up smoking Cuban cigars with him (which I adored), and by and large came to love him and Lillian. He offered to take me on at D'Orsay but I was committed to medicine. As he was dying, he said to me, "Well, now, they're your responsibility," meaning the women needed someone to keep them on a realistic course, and also, in effect, appointing me his colleague and executor. Ultimately, Jack had regarded himself as the one responsible for his immediate family, as well as for his other relatives, and for helping the education of young, poor people. Barbara and I both had similar ideals.

Lillian's Law Career and Barbara's Companionship with Her Father

Barbara adored her father, who also mothered her, compensating for the abandoning, often absent mother, Lillian. She would have been ecstatic had Jack offered to train her in his business. She was her father's companion on many days during her early life, when Lillian spent a good deal of time in Washington. During the Roosevelt administration, Lillian was involved with the writing of the Social Security Act, was the first woman to plead a case before the Supreme Court, and, when her friend, Anna Rosenberg, was the regional director of Social Security and of the National Recovery Administration, Lillian worked together with her as Regional Attorney.

Meanwhile, Barbara and her father were left to amuse themselves. This meant dinners at Chambord and other foodie restaurants in New York, and weekends together in Westport, though Jack spent too much time, so far as Barbara was concerned, at the Birchwood Country Club playing golf and cards, having drinks, and smoking cigars. Westport became a lonely place for Barbara; he made little attempt to engage with her interests or to involve her in his.

Jack lost his enthusiasm for his business in his early fifties and sold it. I was wise not to take a chance on working with Jack, because I wanted to help people directly, not at large, as Jack did in politics and education. Jack gave money to the Democratic party and his educational activities included fundraising and overseeing the investment management at Brandeis and at City University, giving money to the Albert Einstein College of Medicine, the Poses Foundation at Brandeis, and founding a scholarship at Yale Law School.

Lillian's Family

Lillian Shapiro was a middle child. She had two brothers, whom I knew fairly well. I knew her mother, Dora, Barbara's only living grandparent. Lillian grew up in Edgemere, a beach community on Long Island, near Rockaway; her father owned a bungalow colony there. One of Barbara's family tales was a story of Lillian's childhood: a fire broke out, and her father yelled to his wife, "Dora, get the children," as he was attending to the more important matter of saving his precious books, throwing them out of his window. Barbara interpreted this as an illustration of his view of the parental role; books for him to care for, while Dora nurtured the children. Barbara thought that Jewishness is a love of books; the Jews are a "people of the book." Religious observation died out with those who came in the part of the family that migrated across the ocean, but books remained.

Jack's and Lillian's Different Sort of Jewishness

Barbara's heritage was of strong women and men—but it entailed the women, in a way, being servants to the men; Lillian was an anomaly, being a girl between two brothers with whom she competed on their own terms, leading to her successful career, but also to a confusion of roles.

From Barbara's point of view, Lillian was an excellent role model but a poor mother. To Jack, Lillian would say, "I could have been a Supreme Court Justice, but I gave up my ambitions to be your wife"—not only chastising Jack, but failing to recognize that, while ostensibly looking after him, she was neglecting Barbara, leaving Jack to assume part of the maternal role.

Jack's father, a Talmudic scholar, whom I did not know, had two older female children with his first wife, who died leaving a younger sister behind; following the then prevailing Jewish custom, he married her. She then had ten children with him and raised them with the help of her elder stepdaughter, Sonya. Jack regarded Sonya as the person who had most to do with his upbringing in Slutsk, while his mother ran a small hotel and orchard. When Jack's father died, she sent one of her older sons to the U.S. to scout; the report must have been favorable, as she then followed him with the others.

Barbara's grandparents spoke Yiddish as well as English; Jack and Lillian spoke a little Yiddish. Jack knew some Russian, and Lillian did not. The Passover Seder was Jack and Lillian's sole religious observance, and it was chiefly an occasion for inviting the main relatives to a party. Maintaining contacts among family members was important to both Barbara's parents, but religious feeling was totally absent. Every Christmas Eve there was a large party with a huge, decorated tree, dancing, and lots of presents for Jack and Lillian's friends, as well as Barbara. Barbara and I usually went on to El Morocco afterwards with our special friends, Warren and Anita Manshel.

When I met Lillian Poses in 1952, she was forty-four and practicing labor law from an office on Madison Avenue. She and both her siblings had become lawyers. In addition to her law degree, Lillian had spent some time studying social work at Bryn Mawr.

Lillian's elder brother, J. Irwin Shapiro, was a Democrat stalwart with a remarkable mind. He became a Justice of the Court of Appeals, New York's highest court, and was esteemed by his colleagues; his opinions were widely quoted. He looked the part and would have made a great movie actor, with his thick, wavy, gray-white hair, trim white moustache, and a straightforward, direct no-nonsense attitude. Nobody could cow him, except his wife, who was bitchy, cutting, and hypercritical. They had an only child, a daughter, a family court judge. (She was one of the waifs Lillian collected and moved into Barbara's bedroom for a short time. Lillian also brought home babies and told Barbara she was going to adopt them, but of course never did.)

Lillian's younger brother, Abe, was the tallest, best looking, funniest, and most athletic, and a sharp litigator. His first marriage begat two children, an older boy, Joe, and a girl, Beth. Beth at five-years-old was our flower girl; she was adorable. She went on to become another lawyer, married, had children, remarried, was widowed, and litigated formidably. Joe, a college swimmer—swimming was a major sport at Penn—went on to Harvard Law School, then to Donovan and Leisure, a top New York firm. They sent him to Los Angeles to start a branch, where he represented Disney, was hired away and was promoted to be the fourth most important figure in the company and their chief negotiator. He gave a lot of money to Harvard, was charming and mentally tough and swift, but died tragically in 1999, in his forties, of leukemia.

Joe was Barbara's and my favorite of all the cousins. Before he married the tennis star, Pam Shriver, his address book contained the personal numbers of both Xaviera Hollander and Madame Claude, the most well-known Madams of the time.

After Lillian's government years, she was chiefly a mediator who represented management in negotiations with labor, and she created relationships with both sides. As she grew older, she did more work in the field of trusts and estates, but she left her own estate in a mess. It was a case of the doctor who didn't heal himself and showed her ambivalence about money and family, as well as her inability to make plans for her own death. Her previous work in Washington, in the Roosevelt Administrations, was what gave her contacts, friendships, and clout with union leaders and politicos, which helped in her subsequent career. Her early hero, before FDR, was Eugene Debs, the Socialist leader; her desktop held a small bronze statue of Debs.

This burnished her credentials; Jack Potofsky, the powerful head of the Amalgamated Clothing Workers, for example, was a good friend.

Lillian's Admiration of Eleanor Roosevelt; Barbara's Ambivalence About Lillian

Lillian was good at embellishing and used to say that she wanted her stories to be fresh; Barbara, of course, said her mother was a liar. She was a great admirer of Eleanor Roosevelt, talked with her occasionally, and about her more often. One summer weekend, Mrs. Roosevelt came to visit in Westport, when Barbara and I happened to be there. Lillian asked if she might like a swim in the Aspetuck. Mrs. Roosevelt said that would be delightful, though she had no bathing suit. Lillian offered one of her mother's suits, though Dora Shapiro was significantly bulkier than Mrs. Roosevelt, who was taller and thinner. It was of no consequence; she put on the bathing costume and swam.

I couldn't help but note the dissimilarity between Barbara's lineage and mine. My background, in the three previous generations on the maternal side, had fairly uniform standards of education, of material living, and (lack of) religious observance. Barbara's great-grandparents and grandparents on both sides came from small, unsophisticated towns, where the inhabitants were ethnically and religiously homogeneous. My family had lived in the cosmopolitan, multiethnic capital city of an ancient empire. My generation was the third of doctors; before that, there were rabbis. The women were not expected to manage orchards, as in Barbara's family, while their men studied the Talmud. The professional class, indeed, expected their women's lives to resemble more those of the upper-class than being like the lives of their own fathers, husbands and brothers. These women could have musical training at the conservatory, teach, nurse, travel, and entertain. These activities occupied my grandmother and mother; there were plenty of one-parent families, my father's being an example, but I knew of none where the woman had the degree of family dominance that was exercised by Barbara's grandmothers and her mother.

Barbara thought of herself as being a woman in a family of strong women, without needing to compete with her mother's controlling, seductive, domineering qualities. Lillian was not her model. Barbara found other patrons. Not having experienced conditions similar to those of Barbara in relation to her forebears made it a bit harder to empathize. I can sympathize, and even forgive myself a little for my puzzlement at my sense of strangeness, and my distaste for shtetl Jews and theirs for me. Nevertheless, Barbara and I had no cultural differences, religious, intellectual, or moral. We both lacked the drive for money and power that her parents had.

Some stories illustrate generational differences: a joke that captures shtetl life is about a pious Jewish man, who goes to the local rabbi with a problem. His only son, David, has fallen in love with and married a gentile girl. What should the man do? The rabbi ruminates, but can't think of another example of such a disaster. However, he is going to Pinsk, where he can ask the chief rabbi at the bigger town. The Pinsk rabbi is stumped; nothing like that has happened there either. And so on, with a consultation in Minsk, and even Warsaw. The chief rabbi of Warsaw promises to pray to God for advice. When he pleads for help for the pious man in the shtetl, he hears weeping, and a voice says, "He thinks he has a problem? Once I had a son…"

Jewish Jokes Post-Emigration

There are Jewish jokes told about the second generation after emigration. Becky and Abie have been together for sixty years before disaster strikes. Becky has cancer that will kill her soon. At Mount Sinai Hospital, Abie, wracked with grief, sits next to the oxygen tent, under which lies the sick Becky. Becky scratches at the tent and crooks her finger at Abie who comes nearer; and he hears Becky, in a feeble voice, saying, "Abie come into the tent with me." Abie says, "But you're dying." Becky just manages to whisper, "Abie, just this one more time." The next day she feels better; the second day she is able to eat a full meal. After a week, she's out of bed and having rehab; and in another week she is discharged, cured. So, the two go on a trip around the world, and a year later, are in Paris, in a suite at the Ritz, celebrating with caviar and champagne. Abie suddenly bursts into tears. Becky asks why he's crying. It's their anniversary—one year since he saved her life, and they should be happy. "Yes," says Abie, "but just think, I could have saved Eleanor Roosevelt." In the jokes, the second generation of emigrants no longer appeals to God as the grace-and favor-dispensing father; instead they look to inspirational role models among public figures. In the third generation, there were no Beckys and no Abies. How could these three generations understand each other; and what would the generation gap imply for each of them? Barbara and I were of the same generation, despite our somewhat different heritage.

Barbara had a childhood with the Poses and Shapiro family and its background, but her daily life was very different. Her parents looked to be accepted by acquaintances like David Rockefeller, Herbert Lehman, and Eleanor Roosevelt, who also served as models from whom to learn what it was to be cultured and successfully American. Barbara went to school with their children. She grew up with the paintings, the ballet, the literature. Her parents had to absorb and learn about cultural life as adults, while Barbara did this in childhood; for her parents, the arts were like a second language; for Barbara, they were a mother tongue.

The Influence of German Sentence Structure on How I Write in English

I began to learn English aged five years and nine months. I still tend to write as though I were writing in German, my mother tongue. My sentences are often too long, my verbs too often at the end of the sentence, and I like compound words like streetcar, aerospace, and overwhelm. I don't hyphenate when I should. I don't know whether Jack was my *father in law,* my *father inlaw* or my *father-in-law.* I was lucky. I speak unaccented English and these challenges are minor. People who exchange their first language for a second after their fourteenth year like Jack, who spoke English flavored with *Rawshen,* generally have an accent carried over from the *forrrst* language. The brain neural circuits become filled by the late teens, and some have to be deconstructed to make room for new ones.

To be an acclimated Jewish man in Vienna in the latter part of the nineteenth-century and beginning of the twentieth meant to be able to trade, invest, vote, make a career in the army, and enjoy support from a monarch who was willing to empower Jews sufficiently to allow them some prominence in commerce and the professions. After the 1914–18 war, Europeans experienced great changes in the social order: the power of aristocracies was much diminished; the kings were ousted; and the influence of the nobility largely vanished. Dictators replaced kings in Russia, Germany, Italy, and in Spain, partly in response to the political chaos that followed the war, amid the economic disasters that occurred, and in the aftermath of the huge loss of life in the generation of young men.

Though I had the challenge of being uprooted, there was no more than the usual, expectable cultural and social differences between my generation and that of my parents. My parents and I went through many of the same or similar things together: economic depression, recovery, perilous childhoods, Nazism, emigration, and the Second World War. In Barbara's case, this was not so. I might have had difficulty adapting to language and school, but by comparison, the changes for the shtetl and yeshiva generation were very big. Barbara's family went from religious observance and Tsarist persecution to CCNY and Bryn Mawr. Barbara's joining the Harvard and Radcliffe cohort meant more profound chasms between the generations of her family than did the changes from Perchtoldsdorf and Vienna to New York and Harvard in my parents' lives and mine. Barbara had a longer bridge to cross with regard to her experience and her parents' than I did with mine. Barbara was ahead of her time and her generation. She skipped ahead.

Opposites Attract; and Barbara and Jacques Guérin

This difference between us attracted Barbara. From her point of view, I was a romantic figure from a more sophisticated world, a fine amateur pianist, a cultured person from a more gentrified family background. Jack had long had a French partner, Jacques Guérin, who had great appeal for Barbara. He owned one-third of all the paintings Soutine had made, many Courbets, an outstanding collection of books, and Proust's bedroom furniture, cork-lined walls, notes and letters, all in his house in Paris off the Parc Monceau. He had another house in Luzarches, an hour's drive from Paris, which stood on monastery lands with channels in which the monks had farmed fish. His gardens, his collection, and indeed his taste were subtler than what Barbara's parents had created in Westport and New York. Jacques lived quaintly and eccentrically, keeping a donkey, a goat, and a parrot in Luzarches, along with a retainer who cooked and other servants—as well as a younger lover, the eponymous Jean Boy. He knew practically everyone in the Paris artistic world from World War I until his death in 2000. His mother had been a celebrated beauty whose first husband committed suicide, leaving a note that said this was the last and best thing he could do for her, as now she could marry her lover. Mother and son both had Boxer dogs. In an evening ritual, the mother, Madame Monteux, sat in a thronelike chair with the dogs in front of her, being allowed to arise, one by one, to receive a treat.

Jacques was one of several brilliant and interesting men with whom Barbara made strong connections, who appreciated her energy, her smartness, and her work. There were other patrons to whom Barbara would become attached: professors at Harvard and, later on, Joe Baum, a restaurant entrepreneur; Robi Bak, a psychoanalyst and Renaissance scholar; Heinz Hartmann, a leader of the first post-Freudian generation of scholar-philosopher-humanistic psychoanalysts; Jim Beard, probably the strongest influence on the changing food culture in the U.S. in his time; and Leo Lerman, the culture maven of Condé Nast. Barbara evidently regarded me as in a class with such men. Of course, there was also a strong sexual connection between us. And it helped that I had lots of admiration of and appreciation for Barbara's parents, and for Barbara, to go with my love.

Europe With and Without Barbara; 1953

Following our junior year, in the summer of 1953, Barbara and I both went to Europe; we met briefly in London. She lived more luxuriously than I did. I traveled by train and stayed at youth hostels; I made the crossings via student fares on a then Dutch converted Liberty Ship called the *Groote Beer*. Barbara traveled in an ocean liner, stayed at superior hotels, and had interesting people with whom to connect, particularly in Paris.

I went to Vienna and looked up one of my father's orphanage friends, Hermann Schwartz; he had spent the war years in Shanghai, and returned to Vienna, where he opened a camera shop on Rotenturm Strasse. There I spent some of the accumulated pension money my grandmother received at the war's end on an Austrian Eumig movie camera. I photographed Mami's parents' large, dignified tombstone at the Zentralfriedhof, visited my childhood neighborhood, and lots of museums. Like my mother, I was infatuated with cameras and took lots of photos, though now largely faded. I met a girl I knew in Sorrento, wandered around Rome, and went to Florence via the Rome railroad station, where I stared at the schedule boards, trying to understand the Italian words that described the trains. The choices were *Accelerato, Diretto, Direttisimo, Rapido*, which to take? I went for *Accelerato*. It stopped at every hamlet and took eleven hours; *Rapido* turned out to be the right answer.

Eventually, I reached Paris and phoned Marie Fould-Springer, now Mary Wooster, as her Jewish Fould husband had died in 1933, and she had married Frank Wooster a few months later at St George's English Church, Paris. She was at her apartment in the Rue de Suresnes, near the Madeleine; and after some polite catching up about my mother's multiple sclerosis, my brother's army experience in Italy, and my father's activities, the Baroness asked if I recalled Royaumont. I described how ravished I had been by its beauty, back in 1938, and enthused about the tricycle I had been allowed to zoom about with. She asked if I would like to revisit the place and, of course, I agreed. "Unfortunately," she said, "this weekend I have to go to a party my daughter Liliane is giving. I'll show you Liliane's place a bit later, as I have to go by in about a half-hour.

And the weekend following, I have guests at Royaumont. Churchill and René Mayer (then President of France) are coming; you know, Royaumont has the closest hunting woods to Paris, and the old boys love to ride around a bit. But if you're free this Saturday, I'll send the car and you can have lunch and look around."

So off I went on Saturday with a Harvard friend, the son of "Mr. Short's Shirts," Chuck Frankel. The driver was the same as in 1938. The car was newer. We arrived at the same gate, which the same gatekeeper opened, and were at the Château in time to be served lunch, an excellent *oeuf en cocotte*. After coffee, a man aged about sixty entered and told us he managed the estate and the Baroness had telephoned to say we were coming. Were we interested in seeing the place? Soon we came to a hunting lodge with a hallway whose walls were covered, in the old Habsburg fashion, with the horns and feet of animals. Our guide happily pointed out a plaque, inscribed with the Baroness' name, and a date a month past, when she had shot the boar whose feet were already mounted and shod in silver. The next stop was a barn, containing much modern machinery, such as tubes attached to the udders of a dozen or more beautiful cows. Then on we went to the vegetable gardens, and back to the main house.

Our Guide's War Stories

I asked our guide if he had been there during the war, and how the place had survived?

"Oh" said he, "I was the head of the local Maquis, and everything was very quiet." "How so," I asked, "as this is such an accessible place?" "Well," he replied, "It was very quiet. It had to be very quiet, because of the downed English fliers. We stored fliers who had been shot down until we could ship them back to England." How had this come about? The Baroness' daughter, Hélène (1907-1997, "Bubbles") married Eduardo Propper de Callejón (1895–1972), the Spanish First Secretary in Paris at the outset of the war. Brought up Catholic, he was the son of a Bohemian Jewish father and Spanish mother, a career diplomat, a royalist, and a friend of Franco. The Baroness asked Hélène to ask her husband, "The next time you speak to Franco, please ask him, the next time he speaks to Hitler, to ask Hitler to tell [Gerd] von Rundstedt to stay out of Royaumont." According to Marie Fould-Springer, Hitler did that and von Rundstedt obeyed.

The Political Acumen and Influence of the Springers During World War II

A more likely story is that Propper declared the Château of Royaumont his permanent residence before leaving Paris, like the rest of the foreign diplomats, after the French surrender.

The place thus became extraterritorial Spain; and it would seem that the transfer met with the approval of both the Vichy French and the Nazi occupiers. On his way out of France, Propper stopped at Bordeaux, where he found a drawer full of *laissez-passers* at the Spanish consulate. He and the Portuguese Consul, Mendes, issued over ten thousand transit visas to allow refugees, mainly Jews, to cross into Spain, contrary to his instructions from Madrid, and then enter Portugal. In appreciation of this risky behavior (he could have been arrested or kidnapped by the Nazis as a Jew and killed), in 2008 he was recognized as one of the "Righteous Among the Nations" by Yad Vashem, the Holocaust Remembrance Authority in Israel.

Whether or not Franco or Hitler was involved in these events, the story illustrates the international connections of certain families involved in diplomatic and extra-diplomatic activities. It is hard to imagine that, currently, similar behind-the-scenes family connections are as significant in international relations among relatives in élite circles or that these political and personal connections, combined with the power of wealth, can influence conditions for the better, and save many lives.

The meaningfulness to me of the Springers lay in my response to their impressive contributions to the community. They gave me aspirations that connected deeply to ideals already realized by my grandfather's Zionism; my great-uncle Fritz's defense of Jews, in the army; the original Springer, who founded the *Waisenhaus* where my father was raised; and my great-grandfather who was an idealistic teacher at the *Waisenhaus* and in the Jewish community of Vienna. All these people had succeeded in doing their bit; their example went into the formation of my own ideals. They represented possibilities.

Three years later, on our honeymoon in Europe, I would take Barbara to introduce her to Mary Wooster, who showed her pleasure in our marriage and talked about her romance with her first husband, Eugène Fould: "I was born in Paris, and grew up mainly in Vienna. Aged 13, I thought of myself as Marie, my given name, and decided that German was ugly. I determined never again to dream in German. Only in French and English," she said. On a visit to friends in Paris in her mid-teens, Marie met Baron Eugène Fould. The Francophile and the Frenchman fell in love. On her return to Vienna, she told her father about the feelings she and Fould had for each other, but he opposed the match. Baron Gustav knew that Fould was a Baron, but regarded the French title as denoting a lower rank than the Austrian "Baron"; he also regarded the French as inferior. His only legitimate child, however, remained obstinately insistent. Gustav proposed that if Fould wanted to marry his daughter, he would request the Kaiser to permit the Springer baronial title to be passed to Fould. Of course, if the Kaiser were to honor Fould by bestowing the title on him, Fould would have to accept Franz Josef as his Kaiser, and become Austrian. But Fould refused; he was French; France was a Republic. He had no need or desire for a Kaiser.

Not much later, in 1905, the lovers finally got permission from Baron Gustav to marry and went on a lengthy honeymoon. On their return to Vienna, Marie's father (then one of the richest men of the Austro-Hungarian Empire, and richer than Fould) came to meet the young couple. The first carriage was for the men, the second for the ladies, and several others for the baggage. Arriving home, Marie and a companion alit, and saw Eugène and Gustav obviously angry, marching off, one red in the face, the other white. What happened, she asked her husband? "Your father," he replied, "greeted me and said he had arranged a meeting with the Kaiser for us at six o'clock in the morning tomorrow, when Franz Josef means to confer the Springer title on me. Once more, your father said it would be incumbent on me to recognize Franz Josef as my Kaiser, and Austria as my country. Again, I will refuse."

Marie began to telephone everyone she could think of, hoping for some way of averting the imminent disaster; who might be able to help with this frightening situation? No one offered a solution; and finally, she phoned Katherine Schratt, the actress who had been Franz Josef's mistress for years. "Schratti," as her friends called her, listened to the story, and responded that the Kaiser came to her at five or five-thirty in the morning for tea and conversation. As it was the only time he had when nobody could bother him with requests, including her, she could do nothing to help. The next morning, the two men set out. An hour later, they returned. Marie's father looked crestfallen, her husband elated. What had happened? "We arrived," said Fould, "and were met by a majordomo. He explained that the Kaiser was now old and rose from his chair only to greet ladies. We were to enter the audience chamber, bow, and approach. Your father would introduce me; the Kaiser would speak; we would bow and leave. Then we entered, and the Kaiser immediately got up from his chair, came to me, and grasped my hand. He said, *'Mon cher Baron Fould-Springer. Je me rejois à cause de vôtre arrivée chez moi. Parce que, vous savais, nous sommes voisins de Lorraine, l'ancien Lothringen des Habsbourg-Lothringen.'* (I am delighted by your visit, my neighbor from Lorraine, the ancient domain of the Habsburg-Lorraine family). At that point, nothing having been said about nationality or fealty, we were dismissed." Then the Baroness went on, "The next morning, very early, a footman called me to the telephone. I wondered who might be calling so early. When I picked up the receiver, I heard Schratti's voice. She said, 'Someone is here with me, and wishes to speak to you,' and a man's voice came on the line saying, 'Und ist die kleine Springerin zufrieden mit mir? (Is the little Springer child satisfied with me?)" And when I told my husband about that conversation, he said he didn't want a Kaiser, but "if he had to have one, this would be the Kaiser to have." (This story was improved by the Baroness. Actually, the Kaiser's gift came a bit later in her marriage, in 1912, when the couple had already had children, who then became Fould-Springer along with their father and mother. I seem to have known a number of people who embellished their stories!) I was well aware that, when well told, this story deserved to be saved and retold; and that doing so would give me some cachet and entertainment value, as French politesse requires the dinner guest to come prepared with some amusing and useful conversation at table.

My Competition with Debbie Stern for Barbara's Attention

During my college traveling in Europe, I ran into several Harvard people I knew, as well as Barbara, with whom I spent a bit of time in Paris and London. I met other students on the *Groote Beer*, and at youth hostels, but I often felt depressed and lonely. Barbara seemed aloof and occupied with Debbie Stern, a classmate with whom she was traveling, as well as her family contacts. It was my first time on my own, and the first time I realized that I could feel isolated, even in company; I diagnosed myself as depressive, but I didn't have any idea what I could do about it. I did think about whether there might be someone to talk to at Harvard, but I realized that Harvard was a place where students with problems were regarded through a nineteenth-century window: hard work, take yourself in hand, and outgrow it. Skinnerian behaviorist ideas, not Freudian ones, were in vogue at Harvard, as also they were later at the Barnes Hospital in St. Louis. My mind became wounded and twisted in relation to Barbara, and in London infatuation turned to despair. Barbara seemed to have become unapproachable, more interested in Debbie than in me and too rich, staying in luxury hotels, not the youth hostels I could afford.

FINISHING UP AT HARVARD

Senior Year at Harvard

Some important impressions I had in the trip back to Europe were related to the aftereffects of the war. Vespas were a dominant form of transportation, used by most classes.

Mobilettes were all over France. Freight cars were old, rusty, and tiny in comparison to American ones. London had terrific pollution, bomb craters. When I saw my cousin Ruth and her husband, Zerubavel, I was sorry for her because he was so awful.

Barbara and I returned to Harvard. I came back depressed. I broke off with Barbara, thinking I would not be happy with her nor she with me. I got into an excellent medical school, Washington University in St Louis. I graduated from Harvard with honors. Much later, I came to understand survivor guilt and self-punishment. For each of us, to be together was, among other things, an undeserved good thing.

Similarly, post-war Europe evoked a comparison with my undeserved good life. Depression is an ailment, but also a self-punishment. The depressed person's conscious concern about his depression as an ugliness, a pain for others, is another expression of guilt; unconsciously, it provokes other people. Leaving Barbara in order to protect her seemed a generous act to me; I was sparing her my depressed presence. I gave up; I wasn't going to suffer the inevitable defeat of being rejected by her. It was a repetition of denouncing the maid; of running into the lamppost; messing up Nellie's loom in Paris; all of which had resulted in pain and retribution. Unconsciously, it was both self-punitive and provocative: in a word, nasty.

My senior year passed quickly. I got lots of As and A-minuses. For my senior thesis, I elected a topic from the Romantic period. Perhaps it was the languid aspect of the Mauve Decade that drew me to write my senior dissertation about the *Savoy Magazine* as reflective of the Zeitgeist of the 1890s. It iterated the sorrows of the young Werther or Faust.

My personal romantic turmoil was expressed in similar terms in the Romantic period in history and literature. Introspection could be useful, even beautiful, not just selfish. The romantic poets gave me a certain permission to look into myself. One reader gave me a "magna cum laude" for my effort at social study of the "spirit" of the Mauve Decade as reflected in the *Savoy*. "Shows much promise," said that reader. The other reader thought, "Could use more work and thought," and gave it a "cum laude." That meant, one reader pro the inner life, and one not.

An aspect of my interest in the Romantics was their involvement with the inner life; their drug usage I thought of as experimentation about creativity, which also entered into my involvement with the *Yellow Book*, and the *Savoy*, with Beardsley and Wilde, Poe and Whitman. I might have been a candidate for addiction, but I was too frightened about how tenuous my emotional stability might be to risk experimenting as some others were doing in the fifties and sixties, one hundred-odd years after the publication, in 1841, of de Quincey's *Confessions of an English Opium Eater*, and at the beginning of the influence of the Beats and Timothy Leary. I couldn't have become alcoholic, because I never got past the point of getting sick before getting seriously drunk. Marijuana just made me giggly and cookie-hungry.

The important event of my senior year at Harvard was that I was accepted at a first-rate medical school, despite my neurotic tendencies. This had to do with a quirk of my mind—my not so linear thinking—that had the unexpected consequence of endearing me to Gordon Fair, the master of Dunster House, a white-haired, mustachioed South African, of the movie-British colonial type. The amiable sobriquet, "Flush Gordon," referred to an important post in his career.

At a time when Mussolini was doing useful things in Italy, Fair was called to help plan the drainage of the swamps of the River Po, which succeeded in converting a fetid, disease-spreading swamp into fertile farmland. Master Fair followed a British tradition, the Master's Sunday sherry and tea party; it took place every Sunday afternoon, and both students and resident faculty were invited. On the way to the drinks, there was a small entrance foyer, which contained a little table and a mirror. Almost always on the table was the *New York Times Sunday Magazine* section, opened to the unfinished crossword puzzle.

Master Gordon Fair and the Crossword Clue

I would enter, greet Master Fair, start a conversation, exchange some words, and, after a few minutes, his face would light up and he would march off to his crossword puzzle, having solved one of its clues. I noted this but didn't realize that the subjects I brought up gave Gordon Fair clues about the clues, allowing him to advance. Neither of us mentioned this phenomenon to the other.

When it came time to apply to medical school, I realized no Ivy League school would have me, given my poor performance in the sciences, particularly in organic chemistry. That judgment was supported when an interviewer at Harvard Medical School told me, "Don't put all your eggs in one basket," and the Columbia College of Physicians and Surgeons man indicated I had applied rather late. I had an acceptance from Northwestern. Soon I heard from Columbia that I had been put on the waiting list. (I am still waiting, never having had any further word.)

Fair asked me to his office and tactfully said he had some advice. He understood I was applying to medical schools and hoped I was not set on the Ivy League. He had profited by studying in a number of places, and the wider experience had helped him avoid becoming too provincial. There was an excellent medical school in St. Louis and a Dunster House old boy was its current professor of medicine. Fair would write him to recommend me, if I was prepared to go to St, Louis. The Barnes hospital and the Washington University medical school were, I knew, among the five best medical schools in the country. I told him I greatly appreciated his interest and would do as he suggested, should I be accepted there. Ten days later, I received a letter of admission.

I spent four years in an environment where learning was the predominant aim, and where study leading to that aim, to be a learned person, was possible because there was time and exposure to marvelous teachers. I had learned how to study, which led to learning how to take exams and write papers. I graduated with a "cum laude," a Detur Prize, and a John Harvard Scholarship Award. I knew I could have done better. I didn't know why, or how I might have found help.

MEDICAL SCHOOL

St. Louis

St. Louis is one-third of the distance across North America from New York. In 1956, Lambert St. Louis Airport opened a beautiful and welcoming terminal designed by Minoru Yamasaki. It featured two large joined glass-walled spaces that influenced the later designs of the 1962 Saarinen TWA terminal at John F. Kennedy Airport (then Idlewild Airport), and Claude Andreu's Charles de Gaulle Airport outside Paris, begun in 1966. Yamasaki later designed the New York World Trade Center and other important structures. TWA, American Airlines, and Ozark Airlines used light and airy glass-walled buildings as home bases. Lockheed

Constellations were the main planes used between Lambert and New York. It took three hours to fly east to New York and three-and-one-half going west to St. Louis.

Though arriving at St. Louis by air was delightful, my initial, less costly, arrival in St. Louis was by car. The thousand-mile-long drive had been boring, and I emerged tired and hot (the temperature was over one hundred degrees, and my car was the most basic, non-air- conditioned

Chevrolet). I set about finding a place to live; the main criteria were low price and proximity to the Barnes Hospital and the Washington University Medical School.

It took me some time to become used to the climate, the flatness of the countryside, the pride St. Louisans felt in their city and in their well-known, accomplished citizens, their zoo, their art museum, their Union Station, their airport (then being built), and their claim to be "the Athens of the U.S." A St. Louisan, Albert Bond Lambert, learned to fly with the Wright brothers in 1911. Later he flew in World War I, and then, after the end of the war, he bought 170 acres of land ten miles from downtown St. Louis which became St. Louis' airport. In 1920, Charles Lindbergh began to teach flying, to fly the mail between St. Louis and Chicago, and Lambert partly financed the flight of *The Spirit of St. Louis* to le Bourget airfield near Paris in 1927. Now a tourist destination, in 1903 Union Station was the largest and busiest passenger terminal in the world; it is now a National Historic Monument, rebuilt from 1982–1984. In the 1940s it still handled 100,000 people a day. (Railway traffic to and through St. Louis declined and ceased, and Union Station was rebuilt in 1985, and again in 2016; it now houses a hotel and shops.)

St. Louis came to be a place I very much liked—socially, culturally, and in size. It was a provincial capital, quite different from the more cosmopolitan Vienna, New York, and even Boston. The social stratification, especially the southern attitudes towards blacks, and the absence of any large recent influx of immigrants, gave me the feeling of living in what, indeed, the city was: the main city of a border state, with a relatively short history.

Four Nobel Prize-winning professors at the Washington University Medical School, Carl and Gerty Cori (1947), Arthur Kornberg (1959) and Paul Berg (1980), were there in my time and lectured me in biochemistry. The German Expressionist painter, Max Beckmann, was resident during the Second World War. Kurt von Schuschnigg, the Austrian Chancellor ousted by Hitler and interned in various concentration camps until he was freed in 1945, became a professor at St. Louis University. Harry Truman passed through Union Station, waving the newspaper headlining Dewey's victory, a scene which became an icon of his election to the presidency. The city also had the successful St. Louis Cardinals baseball team: Stan Musial, Enos Slaughter, and Marty Marion were local heroes; the football Cardinals did less well, but the basketball team, led by Bob Pettit, was excellent.

St. Louis was also home or birthplace of prominent people, whom I knew in one way or another. A.E. Hotchner was a writer who became celebrated because of his friendship with and biography of Ernest Hemingway. I encountered "Hotch" later as a member of the Elaine's Restaurant roundtable regulars; he was an occasional player at one of my New York poker club tables. He then partnered with Paul Newman (the Poses's next-door neighbor in Westport), in the sauce and grocery business whose profits went to charities. (After Barbara's parents' death, we sold the house and combined an adjoining piece of land that belonged to Barbara, with a piece of land that the Newmans owned. This parcel was partly gifted and partly sold to the Town of Westport, and it became a public space, the Poses Newman Preserve.

Charles Eames was another St. Louisan. He had studied at Washington University. I knew his chairs, on which I first sat at the Lamont Library at Harvard and which constituted my introduction to midcentury modern. (We used them to furnish, in this style, a house Barbara and I owned years later in Garrison, New York.) Other St Louisans I had come upon because of their work included Maya Angelou, Sara Teasdale, Howard Nemerov, Kay Thompson, Helen Traubel, and T.S. Eliot. Masters and Johnson lectured about some of their sexual research findings at the medical school and also collected semen from the medical students for use in artificial insemination. We joked that the donors, though they would long ago have spent the $15 payment for their desirable medical-student sperm, might well bump into younger likenesses in the streets.

Helen Traubel, also a St. Louis native, had been a memorable Brünhilde; during the war, Hans Hopf was her Siegfried. Traubel, looking like the Statue of Liberty posing as a Valkyrie, a heroic, defiantly American singer, played her part standing on a crag a good six inches lower than Hopf's boulder; Hopf, raised a further inch or two by elevator sandals, still needed to look up at her. Perhaps German heroic tenors were in short supply, owing to the war.

When you cross the Mississippi, you arrive in East St. Louis, Illinois, the former largest hog-butchering city in the U.S. (Chicago, or rather Carl Sandburg, usurped the title "Hog butcher to the world.") The nearest natural wonder, the Meramec Caverns, one hour-fifteen-minutes away, was supposed to have been where Jesse James holed up to avoid detection. It became a tourist attraction, popularized by Lester Dill, who invented the bumper sticker to advertise it. It is the largest cave system in Missouri, which has many caves and sometimes calls itself the "Cave State." The Ozarks, 160 miles from St. Louis, are the nearest sites for camping and fishing; there is not much of interest by way of landscape near St. Louis.

The city, though, had many pleasures. The Chase Park Plaza (now Royal Sonesta) Hotel was excellent, with good food and views of the agreeable Forest Park; around the corner were a block or two of luxury shops. Further from the Barnes Hospital, where I worked, was a neighborhood of earlier times, with attractive bargain mansions, mostly no longer occupied by the wealthy people, such as the Pulitzers, who had built them. The suburbs, Clayton and Ladue, and country club life had appeared. St. Louis society was extremely stratified. The old French era settlers, who gave their names to the avenues, were one group, then came later arrivals who made good, then the beer barons, then the department store people, such as the Mays, and, of course, the Pulitzer newspaper magnates.

Next to the Mississippi levee were older buildings that were rumored to have been bought up by Disney, who wanted to tear them down and rebuild a nouveau Mark Twain-era Disneyland; this never happened. Instead, the Gateway Arch was opened in 1965, as a monument to the westward expansion. In my time, the area near the river had bookshops where one could buy deaccessioned library or estate books, like the complete Bulwer-Lytton, Henry James, Dickens, Jules Verne, and Emerson; great works could be bought for pennies, and we did. (Years later this required building many shelves, in which their pages and covers slowly deteriorated.) We were always bookworms, Barbara particularly. There was also a selection of low-life bars, frequented by prostitutes, and shops of various sorts; I suppose these have been torn down and redeveloped. I never returned to St. Louis after medical school.

The Art Museum was a treasure trove, and Forest Park and its zoo were first rate. The Philharmonic was conducted by Vladimir Golschmann between 1931 and 1959. He was a French music specialist, who had been a supporter of "Les Six." In St. Louis, during his long tenure, he never achieved the success of building one of the major American orchestras; he seemed unable to raise the money to do that. It often appeared to me that the orchestra had practiced only half of its program, which was workmanlike, but the other half, not so much. Summer opera in the park was a source of pride; but the climate was too warm for sitting outside on summer evenings.

Medical School, Mainly

When I first arrived in St. Louis with its heat and humidity, the trees and the people in the streets looked equally limp. I found a room in a boarding house three blocks from the Barnes Hospital, the site of the Washington University School of Medicine. The modest room was one of two on the second floor of a nineteenth-century house. The other room was occupied by two Ozark Airline hostesses, who probably provided a cheerful, reassuring, and attractive presence on flights and were agreeable as down-the-hall neighbors. They were not much good for conversation, though, and I felt, as I usually do in a new environment, lonely and unmotivated that year.

I met my classmates: there were eighty-six of us, of whom eighty-four were men, and two women. Five were from Harvard; most were natives of central states, with some from the far west and some from the deep south. Strangely, I remember no one from other Ivy League schools, but several from Mississippi, Missouri, Kentucky, Illinois, and Texas. One student hailed from Rhode Island; there was a married couple from California—the wife was American Japanese; there were no blacks, or Latinos, and no foreigners. I never made close friends with any of them and did not keep in touch later on. Though most were highly motivated, studious, and serious about their future careers, there wasn't a poetic or artistic type in the class.

Carl V. Moore Radiated Dedication, Simplicity, Focus, and Honesty

We were greeted at the medical school by the Professor of Medicine, Carl V. Moore, who spoke for the faculty. I'm wistfully sad that I never met W. Barry Wood, the Dunster House old boy whose intervention had made it possible for me to learn to be a doctor at a top medical school; but I think he would have been satisfied with me. He moved to Baltimore the following year, 1955, to become Vice-President at Johns Hopkins, his medical school alma mater, died aged sixty in 1971, and I never had a chance to thank him. He had an astonishing career, which included becoming Harvard's last All-American football player and winner of ten sports letters at Harvard, three each in baseball, hockey, and football, and one in tennis. He also graduated Summa Cum Laude and Phi Beta Kappa. At age 32, Wood became "Head of Medicine and Physician in Charge" at the Barnes Hospital. He wrote more than 125 papers and several books and might have been a better mentor than I found among the remaining faculty.

Carl Moore succeeded Wood in 1955; he could have been a preacher or a coal miner; he radiated dedication, simplicity, focus, and honesty. In his introductory talk, he explained that he knew we were feeling some trepidation about beginning our medical studies, but that was inappropriate. We only had to remember that the House Staff were all Alpha Omega Alpha (the honorary medical school fraternity) from the best schools in the country, that our faculty was among the best in the world, and all we had to do was to live up to the high standards according to which we had been selected. All this was said humorlessly, without warmth; we had been warned. The future was to be highly competitive and one of great moral responsibilities. I could add Moore's chilling exhortation to my other substantial anxieties, notably the burden of a guilty conscience: I was well aware of the facts that my parents had had hard lives and severe losses, that my mother was looking forward to my finding a multiple sclerosis cure, and that I was a fortunate survivor.

Moore's scary speech was followed by an address by Carl Moyer, the professor of surgery. He informed us that ninety percent of what we would learn would probably be obsolete in ten years, and that scientific medicine was in its early years of development. I took these comments as a sort of hazing, since innocent, idealistic young people were unlikely to feel comforted by such large splashes of cold water. Who wanted to be told we were going to have to work hard, in order to learn things that would rapidly become obsolete, that we used aspirin without knowing how it worked, and that a witch, not a scientist, had given us digitalis? Another side of that comment was to indicate that the Barnes was a locus for training researchers and teachers, not primarily practitioners. Moyer was, nevertheless, pleasantly wry and eccentric; we learned that he, his three children, and his wife each drove a VW Beetle.

The next order of business was to join a fraternity. There were two houses, Nu Sigma Nu and Phi Beta Pi. Nu Sigma Nu was more elite (whatever that meant) and smaller, and Phi Beta Pi had better food. Since the main purpose of these institutions was to provide lunch, I chose the better food. Phi Beta Pi also had a complicated set of recognition gestures and a secret handshake; that was the extent of fraternity fellowship. Life was to be serious. Our curriculum included anatomy, histology, physiology, and biochemistry; anatomy meant two students, each dissecting one side of a cadaver. I shared a body with Alex Gottschalk, one of the other Harvard graduates, and a more devoted and methodical student than I would prove to be. He found his career through his fascination with human anatomy and went on to become a professor of radiology.

My Fascination with Anatomy Study

The complexity of the planes of the body, the spatial relations between different layers, and organs, and particularly the complexity of brain anatomy, were difficult to learn. I was not gifted at three-dimensional visualization—though I found it hard to accept the idea that there were capacities I lacked, spatial relations was one; integral calculus and statistics were others; physical limitations due to a heart abnormality and an over-active conscience I didn't yet know about were a third and fourth. I was further weakened by losses: of language, family, physical environment, and connectedness with parents. I became a collector and warehouser of potentials, sometimes in my good moods and with associated grievances and anxieties at other times.

My new habitat was both an interesting beginning and a threatening novelty that I had to negotiate on my own, another version of being a new boy. I had to learn a new language, or at least a new vocabulary, acclimate to a strange environment, and compete with more focused, apparently less burdened people. In addition, the subjects to be studied were not all that interesting and the highly-stratified St. Louis social structure and the racial division of the population were uncomfortable and foreign.

Gross anatomy was fascinating from the standpoint of how amazing the architecture and mechanics of the body are, but the cadaver was greasy and smelled terribly of formaldehyde; the odor seemed never to go away. And this was all in order to memorize the names and spatial relationships of a huge number of parts that were going to be useful to future anatomists, pathologists, and surgeons principally, and only secondarily to anybody else.

Carl and Gerty Cori, Professors of Biochemistry

Carl Cori and his wife, Gerty, who were mostly known for their elucidation of the metabolism of carbohydrates, taught me biochemistry. Understanding bodily chemical processes is vital, and as Moyer predicted, the progress has been enormous. The Krebs cycle, which the Coris researched, describes a fundamental, relatively simple, esthetically delightful representation of the production-line-like reduction of food to create stored fuel. What we now know of immunology, molecular biology, and the mapping of the genome represents a vast step forward from the work of the Coris. That, in turn, was a great step forward from the material we had to learn in college organic chemistry (which was already history when I was graduated). This supported our perception of the likelihood of a future of greater understanding of normal physiology and pathological variants. Since those days—a long time ago for a person, and a short time for fields of knowledge—we have learned a lot about the action of aspirin, and we have made drugs as important as digitalis without the help of witches.

Washington University has had other great medical researchers, in addition to the Coris. It is to the credit of the medical school that Nobel winner Arthur Kornberg did much of his work on nucleotide metabolism and the construction of DNA there. (He identified DNA polymerase 1.) (His son, Roger, also received a Nobel, in chemistry.) And Paul Berg, a Ph.D. who worked with Kornberg at Washington University, also won a Nobel in chemistry for his work on DNA.

Evolution of Pharmacology; Study of Physiology

I cannot imagine what the course in biochemistry is like now, though if I were beginning medical training I'm certain I should find it much more interesting than I did then. As more has been discovered, our appreciation of how complex physiological mechanisms are—and of the distance to go—has increased, because more questions have arisen. How an overview can be distilled when things are happening in thousands of laboratories all over the academic world, and in more thousands of labs in hundreds of biotech start-ups and giant Pharma campuses, I cannot conceive. But it is the leap from the laboratory to the doctor-patient relationship that really fascinates me. My optimism about progress in medical sciences has been mightily supported by what I experienced happening. As we progress further, technology will, hopefully, make collating reams of data possible where human minds lag.

Experiments on Live Animals; Killing Rats

In those not-so-good old days, the physiology course involved living animals; we had to replicate previous work with live creatures. Reading historical results would have sufficed to convince me of the importance of scientific experimentation, even though it had caused pain and death to the animals, but I failed to accept the usefulness of repeating what had been done. We killed rats by holding them by the tail and whirling them around our heads to crack their skulls on lab tables; we cut up frogs we had used to show the muscular contractions caused by electrical stimulation, and we killed dogs we had used to show the effects of adrenalin on blood pressure. We showed ourselves what we already knew. What I learned from this kind of thing was to wonder what we might learn from these exercises, to find a new reason to feel guilty, and to arrive at heightened sympathy for the animals. This was an example of a violation of the rule, "first, do no harm" without having a compensatory, convincing, positive cost-benefit judgment. On another hand, direct experience and much practice seem to be important to learning, as I know from the repetition required for achieving the neuromuscular training needed in sports or piano playing.

I came away from these early years of medical study with a continuing ambition to be a bit of a Renaissance man. Disillusionment as to the possibility of succeeding at this had begun, but not gone very far. I realized I was a child wonder no more. Nor was I a Barry Wood; many of my areas of interest were complex and, with constant new developments, it was not likely I could master them. I did not yet grasp the full truth—that to achieve modesty would require a great deal of resignation and a great diminution in my sense of responsibility. The old saw is "the quest for perfection is the enemy of progress"—or words to that effect.

More About What I Learned in Medical School and During My Later, Professional Career: Some Experiences and Some Generalizations

While we repeated animal studies in the department of medicine, professors were doing important, and sometimes dangerous, experiments using themselves as subjects. One example was the study of an ailment then called "idiopathic thrombocytopenic purpura." It is no longer as idiopathic as it was at that time. It turned out that in an autoimmune process, antibodies, ordinarily involved in processes that eliminate foreign bodies like bacteria, attack the body's own tissue. In this condition, platelets (which normally agglutinate to further blood clotting in a wound) are attacked by the subject's own immune system. A deficiency of platelets then occurs, together with bleeding. Now, the ailment more commonly goes by the name "autoimmune thrombocytopenia." The Barnes Washington University cardiologists gave themselves thrombocytopenia to demonstrate and study the condition. The experimenter using himself as subject is heroic and sometimes recognized and rewarded: André Cournand at New York University (NYU) in New York won a Nobel prize for performing studies that involved passing a urinary catheter to his heart intravenously to measure intra-cardiac blood pressures in the various chambers, for example.

"First, Do No Harm." Sophie's Choices in Medicine

The alternative to experimenting on oneself is to use other organisms, mice, rats, frogs, or higher forms of life up to apes and humans. The Nazi experiments using humans seem inhuman to us, but perhaps did not to those who performed the experiments; plunging people into freezing water, and worse, was rationalized. The experimental subjects were classed as criminals and lower, non-human forms of life, and the beneficiaries were the good, noble Germans in U boats or shot-down airplanes, who, if dropped into the cold sea or onto frigid steppes, might be helped by information resulting from such experiments. Terrorists, anti- terrorists, and warriors are trained to kill for what they regard as good causes; doctors are trained to "primum non nocere," (first, do no harm—to the patients) so that the "sacrifice" of animals in physiology labs, and the dangers associated with the experiments to which experimenters who use themselves as subjects are associated, are explained by the argument that they serve a higher good. It is necessary to train medical people and to enhance the effectiveness of treatment, despite the physical and moral dangers. "Sophie's Choice" is often the doctor's dilemma.

My medical training exposed me to experiences involving medical research and practice which sometimes caused me serious qualms. In the early days, when my responsibility was to learn, not to act or to judge the behavior of others, life was fairly easy; as time went on and the clinical years passed, I sometimes had to make decisions about actions, and so life became more difficult. My judgments about danger, responsibility, ineptitude, accidents, risk, and fate brought about feelings of uncertainty. When does "teaching" become "training?" I think that to be "trained" is to be forced to make decisions and recognize there is no way to avoid associated discomfort. Medical training is a master-journeyman-apprentice project, with graduated responsibility; so, theoretically, there is always a wiser head to consult. But one cannot ask for help on everything. When is it wise, and when does hesitation indicate unnecessary timorousness?

Making One Choice Eliminates Other Possibilities

One unavoidable part of making a choice is to give up other possibilities. Giving up a tempting possibility was not easy for me, and another reason I did not accept training easily. Also, the mere possibility of doing something, and thereby causing hurt, seemed to me almost as painfully real as doing the deed itself. As in adolescence, when the capacity to act gives the power to harm, learning in medicine can be hazardous to the learner as well as to the subject. Medical school makes it difficult to maintain the illusion that there is a right way, or a wrong way, of dealing with a person or a situation in general, and professionally in particular. A binary system does not work when there is a range of possibilities. To choose one, even though the choice may be relatively harmless, may also close off many other, perhaps more useful, options.

Learning Tact and Kindness Towards Patients; "Medical Student's Disease"

One example: students have to learn to speak to patients, their relatives and their friends tactfully. This is an art best learned by doing it. Giving good news is easy; giving bad news is not. The bad news is always potentially there because every choice involves risks. Often the decision is not difficult to make—the choice is clear; more often, the choice is between possibilities, and is not clear. No amount of tact is sufficient when the choice involves pain and suffering, plus serious risk, but the more tact and kindness, the better. The young medical student has neither the experience nor the capacity to remove himself from excessive anxiety identification with the patients and their families. I learned that, ideally, the doctor gradually learns to titrate his anxiety by calling up his helpful experiences and realizes that it takes time to get over bad experiences. In time, healing happens, but scars remain, both in mind and body.

"Medical Student's Disease" is a not so funny in-joke at medical school. It is self-diagnosed, as when the medical student feels the need to examine himself to see whether unusual sensations he is experiencing indicate that he has a disease, about which he has recently learned, usually by contact with a patient. This happens often: fear is part of being a doctor. There is fear of doing damage, whether iatrogenic—that is, caused by the doctor—or by factors beyond current knowledge. Fear can be useful in motivating a search for causation but can also be a serious impediment to reasonable thinking. Lest I leave the mention of "medical student disease" here, I think it is necessary to point out that this phenomenon is not particular to medical studies.

Anyone who has read Ludwig Bemelmans's *Madeline* children's books will recall that when one child is hospitalized, the classmates will all contract the same ailment.

Learning Patience in Diagnosis

In medical school, time seemed to pass quickly; I often felt that there was not enough time to become prepared. Previous experiences disposed me to feel that time could run out—one could wait too long, and not only in Vienna. I could see that there was a difference in attitudes among the teacher-doctors in different specialties: surgeons like to operate, internists like to wait. The internists call it "conservative," and it avoids operative risk. However, it takes time to see whether the conservative approach is effective. Fear of surgery may cause excessive caution; hurrying into surgery may prove foolhardy. Explaining all the factors which influence a decision to the patient and his family can be difficult; you can share alternatives with the family but, ultimately, the doctor has responsibility and must accept that. The doctor's preference, even if not overtly expressed, will impact how the options are presented. Being ill means being fearful; and fear impels the urge to find quick solutions. The healthy doctor is in a better position to make judgments about what to do than the sick patient—and also than the unwell, depleted, or just plain aged doctor.

The mind, among other things, is a predicting machine. We evaluate, usually without conscious thought, when we are pedestrians avoiding others on the street; sometimes we stop—a moment of puzzlement, of uncertainty appears, we reflect, and a conscious question arises. We consult our memories or the library; we design experiments, limit variables, and work out probabilities. We are curious; we feel motivated. The methods of natural science provide the means for minimizing subjectivity. Thorough assessment requires patience and time. We do the best we can.

Waiting is a capacity that develops over the course of growing to maturity; one passes through stages of bearing delays in being fed, or changed, of toilet training, of tolerating sharing. Patience is a capacity a person must have developed before medical school. To be trained and taught, and to learn and change—by passing through the rigors of the experience of waiting while dealing with danger, pain and suffering, as people in the medical arena do—is to reexperience lifelong challenges.

Early traumata, i.e. unexpected injuries, lead to a feeling that it is necessary to be prepared when one is confronted by a serious problem. The prospect of danger causes anxiety. Anxiety leads to diminished judgment and, often, obsessive thinking. Responses are postponed or hurried. In challenging, especially in frightening situations, a child turns to a parent, a student to a teacher, a patient to a doctor. Those relied on may be or may not be adequately prepared themselves. The result varies between successful handling of the situation, partial success, and none at all.

Frightening Medical School Experiences

Early in my first year at medical school, before I began clinical work with live patients, I spent a free afternoon on a balcony overlooking an operating room. The procedure taking place was a hysterectomy; as the surgeon freed the uterus from its attachments and lifted it out of the patient's body, I began to feel queasy. In my mind I conflated that bloody, large pear with the infants who could never be conceived or born as a result of that operation. I didn't learn about what the indications for this radical step were until months later, though I did know that hysterectomy was an intervention that precluded the possibility of future pregnancy. What benefit did this sacrifice confer?

My First Participation in an Autopsy

A second frightening experience took place a year later: participating for the first time in an autopsy. My first patient was my cadaver; and I was then quite uncomfortable about my cadaver-patient which, when it had been the body of a living person, had been destroyed by lung cancer. Obviously, the unavailability of treatment for the disease responsible for the death had converted a "who"-patient to a "which"-body. My second dead body, and my first autopsy, was that of a beautiful ten-year-old little boy whose death came during a well-meant surgical intervention. He had a rare congenital condition, polycystic liver disease, and had undergone five or six operations to remove large cysts from his liver. What was to have been the final reconstruction of his liver had resulted in an anesthetic death. A successful operation, but the patient died. Nobody could reasonably feel responsible for the outcomes of these cases. All that was possible was to learn more and do better in future.

Life is difficult for anyone who has to make a decision based on insufficient evidence that may have serious consequences. One of the hazards for the physician is making an assessment or decision that doesn't work out well. Practicing medicine is a stressful and anxiety-producing activity. Sometimes the patient has to die before the doctors learn what went wrong.

Autopsies are desirable for teaching purposes; the hope is that anatomic correlations with the pathophysiologic processes that ended in death will cast light on the underlying disease processes; sometimes a diagnosis can be found that was uncertain during life. Dissection serves the purpose of allowing medical students to learn anatomy. It also helps them to learn to objectify the patient to permit a relatively impersonal, and therefore more objective, relationship. In the case of the young boy whose autopsy I attended, I could imagine the feelings of his medical team, and the feeling, even at a significant distance, was one that awoke me that night, in the form of an examination dream: There was a test for which I had not prepared adequately, that was about to happen, that I didn't have time to prepare for. That reflected anxiety but also implied a hope that in some future instance there might be time.

My first cadaver-patient was a man who could not have been helped, and whose diagnosis must have been clear in life. The second was a child who had an extremely rare ailment and an extremely rare, unpredictable surgical death. He had survived previous anesthesia without problems, and there was no reason to suspect that anything was, surgically or anesthetically, done incorrectly. This was a case of good practice with a bad result, and it conveyed a lesson that is good for doctors to learn: harden your heart and try not to become too much or too little emotionally involved with the patient. Freud cautioned students to treat the patient as surgeons try to do when they isolate an operative surgical field and have it draped nicely, so the hidden face of the person is removed from the vision of the surgeon. Still, even if, as happens these days, the surgeon has never had personal contact with the patient, he knows, as I knew that Siegfried and Fafner were hidden behind the thin paper my mother had pasted over the picture, that he is working on a person, covered by a sheet though he is. I did learn that empathic contact with a patient is essential, and the doctor needs to be able to keep a distance, while communicating an inner self-assurance that is in tune with his patient.

A third instructive case, again surgical, was a middle-aged patient with a simple abdominal hernia. Having gone through the preclinical studies, the course in physical diagnosis, and having participated in autopsies, I entered the phase of working with living patients. You rotated through various departments; you scrubbed and participated in operations; you held retractors and learned how to tie knots in sutures and how to clamp arteries. I had a chance to work with a surgeon who was known to be kindly and experienced; we were to perform a simple hernia repair.

The surgeon went over the procedures to ensure a sterile operative field and reviewed the simple anatomy involved and how the operation was meant to go. He reminded us that there was one factor to be considered: a recurrent sensory nerve, which innervated a part of the lower right quadrant of the abdomen, should be identified and not cut; otherwise, the operation would leave an area of lack of skin sensation. He made his incision and cut the nerve. He touched his head in shame, his surgical hat fell off and landed in the operative field, followed by a piece of potato chip. The patient survived and left the hospital without a complication, completely satisfied; the surgeon probably gave a sigh of relief. This was one of many examples of how imperfect people are. This physician's warmth was appealing, and he had a good, busy practice; a more serious—obsessive even—attitude about work might have been helpful. This man was a good doctor who made a minor error. I increasingly felt that, when seeking professional help, consulting senior members of the house staff about looking for a personal doctor would be a good idea.

CPCs, Clinical Pathological Conferences, are standard procedures, often dealing with mysterious cases, at which the pathologist can discuss the findings. Some patients have had biopsies that were intended to resolve questions of diagnosis; sometimes the last word is issued by post-mortem findings. After death, the puzzle is solved most of the time; even then, though, questions can remain. The microscopic evidence at one particular CPC case was so much the same in benign and malignant cell appearance that the professor of pathology, Loren Ackerman, stated, one could not explain how to decide which was which. Someone raised a hand to ask, "If benign is indistinguishable from virulent, how do you tell the difference?" To this, Ackerman replied, "Great intelligence and long experience." In this case, it turned out that the benign diagnosis had been made on a biopsy specimen, and the patient was alive and well.

Medical school, becoming a doctor, spending a great deal of time supervising the work of others during further training, and working on research projects eventually gave me plenty of experience of the doctor's various roles. I felt the weight of the responsibility the doctor bears; the doctor must teach the patient to participate in the management of his illnesses and, at the same time, to consider and generally accept professional advice. Patients idealize the professional helpers but resent having to depend on someone else. Gratitude may be too much to expect after a frightening diagnosis, followed by a painful procedure, followed by a painful recovery, in which passivity and dependency become traumatic memories. That is sometimes the case when the doctor can help; what happens if the encounter fails to help? It partly depends on the patient and partly how the doctor has dealt with the patient.

Both doctor and patient are susceptible to lurking fears of failure, and sometimes the doctor must understand that the patient's apparent love for him is close to hate. Neither positive nor negative feelings for the doctor are wholly realistic or personal. The bedside manner—the positive, "placebo" effect, and the fearful suspicion toward a doctor who fails to connect—are both important; however, the patient also partly determines the doctor's role. The student relates to the teacher's role;

the doctor is a teacher and trainer, at the same time as he is a performer and a student. As a teacher and a sometime student, he has experience of both conditions. It is similar to the experience of a parent, who has an opportunity to recall, even re-experience, many of the feelings of childhood: the awe, the admiration, the love, the competitiveness, the resentment, and the dependency of the child and can, hopefully, take advantage of his greater knowledge.

When Doctors Become Ill

On the other hand, doctors get ill, and become patients, subject to the conditions that patients encounter—busy offices, coping with insurance questions, undergoing procedures, dealing with doctors often displaying lamentable limitations in their communication abilities, and too busy or too tenderhearted to proffer explanations. They are excluded from discussions among their colleagues; they find themselves exhibits on rounds; as a patient, they have to deal with a sudden demotion—their charts are not available to them.

History of My Motivation Toward Medicine

Late in my working career, I chaired an admissions committee, in which we interviewed and evaluated applicants who wanted to become psychoanalysts. A large majority had family members who had had major illnesses, and many had come from families where alcoholism or psychosis had afflicted important family members. Having a patient or two in a family, and having been a helper or a patient oneself, were powerful motivators for wanting to become a doctor; this was certainly so in my case. A good part of my interest in writing a memoir is thinking about how those experiences affected me; going over my personal history, if it has not opened my eyes, has at least cleared my vision.

Another thing I learned early in medical training is that there is nothing as reassuring as creating a mutual understanding between two people as shared experience. Usually, the patient can express his experience directly, if he and the doctor feel they are collaborators. Many intangibles connect and separate people.

Childhood Medical Models

There were four doctors in my childhood who served as models: Edi Ehrlich, my uncle Gusti, my grandfather Tatti, and Otto Gersuny. Gusti never talked to me about his professional work, not in Vienna, nor in 1957-9, when he lived in New York alone, having been divorced by his wife, Lisa. He had lost his younger daughter, Naomi, to glomerulonephritis, and the older, Evi-Ruth, to her husband, Zerubavel. Gusti worked as an anesthesiologist until committing suicide. My last memory of Gusti was of him at one of the Poses's family parties, looking through the window at the view of Central Park, not responding to efforts I made to talk to him.

Years later, my cousin Ruth came to visit the USA, to spend some time with her daughter who was studying in Cambridge. She took the opportunity to make her trip during the first Gulf War, since there were few tourists, German or other, for her to guide around Israel, which had become her career. I took her on tours of New York; I drove her to the Statue of Liberty, the Aquarium, and other tourist desiderata. Those hours with her were a time when I felt absolutely no internal pressure to be amusing and agreeable; I didn't have to do anything to be accepted, nor did I have a feeling of having a burden I resented. Evi and I fell into a relationship, such as we had before the war, and before we had to begin to accommodate to the complex world beyond the family, as well as to the family. I felt tranquil with her as I would not have felt at re-meeting any of the family adults.

Her mother, Lise, moved back to Vienna after the divorce from Gusti. She wanted to restore the bonds between the Austrians and the Jews; she wanted to get the Austrians to regret what they had done and make peace, and she had a radio program, which broadcast discussions intended to re-create bonds. She saw herself as a missionary of healing. I cannot remember ever thinking of or reminiscing about her.

Tatti I knew from afar and through my mother, grandmother, and his friends; everyone described him as the best person they ever knew, devoted to patients and refugees, an alpinist, mushroom collector, gymnast, tulip breeder, an "idealer Mensch." My mother's eyes went misty when his name came up, and she sighed and grieved, until she died. Tatti continued to be an occasional model and presence in my memory.

Otto Gersuny was a good family friend. I loved him. He knew Gusti from medical school; he did not love Gusti, but respected his intelligence. Gersuny was my pediatrician in both Vienna and Jackson Heights until he died. His wife, Fritzi, *née* Kafka—no relation—was a sweet and gentle lady, whom I saw years later at my admired teacher Heinz Hartmann's funeral. Hartmann was Freud's last important potential heir and one of my most important and loved teachers in psychoanalysis; Fritzi Gersuny had tears in her eyes as she greeted me, and they were for Hartmann, who might have been her lover or maybe her analyst in Vienna, or perhaps both.

"Bauchreden" with Otto Gersuny; Anger at Incompetent or Dishonest Doctors

Otto Gersuny is another who is still with me. He was a cuddly, stocky little bearlet of a man, always with a little sly smile on his face, bald head tilted to the right. As he entered my room, out came the stethoscope, up went my pajama top, and he bent over, saying, "*Noch, Ernstl, was hast du denn"*; then onto my chest with his instrument, whereupon my stomach would speak, saying something between a growl and a laugh. Then he might look up and say, *"Ruhig, Ich will doch hoeren,"* ("Quiet, I need to hear"), and then lower his head down. How could I be quiet so that he could listen to me while my tummy seemed to be making funny noises? I never had anything important—just the usual measles, chicken pox, what you have as a child.

Gersuny could be playful on a child's level; his "Bauchreden" added one of the German words that still elicit a world of meaning beyond the simple translation, in English: "ventriloquism." "Belly-speaking" is the nearest literal rendering in English; but my German childhood word for the inside middle part of me was "Bauch," and that associates to childhood illness—and the relationship between me and my friend the Herr Doktor who "got" me. Through his manner, his way of moving, and the feeling of his touch, Dr. Gersuny was able to make an authentic connection. I consider Dr. Gersuny my first teacher of medicine.

In medical school I tended to be pleased, proud, and reassured by good results and to blame the patient or myself for disappointing results. I tried to control my egotism and convince myself that "the doctor dresses the wounds; nature heals them," but generally failed. Few doctors are so humble about the significance of their work as that. I was (and continue to be) angered by experiences with doctors whom I found to be incompetent, dishonest, hypocritical, or unethical: "inauthentic" is a critical word. I also had extensive experience with other, partly cultural, partly personal styles of relating to patients. They were not all designed to create a cooperative relationship between doctor and patient. Frequently, doctors displayed the attitude: "I'm the authority and you need to obey. I know what I'm talking about. You don't." This confuses authority and knowledge. Authority is powerful and more or less effective, but often it elicits more resentment and fear than willing collaboration. As I passed through immaturity and change, Dr. Gersuny was a model to follow, *"ein idealer mensch."*

I had a good doctor, Gersuny; a model doctor, Tatti-Gottlieb; a difficult, spoiled mother's older brother doctor, Gusti; and a somewhat bad doctor, Edi Ehrlich. His attitude, including the lack of information or warnings surrounding my operations, certainly affected me, but I didn't understand this at the time. After emigration, Edi spoke about really bad doctors in Newark—doctors who had ghost surgeons operate for them, split fees, prescribed useless remedies or procedures and overcharged. Edi himself never did anything like these bad things; however, he did other, not good things: he certainly had an unpleasant, hypercritical attitude.

Recognizing the impact of Ehrlich's attitude required my medical training, and my later personal therapy experience. I needed to undo my childhood mis-learning; I had to examine the attitudes of my parents as teachers, counselors, and guides; I needed to realize that I was experiencing a natural course of events and should not expect more. My childhood idea was simple. My role was to be around for my mother, to keep her company, and eventually to be her doctor. Hers was to be there for me. That not being the case, I needed to escape—to college, to medical school. I needed to learn to believe that my parents had inner needs, and also that they acted according to cultural norms, but in error. The theory that children are harmed by knowing too much too soon was a widely accepted belief among my parents' generation; it supposed that children needed to be protected from information, not to share in it. Much later, I came to realize the roles and attitudes my parents adopted were useful for them, not necessary or beneficial to me. I learned that to be responsible one had to be able to wait and to act, and to decide when to do which, while accepting fallibility and the pain of failure.

What went on in my head during my time at medical school included becoming aware of the matters above. There was much that I realized only in retrospect, with the still later advantage I had of being able to lie on a couch talking to someone who paid attention and encouraged me to express ideas and of listening to myself saying things I never would have imagined I should say. Of the many things I later found remarkable, one was realizing that, in medical school, I lost my uncertainty about my work life. I stopped worrying about my future; it was going to be in one specialty or other, perhaps with teaching and research as well.

Understanding how that came about was gradual, and crystallized later; indeed, much of what I now understand came to me after I started writing this memoir.

One lesson I took, at least in a modest way, was that only a degree of success is possible, fear of failure is inevitable, one can only do as one can do, and I was more able than I often felt. A lot of that came from my conclusion that Barbara, who had a good head for quality, believed I was quality.

My uncertainty about becoming a doctor disappeared in medical school, but my anxiety and uncertainty about my capacity to love persisted. I was as yet unaware of the degree of underlying passion I was capable of harboring, and equally unaware of how attached I was to my mother, to Tatti, Gersuny, Hartmann, and several others. I discovered my buried passion later, when I uncovered my buried losses. At the time, I was also not conscious of how angry I felt, toward those I—often unknowingly—classed as hypocrites, liars, and phonies. These were people who held themselves out as authorities and demanded subservience, but whose powers were feeble; what they offered was tempting but represented a swindle. Sadly, I later discovered my parents were among the disappointers, as all parents (and all children) must be.

At Harvard, and in my first year in St. Louis, I had periods of depression. That meant lack of energy, a lot of time spent at the movies when I might have been studying, insomnia, a deep sense of aloneness tinged with a scary feeling that I was lacking in real feelings of affection for and connection with other people, and a lot of frenzied activity, all at the same time. Nowadays, I know better. Behind the fear of being a cold fish was a lonely, frightened child trying to hide from the prospect of the next important loss.

MARRIAGE

Reuniting with Barbara

Barbara had never left my mind. In St. Louis, at medical school, my love for and fascination with her revived. We had become seriously attached during our junior year at Harvard, but the relationship was not easy for either of us; we both behaved as though we were friends, but we failed to discuss our deeper, more dangerous, romantic feelings for each other, and we hid our anxieties. Barbara and I had classes together and saw each other a great deal, but there was no idea of going steady, or of being boyfriend and girlfriend, though, really, we were.

While we were at Harvard, Barbara visited at Dunster House from time to time, sometimes because she had been contacted by one or the other of my roommates. John Hirsch, in particular, liked to talk to her about papers he had to write. One instance was when he had a paper he was working on about Georges Braque. She came to Dunster House, they went off to the Fogg Museum to look at Braques, and Barbara gave John a disquisition about Braque. I felt envious; it never occurred to me that her visits were pretexts to be with me. John got a good grade for the paper. A relevant factor: her parents had been to Europe and asked her what she wanted them to bring back, and she answered, "a Braque." They returned with an excellent painting they had acquired through François Reichenbach, a cousin of Jacques Guérin, her father's Paris perfume partner. François was making documentary films and dealing in pictures at the time. Barbara had stayed at a huge triple apartment, which François, his brother Phillipe, and his father Bernard shared, during the summer of our junior year, when we were both in Europe independently, but meeting in Paris and later, in London. François was also dealing in paintings, hence the Braque. Though dealers, François among them, are not always reliable, this Braque had a provenance: it passed from Braque to Walter Chrysler. This present to Barbara hung on the wall of the Poses's living room until they both died. Some things, like useless gifts parents really give themselves, seem not uncommon. Barbara had been given other gifts, such as dolls, but these were too fragile to play with, and for observation only. I never saw Barbara with a toy. There was one usable doll, the only one, and it was dilapidated.

Barbara, I felt, flaunted her brilliance, family connections, wealth and sophistication, and flirted with John. She left behind the potent aroma of her perfumes, *Intoxication* and *Le Dandy*. All that left me in a high dudgeon of envy, jealousy, and impotence, as well as anxiety about what I thought she would not be able to afford, if I pursued her with the idea of making a permanent relationship. I feared that she would feel that life as a doctor's wife was not for her, and that I would not be able to provide the milieu she was used to. Actually, Barbara was driven by a need to feel accepted, and went out of her way to give gifts to other people, having previously experienced her own longing to be given real gifts. In fact, of course, she wanted what, naturally, children need much of: parental support and understanding. Neither of us was greedy. We *felt* greedy. I never forgot that my mother had called me a thief: "*Du bist ein Dieb!*"—treating me as though it were I who had taken her health from her. As for Barbara, her parents lacked interest in and aptitude for parenting.

An added problem for me was that Barbara had been a child and teenaged dancer with the Ballet Russe, a protégée of Danilova and Léonide Massine, and she relished being the star. She shone in performances in the Dunster House Christmas play, and the senior yearbook had a large picture of her on the first page of the Dunster House section, costumed as a Valkyrie, in an extremely décolleté dress and a Viking helmet. In addition, knowing that the daughter had a certain similarity to her mother, Lillian Poses, another seductive star, what did I imagine I could do with such a creature? In truth, I had plenty of ambition, and plenty of anger, and plenty of anxiety about it all, and I wasn't sure I could keep up with Barbara, in social status, financial habits, or intelligence. In a way, it was a rerun of the Fafner story. But, basically, I was jealous and didn't want to share—and never far from my refugee fear of loss.

After I settled into the medical school routine, my orientation began to change; I began to feel that life was going to be manageable. I felt that though I didn't seem to be studying very hard, I was handling the frequent exams reasonably well. I managed to learn to ignore the formalin smell and also to endure either the absence or the presence of Barbara's inviting aroma of d'Orsay perfumes. I missed her cheek, her intelligence, sexiness, and affection, and I began to write to her. She replied; after a couple of months, the correspondence became warmer. In writing, Barbara and I both grew more revealing and conversational. Barbara had become transformed in my mind. No longer was she unreachable, unattainable, too brilliant, and too rich; in fact, she was not simply brash and self-confident, but also timorous and uncertain: more like me.

The conditions of my life during my first year at Washington University Medical School and Barbara's postgraduate fate, to live with her parents, broke through both of our resistances to coming out of hiding and making the risky venture to marry. I began to correspond with her and amassed a hoard of her letters. Soon we were flying between St. Louis and New York. I had some time off at Christmas and the New Year, and we became a romantic couple, much in love. Jack Poses was encouraging. He gave me a D'Orsay credit card to use for airplane tickets, a gift I was not too proud to refuse. What happened was that we loved each other, trusted each other, and trusted the feeling that we deserved each other. That was basic and carried us through what were transitory moods and quarrels.

I was not, however, attuned to Barbara's ambivalence about marriage. It did not occur to me that she had had a miserable relationship with her parents, who had a tempestuous and rivalrous relationship; I failed to realize that her family tensions were frightening her about the prospects of family life. She was angry and fearful and dreaded a replication of her own family history, and I did not really understand what a difficult and painful childhood Barbara had had.

I didn't perceive that I had an "attitude," meaning that, among the various personae that I constructed of Barbara, was one of Barbara as a spoiled rich kid, who'd had everything material anyone could want, while I had to fight my way into a family (without great success), and a community. Concerns about keeping up with the rich and well-connected Barbara were certainly part of the story; I resented what I saw as her social and economic freedom was another factor. I liked the material aspects Barbara enjoyed and was worried about my capacities to maintain them, but that didn't mean that I was not eager to enjoy those things myself. When I proposed marriage, I did so despite the fact that I felt I was motivated by greed as well as by love; I did not like what I then felt was a whiff of hypocrisy about my attraction to Barbara. That life is something that takes place in material reality, and that motivation is complex and conflicted, was not really a powerful enough way of thinking.

In retrospect, I was thinking and feeling like the adolescent I was, a hypocrite, because, really, I wished for these opportunities. Years passed; these callow ideas passed, the materialistic nonsense passed, and the partnership remained. Around Christmas we talked, and I proposed; Barbara hesitated. On the phone, on February 2nd 1955, Barbara accepted; I was rapturously relieved and happy. Jack sent her yellow roses, and we decided to marry on June 19, 1955, in Westport, at the Poses's home there. Barbara was twenty-one years old and I twenty-two. We found a rabbi who served at Columbia, and we had a brief conversation, of which I remember nothing, about religion, but also about loyalty, togetherness, patience and compassion, more of which than most we ultimately achieved.

We were married, but my mind was not uncluttered. At the time, I was ashamed of my father and guilty about accepting his support. I wanted to be self-sufficient. I didn't quite realize or accept that this could not happen—that dependence was inevitable, and inevitably intertwined with fear of loss. Jack's air travel card affected me insofar as it meant I would not be able to provide for Barbara in the way her parents could. I would remain a charity case, in debt as a child is—or a Jew or a refugee. Probably the fearful reluctance to understand that one is always attached to and relies on other people whom one can lose is intertwined with a fear of cowardice and consequent shame. I had experienced the pain of being jealous about Barbara's other friends and suitors and the distress of having been separated from her in the first place. I was not willing to lose her again, and that required a sacrifice which I experienced as humiliating. Was it braver to try, or to do without? I accepted the air tickets—a stage in a lifelong struggle against a fear of inadequacy. In fact, Barbara was not a spoiled Jewish princess. We both liked luxury, but other things were more important.

Jack Poses provided one piece of advice, which was that neither of us should enter a bathroom when the other was using it. This suggestion left me bemused at the time; I didn't realize that more thought would have produced an understanding that this advice revealed something substantial about the atmosphere in which Barbara grew up. Later, when I observed that he carefully emptied ashtrays and removed leaves and twigs from around the swimming hole in the Aspetuck River in Connecticut, I realized that this was an obsessional characteristic, and that both senior Poses were prudish and physically uncertain.

The Wedding

The wedding impressed me. It seemed to Barbara and me that Lillian, who had not had a proper wedding of her own, was designing a wedding for herself. Lillian was involved in every detail of the planning; the choice of the wedding dress, the bridesmaids' gowns, and everything else seemed to be more important to Lillian than to us, the to-be married couple. We, Barbara especially, felt dominated by the director of the drama, which made us actors less significant. It was supposed to be our duet, chiefly Barbara's (I never quibbled about that), not Lillian's solo; this reflected our ignorance about what the marriage of children, especially of an only child, might mean to the parents. There was a marquee with a dance floor; the apple tree on the lawn was decked out with paper apple blossoms (June 19 was not a date when natural blooms could be expected), which served as a canopy-chuppah. There were a lot of guests, including Abe Ribicoff, then a senator from Connecticut; Chester Bowles, a former senator; Bob Wagner, the New York mayor; and Jack Potofsky, the head of the Amalgamated Clothing Workers union. The rabbi not only looked, but also sounded, like Robert Taft.

The band played, people danced, and everyone enjoyed the party. I snuck off briefly to take a swim in the river to cool off and to relax before returning to greet all those whom I had missed before.

Happiness at the Wedding and Our Getaway Car

The food and drink gradually disappeared; people began to leave, and John Hirsch bombarded us with rice and flashed a happy grin, as we got into the getaway car. Barbara and I were happy, and happy that the day came to an end, with the Sherry Netherland Hotel for the night, and Europe for our honeymoon.

When we came back, our plan was to live in St. Louis until I finished medical school, and then return to New York. I would then have left the strain of conflicted preparatory years behind, have a chance to work as a fledgling doctor in an internship, and deal with people more personally; I might lean towards an academic life, or maybe not. Barbara had a job in New York working at Farrar, Straus, & Giroux, doing public relations under the supervision of an alcoholic and difficult woman, and she wanted to see about getting a graduate degree in English at Washington University. We were going to have an allowance of $5000 a year from each parental side; this would allow us a comfortable, if not luxurious, life. Barbara would escape from the parental nest on Fifth Avenue, and I would be freed from my boardinghouse room; we would be together, and have each other as lovers, companions, and best friends.

Our Honeymoon; My Bout with Paratyphoid Fever

We had a two-month summer vacation qua honeymoon, which we spent traveling around Europe, mainly in a Renault Quatre Chevaux, a tiny car with an air-cooled engine that often overheated. When that happened, we had to stop by the side of the road and wait for the engine to cool. The trip was uneventful with two exceptions. After eating a paella in Spain on the way to Catalonia, I developed a high fever with delirium. The diagnosis was paratyphoid fever, and we had to spend a week in a mountainside hotel, where we were alone with the heat and mosquito netting and my delirium. The American Consulate found us an English-speaking doctor, who prescribed achromycin, which cured the problem, but not quickly enough to spare us two or three nights of my raving in German.

A frightened Barbara stayed up with me, properly distressed about having a delirious husband but after a few days, I was clearly recovering. She reported that she had had thoughts that I might die and begun wondering about how she was going to get my body back to New York. When she told me this, we laughed at how silly it sounded, but my next reactions were fear and anger, as though Barbara had been thinking about herself, and not feeling sympathetic to me. That was one of many similar, unattractive, painful misinterpretations. Should a twenty-two-year old medical student know that it is healthy to deal with fear by shifting thought to practical, administrative, controllable matters? Should a recent recovery from an illness excuse taking one's anger out on an innocent wife? We got over the unpleasantness of that week or ten days quickly, went on to the Riviera, and back to honeymoon-vacation happiness. I rarely thought about this event afterward; it became a remembered, but not weighty, moment for me and for Barbara, as we remembered that we had been afraid, but the memory no longer came with fear. But as I write, I realize that the illness in Spain became connected with other events, in a kind of semi-conscious, voluminous file of experiences.

Theft of Barbara's Engagement Ring

While we were at Juan les Pins, on the French Riviera, where our outstandingly powerful American dollars made this luxury possible, Barbara lost her engagement ring. It simply disappeared from our hotel room in Juan les Pins. Was this an omen? I wondered how she could be so careless (read, "heartless") as to lose the ring I had given her. Had there been a safe in which she could have kept it? In the midst of even such comfort and luxury, I found a way to feel put-upon, to assume the role of victim. At a time of great pleasure, leisure, and independence, I had to suffer; it was more than I deserved, and too good to be true.

An equally important issue was that the ring represented my connection with Barbara, not only her connection with me. Whether she had it on her finger, or in a drawer, to me that meant a part of me was with her. At least, so I knew later. It was not simply the loss of a ring; the problem was my fear about losing Barbara. In retrospect, losing the ring stirred the pain of past losses, by reminding me of what had happened, and might happen again. It seems to me now that a more complete explanation of my fear of and anger about loss is that it is largely a consequence of having not settled the feelings about earlier losses, combined with the ever-present guilt about having when others had not, and knowing that, after all, one is hardly very able to control one's fate. The burnt child doesn't always shun the fire; instead the burnt child sometimes keeps testing the flame, to try to inure himself to the pain, to remind himself to be cautious about how close to the flame he can afford to let his passions lead him, to remind himself that he has the capacity to suffer, and yet to survive. Losses result in efforts to distance oneself, blame someone, and avoid too intense connection. But you also reassure yourself that you are still alive; all is not lost. Is there ever a really safe safety? Apparently not. Does one always make correctly cautious decisions? Apparently not. Sometimes, the flame is too hot and calls up old wounds. The capacity to employ the learned method of management is overwhelmed. Anger, deflation, and self-destructive behavior follow. With time and help, I have come to revisit my happy memories and grieve over the losses I have had; I revisit my sorrows as well as my joys, reassuring myself that, as I have in the past, I will cope with my future.

Eden Roc and Hôtel du Cap d'Antibes

We discovered Eden Roc and the Hotel du Cap d'Antibes; the continuing desirability of American currency let us spend days of luxury there during several subsequent holidays. We met and befriended M. Sella, who had known the Fitzgeralds and Hemingway, and other interesting and celebrated people. We were bright, young, and attractive; we spoke French; I had escaped Hitler; these were both good (I felt comfortable and Barbara felt comfortable) and bad (why us?). M. Sella had presided over the place long ago, when the English favored the region in winter and buried their little dogs in the faithful dog cemetery on the grounds. France passed a law prohibiting this interment practice in 1916, so no faithful canine friends were added subsequently. We could imagine future trips, which would make us "habitués."

Schoenbrunn, Private Theater; Performance of *The Abduction from the Seraglio*

We went to Vienna, arriving late in the day, without a hotel reservation; so, I decided to stop near one of the railroad stations, the Westbahnhof. When I saw a hotel sign, I went in and asked if they had an available room and was smilingly received by the man at the desk. But when I said, "Good, I'll get my wife," he turned sour, and informed me that this would not be a good idea. The penny dropped: the "hotel" was a place of business for ladies of the evening, and any wanderers who might call on them. We heard *The Abduction from the Seraglio* at the Kaiser's charming Baroque private theater at Schönbrunn and visited some of my childhood haunts: the zoo and the Wurstelprater (the setting of both *The Third Man* and of my Grottenbahn which, to my sorrow, seemed no longer to exist). The Matador store in the Graben had also disappeared, along with its window display of the marvelous things a child in Vienna might want to construct, especially a child like me who shared his mother's liking of the toy cable cars, trucks, and railroad engines that had adorned the shop's window. Demel, the pastry shop with its *Indianer* (balls of pound-cake sliced in half horizontally, filled with *Schlag* and covered with chocolate), and the antiques shops, at one of which we almost bought a Riemenschneider but decided we couldn't afford the few hundred dollars it cost then, were still there. So, too, was Montezuma's cape, made entirely of exotic bird feathers, given by Spain's king to his Vienna Habsburg relative when Pizarro came back from the conquest of the Incas. It was now displayed in the ethnographic museum.

Vienna: So Familiar and Yet Very Strange

I felt odd in Vienna, then, and in my few later visits. The place was familiar, yet strange. Strange partly because I felt the place was so familiar, more so than, say, St. Louis: the smells, the food, the way people walked and talked, the manners, the humor, the trolley sounds, and the people jumping on and off between stops. I seemed to know my way around. Talking to the locals in shops, I would be asked what part of Austria I came from; the argot had changed. Familiarity did not make me comfortable; not as comfortable as I felt in France, which was familiar and agreeable. I was neither comfortable nor uncomfortable in Vienna; I was not a visitor or a guest. Spain was definitely a foreign country; England was different but much like the States; In Italy, in 1952, I felt that the country was not really a serious place with serious people. In Vienna and in France, I retained a good feeling from my years of protected childhood; I also had a puzzlement. I felt it was now familiar but strange. Despite the undercurrents of anxiety and secrecy I felt, my family had made it possible for me to have a comfortable childhood in Vienna, while in the early years in the United States I was clearly a refugee. I was not still the child of Vienna, yet Vienna was the place of my childhood.

Brigitte de Vallee and Cecil Altman

Barbara and I looked up a couple, Brigitte de Vallée and Cecil Altman, to whom we had been introduced by mutual friends at Harvard. We got along famously and after a few days together in Vienna we were close friends. Barbara and Brigitte were both excellent cooks who liked to entertain, trade recipes, and tell stories. Cecil was Viennese; a child of his father's second marriage, he left a Harvard Ph.D. program, married, and went to work for his father, Bernhard, a plutocrat, who had a large international business in cashmere. Cecil was managing the business in Vienna and living very nicely in a house in Schönbrunn. Later, he became a wheeler-dealer—dabbling in, owning, and running hotels, restaurants, and a ski run, and making plans for projects all over the place. Cecil was also a storyteller, a very Viennese trait.

Cecil's Story About His Onkel (Uncle) Fritz

Cecil and I both had an Uncle Fritz. When the Nazis took over in Austria, they went into the business of extortion; if you wanted to leave Austria, you had to leave your money behind. If you had money outside Austria, out of the grasp of the Nazis, they made sure you or your family didn't get out of the country until you paid a large ransom. They arrested Fritz and imprisoned him while negotiating with Cecil's father, who had been clever enough to get himself and a substantial fortune out in good time.

In prison, Cecil's Uncle Fritz had a cellmate, a Viennese criminal with Viennese charm. When Fritz learned he was going to be released, he told his cellmate, and said that their friendship had made his stay bearable; he had become very fond of the man. The newfound friend responded sheepishly, asking forgiveness for something he had done which he wanted to confess. He asked Fritz if he remembered a robbery at the Altman office, when the safe had been blasted open, and the payroll stolen. "Of course," said Fritz. "We did it,'" said the cellmate. "We knew everything about the payroll. We knew about the old lady and the basket she carried to the bank to get the money, the route she took to get back to the factory—everything." "But if that was so, why didn't you just knock her on the head, and take the basket when she was carrying it back from the bank?" And now came the answer (which needs to be told in the original Viennese German, "Nah, was glaubst den, wir sint doch nicht g'wönliche Strassenreuber!" What are you thinking, we aren't ordinary street thieves!" Almost a Graf Bobby-Rudi story, and very typically Viennese.

A not-quite footnote that gives another example of the small world of the time: Edmund de Waal, in his wonderful book, *The Hare with Amber Eyes*, wrote about his family, the Ephrussis, who had a wealthy Vienna banking branch. He describes the head of the family who receives a friend in his library of rare books. The friend tells him, "You have to leave. Mitzi Springer and Bernhard Altman have already gone." Another link in the chain of connections in the group of acculturated Jews, which included my family in the Vienna of the time: Cecil, the son of Bernhard, was a great-nephew of Adele Bloch Bauer, whose portrait by Klimt was returned to the family as the result of a lawsuit pursued by a California lawyer. The lawyer was a son of Arnold Schönberg. Schönberg and my piano teacher in my teens, Edouard Steuermann, were best friends.

In looking back to the eighteenth century in my ancestry, I found distant connections to Springers, Ephrussis, Rothschilds, Kafkas (including Franz), Freud's children (by way of the Bernays family), and many other notable (as well as unimportant) Jewish inhabitants, whose Austria-Hungarian families date back a few hundred years. After all, there were only ten or twelve-thousand such families; and every connection I found was Austrian or Bohemian. Many of those who lived in the Hitler era met their ends at Theresienstadt or other camps.

Barbara's Minor Car Accident; Gendarmerie in Passau

From Vienna, Barbara and I drove to Munich to buy a Zeiss microscope for my second-year pathology course. Barbara, driving, looked at me and, making some comment, crossed the center of a narrow road and sideswiped an oncoming small truck. A local policeman rolled up on a bicycle; he joined us while we were looking at the damage and discussing what to do next with the driver of the injured truck. The officer told us that Barbara had committed numerous crimes. She had caused financial damage, risked injuring herself, her passenger, and the truck driver—that made four crimes he could think of. We had to visit the local Gendarmerie just short of Passau, the German border town through which the Nazis had invaded Austria in 1938.

By the time we got there, it was dusk; we were in a deserted, gloomy square and the street lights had not yet come on. We came to a building, climbed some stairs, and sat to wait for the local commander; after a half-hour, a tall man arrived, wearing high boots, a long coat, a serious expression, and a dueling scar. This man might have played an SS officer in a Hollywood movie. He asked for passports. He looked at

Barbara's and muttered, "Hmmm; tourist"; and then mine, which of course indicated that I had been born in Vienna. He said, in German, "So you are Austrian." I agreed, also in German. He asked where we were going, and I explained. In an ironic, suggestive, regretful, and meaningful tone, he said, "Well, you missed a great deal," and waved us on our way. He probably meant: we missed being murdered, or killed in an air raid, or having too little food, and being overrun by Russian looters and rapists. One thing was clear; the commander was certain that whatever we had missed—which he had not—had been awful, was now gone, over, finished, and worth having missed.

We got to Munich, and I bought my microscope, which was an excellent piece of optical engineering, the price making it financially well worth the trip to the Zeiss shop. But when we left, at a red light, a group of young men started rocking our little 4CV Renault and jeering at us, thinking we were unwelcome French. We hurried back to France as quickly as the car could safely take us.

Border Crossings Past and Present

Crossing the border gave me a sensation similar to one I had years later, when we flew over the Channel from a dark, damp, wintry London, and midway over the Channel the sun broke through the clouds. It also reminded me of the train, as we exited from Austria, in 1938; then I looked through the window and saw a long curve and a tunnel ahead. I asked where we were, and my father said, "On the other side of the tunnel is Switzerland." I felt glad to be out of Germany as I had been happy to leave Austria. Brigitte Altman told a story about leaving Germany for France with her small children, a similar experience for her. They crossed the border at an ugly crossing point, and Brigitte drove on until she came to the top of a hill. There, she stopped, got out of the car with the children, pointed ahead at a prospect of fields, hills, and a charming village, and said, *"Et, mes enfants, regardez,* ça *c'est la France."* Brigitte and her family—parents and two brothers—were in hiding and often hungry during the war. The father had been a public anti-Nazi.

Crossing borders still triggers a mental catalogue of bad things for me—enforced immobility and associated pain and fear, night terrors, fears of going to sleep, fears of a latter-day Gestapo, ideas of being buried alive (reviving ether memories), being lost, my mother's fragility, and being confined in a hospital. I can counter with a catalog of good things: waking up, and realizing I had been having a nightmare; recovering from anesthesia, and slowly realizing where I was, and what had happened; participating in some group effort that comes out well; having a reunion with old friends, or making new ones; or hearing or playing a piece of music that sounds almost exactly as I want to hear it. And that I am still here. I and mine might have been made extinct.

As for the Austrian police near Passau, I had no need to fear them; nevertheless, I still get a frightened chill whenever I encounter police, immigration officials, and customs officers, or if I pass by someone by the side of the road stopped for a traffic offense. This has more than a bit of the post-traumatic about it.

I feel about France, and the French, as I remember having felt in 1938, in the month of August in Paris; I remember relief and escape, as I felt in leaving the dark tunnel into Switzerland and entering the world of sunshine; I remember the joy at the beauty of Paris, the street sounds, the odors of wet horse chestnut trees. It was a time when I still had the comfortable, child's understanding that there is a simple yes and no, a right and wrong, and a good and bad. "Those were the days, my friend, I thought they'd never end…" but they did. Things became a lot more ambiguous and complicated, and choices became more difficult.

My Grudges and Guilt: Effect on Relationship with Barbara

I was conflicted in 1952 when I made my first trip back to Europe, and, again, on the second, our honeymoon. I knew that the war had left many people bereft and impoverished, and likely to purloin a rich American's ring. I didn't realize how guilty I felt about not being poor, not being dead, stupid, diseased, deformed, or a variety of other things. I was still in the self-induced state of feeling put-upon. I could not simply brush other peoples' situations or reactions aside.

By then, I had spent enough domestic time with Barbara to realize that putting things aside was not her style either. Being more than a little self-punishing was her style, as mine was too. I now see that we were two of a kind; I put our unconscious guilt-quotient far higher now than we would have estimated at that time, had we thought about why we were feeling as we did. We knew we had problems; we regularly explained our moods and tendencies to feel put-upon or neglected as responses to passing problems. We tried to explain away the dips, considered them normal, understandable reactions to actual insults and disappointments; there was enough truth to these explanations to make them seem sufficient.

The Hotel Bisson in Paris

Back in Paris we stayed at the Hotel Bisson, on the Quai des Grands Augustins. We felt very Parisian, what with the Seine and the traffic with its cacophony of Gershwin-like noises outside our windows. Gershwin brought the Parisian car horns into *American in Paris,* a good example of the working of a musician's mind, of taking in sounds, pushing them into internal listening, and moving them back out into honored places in works. I was pretty good at hearing music in my head myself. The sounds of the cars, of which I could identify quite a few makes and models, as they drove by our open windows, joined my internal music, which had been influenced by Gershwin's conjuring trick of mixing styles, to my delight, years before. Besides, had our stay in Paris not been in a house on the same Quai? Had I not heard the same horns as a little boy? Had that led to my enjoyment of an *American in Paris*?

Gershwin and Other American Composers; Visiting Mary Wooster in Paris

I had persuaded my mother that the U.S. harbored real composers by playing her Gershwin; she admitted that he was pretty good, though not as good as Brahms. When I added that I knew she had marveled at a performance of Ravel's *Bolero*, led by the Italian conductor Victor de Sabata in Vienna, and that Gershwin and Ravel had made friends in Paris, each congratulating the other on his mastery, she was happy to ask me what other American composers she might enjoy. I recommended Aaron Copland, Samuel Barber, Walter Piston, and musical comedy; I hadn't yet heard Dixieland, jazz, and folk music. Later on, I brought my mother a recording of *Candide*, to go with my general attempt to please her by bringing home wildflowers, good grades, and so on. But on the guilt front, I never did find a cure for multiple sclerosis.

We visited Mary Wooster in Paris and made friends with John Levee, a painter friend of the art dealer, André Emmerich, who was showing John's work in his new gallery in New York. John was a freckle-faced Californian, a former air force pilot who had flown the hump across Burma and the Himalayas, on to Chungking in China, during the war in the Pacific. He looked like an adolescent, so it was hard to imagine him as a hero but I knew that route was hazardous. I always assumed his freight had been arms. One day, when he informed me that he was buying gold to try to compensate for the continuing devaluation of the French franc, he said it reminded him of when he had delivered to

Chiang Kai-shek gold bricks, with which to pay his soldiers and officials and presumably himself.

Though a pilot himself, John was not at ease in airplanes, which became evident when he came to New York for one of his showings chez Emmerich. I knew a wartime comrade of John's, Howard Sloan, who had just taken delivery of a brand-new twin engine Cessna. Howard and I were both thinking of renting houses on Cape Cod for a summer vacation, and we had agreed to fly there to look at possibilities. I told John about this plan, and he was eager to join. When the weekend for the project came, we three trundled off to the Teterboro airport. The Cessna still had plastic sheeting in the interior and was about to be flown by its new owner for the first time. I learned that once in the air, you are surrounded by noise; transponders were working, voices were telling us where other planes were flying in the vicinity, as "TWA (some number) is proceeding south at 30,000 feet at eleven o'clock one mile away" from us. The air was rough, and we were bouncing around.

Suddenly, something went wrong with our electronics, and everything became much quieter, and Howard had to radio Logan Airport in Boston for permission to land to deal with this fault. Howard and I were quite calm but John, the old experienced pilot, greatly embarrassed, vomited. Howard moaned, "Oh no, my new plane, thank God for the plastic on the seats," and we landed at Logan. A minor electronic fault was repaired, but we failed to find appropriate properties to rent on the Cape.

My appreciation of John's bravery was enhanced; his air exploits during the war had placed him quite high up on my hero ladder, together with the RAF fighter pilots with their Spitfires and Hurricanes. John was a sort of adopted older brother, though we referred to each other as "cousin." (His father was M.C. Levee, one of the founders of the Hollywood Academy that awards the Oscar. John died in Paris in 2017, aged 92.)

The Honeymoon Ends—To St. Louis With Barbara

As Barbara and I learned more about each other, I came, more and more, to sense what brought people together and what kept them apart. One thing was similar experience, whether with women and women, men and men, refugees and refugees, or artistic types, or obsessionals—all having empathy for people like themselves in important respects, whether anatomical, intellectual, or cultural. Many factors are intangible; I learned ever more about how important these mysterious qualities were in relationships, between doctor and patient, no less than between civilians. Barbara and I knew too little about our inner selves to be able to tell each other about our ideas and feelings clearly; a good deal of flailing about would, eventually, improve this, with a good deal of psychoanalytic help.

Barbara's Cognitive Issues, Some Noted by Me; Others Not Diagnosed; Jack Taught Barbara to Drive

I realized that Barbara suffered from a mild right-left confusion. She had never been able to subtract serial sevens from one hundred, a standard mental status exam, which was supposed to show whether one was free of brain disease (which she was). She also had trouble paying attention while driving, which had resulted in a fender bender when she ran her mother's Cadillac convertible into a car she was following on Fifth Avenue, at the same time looking at the back-seat passenger, and making conversation. A similar accident happened another time and, of course, there was the one in Austria. I was not surprised to discover that her father had an even more severe right-left problem, and frequently got lost. I regarded this as an amiable eccentricity of the British type, a quirky quality of the sort we had appreciated in people during our time in England. I did not yet realize that such cognitive defects are powerful self-esteem busters.

Jack had felt it incumbent on him to teach his daughter to drive. On entering the driveway in Westport, he famously insisted that she turn left, which she did, into a stone wall. It also provided a good story. The "I-must-be-right" pressure in the family caused unnecessary trouble by way of arguments about who knew something better, or first. Control was the issue. Jack's cleaning-up symptom went along with the rest. The need to be right serves to cover and deny the sense of deficiency.

Much later, it turned out that a patient of mine—who often came late as a consequence of leaving subway stations and walking in the wrong direction or entering and taking the wrong trains—had a right-left problem. The patient, unlike Barbara who had fine handwriting, also had undecipherable handwriting. We defined his right-left problem, and the writing difficulty, as analogous to dyslexia. At that time, it was becoming more apparent that definable focal cognitive deficiencies, including difficulties with spelling, writing, numbers, and names, among others, could be identified by psychological tests. They could be remediated. They were familial and heritable. The defects certainly did not mean the man was stupid or obstinate, as teachers in his childhood had assumed. I published a paper about this that became something of a classic.

It turned out that, in addition to her right-left issues, Barbara had the recently recognized condition ADHD. Observation of Barbara and her father gave me sensitivity to the small symptomatic traits they showed and sensitized me to the importance of the kind of problems that appeared as a consequence. Low self-esteem often underlies an exaggerated need to be right, which sometimes leads to trouble. Self-medication can appear in the form of drugs, especially alcohol, or strenuous exercising. I seem to have another sort of cognitive arrangement: I find it difficult to think in straight lines. "A" may lead to "B" and then to "C," but I find it difficult to keep it simple. I usually think A leads to X, P, R, and maybe B. In other words, I don't know how to accept that A leads to B but instead see that as only one possibility, and I can't help thinking of other factors that are involved.

Barbara's Need to Know

Barbara had an impatient need to know, and to be right, which often seemed to impel her to invent stories, or serious-sounding rationalizations. Again, much later, I began to teach that this characteristic is typical of people with what came to be regarded as focal cognitive problems, such as difficulties understanding written words, though the same words, when heard, were easily understood or, in the case of names, not easily remembered, or numbers, like serial sevens not easily manipulated. On the other hand, Barbara had an amazing ability to picture the arrangements of furniture, or the potential arrangement of garden plants and flowers; the contrast with her relative difficulty in planning a trip, or reading a map, showed how focal talents, and troublesome cognitive capacities, can coexist.

The diagnostic question—how much is physiology and how much is nurture and how do they interact?—is an important one. Another matter: physiology has something to do with the capacity to empathize, the grossest examples being autism and Asperger's Syndrome. A reasonably accurate judgment about one's own capacities is useful. Is there a physiological factor involved here as well? Is a self-judgment a cognitive element, an influence? Certainly.

I now think that it is hard to avoid the conclusion that variation in cognitive characteristics has a profound influence on who is empathic with whom, and how much differences in thinking styles affects social connections. The interconnectedness of people depends on processing ideas similarly. "You don't get through to me, and I don't get through to you" dissonance may result in pathologizing attitudes towards absent-minded, nerdy-genius-professor types, who are easily both feared and envied. I think interpersonal failures to connect are very important. Straight-line thinkers seem to me to be uncomfortable with my loose, complicated way of thinking, fail to get my jokes and puns, avoid color and hyperbole, and tend to regard me as odd. To the extent to which I see myself as others see me, beginning with my parents, in their overdone concern about me, it makes me shy and overbearing. I find it hard to persuade and easy to harangue, which does me no social good.

Eventually, the left brain-right brain notion became an in-vogue oversimplification of functions, which initially made something that had been unclear, clearer. Paradoxical qualities coexist, talents and deficits together, so a taxonomy of mental characteristics has to take that into account. One pretty common picture is left-handed, enuretic, left-right confusion, reading difficulty, letter reversal, anxiety about "defects," impatience—and self-medication by means of exercise or drugs.

Barbara also had a capacity to respond to language, in the poetic realm, with intense feelings, and to have remarkable insights and responses, shown in a thesis she wrote about Emily Dickinson, and in her own poetry, and, later, in her hundreds of articles, reviews, and a dozen books. Organizing longer pieces, however, was always difficult for her.

Barbara's Uninteresting Ph.D. studies at Washington University

In St. Louis, Barbara enrolled in the English department at Washington University. Her mentor there wanted her to work on a subject that held no interest for her. He was involved in studying English commonplace books of the 18th- century. He had Barbara sitting in a library reading fiches, a sort of slide photograph, hard on the eyes and, probably, her back, which had a propensity for responding to stress, rain, and awkward positions by creating spasms.

Going over these sociologically fashionable, but unliterary and unpoetic publications, Barbara thought, was like having to read the weekly women's magazines as though they contained important literary products—of a period when there were plenty of unexplored important writers to investigate. Barbara and I shared a dislike of collecting, listing, dating, and categorizing information—as though that would lead to understanding meanings, and cause-effect relationships. Lack of patience was another quirk. Had we seen commonplace books as culturally interesting, and as culturally equivalent to so-called high art, we might have been part of a majority; but we were the kind of people who did not wish to conflate popular art with high art.

Barbara's disappointed feeling that her academic work was a waste of time and effort (very different from what had been the case for her at Radcliffe, where professors recognized her talents, and she felt understood), led her to drop out. This was reasonable and realistic, but she interpreted it as a shameful sign of weakness. She pretended that she had a sprained ankle as part of her repertoire of obfuscations; this confused me, and, when she finally explained herself, I, as usual, took the delay personally. It took me a long time to reach the conclusion that the need to be correct can be extremely pressing, and the feeling of being defective extremely painful to people with cognitive deficits. For Barbara, considering herself a failure or feeling she was shirking a burden, or causing a problem, was untenable at that moment.

When I was given to pouting as a child, I was called a "*Beleidigte Leberwurst*," a sulking liverwurst; this was a jeering insult, of an ironic poor-little-baby type, meaning, "He's not the center of attention." I felt Barbara didn't trust me; how could she have done this, and did she love me? Had I failed her? What I failed was to see that I was thinking as she must have been. If she felt she couldn't trust me, wasn't she right?

Wouldn't I have reacted egotistically, as with the engagement ring? I hadn't yet come to my gradual, progressively brighter, illuminations about cognitive defects; I had not yet started gathering together ideas about low self-esteem. I was self-important, felt easily ignored, and prone to feeling unwanted. Step one: I really wasn't that sympathetic, and she was right to fear my disapprobation. Step two: I was a victim, not a danger—wasn't I? Step three: I was the victim; Barbara was the villain. If I was the victim, I couldn't be the bad one, who hadn't been good enough to Barbara. Of course, she was living a similar story. Barbara and I both enacted scenarios playing with victimhood, in a sadomasochistic role playing, in which we each were both partners, sadist and masochist, within our own minds, while trying to project one of the roles, that of bad sadist, away from ourselves.

The practical outcome of the situation was that more truth came out. I soon calmed down, while feeling disappointed about her having wasted her time, and empathic about how hard it had all been for her. We both returned to reality until, naturally, the next time. Barbara did a similar self-renovation, by concluding that she hadn't really needed to be so timid about how I might react, but there came a sour note with the harmony. She remarked that I had, after all, broken up with her at Harvard. I did not bring up all the people (and there were a few) whom she adopted, and all the times she made me wait for her while she was helping somebody with an essay or arranging something else for somebody else. I had more reasons for my feelings, but I still had a lot to learn about what they were. We both could have used a good therapist.

Barbara dropped out of university officially, gave up the idea of an academic life, and never looked back. She got a job in the public relations group at Ozark Airlines, which made her part of a social circle, brought some income, and amused her. She continued to write poetry, which she had begun to do in adolescence. She thought of herself as a poet. I found her poems dark and gloomy, even frightening. I did not want to think of Barbara as a depressed person. I, as a depressive person, thought that one was enough. Barbara never tried to publish these works, and after her death, on June 1st, 2018, no amount of searching produced her manuscripts.

Another issue was having children. We both occupied ambiguous places in our families. Barbara's mother was clearly extremely career-oriented, and, as the middle child between two brothers, always uncomfortable about her place. Barbara, as the only child of the most socially successful and materially well-off members of her parents' family generation, was, unlike her cousins, raised by servants. Her mother was largely occupied by political life in Washington. Her father drank too much and had a difficult, competitive relationship with his seductive, but sexually fearful, wife. He understood little of parenting. He had no father figure, his father having died in Russia, and his oldest sister and his mother also had twelve others to bring up. Besides, there were the defective and genius aspects of Barbara's thinking process to contend with, as well as a toddler affliction, coeliac disease.

Neither of us consciously considered that a child would come between us and reduce our importance to the other. We both neglected the understanding that children are burdens as well as blessings. The idea that my father might have had, in the material situation in the Austrian state in the late 1920s and early 1930s, a good reason for concern about adding a child took a long time to pop into my head. In any case, to have or not have or when to have children should be an important question, worthy of exploration.

Barbara's Childhood Amid Anti-Semitic Social Snobs

As a child, Barbara was plunged into Manhattan social circles where a good deal of snobbery and anti-Semitism were displayed. Her parents wanted to be part of the society of fancier and more integrated people though, economically and socially, they were arrivistes who, having been strivers, once having arrived, still felt inferior. They had the disadvantages, as well as the benefits, of having unusual gifts and unusual weaknesses. So did Barbara, who grew up with plenty of ambiguities and ambivalences of her own. As did I, of course. The question, were we a part of the community—or not quite?—was important to Barbara, her parents, and me. We became a mutually supportive arrangement, but our deficits interfered with some potentially useful, effective, and mutually supportive, theoretically possible meditations.

In the early years of our marriage, I was eager to have children—not immediately, but some time not too far off; and Barbara was more hesitant. We failed to find a way to discuss the question realistically. When we were writing letters to each other before our marriage, Barbara said she would like to have five children; she wanted to be like a peasant, to pop babies in the fields, and return to work within days. We both failed to notice that rearing children might mean someone had to be there to do the rearing, and it seemed that neither of us was thinking about playing the part. I was not that much in a hurry, nor did I take her seriously about five children, but I did not expect having no family at all would be in question. But then, I was embarking on a professional path; Barbara was all at sea.

I took it for granted that I would not be the main parent. I didn't worry about feeding a child, getting up at night. That was what doctors did with patients, not at home. Times had not yet changed. When they did, and we had a daughter in 1962 and a son in 1964, both of us had offices in our house. Barbara worked at home until 1970 and then travelled more and more. We were both happy with our arrangements.

Barbara's parents were pleased about us and generous. The annual $5,000 each they and my parents contributed made our lives easy. This money was ours to manage and went to living expenses. There were also gifts—the Poseses gave us a car and me a piano as wedding presents.

In addition, Barbara was the beneficiary of a trust, which had been growing for years. As Jack had been able to carry on his career during the two wars and was clever, hard-working, and conservative about money, endowing Barbara in her early childhood led to the trust being worth about a million dollars twenty years later.

However, his faith in our capacity to treat the money sensibly was not great enough, and his need to control did not loosen enough to permit Barbara, or Barbara and me, to make decisions about the funds. The idea that wealth is likely to promote waste or fecklessness probably infects most parents who have material assets to transmit; they don't want to have the King Lear-like results that worry some wealthy families. The Poses's public benefactions were many—mainly to educational institutions such as the City University, Brandeis, and Yale Law School, but also to the Democratic Party. We, in effect, had to apply for grants from Barbara's trust.

Married Life in St. Louis: Our Landlords and Friends, the Landesmans

In St. Louis, we moved into what was, for us, an ideal apartment, and took up new lives at 326 North Euclid Avenue. Our Victorian three-story walk-up had a front living room with a large bay window looking onto the street, a large bedroom, a bathroom, and a good-sized kitchen. The hospitals, Barnes and the Jewish, were a few blocks away, and Forest Park, one Block away, as was the Chase Park Plaza Hotel. Our building was in the process of being refurbished by Fred Landesman who, with his wife Paula, his brother Jay, and Jay's wife Fran, owned it.

The two brothers also shared an antique shop that had belonged to the Landesman parents, the Crystal Palace, a bar and cabaret, and another apartment building on Olive Street. The area gradually acquired a restaurant and other shops, and became a pleasant, moderately late-night neighborhood called Gaslight Square. Moving into Fred's house was rapidly followed by our moving into his social circle. Paula and Fred Landesman gathered a circle of actors, literati, and artists around them, We too became part of a crowd that made our lives pleasurable and interesting.

The atmosphere around these people was artistic-nouveau-bohemian. The group was not large; it was independent of the larger community and indifferent to it. The Landesman brothers were St. Louis natives, but they had little to do with the society around them. Their attachments were to theatre, literature, popular music, folk music, and the people that made them. The Crystal Palace had a bar, a smallish stage, crystal chandeliers and sconces, good service and good shows; it also had a clubby atmosphere, something like Elaine's had for us in New York later on.

Jay had published a magazine called *Neurotica*, an avant-garde literary journal. Fran was a songwriter who had a hit, "Spring Can Hang You up the Most," and Fred was a playwright and artist. Their social life was active, and sexually a bit advanced for my and Barbara's tastes. To show what a naïf I was (or, at least, where my mind was not), an extremely beautiful young woman, who had a lovely face and a striking, brown body, was a Landesman friend. At one of their parties she asked me for a cigarette, and I responded that I had none with me but had some at home. It was a ten-minute walk. I'd like a cigarette myself and said I'd go to get them. She said she'd walk with me. We arrived, found the cigarettes, lit up, and, when I turned to leave, she looked surprised and asked me if all I had had in mind was a cigarette. It took me some minutes to get over how flabbergasted what she had suggested made me; sexual curiosity and expectation had motivated her, and I had obviously been flirting, but where had I been? How came it to be that I processed our invitations to each other as though I lacked sensory organs?

The Crystal Palace on Olive Street

Fred and Jay housed the performers for the Crystal Palace at the building in Olive Street. Fred, Paula, and their three sons lived nearby in a late 19th-century Henry Hobson Richardson designed house with a small private theater; they entertained their guests, performers, and friends including us. We hung out with the Compass Players, a Chicago Second City touring offshoot, including Mike Nichols and Elaine May, my Beacon Hill–Scollay Square friend, Severn Darden, Alan Arkin, and Del Close—all of whom went on to movie and stage careers; a Viennese chanteuse, Greta Keller, who assured us that she had been more famous than Marlene Dietrich; the folk singers, Susan Reed and Jean Ritchie; and Miles Davis, who had lived in East St. Louis as a child.

Chevy, Our Beloved Child Substitute

In St. Louis, we enlarged our two-person unit by acquiring a puppy, a standard poodle, who became as human as dogs can be, which means a lot. I suggested we name him Chevy, partly to try to flatter Jack Poses, by calling the dog after his men's fragrance brand, the "Chevalier D'Orsay," and partly to thank the Poseses for their helpfulness. The dog, Chevy, the child substitute, proved to be the wisest and least neurotic, if not the smartest, member of the now three-being family. I think he felt no sense of not belonging; he enjoyed most of his moments and expressed himself clearly when expression was called for. He showed when he wanted to go out, and when he did not want to go out. When he wanted petting, he presented himself and nudged with his nose. If you threw a stick or a toy, he chased it, brought it back for another toss, and indicated when he had had enough. When we visited New York, he calmly went for walks and when we went to Westport to visit the Poses, Chevy came along happily.

We swam in the Aspetuck River, which was dammed up nicely—long before the wetlands around the stream had been defined and decreed to be in need of protection—with the occasionally catchable trout living in the swimming hole. When we swam, Chevy leaped into the water after us; whether he did this to stay close to us humans was unclear. When we imagined he was protecting us like a sheep dog, or had both motives, we were wittingly spinning egocentric tales. He was, after all, a dog. Did that mean he could feel protective? Or left out? Nowadays, I know—of course he could.

Even when left alone, Chevy behaved. However, once we put him into a crate, taking him with us to New York for a few days, traveling in the dog compartment in the belly of the Constellation. When we returned to St. Louis, with Chevy again in the crate, we left him and went out to dinner. While we were gone, he invaded Barbara's closet, and chewed one shoe—of each pair of her shoes—for as long as time allowed before our return. He must have wanted to join us and resented being left alone. Was he joining us for a few bites without having been invited? Attached to us as he was, when we went to Europe, he nevertheless quickly seduced the friends with whom we left him, and pointedly ignored us for a few days after we returned. He was altogether a reliable, trustworthy, straightforward animal; and Barbara, who had worried that she might not become a satisfactory mother, took comfort from the fact that she had mothered an excellent dog.

The major disadvantage in our relationship with the dog was that he could not speak. If we were not especially interested in conversing with each other, but still wanted company, conversation with the dog was not possible. He could not obey the rule that a polite invitee is responsible for initiating interesting conversation with the host. What Chevy was able to communicate by sounds and body language was limited; but that did not mean that he had no conscious feelings, or that he was incapable of experiencing and communicating feelings in such a way as to evoke an understanding response from his companions, and he could respond to some of our affective messages too. All this interaction was to be important to us when we had children, and when I began to treat patients. Especially when one gets down on the floor to play with child patients, one needs to be attuned to the un-verbalized meanings of what is being played out. I soon learned that how patients organize concepts, how they spin ideas, both conceals and reveals a world of thoughts and feelings. In St Louis, we had a dog, friends, a good life—pigs in clover—why add a child?

Dogs and humans are both sociable animals who live in groups, hunt together, play together, compete for territory and sexual partners, and establish hierarchies within their tribes or packs. Unlike other animals, they look into our eyes; they also recognize us through sight, smell, and taste, and by the way we move and gesture. They respond to teaching, can identify as many as five hundred words, know when it is time to drive to the country, when to expect the dog walker, and when they are nearing the house at the end of a weekend trip. They obey hand commands and cuddle and lick us when we are ill or hurt. They react positively and negatively to music. They accept us humans and seem pleased or not to be with us. Unfortunately, they also die.

Chevy's death was Barbara's and my first major shared loss, and it caused our first mutual grieving. He died of kidney failure in his ninth year, when we had the two children his excellent dogginess had made it easier to produce. Success with bringing up the dog lessened the fear of becoming bad parents. It did not speak to the question, why take on the lifestyle limiting responsibility of parenthood? Another later event, years later in 1961, had to happen for the first child to be conceived.

MARRIAGE

A History of Our Families' Love and Attitude Towards Dogs

My grandmother took in stray dogs at Perchtoldsdorf; three or four rescued dogs usually lived in my grandparents' house. There were Milly, Fipsi, and Mitzi, but my grandmother's favorite dog during my childhood was called "Bello." Bello had a blue tongue, part of which needed to be amputated because of a tumor or cyst, which interested me greatly, and scared me more than a bit—probably related to my adenoid surgery, which came just before Bello's operation. He recovered, and everyone was pleased.

My mother had a way of scrunching her face around her eyes when she was reminded of a particularly beautiful and important experience. Then she would say, "Ach," and perhaps mention a name, with wistful nostalgic passion; at such moments, it was impossible not to be touched by the love in her bones, muscles, and voice. "Ach, Huberman" (a favorite violinist) or "Maloja," or "Venedig" (holiday spots), "Ach, di Sabata's *Bolero*" (a conductor's performance of Ravel's piece). One of her most heartfelt was "Ach, Fipsi" (her favorite dog). Her "Ach" experiences reflected things I later came to love as well.

In the time of our poverty, at age seven and eight in Jackson Heights, I walked an aged wire-haired terrier, or, rather, coaxed him along the street and carried him when he was tired. I begged to be allowed to do this, and the old lady who owned him paid me twenty-five cents for five walks a week. He was my friend at a time when I had few friends.

Barbara had a childhood dog, Ronnie, still a companion in memory and photographs. Ronnie died while Barbara was away at college, and Lillian told Barbara that Ronnie had missed her so much that he stopped moving his bowels and died of constipation. Barbara believed that her mother had the dog destroyed. Lillian disliked house-pet animals; she absolutely hated cats, and lied about it, claiming allergies. In Venice, a city with many wandering cats, free-ranging felines seemed to be everywhere; and when we were there with Lillian one summer, she would scream, "Go away, go away," and find things on the ground to throw at the cats (Venice also has plenty of things that one can find on the ground). Lillian found cats dirty and noisy, and thought they carried diseases—like children. My mother thought similar things about dogs, with the additional disgust that they seemed to like to smell feces and might even eat them. Nevertheless, these feelings didn't prevent her from loving dogs.

Having dog companions taught us lessons. Even though one sometimes doubts one's capacities to love, really love, it becomes hard to believe this doubt is valid when one has a dog one loves and grieves over. Some people claim dogs are dumb animals who have no feelings and behave as though they do only because we feed them, and they need and enjoy food. Then why does the dog want to sleep in our beds with us? The dog would have to be a brilliant actor to dissimulate so successfully. We love our dogs and mourn their loss. When we have forgiven the departed for leaving us, then, *de mortuis nil nisi bonum*, they return to us, called up in nostalgic memory and dreams. Recovery from the loss proceeds, the pain recedes, and we accept the reassurance the process illustrates—that we have an ability to recover, even though, as with physical wounds, healing leaves scars behind. A lesson about ends and beginnings? Survival?

St. Louis: Lessons from A Border City

The St. Louis years presented me with changes of a kind I had experienced before: the move into a new physical environment, the adjustment to a new set of friends and teachers, and a geography to learn, both in material and in social structure. St. Louis, as Gordon Fair had suggested, was not Cambridge, nor New York, nor an extension of New York like Mon Amour Lodge in Lake Placid. It was St. Louis as it was. Perhaps the strangeness I felt in Vienna came not only because I was different, but because Vienna was different. The need to adapt, the sorrow of giving up the attachments to the past, and the difficulties in venturing attachments to the new remain to this day.

In 1954 St. Louis, the black-white and male-female separations were much more evident than in the East. There were no blacks studying medicine at the Barnes Hospital, nor were there any on the faculty. Our medical school class had two women out of eighty-six students. One was a California Issei, married to a white classmate. Social class distinction was more evident to me, on a large public scale, than it had been anywhere else I had been. Of course, Harvard had its Final Clubs, which took some Jews but were mostly for old-line alumni offspring, and they were largely regarded as anomalies. Greenwich kept out Jews. Vienna had an only slightly porous ruling-class, and lots of anti-Semitism. The U.S. had race, anti-immigration, and no-Jews-allowed problems. St. Louis had all those and, in addition, the annual Veiled Prophet celebration was public—parade, floats, debutantes, queen of the ball, and all.

This was a contrast to my boyhood and adolescent experience of the American northeast, where public celebration of exclusivity was not flaunted. Quotas and exclusion were quiet, not public, though this did not mean that quotas for Jews needing to escape from Hitler were actually filled. The State Department excluded genuine refugees; America-Firsters argued against immigration; American blacks' civil rights were restricted; and Father Coughlin encouraged prejudice on the airwaves but without St. Louis' fanfare. In school, we recited the Pledge of Allegiance, "to the flag and to the republic for which it stands," a vague concept. Missouri was clearly a border state—segregation was still practiced. All this tribalism and bigotry was as nothing, compared to the depravities of the dictators, Hitler, Mussolini, Hirohito, Franco, Stalin, and Mao. Still, our republic has the usual divisions that nations survive (or not, as Austro-Hungary did not).

St. Louis was complicated; for me, there was too much sub-group self-definition and also too much collectivization of groups other than one's own. There were too few subtle distinctions. I preferred having loose definitions and unconfined categories, but St. Louis was an example of the reverse: groups were separated by race, economic level, educational level, gender and religion, and, in addition, there was stratification based on *when* migrants of different groups had arrived. Inclusion, which seems a more accurate term than integration, was unlikely. First came the French: the Chouteaux, Ladues, Lindells, for whom the main Avenues were named; then the English; then the beer barons; then the department store founders, and newspaper-owning Jews (pretty distinct from each other). By and large, they did not play together like the instruments of the orchestra do. The strings, brass, woodwinds, and percussion of an orchestra harmonize; orchestras, however much the instrumentalists compete, are composed of people who want to play together, and the exclusion of others is not a main source of satisfaction for the musicians. Of course, and in general, orchestras were then still largely made up of white men. Women were limited to their own instruments: their voices. I had not lived in a community like St. Louis, where successive groups had moved in, but previous groups had not been displaced; they remained, but mixing was not much done—St. Louis was not a melting pot. St. Louis prides itself (or at least presents itself) as a gateway, a way-station, not only between East and West, but also between North and South.

Early Huge Global Migrations

Large migrations occurred to and within the Americas. Millions of black Africans were transported to the American mainland's south and enslaved; Germans, Norse people, Italians, and Chinese arrived from distant foreign parts. After the Civil War, migrations from south to north, and from east to west—with the opening of the west by railroads—meant great numbers of people, with changed living conditions, social expectations, occupations, and economic possibilities. Migrations and changes in social organization and attitudes, over similar periods of time, influenced the cities of the American northeast, and Vienna in Austria, which led to them being final destinations more than were places like St. Louis, which built an arch to represent the city as the "Gateway to the West," not a receptacle for the east. The Native Americans of the West were not particularly receptive to the settlers, who were not interested in becoming Native Americans, just as the majority of eastern immigrant Jews were not interested in becoming part of German Austria. It was understandable that St. Louis, more torpid, and less dynamically changing as to population in recent times, would be different from New York, or Vienna; New York and Vienna were havens for escapees as well as passageways. Often, the earlier arrivals would prefer that the newcomers move on. St. Louis, as had Harvard and Boston before, put me into a mélange of different colors, backgrounds, social and educational variations, and vagaries of food and dress.

BACK TO MEDICAL SCHOOL

Lessons from Hospital Life

The hospital environment was much more intense than any experience of communal daily life I had had before; if you want to see and live human drama, go to medical school and work in hospitals. The hospital is a place where the most important distinction is between two sorts of people, the sick and wounded, on the one hand, and the well on the other. Sharing a ward with others is less comfortable than living in a private room with a private nurse, but all patients, rich or poor, share a more important misery than the private group can overcome by their advantages. The sick confront the dark side of life. Pain, fear, suffering, the perils of aging, and the experience of fragility are uppermost, and the relative dependence, and reduced capacity to manage one's fate, become paramount. Being ill is traumatic, and the more so because the mind does not function as well in periods of pain and stress as it does under more normal circumstances. Anxiety defeats better judgment. The caregiver is in the position of *The Wound-Dresser;* I reread that work by Whitman several times. The caregiver has a much easier time than the patient, as he concentrates on giving care; the patient cannot concentrate on anything, and lives in fear, relative ignorance, and helplessness.

Challenges to the Healthy in a Hospital Setting

The healthy in the hospital are not exempt from painful challenges, for they are reminded constantly that what they are trying to ameliorate is that to which they are susceptible as well. Empathy and sympathy are natural responses; the helpers want to help, but their ability to do so is severely limited—despite the high success rate presented (with caveats) by drug manufacturers in television advertisements. Medical training shows how little we know, and how much we wish to accomplish but cannot. I think there is a similarity in the situation of medical workers and soldiers at war; in both cases there is the constant presence of pain, maiming, and death. There is also a tendency to form exclusive groups made up of those with similar experiences—operating-room and emergency-room teams, for example. Doctors, in general, prefer to share war stories of cases with other medical professionals. In addition, patients' rights to privacy limit medical people's choice of confidants; protective attitudes among colleagues encourage secrecy; and the expense and annoyance caused by lawsuits, and fear of lawsuits, add to the pressure toward isolation.

The Meanings of "Provider"

Medical school, and doctoring, impose situations where matters of life, illness, death, privilege, social level, race, gender, and educational opportunities are all present together. Childhood morality, with its wait-your-turn and share-alike principles, doesn't work when it turns out that life can't be fair; the fair thing would be—in the attitude of many sick people—the greater the pain and danger, the greater the right to be attended and cured. The sad fact is that, often, the greater the pain and danger, the less likely it is that full health can be restored. Life becomes difficult to deal with in terms of usual moral ideals about reward and punishment; health may be regarded as a right, but the best medical care, though desirable, is in practice not available for everyone, because of the limitations of people working in the field. Not everyone can be the best. The same is true for education. There are not many "best" doctors, teachers, and athletes to go around. There are not many "best" providers of anything.

Every person, nowadays commodified as a "provider," is still a professional, no matter what he is called. Professionals, tradespeople, craftspeople, service providers, and tax collectors are all described in terms of the work skills they offer. I take the simplification implied by the dichotomous description of providers and consumers—as a reduction, to serve the purpose of reducing more complex thinking to simpler categories. We are all workers. However, we like to be allowed the individuality communicated by titles such as firefighter, police officer, doctor, or mayor. "Provider" should have remained a word meaning "one who provides," as used to describe any product or service; professionals deal in highly technical services, and we hope these incorporate humane, caring attitudes. Yet, a nurse is still a nurse, a phlebotomist still a phlebotomist, and an X-ray technician remains an X-ray technician. It is demeaning to have one's service reduced to an all-inclusive consumable commodity for simplicity's sake.

People who apply to institutions to be educated to become able to form a complicated relationship in which they deal with frightened, suffering people, are understandably vexed. This is a trying interpersonal role, more like that of a priest, than that of a grocer (or any other tradesman). Medical people submit to a triage, designed to accept and train the most able of the lot, and, when selected, they in turn accept the subsequent benefits and disadvantages. Those who succeed are not simply "providers," because their skills are diverse and difficult to acquire. Professionals in the healthcare world are highly trained people. They are required to subscribe to ethical rules, and they have earned the historic classification as professionals, like teachers, airline pilots, judges, or at the very least, craftspeople.

Everyone is a "consumer." Nobody needs to be dissatisfied by that description. Everyone has the same basic needs; people cannot be distinguished on the basis of differing needs. There are, of course, people with special needs: children, the aged, patients. "Special needs" are merely newly recognized needs; nothing else makes them "special," though some needs may be more pressing than others. Triage is employed in assessing capacity, whether for being helpful, or being capable of responding to help. In patient-prognosis, those who turn out to be less capable of responding to the available help are clearly in a worse situation than applicants who don't get accepted by the educational institutions they hope to enter. Reality impinges on health and treatment all the time. Ultimately life is fair, to the extent that everyone is born, gets old, and dies; however, that is not soothing to doctors and patients, who find it difficult to accept their limitations. They also find it difficult to be treated like commodities. All these things I learned in medical school, and in subsequent training and practice as a doctor. I concluded, too, that those who seek to befuddle, by promoting the desirable—achieving equality in having the best of anything available—are lying.

Confronting and Learning About the Unknown; Health Workers Are Animals Too

A certain amount of avoidance, and denial, is common in the responses or lack of them, which doctors employ in their work and social lives. This involves accepting a role; the physician is operating (double meaning intended) in a particular capacity when he serves as a source of help to the patient. He also has to be a scientist, who trusts in studying the natural order of things; he needs to see the patient, to the best of his ability, as objectively as it is possible for a subjective person to do with an experimental subject. Yet he is a human still, and one often uncomfortably aware of the fact that we all live, die, and depend on each other in the material and emotional realms. We are all subject to factors we do not control, or even know, but need to learn more about. We learn about the unknown only by facing our subjective inclination for simplicity, dependable order, and equity; scientific study must be as objective as possible. Health workers are not immune to (instinctual) grandiose demands. They have narcissistic desires and, usually, overactive consciences, and few things distress them more than a patient who doesn't get better, except a patient who not only doesn't get better, but also sues for damages. Further, there lurk the sexual and aggressive inclinations, aroused in adult-child relationships and their analogues: the teacher-student, and other power-imbalanced situations, which challenge the force of ethics. I apprehended a good deal of all this during medical school.

Medicine involves a great deal of time away from family for work, as well as death or discharge of patients. There are constant reminders that every gratifying attachment carries the probability of separation and loss. When I do not meet my expectations, I feel loss. I suffer from my felt failures, rational or not. There is, for me, always a hesitation, as though a premonition that my refugee experience, the loss of people, scents, food, smells, and particularly of my gradually increasingly absent mother, and of my departed-to-the-war brother, is going to recur. I feel that as the most important person in my own life, I ought to justify that importance by performing great deeds.

Carl Moyer said that much of what we did and thought we knew then would have become obsolete by the time we finished our training.

The implied meaning was that we should remember that we would never stop needing to learn, and that we would never know enough. Perfection is an ideal; progress in gaining wisdom and knowledge inevitable. With many stops and starts, I'd even say I became more modest and, therefore, more content.

My brother had a more realistic attitude. He came back from the war in Italy determined to live a quiet life in a suburb, surrounded by his family. He lived his post-war life with his wife and children, and now grand-and great-grandchildren, and without obvious grander ambitions. Maybe he felt he had paid his debts by soldiering.

My father, the orphan, always wanted to enjoy family, but Hitler made that impossible. My father thought like a doctor insofar as he lived by the professional fiduciary code (not the "Provider"), the ethical code that puts the client's, or patient's interests ahead of the banker's and the banker's family's. He, like Fred, seemed to feel he had no unpaid debts.

Summer Work at NYU Lab with Jerry Lawrence

In the summers of my second/third and third/fourth medical school years I worked for H. Sherwood (Jerry) Lawrence in a lab at NYU. We were trying (it turned out, unsuccessfully) to create autoimmune responses in frogs, in the hope that the frogs might help us learn about autoimmune processes. I turned to an interest in autoimmune disease because multiple sclerosis seemed, possibly, to be an autoimmune disorder. My mother often asked me what was happening in the understanding of MS; unfortunately, at the time, it was not much. Lew Thomas was a beloved teacher and writer on medical subjects for laypeople and a figure around the lab. I appropriated him into my personal Hall of Fame because I admired his attitude, which was to explain what really was known and what was not; he was an exponent of the idea of pursuing only what it was *useful* to understand. The frogs failed to provide leads.

The Lessons of Queen Square, London: Social Life

The medical school curriculum reserved time for individual projects, which students could design and execute. I arranged to join a group of people from several parts of the world who wanted to study neurology in London. The Hospital for Nervous and Mental Diseases in Queen Square was where patients with neurological problems were referred from all over Great Britain, for consultations and treatment. Barbara and I spent the period January through March of 1958 in London. In April and part of May, we traveled to Lech am Arlberg in Austria, and to Greece, where we met Jack and Lillian. Graduation from medical school took place in June, and my internship in New York began in July.

In London, we had introductions to Irving Kristol from Warren Manshel; to Greville Janner, a Labour MP, through someone else; and to an Asprey scion, who came by way of yet another. Each of these invited us once, asked whom else we knew, and seemed not very interested in further contact; we were, of course, Americans of little importance. Janner was the only one who seemed interested in talking to us. The British had royalty, nobles, and real social classes, and felt entitled to be snobs even without having titles themselves. I saw another example of crowd psychology, in the feeling people had that to be British was to be superior. To have a royal family made everyone a member of an Empire. It seemed the ultimate fandom.

The Kristols were from America, where social classes were more loosely defined. My father had been almost overjoyed when he found that, in New York, people called each other by their first names. Can one have snobs in the absence of an aristocracy? Could people who knew more than others, or were more talented, reasonably think they were better than those who knew less or were less adept? I concluded, "Apparently so." The Kristols could not have been defined as snobbish, but they had little modesty about exuding self-importance.

Encounter Magazine, Edited by Spender and Kristol

Irving Kristol edited *Encounter* with Stephen Spender and Harold Laski. The Congress for Cultural Freedom was an organization whose mission was to provide a public forum for left wing, anti-Stalinist intellectuals. The magazine *Encounter* was one of its projects, and Warren Manshel, my close friend, was its administrator. The Kristols invited us for cocktails. They were clearly not interested in us. I had the impression that they were both too involved with their political ideas to be bothered with non-political people. Our new acquaintances were not interested in us once they discovered we were not useful, and whether we were ignored out of lack of interest or assumptions of superiority, it made for quick, disappointed endings to our evenings. They probably missed out by underestimating us.

Perhaps similarly to Kristol, I often feel smarter and more capable than others. I have great pleasure when I can excel. I sympathize with those angered by what I deem injustice. I feel justified in feeling resentful when I see what I regard as unearned satisfaction in privilege, enjoyed by whomever. I saw other people mingle self-satisfaction with a sense of superiority and, unfortunately, I suffered from attacks of irritability and anger when confronted by bumbling, especially if it was accompanied by self-satisfaction, which I felt was undeserved. Unfortunately, I also envied self-satisfaction among people who I thought were entitled to it. I had such difficulty with respecting myself. Enough was not enough for me.

I did not have the idea that social connections should provide standing, and therefore I felt that social climbing was mainly a waste of time, even though it clearly helped to facilitate careers. I had the idea that other people should recognize my talents and assume, as I did, that my application of my gifts in the future would make investing in me a good bargain.

Performance may bring recognition while talent only signals possibility. Talent does, however, lead to patronage. It did happen that some who knew me helped me get into the better colleges and universities. Some people did give me the benefit of the doubt: my not entirely impressive past application of my supposedly strong gifts might indicate the immaturity of a late bloomer. (That I had been hindered by my war-wounded neurotic character would have been a more accurate description.) I did not understand why chance, as in having talents or connections, could be taken as justification for feelings of entitlement, though I had some. I missed the point that how one performed was the key; I also missed another point. I had benefited greatly by having generations of fortunate ancestors and parents who invested in me and sacrificed for the future.

I was certainly indignant at the cool reception Barbara and I got in London. I was no stranger to the burdens of good fortune, or the wounds caused by discrimination. I held no brief for the rule of the anointed. But maybe the British had been so wounded in the war, and by losing the empire, that they found it difficult to deal with those lucky Americans who had largely escaped those disasters.

It isn't rational that I expected inclusion before I passed the entrance requirements. I understand clannishness or tribalism as part of human nature. Juvenile idealism is common, and includes the ideals of meritocracy, equal rights, and a chance for everybody to pursue happiness, but I also know that we don't choose our parents, genes, or times. We have to establish credentials. To be needy, at least after early childhood, is not enough. In fact, how much time and effort is required before one is entitled to respect and inclusion is hard to know, when one is a precocious person, as Barbara and I were. We were in some ways children, expecting to be applauded, not expecting to have to learn or conform.

Amusing Acquaintanceship with Elizabeth Hardwick

In later years, we saw Irving Kristol sometimes in New York, when he worked with Warren at another magazine, *The Public Interest*. The practical idealism of Warren, Sam Huntington, Daniel Moynihan, and the others with whom he collaborated appealed to me. We met the Kristols several times at Warren and Anita Manshel's homes, and they never seemed to know who we were. I think Kristol thought of himself as a New York intellectual who had made it, but wanted more influence than he had. Maybe he thought that, once he had achieved enough, he would get over his grudges. Dream on, Irving, wherever you may be.

Another example of this childlike form of thinking came at a dinner given by Helen Frankenthaler years later. I was seated next to Elizabeth Hardwick, who had had just about the right amount to drink. She told me to call her Lizzie and launched into a hilarious discussion about her earlier life and her coming to New York. She wanted to get away from her too large, too provincial, too unintellectual, too southern, Lexington, Kentucky, family. She dreamed of meeting brilliant, stimulating people in New York, and thought such people were likely to be found among New York Jewish intellectuals. "But you can't imagine how disappointed I was when I knew them," she said. "They didn't know all that much. They didn't know how to swim. They couldn't even float!" Raucous laughter on both our parts. Lizzie and I were partners in making fun of people whom we had idealized, envied, and wanted to emulate and join, but who had disappointed us, by just being real. I stopped being bothered about Irving Kristol. It wasn't my doing that he couldn't float.

On my other side was Claire Bloom, who was complaining about her former husband, Philip Roth. I was sympathetic; the beautiful, gifted Claire Bloom had chosen a difficult and angry genius as a husband, with whom she had suffered.

The Issues that Come with Knowing Powerful and/or Influential People

This time was the acme of the era of Irving Howe, Lionel and Diana Trilling, Clement Greenberg, Harold Rosenberg, and the *Partisan Review*. A lot of these people were open-minded, receptive, and likable. Knowing them was a privilege, which also brought disappointment for one came to see the warts. I determined to rid myself of my seeming need for wartlessness. Still, that continues, with modest improvement, to the present.

Queen Square, London (continued); Barbara at *Encyclopedia Britannica*

In London, Barbara worked at the *Encyclopedia Britannica*. She did research at the Reading Room in the British Museum and wrote entries for the coming edition. As one might imagine, outwardly assertive but inwardly shy, Barbara was astounded that she was actually doing this. That she was, despite her doubts, good. On the other hand, she had to put up with being a woman and an American at work, which was a downer.

The *Britannica* office was British: it had central heating, but everyone threw open the windows and wore sweater twin-sets or jackets. After a few weeks, a fellow worker invited Barbara to lunch and explained that she had been deputized to do this. An American, she had been living in London, married to a Brit, for many years; she dressed and lived British sweater set, but continued to be treated as "the American woman" and was, therefore, the one to be given the responsibility to offer lunch to the other American. "Aha." Was this a case of misogyny? Barbara certainly thought the two-women-at-lunch idea was demeaning. On the other hand, why did the office have to be chilly? Because to be comfortable is to become soft.

My Experience as a Student at Queen Square Was Not as I Had Expected, in Terms of Socializing, Manners, Behavior, or the Professional Approach

Being in London had its professional side for me; after all, we were there because I had career prospects to explore. I was still uncertain about my direction, whether to go into a subspecialty, a laboratory, clinical research or an academic career. My experience as a student at Queen Square was not as I had expected, in terms of socializing, manners, behavior, or the professional approach. The atmosphere was formal; the hands-on contact with patients, such as took place in the clinical years of medical students' experiences in hospital work in the U.S., was non-existent. I had become used to having patients assigned to me, interviewing them about their complaints, doing physical examinations, and having the records of laboratory work and notes by house staff available to me in the patients' charts. In addition, in the U.S., the entire group of those concerned in the care of the patients made rounds with the attending physician and would see the patients and go over the case. The interns and resident physicians and medical school students followed the procession around the wards, had plenty of opportunity to talk to the patients, and to discuss problems with the teachers. Not so in my taste of Queen Square.

I had written an essay about amyotrophic lateral sclerosis, a disease of the axons of motor neurons, which causes destruction of the myelin sheaths of those neurons, resulting in neuron loss, denervation of voluntary muscles, and therefore, atrophy of those muscles and consequent paralysis. Commonly known in the U.S. as Lou Gehrig disease, the course is variable but generally kills within months, or a few years at best. (Stephen Hawking's situation was unusual, in that he survived over a much longer time than is characteristic. Though he was paralyzed, Hawking lived many productive years.)

It seemed possible to me that ALS and MS, another demyelinating disease, are somehow related. At the time I was working on the subject, it appeared that in certain South Pacific islands, there might be a strong inherited tendency to develop ALS. Given my mother's MS, I had a personal reason to learn more. Nowadays more is known about MS, and some treatments that mitigate the symptoms are available. I should have loved to talk about the subject with instructors at Queen Square, but that was not possible.

The teaching at Queen Square was both exciting and disappointing. It was exciting because of the wisdom and finesse the instructors displayed. They were able to localize lesions and make diagnoses, using mostly minds, hands, percussion hammers, and tuning forks to examine patients. The plucking of diagnostic rabbits out of the hats of patients' physical signs, or from their histories, while sometimes awe-inspiring, was also disappointing. The diagnostic acumen seemed almost magical, but the diagnoses that came out of the hat were often not very useful as, unfortunately, they often labeled untreatable conditions.

Disappointments regarding patient care were one matter. The rigidity of the teaching was another. There was a disappointing pattern that I regretted about many of the English, which constrained my Anglophilia: there was no way those of us who were sitting, watching the consultants do their work and listening to what they said, could ask a question or discuss a problem.

For all my social bearishness. and off-putting quirks, I like people—at least some people—and I need to have personal contact with them. I also find it important to be able to ask questions and challenge those in authority, who may be incorrect. I have had three major depressions triggered by missteps taken by doctors caring for me, and Barbara and I are still susceptible to strong feelings of indignation.

My Anger and Disapproval Towards Doctors Who Work Past Their Viable Years

Nowadays, I talk to friends who are doctors, who are out of touch with the developments in their fields, or who are overworked, or who should retire because of the effects of age. I have an irrational anger about colleagues who continue working and writing, when their faculties are not as they once were, who explain that their memory may have become porous, and their hearing weak, but their wisdom makes up for it. I cannot forgive myself for my professional errors; and I still often remember, to my horror, that when I was at the beginning of my training, and still believed that nothing but Oedipal experiences mattered, I saw a concentration camp victim who needed certification that this had caused him harm and turned him away. That happened because of ignorance and lax supervision, but knowing that did not prevent me from continuing to feel ashamed.

Any similar blundering by doctors arouses rage in me; failing to refer sick people to competent doctors is not simply a sad state of affairs. I feel guilty about not having tried to do more to institutionalize ways of dealing with the assessment of competence; but finding reasonable criteria, for judging and enforcing decisions, has eluded me and, seemingly, the profession at large. Many retire in time, but many stay too long. When I am with someone who keeps working, while relying on the idea that mental slowing is more than counterbalanced by wisdom,

I tend to become tactlessly argumentative and unpersuasive. This irascibility I construe as a sign that I have become a crusty anachronism.

Helping patients or even mentored colleagues to move away from failing training analyses to go to a consultant is difficult. A friend told me the most helpful part of his analysis occurred after his therapist became quite infirm after a stroke. How so? My friend's father had died while he and my friend, the son, were at odds. Caring for a fatherly analyst allowed the patient to feel guilt, and repay his debt, using the analyst as a proxy.

A particular bone sticks in my craw when extensive study is ordered, with lots of tests, expensive and also uncomfortable, especially when the tests are unnecessarily repeated. I am referred to a cardiologist, who refers me to a hematologist, who refers me to a sleep specialist; and they all order tests, some repeating what someone else has already done. I travel to Florida to spend the winter with the other codgers, and my disabled wife; of course, we need to be monitored by a doctor. What happens? The tests that we had in New York are repeated. I was put in hospital; lots of tests were done, and I was discharged. I had spent many days with an indwelling urinary catheter following a surgical procedure; as often happens, the catheter produced bleeding and clots obstructed the urinary flow after removal of the catheter, so back to the hospital for another two days. Following a battery of blood tests, I was discharged, but on the way home, another blockage occurred, so back to the ER: another doctor, and another round of tests identical to what I had had a few hours before.

At least we, in the U.S., who have plenty of social, racial, and gender inequities, don't have the class problems they had in England in 1958. At Queen Square, we sat in a theater like the one painted by Thomas Eakins, entitled *The Clinic of Dr. Gross,* which shows Dr. Gross demonstrating the dissection of a cadaver for the benefit of a group of students. As in the painting, Queen Square had an auditorium with a stage, and the students sat in semi-circular rows, looking down at the scene below. On the stage were two desks, one for the instructor, and another for a clerk who made notes; a patient would be led in, and the lesson proceeded with the demonstration of reflexes, visual fields, and gait. Then diagnosis and prognosis would be discussed by the presenter, but hardly ever in conversation with the students.

Contrast Between Elkington and Cameron at Queen Square

The attitudes of the presenters varied. At the extremes, one man with the imposing name John St. Clare Elkington was curt, gave the patient orders to do this and do that, and was quick to berate the man for being slow in responding. He had no hesitation about showing his own superior position and the patient's "stupidity." "Don't be stupid, man, do what you're told, and hurry up about it," for example.

A different and really excellent performance was that of the Scottish Dr. Cameron who brought out a patient with a wobbling walk. He took the man by the arm to help him move to center stage, meanwhile encouraging him and passing a few words about the rotten weather, and then about a football game. He sat the man down, tested reflexes, found some of them awry, went over the visual fields to show a defect, mentioned the gait, got the man up on his feet to show he had a problem balancing, thanked the man for coming, and led him away. He returned and asked the assembled group what the diagnosis might be. Various possibilities were suggested but, because there were so many sites of damage, the majority opinion among the students was disseminated sclerosis. I realized that we had not heard a history, and there might be a catch somewhere.

At last, the lecturer, Dr. Cameron, told us: "I didn't bring this chap here to point out that it's always a good thing to take a history. But I'll tell you this. The man was a soldier in the Finnish army and fought against the Russians. He was wounded and captured; he escaped and traveled overland till he came to the sea, where he stole a boat and set out. He almost reached Sweden but was captured and imprisoned by the Swedes. At that, "in prison again," Dr. Cameron wheeled out a blackboard on which in one sweep, he drew a half brain, and he went on—dot, dot, dot, dot, on the blackboard—"He thrust an ice pick through his eye." He pointed to the dots, "causing lesions here, here, here, and here," thereby accounting for the damage at different points in the brain. "And once again, he escaped to the sea, where he was rescued by Scottish fishermen, and brought to Scotland. The point is, the Scots are a free race!"

Dr. Cameron's Empathy and Humanity Towards a Badly Damaged Patient

That teaching exercise has meant a lot to me. Dr. Cameron was my sort of person, with a good amount of interest in people and their lives and, also, a strong sense of individual integrity and freedom. Queen Square gave me a lot of knowledge about neurological ailments, about symptoms and signs. The diagnostic tools were physical: the Queen Square percussion hammer had one large discoid end, carrying a semi-soft rubber ring for banging on body parts, which elicited reflexes; the other end of the slightly elastic wooden shaft was pointed, for testing for failure of fine sensitivity. In addition, a tuning fork could be struck and pressed on a bony part of the patient, who was asked to report experiencing the vibration, or not. Then there were wiggling fingers above, besideor below the patient's eyes to determine the state of the visual fields. And then there was the history—how had his problems with balance begun, and how had they changed over time? When had he noticed that tingling in his arm, and had he had any trauma at that time, or had he lost consciousness after falling down and hitting his head?

Artistry of Simple Procedures at Queen Square

One good effect of my sojourn at Queen Square was to show me what a highly refined use of simple procedures could accomplish, in practiced hands, manipulated by wise, anatomically sophisticated minds. These doctors could locate lesions, and make diagnoses of illnesses, and predict what a patient might anticipate that his future would be like. They seldom used X-ray studies of the central nervous system, which at that time involved injection of air into the central nervous system's fluid-filled spaces, diagnostic means that were commonly used in the U.S. These were, at the least, unpleasant experiences for patients, and, at most, risky and were out of favor at Queen Square. In that regard, the Queen Square attitude, so arrogant in the Elkington manner, was more humane than the American, in that it spared the patient. In that case, modernity was less an improvement over the older ways of the clinicians than one might have thought.

Some Neurology Treatment at Queen Square Taken Over by Surgeons or Internists

I appreciated the artistry of the Queen Square approach. However, another aspect of the neurology situation was that if a disease was treatable, the treatment could be employed, or taken over by internists or surgeons. Great diagnostic expertise at great expense was not necessary for prescribing anti-seizure medications for patients with seizure disorders, or dietary restrictions for those with metabolic disorders, such as iron metabolism defects. Management required expensive neurosurgeons, when surgery was indicated, as for tumors or clots. When I came to this conclusion, I realized that I liked the idea of helping patients get better but, as they had to have treatable ailments for this to happen, neurology seemed to me a not very appealing specialty. Diagnostic capacity was a limited good—what was needed was, more and better science. This was a negative point about neurology as a clinical field, though scientifically, there was a great deal to be studied. I gave up the idea of neurology and attended fewer neurological demonstrations. An alternative life, in a basic science laboratory, was not what I wanted either.

The two earlier summers with no positive results, working at a dead-end research project at NYU, were discouraging.

That was then; this is now. Now is an age of machines—CAT scans, MRIs, robotic surgery, clot-busting drugs, and more. The current medical state of affairs involves a growth of sub-specialization, with at least one specialty for every organ—we know so much that it has become nearly impossible to keep up with advances—but we have difficulty integrating the specialties into an overall view of a patient. Had the techniques and technologies we have now been available sixty years ago, I might have made a different decision and gone into neurosurgery. But probably not; in retrospect, my history, interests, and strengths led me to take the path I followed.

Much later, some of my thoughts generated at Queen Square coalesced into an idea: that the so-called "placebo effect" was not a bad thing, which needed to be discounted in drug trials. It is a good thing, if it occurs when doctor and patient are acting together as colleagues, not as expert and naïf, where the expert presents the rules. If part of the reason a patient gets better with treatment is that a good relationship has a beneficial effect, then the good relationship should be counted as part of the armamentarium of healing. How do we compare the impact of technology and science with the less understood factor of the role of the doctor-patient relationship?

My experience with Cameron was infinitely more comfortable, even inspiring, than that with Elkington, who evoked fear, resentment, and disdain as responses to his own disdain and to his arrogance. Cameron induced a desire to collaborate, to accept what needed to be accepted of his message—even the parts that were painful to hear. Could one ever quantify the degree to which a patient reported feeling better, simply because he found someone he felt he could rely on; how much resulted from his cooperating by accepting treatment suggestions; how much had to do with his receptiveness; and how much was a response to how the treatment protocol?

Where are the studies that compare two groups, one subjected to an Elkington and another to a Cameron approach, with both groups given the same medication, the same sugar pill, to measure the healing effect of the good relationship? I should not be surprised to find that the effect would turn out different between the two groups.

After Queen Square: Travels to Austria, Greece

When not at Queen Square, I spent the rest of my time exploring London; while Barbara was at work, I went wandering in museums, auction houses, and galleries. Our time in London ended in March, 1958. We had had an interesting and fruitful few months in London; I had benefited by my time at Queen Square, and I had arrived at some conclusions about what I was and was not.

Barbara and I packed up our stuff, got into our Morgan, and went off to Lech am Arlberg to learn how to ski better; or, in Barbara's case, to learn the basics. There was an airfield at Lydd Ferryfield on the Channel, from where you and your car could be flown to Calais; and we were delighted to leave the fog, rain, cold, chilblains, and the shilling-heat behind, especially as the bank never had enough coins for more than a few hours of warmth. Halfway across the Channel, the bright sun appeared; a pleasant few days in Paris, then a drive south, and we were in Austria in a snowstorm. The canvas clipped-down roof on our Morgan sifted snowflakes into the car, and onto our hair, as we rose, glistening, up an alp, on a road partly covered by avalanche-deflecting roofing, and partly by a powdery snowfall.

Barbara enrolled in a class of advanced beginners. She soon fell, sprained an ankle badly, and spent her time in front of a fire. I was on my own on the mountain. We made a new friend, Victor Stone, who had been careless about the sun and had a terrible burn. In the two following weeks, Barbara, her ankle recovering nicely, acquired an impressive gait of limp and cane. The car sent home, we met the Poseses in Greece and had two more weeks' vacation there and on Crete. Though we did the usual tourist things, there was one event that was psychologically meaningful—another example of how long the effect of trauma lasts, and how easily later analogs of very early experiences revivify the ancient experiences.

We were in Athens at Easter, and we sat on the roof of the Grande Bretagne hotel at dusk, watching the traditional parade up the traditional hill, which represents and mimics the climb to Calvary. The torches flickered, the funeral march played, and Jack turned white; he muttered, "This is the way the pogroms began." The symbolic Passion re-enactment revived terrifying moments Jack had as a child in Russia, when such a scene preceded the Cossacks' storming the town, looting and burning. My variant of response to triggers that recall earlier traumata doesn't involve pallor; after something sets me off, I become angry by day, and at night I have anxiety dreams and, sometimes, insomnia, for a few days. If the stimulus is acute enough, severe depression can strike.

The Nazis, or analogues of the Nazis—particularly doctors when they mistreat, or policemen who set up speed traps, or friends who act unethically—stimulate my automatic negative responses easily. Often, I have to puzzle out what happened to set me off; I have become progressively quicker at that. In Athens, Sounion, Delphi, and Crete, Jack recovered his aplomb. In photos, he gestures happily, Cuban Claro cigar in his hand, sitting on what was supposedly Agamemnon's throne.

Graduation in St. Louis; My Father's Death

And so back to St. Louis, for my graduation, a chance to wear a doctoral gown with velvet sleeve stripes and a mortarboard with a gold tassel, kisses and hugs all around. It was to be the last happy family rite when we were all together: Jack and Lillian, my father and mother, Barbara and I, at the farewell to the Barnes Hospital, and the end of my student times. My father was the first of us to die, the following spring. Mami, who had been at our wedding, was already dead and so, too, was Gusti.

RETURN TO NEW YORK – INTERNSHIP AND RESIDENCY

Return to New York; Warren Manshel; Artistic Circles in New York

Soon after Barbara and I returned to New York, I began my internship, and we looked for a place to live; in the meantime, Barbara's parents put us up. We found a nice apartment at 130 East 67 Street, on the second floor, facing the Armory on the other (west) side of Lexington Avenue, in a building designed by Charles A. Platt, in American Renaissance style. Barbara plunged into making it suitable for us to live in and the walls were taken back to the bricks. One of the two bedrooms became a study while the other remained a bedroom. The kitchen was lightly redone—some of the walls were covered with burlap. The living room was continuous with the kitchen and now boasted a carpet obtained from Julius Rosenberg, the rug manufacturer-husband of Anna Rosenberg, Lilian Poses's old friend from Washington New Deal days.

Local shop outlets included Paul Molé, the barber; Colette, the bakery for quiche and roulades; and Lehmann for wine. Then there were institutions: the residence of the USSR UN personnel (and possibly also for troupes of spies), an Orthodox Synagogue, the local precinct police station and fire department. Also, nearby were Le Veau d'Or, Bloomingdales, Central Park, and the William Poll food shop, a virtual catalogue of New Yorkiana.

Warren Manshel, now in New York, continued to be important to me, through the many years of friendship that began at Harvard and lasted until his death in 1990. Warren, his older brother, Ernest, and their parents had migrated from Berlin. Weirdly enough, Warren had gone to the same high school, Newtown in Elmhurst, as my brother and I. Harrison Dillard, Leo Lerman, and Rise Stevens were also Newtown alumni.

Warren was nine years older than I, about the same age as my brother. He had enlisted in the U.S. Army and been in an early wave of the June 6, 1944 invasion of Normandy, in which he suffered a minor wound, for which he received a Purple Heart, and, later, a modest disability allowance. That was like my brother, except that Fred fought in Italy, not France, and received no disability money.

Post-war, Warren worked for *Stars and Stripes.* Then he went to Harvard, where he took a bachelor's degree, and subsequently, a Ph.D. in government; his mentor was Arthur Holcomb. Warren also wrote for *The Christian Science Monitor.* His dissertation was on European integration, written at the time of Adenauer and Schumann, when the subject was at the forefront of post-World War II European reconstruction.

When I graduated from Harvard and moved to St. Louis in 1954, Warren took a job that separated us for a few years. He was the administrator of the Council for Cultural Freedom, and his office was in Paris. This organization was ostensibly financed by the private Kaplan Foundation; Jack Kaplan was the head of the Welch's Grape Juice Corporation, and it was later revealed that the Kaplan Foundation had been used as a conduit by the CIA. Arthur Holcomb had contacts in Washington, and apparently helped recruit Warren.

Warren married Anita Coleman and returned to New York, where the couple settled in 1955. He joined Anita's family brokerage, Coleman and Company, which had been used primarily to manage the family finances. Warren had a gift; he was able to communicate with almost anyone and create relationships with amazing ease. He turned a small enterprise into a large research-based institutional firm.

Thiokol Makes Us Comfortably Well-Off

When Barbara and I had been married for about two years, Jack Poses made us a gift of shares of stock. Shortly afterward, just as 100 Allied Chemical and 200 International Harvester shares arrived, we were in New York having dinner with the Manshels. I asked Warren's advice about what to do with my new shares.

"Sell," he said.

"Sell how much?" I asked.

"Sell it all: those are good conservative companies that will pay nice dividends but won't appreciate in value."

"And what shall I buy?" "Thiokol."

"And how much Thiokol shall I buy?"

"Use everything you get from selling the Allied and Harvester."

I was put in mind of the movie, *The House of Rothschild*, a 1934 film about how Nathan Rothschild (played by George Arliss) had just been informed, via carrier pigeon and semaphore signal messages coming from Waterloo, that Napoleon had lost the battle. He stood, partly concealed, behind a column at the London Stock Exchange; agents were running to him saying, "The market is collapsing, what shall we do?" In a rasping guttural voice, Arliss says, "Buy." Again and again, they ask, "What shall we do?" "Buy, buy." But, like Rothschild, I wanted information.

"What is Thiokol?" I asked.

"Oh, it's a rubber company. They boiled rubber with some chemicals during the war, and they found out that they could make the rubber gooey that way. So, they used it for airplane gas tanks. Bullets going through the tanks made holes, but the holes sealed up."

"Yes," I continued, "but do we need lots of this stuff now? Are we building lots of airplanes that have gasoline tanks that need to be self-sealing?"

"Well, maybe not. But then they boiled the rubber with some other chemicals, and found that the stuff burned very fast, with a very hot flame. Since Sputnik and Laika, the dog, went into orbit, we're having a space race. We have a choice between liquid fuel, which requires very low temperatures, and is hard to store, and move around, and solid fuel. If we decide to use solid fuel, that's Thiokol. Besides, not many investors seem to be aware of this yet, so you're getting a decent rubber company with big possibilities at a fair price."

"All right," I said, inspired both by the movie of Wellington and the war against Napoleon, and by Churchill and the war against Hitler. So, I bought. This stock simply had everything, including a romantic story that was not yet generally known; it was a war story—Sputnik, the Cold War game—a story Warren understood well.

Warren was used to talking to people who shared his interest in politics, economics, and foreign policy. In his own way of making contacts and friendships, he met Jack Kennedy, befriended him, and helped him at the beginning of his political career. During the second Eisenhower administration, Kennedy was a senator, greatly involved with the space competition, which was becoming part of the rivalry of the U.S. with the USSR. This was a time of open debate; discussions between Secretary of Defense, Charles Wilson, and President Eisenhower, about how to deal with the space race, were much in the news.

Warren Founds *Foreign Policy*

With the help of Patrick Moynihan, Samuel Huntington, and others, Warren founded and became publisher of *Foreign Policy*, a companion to *The Public Interest*, which he had founded earlier. *Foreign Policy* was meant to print opinions different from those of the State Department establishment, which tended to appear in *Foreign Affairs*. Both these publications were intended to be read by academics, government officials, and members of Congress. When Frank Church decided to try to become the Democratic presidential candidate, Warren was one of his foreign policy advisors; and when Church became chair of the Senate Foreign Relations Committee, Warren was made Ambassador to Denmark.

In the 1950s, at another dinner in New York a few months after my stock market trade, I thanked Warren for his advice. I told him I looked up the Thiokol stock price every once in a while, and it would be selling at twenty, then go up to thirty, and a month later, still thirty, and now thirty-two. I thought that was a very good result. Warren smiled, and said, "You don't know! The stock split two-for-one, three-for-one, and again, two-for-one; so now you've got about three hundred thousand dollars. Wait until it's long-term. and then sell some. You might buy some shares in Control Data and some Chock Full o' Nuts." Thereafter, I became more conservative and, with our investments, Barbara and I lived well on our incomes, increased as they were by capital gains. That was a time of rising prices. The 67th Street apartment cost $17,000 when we bought it in 1958 and brought twice that when we sold it in 1962.

Knowing Warren meant I had a friend with whom I could talk about, subjects in which I was extremely interested. Years later, in the 1990s, I would have another great stroke of market luck. Thanks to my tutorials with my father, I enjoyed following the markets and thinking about possibilities in investing. In the early nineties, I made some good bets in technology stocks. I was an early advocate of computers and the internet. I took, for me, significant positions in SUN Microsystems, Applied Materials, Intel, Qualcom, and other shares, some of which worked out amazingly well. This was another exciting story, such as the space race had been, a new world opening up. Internet discussion groups began to flourish, and I joined groups about gardening, music, and photography. I learned enough UNIX commands to become able to make some use of university libraries. There were also market-oriented discussion groups to follow.

Art is Cool

Barbara and I had been living in New York for enough time to appreciate the contrasts with life in St. Louis and London. We came to have artist friends who lived and worked at Bennington (where we sometimes spent time in the summer), or, in the case of David Smith, nearby at Lake George. One such was Ken Noland and another, Tony, later Sir Anthony Caro OM CBE. He was a Sephardic British Jew, a sculptor who welded and painted steel. Part of the circle of the Abstract Expressionists and Color Field painters, he became one of a group of artists who showed at galleries in New York (Emmerich), London (Kasmin), Toronto, and elsewhere. They included Helen Frankenthaler, Morris Louis, and Noland, with whom Barbara and I became particular friends at that time (1963–1965).

Friendships with Motherwell, Noland, Kulicke, *et al*

Some of us: Motherwell, Noland, Bob Kulicke and his wife, Barbara, Sam Hunter (a museum director at Princeton and Brandeis) and his wife, Edis, Bernie Brodsky (a psychoanalyst) and his wife, Marilyn, and Paul Brach and his wife, Miriam Shapiro, had a rotating-venue poker game. It was very informal; smoking and drinking were not just permitted, but almost universally enjoyed. Feminism was in—all the women worked or were artists—but PC was not yet a common contraction for Personal Computer or Politically Correct.

There were two unusually memorable poker evenings at Robert Motherwell's place uptown. The typical stakes were one or two dollars, with three raises allowed; but on one particularly entertaining occasion, Bob Motherwell and Ken Noland were in particularly feisty moods. They competed vigorously, and in a deal when everyone but those two had dropped out, they agreed to raise the stakes. It came to the point when each bet a refrigerator (incidentally, we were all quite involved with gastronomy). This was an amusing high point for me. I found it charming and funny to see these two celebrated artists behaving like children in a playground. Another poker evening, though, ended on a low point, with a telephone call to Bob. David Smith had died, when he went off the road into a tree, en route to his home in Lake George, after a night's carousing with Ken Noland and other friends in Bennington. Having heard the news, Bob presented me with a small painting; he had meant it to be a birthday present but felt David's death should be commemorated by an act of friendship.

Bob gave us other gifts, thanking Barbara for a good dinner, served with a particularly good wine, by taking home the bottle, and sending back the label as part of a collage. We have a cigarette package collage, as well. Bob and I had common interests: We liked to go to baseball games together, and we loved cars. My involvement with wheels has a long history. It progressed from tricycle-rocketing around the Vienna living room in winter and perambulating next to the Donau Canal in summer, to watching the Orient Express on the tracks near Perchtoldsdorf, to bicycling to Long Island Sound to watch the Pan Am Clippers land and take off from the water, to memorizing all the models and makes of cars in the streets, and then to owning my own cars.

Bob outdid me as a car freak. He seemed to buy a new car every few months; he'd have the chrome removed to simplify the appearance and then lose interest and buy another. He offered the outmoded cars to me. I owned a huge Oldsmobile convertible and two Jaguars that I bought from him, at market prices, but I had to refuse a special-body Bentley Bob had acquired when he was older and more prosperous (after he married the photographer Renata Ponsold and moved to Greenwich). Though he offered it to me at a special price because it caused him a backache (he could only tolerate Saabs), even a bargain Bentley was too expensive for me.

Bob had had two marriages before we met. I know little about the first. Though she was said to have been a beautiful, fiery Mexican woman, after they divorced in 1949 Maria Emilia Ferreira y Moyeros was never a significant figure in Bob's life. He never talked about her, and the marriage had lasted only a short time. I do know a bit about Betty, the mother of his two girls (Jeannie, the elder, and Lisa, the younger), whom he married in 1950. Both came from upper middle-class families, she from Virginia, he from California.

Barbara and I got to know Bob when he was married to his third wife, Helen Frankenthaler, from 1958–1971. Quite a bit junior to Bob (b. 1915), Helen (1928–2011) was the youngest of three sisters. Her father was a judge, and she had been educated at private schools and, later, Bennington College, of which she became a trustee and great supporter.

We spent many happy hours with Bob and Helen in New York, and also when we rented a house in Provincetown, across Commercial Street from one of their houses, set up as studios on the seaside. Their studio house had a weathervane in the shape of a fish. Just across the street was their second house, where the four of them lived. For two

RETURN TO NEW YORK — INTERNSHIP AND RESIDENCY

summers, with all the children, our own two toddlers and Bob's two preteen daughters, we saw a lot of each other. At the end of the working day, there were frequently drinks on their lawn and croquet games with the Motherwell children. Ours were not yet big enough to play.

Bob's younger daughter, Lisa, works as a psychotherapist, and she has written about typical issues that children of famous parents face. Shortly after Bob died in 1991, I sat next to Lisa at a dinner given by Helen (who remained a good stepmother to the girls). I told Lisa that I knew the relationship with her three-times-divorced father had been difficult, and I sympathized with her all the more because I understood what mixed feelings she must have—whereas I had enjoyed a trouble-free relationship with Bob and thus had grief, but not grief mixed with relief. "I hope, at least you won't want for money now." "Oh," said Lisa, "he left his work to himself. It goes into a foundation to manage his history and reputation. Renate [wife number four] lives in the house until she dies. We have our trusts." Bob made Barbara a trustee for his daughters' trusts; her reward was an etching.

Then too, there was a small *Spanish Elegy* inscribed "for Michael," when Barbara gave birth to our son in 1964. It wasn't clear for whom the picture was meant—for Barbara, as a reward for having Michael, or for Michael, to encourage his esthetic future. Michael received the picture when he and Jill Gaydosh married, and they set up their household. Bob was never unproductive; he could give away his work whenever he felt like it, as he could always go into his studio, turn on the classical music, and paint. One time I arrived early for a poker night, and asked Bob how he had spent the day? "I made thirty-seven masterpieces."

In retrospect, I might have been be wrong in thinking Bob always had as much confidence as he projected. He sometimes drank too much and went through periods of depression. Another of Bob's gifts to me was *Born Under Saturn: The Character and Conduct of Artists: A Documented History from Antiquity to the French Revolution* by Margaret and Rudolf Wittkower, detailing artists' tendency toward depression, another characteristic we shared.

At one point, Motherwell was interviewed for a public television series. The interviewer approached the work by saying he understood that the work of art was intended to express something of the artist's inner life, but exactly what did it represent? Motherwell replied, "And what do you represent?" and, at another time, "If I could express what I was doing in words, I wouldn't have to make the painting." Creation is an element in mind-brain life. I think the unconscious is much involved in our creative capacities, including synesthesia and symbolic language (visual art, music, dance, poetry, and mathematics are areas that involve multiple interrelated sensory pathways).

That Bob could deal with words well is evident in his published writings and editing. It was clear to him that his painting expressed something that words could not. "If I could tell you what it is, I wouldn't need to paint it." It was a period when I was interesting to artists and writers, because the unconscious was interesting to them. I was confident that I was responding to something Bob had felt, when looking at the marks he had made on canvas. Not everyone has a gift for imagery. That was apparent later, when I was doing research that involved imaging.

In those years of the early 1960s, being a psychoanalyst, even if a student, was a good thing. Later, when I replied to a question that I was an analyst, the response would likely be, "And what stocks are you looking at?" I had answers to that question too, based on experiences as a refugee from the disappeared Europe of the inter-war years, about which my father had opinions, as did I. The shenanigans and interferences of governments were more evident to me than to most of my contemporaries. It was easier to use words about an external phenomenon, such as the economy or political ideas, than about esthetic experience, and nobody said that the conversation about the latest démarche by the Secretary of State was about nothing but words and postures, unless they took diplomats' words figuratively, not merely literally. In other words, words are not just words, though one can claim that that is just what they are. One can also say, ink blots can be claimed to be just inkblots, or cigars as just cigars. Diplomats, subjects, and the rest of us use words to conceal as well as to reveal. Those who saw only shapes in the experiments evinced unpredictable physiologic responses. Some had elevated activity, some not. We were at liberty to assume that defensive aspects of response to the experiment could mean that being literal was a way of shutting out by shutting off, as diplomats do. The arts communicate more by sensations, the sciences more by sensibility.

Helen Frankenthaler went through periods when she was very prolific, and others when she was not. Generally warm and gracious, she, too, was a generous friend. She could, though, have flashes of anger. Meticulous about her work, she made many multiples, was a perfectionist about how her prints were made, and participated in the process of printing them.

Henry Geldzahler; Barbara Rose

One August in Provincetown we gave a party and, among the guests, were Motherwells, Henry Geldzahler, David Smith, and Barbara Rose. Our little house had several small rooms; in each sat one of the Masters, surrounded by eager acolytes. Afterwards, my Barbara vowed she would never give another party with more than one genius guest. David complained he was not able to sell much of his work. I mumbled, wistfully, that I would be happy to buy a piece myself, but I couldn't afford the forty-thousand dollars his sculptures typically cost and, anyhow, I would have no place to put it. David said, "Of course not, but any architect who puts up a building can afford to put one in front of it." Probably on second thought, David gave me a propitiatory drawing, for which there was room. He was never shy about what he thought of the importance of art. At David's funeral, one of the speakers told a tale of going with him to an artist's supply store, where David filled two shopping bags and left without paying. The rationale for the shoplifting was simple: "It's all for the sake of art!"

Stella, Johns, Hockney; Castelli

Henry Geldzahler was similarly enthusiastic about art. One of those unusual people who managed to know everybody and befriend many in the world of art and artists, he was part of a circle that included Warhol, the Colorists, Frank Stella, Jasper Johns, Dick Bellamy, the Green Gallery crowd, and the English artists, Dick Smith, and David Hockney. As the first curator of contemporary art at the Metropolitan Museum, Henry organized an astonishingly noteworthy show, which I liked particularly because he included the large 1964 Frank Stella irregular polygon, which hangs in our living room to this day. I read this as a friendly gesture on the part of Frank's dealer, Leo Castelli, signaling that we were accepted members of the crowd; earlier in Frank's career, Castelli had denied me and Barbara the chance to buy a Stella at one of his gallery's shows. He was meting out works only to more important clients, in the service of steering the market; at last, he said, "I think it's time you had a Stella."

I had much in common with Henry Geldzahler, (another example of how similar experiences and background equal glue). Henry was a refugee, as I was, and had had a distant father as I had. His father was an Antwerp diamond merchant who had been able to get money out of Europe, and Henry reported a conversation he had with his father shortly after his appointment at the Metropolitan. His father said, "You know, Henry, I have lots of money."

"Yes, father."

"And I hardly ever give you any of it."

"Yes, father."

"If I thought you didn't need it or want it, I'd give you lots of money." "Yes, father."

He wasn't really a Jewish believer, but another Jew who found out he was Jewish because he was defined as a Jew by Hitler. Unlike me, he had Orthodox relatives. Once, while showing some distant Orthodox relatives around the museum, Henry pointed out some columns, and said they came from a temple. "First or Second?" asked a cousin.

Henry's Homosexuality; Mark Rothko

Henry confided that he had always felt he was between two worlds; he meant between his father and mother, between Europe and America, and between homosexual and heterosexual. Never having felt sexually aroused by another male, I understood all but the sexual confusion. One day, climbing up a dune from the beach up toward our car and Truro, one of our company complained of a sudden back pain, and Henry said, "That comes from being followed by a good friend with a knife." I had a similar thought at the same moment; similar backgrounds bring about similar thoughts.

Mark Rothko and the Motherwells were friends, and we met him at dinners with them. Rothko won a Brandeis University award, via a Foundation set up by Barbara's parents. Brandeis was a non-sectarian institution, established primarily by Jewish donors to be a liberal arts center. Jack Poses served on the board and led the investment committee; Abe Sacher, the president of Brandeis, was a valued friend. Each year there were two groups of awards for creative arts, one for established notables, and one for young achievers. In 1965, Mark Rothko (born 1903) received the medal for painting in the established classification, and Kenneth Noland (b.1924) the citation for painting in the younger category. (That year Stanley Kunitz took the medal for poetry, Tennessee Williams for theater, and Elliot Carter for music.)

Rothko and Jack Get Along Like a House on Fire

Jack and Lillian held an annual reception in their apartment for the award recipients. At that year's, 1965, Mark Rothko and Jack were introduced to each other, realized they were both Russians, launched into an hour-long discussion in their mother tongue, and were obviously very happy to meet each other.

Mark Rothko's death led to an awkward result, like Bob Motherwell's, with regard to family arrangements. He established a trust to help needy artists, and also, like Motherwell's, to manage his posthumous reputation; the trustees he appointed (including his accountant, Bernard Reis, and his dealer, Frank Lloyd, supposed friends) enriched themselves at the estate's, and his children's, expense. A lengthy suit filed by Rothko's daughter and son was eventually settled in their favor, and the trustees' reputations as well as their bank accounts suffered greatly.

Sir Anthony Caro

Born in 1924 (as was Ken Noland), our poker friend, Tony Caro was then a youthful 39-year-old, and taught at Bennington between 1963 and 1965. The son of a Jewish stockbroker, Tony had been educated at Charterhouse, a smart but spartan public school in England. He told me there was no heat in winter, and when it snowed the boys made snowballs, stored them under their beds, and later sold them to their schoolmates.

In Bennington, his children attended a school which included children from different origins and classes where there was no corporal punishment and much freedom. He found it wonderful. Years later, having returned home to England, Tony came to New York for a show. I asked him about his children. He had sent them to Charterhouse, his old school. (Tony was knighted in 1987, and in 2000 the queen awarded him the Order of Merit, the highest honor in the UK, restricted to twenty-four, and given for intellectual or creative endeavor.)

Leo Lerman, Jacques Guerin, Frank Stella, and Barbara Rose

Of our close friends, Leo Lerman was another who knew everybody, Jacques Guerin was still another, as is Barbara Rose. More than a muse, she has written about her discoveries, as well as inspiring them; she also married two great creators. One was Frank Stella, with whom she had two children about the same age as our two. The other was songwriter and record producer Jerry Leiber. This, and lots of common interests, made for an on-and-off connection in the case of Stella, which has lasted to the present day. Leiber died in 2011.

Helen Frankenthaler gave a fortieth birthday party for me and seated Barbara Rose—Frank Stella's then-divorced ex-wife—to my right, and Jerry to her right. At one point I noticed they had both disappeared. They were having their own party in the basement and married a little later.

The Downtown Poker Game

There was also a downtown poker game, with a different crew of artists, among them some lesser-known ones, including Herman Cherry, (1909–92) an abstract painter and poet, the sculptor, Peter Agostini (1913–1993), and Matsumi Kanemitsu. Kanemitsu had an unusual background. Born in Ogden, Utah, in 1922 (died 1992), his family moved back to Japan three years afterwards. He left Japan in 1940, came back to the United States, and served in the American army in

World War II; at the end of the war, he studied with Fernand Léger in Paris, and then with Yasuo Kuniyoshi in New York. His loft apartment in Soho had a Japanese room at the back; you climbed two steps, and entered a tatami-covered space with bamboo walls, on which hung a pair of Samurai swords with pearl-encrusted hilts that, Kanemitsu said, had been handed down through generations of his family.

He said he had left Japan for political reasons, following a brief time at the Imperial War College, where, among other things, he learned to break down and re-assemble Garand Rifles. He left a large family behind in Japan, including several relatives who were to be hanged as major war criminals. He told us he had been promoted to corporal in the U.S. Army because of his own previous history in Japan; he knew how to drill draftees, some of whom were illiterate, and wrote love letters for them to their girlfriends, translating from a Japanese volume of Shakespeare. He reveled in telling about an occasion when General Mark Clark was inspecting an army group in California. He espied Kanemitsu wearing Corporal's stripes, and, according to Kanemitsu, Clark haughtily called him to approach and asked, "You cookie?" (i.e., one of the unit's cooks). Whereupon, Kanemitsu said, suppressing his highly educated English to mock Clark's manner and affecting a fake Asian intonation, riposted, "No am cookie," and with a toothy smile, "Me Colpolal." Following Pearl Harbor, Kanemitsu was interned and, when released, re-enlisted in the U.S. Army.

At dinner with us at home, he and Barbara, who had recently returned from a trip to Japan mentioned that there were there were a substantial number of Jewish-Japanese working in the food world. Kanemitsu replied that though he himself was not religious, his mother, who came from Macao, prided herself on coming from a long-established Jewish background—in contrast to the recent converts who were merely following a fad. Barbara's take was that Kanemitsu's mother was a Portuguese-Macao Sephardic Jew—and a snob. Kanemitsu, as had Bob, presented Barbara with a painting to mark Michael's birth in 1964.

Our House on 92nd Street

In 1962 we bought a brownstone on 92nd Street near Madison Avenue. It accommodated offices for both of us, plus children, plus dogs, plus tenants (whose rent helped pay our expenses, many of which were tax-deductible). The seller was our former St. Louis acquaintance, Mike Nichols. He had been engaged to a woman who wanted to live in a brownstone; when the engagement flopped, Mike sold us the house.

It was in a neighborhood not, at the time, as enriched by Wall Street moguls as it became, but also not as arty as a mansion near Gramercy Park (which Barbara preferred) would have been; that, however, was too big and expensive, and therefore impractical for us. It was also around the corner from Barbara's parents. One day, when Nicole was three years old, she was walking down the block with Lillian when she saw a pigeon, lying on the steps of the Jewish Museum. "What's wrong with the pigeon?" she asked. "It's just sleeping." When Nicole returned home, she told Barbara somberly that the pigeon did not look like it was sleeping. Barbara, who had fortunately walked down the street earlier in the day, told her the pigeon was dead.

Brigitte Altman and Barbara Compete at Cooking

We were emotionally, and now physically, close to our recently-made friends, Cecil and Brigitte Altman, who bought a brownstone further east on 93rd Street. Brigitte (1933–2018) and Barbara vied with one another in the kitchen. Brigitte was a very good cook and made unparalleled orange sorbet in hollowed orange skins; Barbara made

Opa Alexander Hecht

Oma Clara Hecht & Adolf

1910 Uncle Gusti and Mother Hanni

1910 Hecht and Stern Family

Hanni as a child

1923 Hanni and Adolf Kafka

c. 1931 Fritzl with Sterns & Dogs

1932 Hanni Stern, Mother

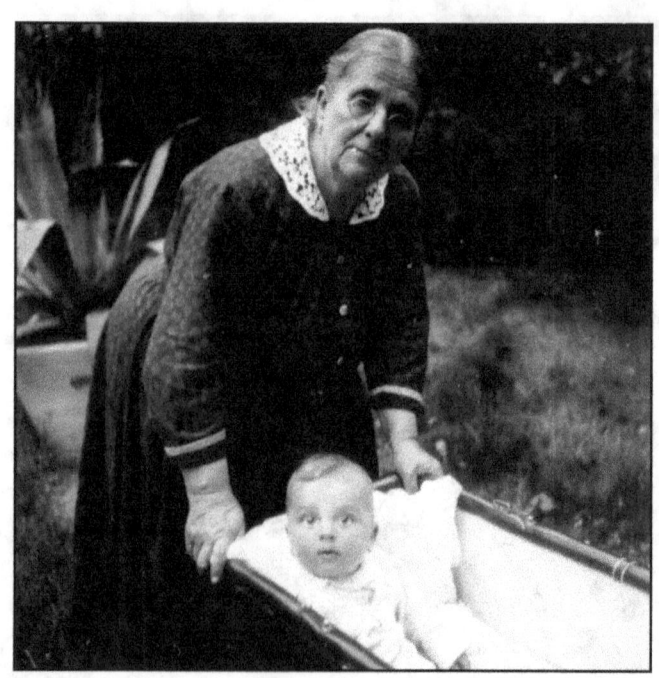

1933 Great Grandmother Klara Hecht with Bubi as a baby

1933 Mother, Fritzl, and Bubi

1934

1934

1934 Ernsti and Evi, first cousins

1935 Vienna Balcony from which I saw Parades

October 1935 at Donau Canal

1936 Ernsti

Barbara Joan Poses, age 4.

**1935 Austrian Alps
Photography by Gusti Stern**

1938 Family on the eve of leaving Vienna

c. 1939–1940 Mary Wooster,
Baroness Fould-Springer

**1937 Millstadt, July
Photography by Hanni Stern**

**1937 Millstadt, July
Photography by Hanni Stern**

**1937 Millstadt, July
Photography by Hanni Stern**

1935 Photography by Gusti Stern

**1955 Ernest and Barbara's Wedding
Hanni and Adolph Kafka**

1955 Barbara & her Parents

1955 Grandma Shapiro, Lilian Shapiro poses,
Jack Poses, Barbara Poses Kafka, Ernest Kafka,
Hanna Stern Kafka, Adolf Kafka, & Margaret Hecht Stern

1955 The Groomsmen: Chuck Frankel, John Heiman,
Gaynor Bradish, Stuart Byron, John Hirsch,
and Michael Halberstam

1956 "Chevy," Barbara and Ernie's first dog

c. 1950s, Heinz Hartmann

c. 1950s, Paul Desmond

1960 House Staff at Albert Einstein / Bronx Municipal Hospital

Freud Photo with inscription on the back, Gift from Harry Freud, Alexander Freud's son

To a scholar of the
major Freud with
best wishes from
a minor
Freud

Freud inscription on the back of Freud Photo

Mid 1960s Barbara Rose

1966 Nicole Kafka

1960s Jack Poses

**James Kirkman (British Art Dealer)
Represented important British painters,
including Lucien Freud**

Stubbs, second dog

c. 1969 Michael Kafka with Chameleon

c. 1966 Ernie & Michael Kafka in Vermont

1969 Helen Frankenthaler and Robert Motherwell in Venice

1970s CAPS Group

Nicole Kafka, 1970s

1970s Robi Bak

1970s Mort Reiser

**[Christie &] Andrew Wyld
taught me English Watercolors**

Late 1990s Barbara at the Microphone

**1992 Michael Kafka, Helen Frankenthaler,
& Ernie Kafka at Nicole's wedding (Vermont)**

c. 2000 Barbara & Ernie at Cap d'Antibes

2006 Voyage to Greek Isles

2018 Oliver's Graduation
L to R: Jill, Oliver, Lily, and Michael Kafka

2016 Sander Abend

Marilia Aisenstein

Show at Walter Randel Art Gallery
Left to right: Walter Randel, Mindy, and Fred Kafka

Ernest Kafka Exhibition

Peter Galbraith at Little Dix

Ray Sokolov, Journalist

Michael Kafka, Ernie Kafka, & Sander Abend at 50th Birthday

Nicole Kafka at Garrison

Jay Greenberg & Bob Michels

Arnie & Arlene Richards

**Paul Levy,
Journalist**

**2011 Howard Stein
of the Dreyfus Funds**

Ernie Kafka

RETURN TO NEW YORK — INTERNSHIP AND RESIDENCY

outstanding everything, including an amazing Dione Lucas chocolate roulade.

The Altmans remained in New York for two or three years, and we met their friends. In those days there was a little circle of children of French, or mixed French and American, or French and some other European country, who had spent the war in the U.S.; some had gone to secondary school at the Lycée Français in New York. Some, like Cecil, had gone on to college and graduate school. Another such, Philippe Dennery, earned a Ph.D, and went on to become a well-known physics professor, represented France at the Centre Européenne de Récherches Nucléaires at Geneva, and advised de Gaulle. Another, Bernard Hanon, became head of Renault. Brigitte's older brother, Patrice de Vallée (died 2018), became an economist. He could transform himself into a fish, swimming and gulping water for air—in a very realistic way—for an appreciative audience of children and adults; his performance was often requested, and the response was always awed applause.

Patrice always had a story to tell. For example: the U.N. had sent a large amount of money to an African country, to help build a highway from its capital city to a new airport. The U.N. deputized Patrice, then a banker in Paris, to investigate the progress of the work. He returned and reported there was no airport, but there was a road connecting the capital and the President's palace; was there a coincidence here? Were two old friends involved in opposite roles in this everyday story of corruption? Phillipe Dennery had, by that time, decided he would either have won a Nobel Prize in physics by predicting a particle that might be found (it was)—or he would not. In either case, he thought his talent for physics had reached an end. At the same time, his father died, leaving Phillipe the business, which he took over; the firm was a construction company that specialized in the design and construction of interiors of large buildings, mainly museums and palaces, especially in Africa.

Brigitte's Affair with Bertrand de Saussure and Later with Edward Sniders

Brigitte and Cecil Altman divorced. Cecil discovered that he was the last to learn that Brigitte was having an affair with Bertrand de Saussure, the son of Raymond de Saussure, an important follower of Freud, the grandson of Ferdinand de Saussure, a founder of 20th century linguistics and semiotics, and the great-grandson of Horace-Bénédict de Saussure, the first "Savant" to climb Mont Blanc for scientific purposes. (The party carried barometers and other instruments, which showed that altitude was correlated with barometric pressure.) Brigitte and Bertrand married and lived in the Palais de Saussure, at the top of the hill in the old part of Geneva, with a view over the city, where Barbara and I often stayed with them. We also visited them in Gstaad, when Bertrand was suffering from a cancer that eventually killed him. Brigitte was his devoted nurse, but at the same time carried on a relationship with another remarkable man, Edward Sniders.

Edward (1920–2003) had a wife (Mary, who died in 1984), and two daughters and had to give up his career in the British Foreign Service, owing to his wife's illness. During the Second World War, Edward had lied about his age and became a pilot flying the Mosquito—a light, largely wooden aircraft, designed for speed and bombing. The average life expectancy for Mosquito pilots was six weeks, but Edward survived being shot down by Germans twice, and was one of the group who made a famous, but unsuccessful, escape attempt from Stalag Luft III. They were caught. Edward wrote a memoir, *Flying In, Walking Out*, published in 1999. He often came to New York on business; he was one of the first to promote the use of algorithms to analyze markets. We used to have dinner in a wonderful restaurant that Barbara had designed—interiors, menu, wine lists and all; it was called le Plaisir, and the name was justified. (It closed when the chef moved to California, and one of the owners died of AIDs.)

Our last contact with Brigitte and Edward as a couple was when we rented a clutch of buildings on a secluded cove in Saint Lucia, and I swam as a companion-cum-lifeguard to look after Edward, who had suffered some strokes and was worried about swimming.

Robert Haas; Oenophilia

Another of Barbara's finds was Robert Haas, a Yale baseball player who, though he'd had a minor-league tryout, preferred to take over M. Lehmann, his father's wine shop on nearby Madison Avenue. It was there that Barbara bought one of the greatest wines ever, 1952 La Tâche, which she served at my next birthday dinner. This was a time when a bottle of the most extraordinary wine could be had for under $12. (Of course, my monthly salary for one hundred or more hours of learning, drawing bloods, taking EKG's, staining slides, and missing whole nights of sleep, was similarly distant from today's salaries. I was paid $72 per month; but we were still subsidized by my father and Jack Poses. (My father's stipend ended with his death in the spring of 1959.) Another similarly priced wine was *Cheval Blanc*, 1947.

Bob Haas's second wife—another Barbara—and their two children were close friends of ours. Bob and Barbara's wedding took place in our brownstone, and they moved their family and business offices to a beautiful eighteenth-century farmhouse in Vermont, after trying out the idea of moving there from New York one summer by living in our Vermont house while we were away in Europe. They celebrated their fiftieth wedding anniversary in January 2018, a few months before Bob's death in March 2018.

Bob became a major wine importer, and he persuaded Barbara to edit an American edition of the French trade magazine *Cuisine et Vins de France.* This led to an invitation to attend the annual Paris dinner, sponsored by the French wine industry, conducted on the lines of (the later) *La Paulée de Paris,* where growers and shippers met to taste the wines of the year. There were probably thirty reds, and the same number of whites, to be tasted and evaluated; and two *vins mystères* to be identified. I won second prize by identifying the white as a Savennières. The winner identified the vineyard from which this Loire white had come, and word spread that he actually owned the property next door. This was one of my proud moments.

During Barbara's tenure as editor of *Cuisine et Vins de France,* we often vacationed in France, and we sampled the foods and wines at restaurants in several regions. The lucky financial break that came from the investment in Thiokol allowed us to enjoy luxuries in then- Europe with our then-strong dollars. One of the things I learned from Barbara was to expand my palate to appreciate a wider range of cooking than my mother's more than adequate central European cooking and baking had provided.

The Commanderie de Bordeaux

When Bob Haas asked me if I wanted to join the *Commanderie de Bordeaux,* I happily did. This organization's members were wine lovers, both professionals, such as Bob Haas, Alexis Lichine, and Julius Wile, and amateur afficionados. It was a commercial organization to the extent that it was partly supported by the French government as a vehicle for promoting French wine, but it was also a convivial opportunity for people in or around the trade to get together and be clubby. There was an annual dinner at which we became "Langoustes," greeting each other by mimicking antennae by wiggling our fingers on the top of our heads.

The leader of the club was H. Gregory Thomas (1908–1990). He was a tall, elegant, charismatic, American-born, European-educated

(Cambridge, Switzerland, Salamanca) man who had practiced international law, headed Guerlain and, later, Chanel perfume companies, and spent the war as an OSS officer. But I had a problem with my membership: no women were members. I never liked it when no women, particularly my wife, were part of my social activities and so, eventually, I dropped out.

Bob was also a great sailor; I crewed for him in International Class races, and on a Block Island race, and loved sailing. But his rarest gift was his ability to taste; he could differentiate between Bourbons at blind tastings, far more difficult than remembering the tastes of wines made in different vintages and varieties of grapes. For years, he longed to own a vineyard and make his own wines, and we always accompanied him in his various attempts to make a deal.

There were a couple of "almosts," one in Burgundy and another in the New York Finger Lakes. Eventually, in partnership with the Perrins, the French family who owned the renowned Châteauneuf du Pape vineyard, Beaucastel, in the Rhône valley, he found a property in the hills above San Luis Obispo in California, with soil and climate similar to that of Beaucastel.

Tablas Creek

The two major partners, plus a few friends, including us, founded a vineyard called Tablas Creek in 1989. We imported vines and rootstocks from Beaucastel, sent them to Ithaca, New York to be quarantined (as was required to protect the U.S. from plant infections), and then reproduced the plant material by meristem.

Our son, Michael, and I went to California for the first vintage. A winery had not yet been built, but enough of our French grapes were ready to be pressed and made into wines. They were picked and meant to be transported to a nearby hired winery, by Jeep and trailer. We were in a group with the Haases, Barbara and Bob, and the older Perrin brother; we awaited the arrival of the grapes—and waited and waited. Eventually, we learned that the trailer carrying the first load of grapes had overturned, spilling the grapes onto the oily road, making them useless. A second trip was more successful; the grapes were loaded on a forklift, lifted, and fed into a crusher and the juice pumped to the vats. The forklift broke, and the grapes had to be raised by manpower; the pumping proceeded. Bob reminded everyone that one particular valve needed to be closed, and then Bob failed to close it, causing juice to be lost. I was pleased that we had experienced professionals doing the work; it would have been much worse had the workers been amateurs. Fortunately, this was our last disaster; we built a winery, a showroom, added more vines, more acreage, and now have a prize-winning, money-making operation. All of us are happy.

Barbara's Career at Conde Nast; Beginning of My Internship at Albert Einstein

Another success: Barbara began work at *Mademoiselle*, a Conde Nast magazine. Owned by the Newhouse family, Conde Nast was run by Si (1927–2017), the elder son. Leo Lerman (1919–94) was Si Newhouse's culture guide and scout for young talented newcomers. Barbara and Leo soon discovered they were kindred spirits, and Leo took her under his wing.

Barbara's *Vogue* connection began when Leo asked her to come to his office and asked what work she would like to do. "To write," Barbara replied, unhesitatingly. Leo said, "And if I sent you to Allene Talmey (1903–86), (the Features Editor at *Vogue* in 1958), what would you say you would like to write about?" "Art," said Barbara.

"Oh, no, you can't write about art for *Vogue*."

"Why not?"

"Because Allene Talmey writes about art for *Vogue*. You're a very good cook," said Leo, having sampled a few of Barbara's meals. "Why not say you'd like to write about food?" "Fine," said Barbara.

Off she went to see *Vogue's* features editor, who asked her what she might want to write about. "Food," said Barbara.

"Yes, dear, but what about food would you like to write?"

Unprepared but unperturbed, Barbara rattled off three ideas, all of which Allene Talmey bought.

As Barbara began at *Mademoiselle*, I began my internship at Albert Einstein College of Medicine's affiliate, Jacobi Hospital in the Bronx. I thought a city hospital (and Jacobi was part of Bronx Municipal) would provide lots of experience with full-time teachers and public hospital patients. These patients didn't have private doctors, which allowed the house staff, even including interns, more responsibility and hence experience, than private hospitals could. Besides, its reputation was of having the best psychiatry program in the city (or, actually, anywhere at that time) and also first rate, relatively youthful teachers—mostly Columbia College of Physicians and & Surgeons, Jewish doctors in a hurry to rise, and not likely to do so at P&S. I proved to have made a good choice from the educational standpoint, if not from the practical, patient-attracting-after-training, standpoint. For this, it would have been better to train at a private hospital, with private doctors having admitting privileges, thus making contacts for later on. But I was too idealistic for that, probably not hungry enough to need it, and with a strong hankering to be a manly man—a real doctor.

The internship at Albert Einstein was a year of hard work; many weeks interns worked a hundred or more hours. The system was pretty foolproof; for one thing, no fools were accepted for the program: the standards were as high as they had been for the Washington University Medical School, which was, and remains, one of the most desirable in the U.S. We interns rotated through various services; medicine was the most important and longest, lasting six months.

There was an easy month in the Nathan van Etten Hospital. A planning white elephant, it was a tuberculosis hospital, which opened in 1954, at the same time as the new medical school. It had five hundred beds but housed many fewer patients, and, though some of them stayed years, most were there for a shorter time. Tuberculosis had become much less common since the hospital was designed, and there was not too much to do for these patients except give them a tranquil place to rest, take antibiotics, and heal. They were usually treated with streptomycin and isoniazide. In the past, but not in my time, there had been patients who had surgical procedures to collapse infected lungs, in order to encourage healing. One Haitian doctor was learning how to deal with tuberculosis, intending to practice in Haiti, where the disease was more common; a pleasant fellow who smiled a lot, and spoke in a slow Haitian tone, he had practically nothing to do. Our function was simply to staff the place, and that was not going to be necessary much longer. Later, Van Etten was reconfigured to house a number of other services.

Life on the Wards

All the other services, including the emergency room, surgery, obstetrics and pediatrics, were staffed so that every patient was examined and followed by a hierarchy of people. There was a rotation in the out-patient clinics, where we referred new patients to the various specialty clinics for appointments. Lowest in the hierarchy, and least responsible were the medical students; they were predominantly responsible to the interns, and above them, the residents in order of seniority, then the chief residents and the attending faculty. We had daily patient rounds which were attended by a crowd of medics, who heard the story of the patients' problems, treatment, and progress, and diagnostic and treatment possibilities, and plans.

Clinical-pathological conferences were teaching performances, where autopsy or biopsy information was available, so that (generally) a retrospective understanding of the course of patients' medical events could be made known. Other conferences used journal papers for discussions; and when I went on into a three-year psychiatry program, we saw visiting experts interview patients and discuss their problems.

Daily life on the wards followed a consistent schedule. The day began with drawing blood, sending some to labs for testing, using some to find the hematocrit (the ratio of the volume of cells, primarily red, to the volume of serum), preparing samples for culture of possible infectious organisms, and separating out white cells and staining and counting them to determine the number of the different forms per cubic centimeter. Urine samples needed to be collected, cultured, centrifuged, the sediment examined microscopically, pH determined, and white cells stained and identified. We had to prepare necessary instruments for biopsies, spinal taps, and a host of other procedures. We also managed infusions. We stained bacteria to identify them and planted them on agar media where they might establish colonies, so they could be better identified and examined to see to what antibiotic they might be sensitive to. We did EKGs. Sometimes medical students on clinical rotations did some of these tasks, in which case, they might need help and supervision. I discovered Harry Freud's very attractive Austrian wife was an EKG technician there. All or almost all of this "scut work" took a significant amount of time; most of it is now done by technicians. As interns, there was no limit to the number of hours we worked. When we were posted to the Emergency Room, the most arduous of the rotations, or when we were on call for the wards, we sometimes worked twelve or more hours every day, plus every other night. When the lab work had been done, we followed the ward chiefs and residents on rounds. Each patient was visited, often some physical examination took place, the course of the illness was assessed, and plans for needed tests were agreed upon. There were notes to be filled in on the patients, new patients to be admitted, examined, and written up in charts, consultations to be organized, and discharges to be made. In addition, there were autopsies to be observed, conferences to be attended, and reading to be done.

I was frequently exhausted, but in general I had a wonderful time. There was a camaraderie among the older and younger residents and interns, among interns with each other and with the medical students, and, gradually, the whole community, including the faculty. When I started in 1958, the first group of students was graduated, and there was something almost spiritual about the atmosphere of being near the beginning of a new institution, which seemed to touch all those involved—everyone from professors and staff members down was eager to learn and to teach. I cannot think of a chair of a department who was as old as fifty, other than the neurosurgeon, Leo Davidoff, who was sixty in 1958. It was a year of great privilege for me.

My Home and Social Life with Barbara Suffers

As I came to honor Harvard for achieving the success of its search for Veritas as an ideal, I honor the medical ethos I experienced at Einstein and Washington St. Louis. It was more difficult for Barbara. How could it be otherwise, given that I was deeply engaged with my patients, comrades, and work, and not awake much of the time I was at home? That is not to say that we lacked friends. I managed to get to a few poker games. We entertained, and were entertained, and I had a month off a year. Things became much easier after the first, intern year; night calls were less frequent.

Perils of the Medical Profession

Doctors have more divorces, and suicides, than people in other professions. There is also a correlation with the pressure of the kind of work they do: surgeons are said to compete for numerical victory in the number of divorces they have. The probability of receiving a call that requires getting out of bed and rushing to a bedside during the night is reduced now, because a specialty of emergency-care doctors has arisen. Also, more deliveries are induced, more doctor groups have sprung up with rotating on-call coverage for existing patients, and more answering machines offer office hours, and those who need immediate attention are now advised to go to an emergency room. None of these things applied then to the people who cared for the patients who lived in our public hospital catchment area.

There were funny stories about intern-patient interviews, which determined assignment of patients to the proper clinic. You conducted an interview and tried to make a diagnosis to enable triage—to sort out who went where, and how quickly. There were always patients who replied to the routine first question, "What brings you here?" with "the bus." And when the intern revised the question, "I meant, what's the medical problem that brought you here?" someone would invariably say, "You're the doctor." Then there was invariably someone whose answer was, "I'm feeling sick, so I came here; it's the Johns Hopkins for the Jews." The answer to the question, "Can you tell me the name of the Governor of New York?" was likely to be "Rockenfeldberg." "Can you tell me where you are?" Again, "Johns Hopkins for the Jews." One would be justified in thinking that most of our patients were Jewish. It's possible, but there was a good urban mix. Perhaps Jews are more inclined to *try* to be funny. Barbara, in her later stages of dementia, responded to her neurologist's questions, "Can you tell me the name of the President?" with a snappy, "Of what!?" when she was more than a little disoriented, and I appreciated that that part of her was still there.

The House Staff had meals in a large dining hall, and loudspeaker calls were frequent. For months, I thought that we had a Dr. Philip Cates, but he turned out to be a Canadian who spelled his name Katz, but explained that in Canada it was pronounced Cates. Then there was Dr. Hama Schnickel, which I thought was an unusual, but definitely Jewish, woman's name, until I realized he was really a Scot, Hamish Nickel.

My wish to have lots of encounters with lots of patients, and lots of responsibility, was certainly gratified by working in a public hospital; but until I was actually there, I didn't grasp what degree of stress and strain, for man and wife, was going to follow. I now know that experience is a lot more important than one imagines when young. Being married means making compromises and sharing space and responsibilities. Among the compromises are giving up a degree of privacy, relinquishing some control over budgets, and welcoming the crew of friends and relatives that come with your spouse. The need to adapt has to be felt before it can be acted on, and there have to be frequent negotiations over unexpected conflicts. Sometimes accommodation is impossible. I was accustomed to having my own toys, books, and food on my plate. Barbara seemed to feel free to reach onto my plate to taste what I had ordered, to grab the salt and pepper for herself as she wished, to leave her clothing all over the place, rarely to close closet doors or bureau drawers, or turn off lights. She tended to greet me when I came home tired or randy, with the instruction, "Take out the garbage." I persuaded her to add, "You don't have to do it right away. Whenever." But ten minutes later, she'd ask if I'd done it yet. Barbara had work as I did. She liked what she did; but at the end of the day she had an exhausted husband, or one of many nights alone to look forward to. Barbara could be patronizing about being smarter, and knowing more than most other people, though she never thought that with me. Actually, in many ways she was smarter than I. She hated the quibbling that her parents did; their arguments about who knew what first were really annoying, though they could not have managed without each other. It was partly a class issue, as both Barbara's parents had to sacrifice and work their way up, and neither developed the confidence they should have felt, reality-wise. It was also true that they never reached an accurate view of Barbara, who was certainly given every educational advantage and financial support anyone could have needed, but to whom respect was not freely offered. Guilt-inducing remarks about the need to pay back, once privileged, on the other hand, were frequent.

On our honeymoon visit to Baroness Mary Fould-Springer Wooster, Barbara had enacted both sides of her ambivalence (enjoying the pleasures of good taste and wherewithal, and suffering from guilt). She listened to the Kaiser Franz Josef story with tender rapture, but when the Baroness handed her an envelope containing money as a wedding present, Barbara immediately took it to a flower shop nearby, converted the money into a bouquet, and sent it off to the Baroness. Barbara felt she was being patronized. She failed to understand that Mary Wooster was a lifelong patron; she knew no other life. For my part, I had been rich, then poor and vulnerable (enough to know the difference), and then rich and fortunate again, I knew both fear of one and guilt over the other, so I felt sympathetic and annoyed about seeing Barbara, like me, hopping between self-indulgence and self-punishment. This made us good candidates for psychoanalytic treatment.

These have been irritants to which I am unduly sensitive, but, of course, there have been other things of importance that we settled or came to ignore. Those included where to live; our New York brownstone, for example, when Barbara coveted a mansion near Gramercy Park. On the other hand, I would have preferred a place within commuting distance as a second home, while Barbara, who had been dragged to

Westport every weekend with her father, wanted nothing to do with commuting, or settling near her parents.

Barbara also had a strong influence on my choice of profession, partly indirectly, in that my going into analysis had to do with marriage, dog ownership, patient-versus-relationship conflicts, as well as with Fafner fantasies, Nazis, my mother's multiple sclerosis, ether anesthesia, emigration, and my outré way of thinking (using outré is an example of my annoying propensity to complicate things by enlarging because I like the special flavor of the sound of the word, and its not easily translatable meaning to me). My professional work and my personal neuroses were much of a piece. Barbara also thrived with the aid of her analyses. However, both of us, given the scarcity of gifted and experienced practitioners at the time, had not so good luck with our first doctor experiences and had to try again.

Back to My Internship—The Effect of Chronic and Repetitive Health Problems in Patients

Something inherent in the work we did in the department of medicine led me to the discovery that, when we treated infections successfully (the organisms involved were sufficiently sensitive to the agents we had available to dispose of them), the patient could find that he was, once again, as he had been before the illness struck. There were two other possible outcomes: either the infection progressed or it had already caused permanent damage to an organ or organs. An example might be endocarditis. A particular bacterial infection could be eliminated by antibiotics, but valves might have been damaged. This might predispose to reinfection, which might or might not be drug sensitive. Valves might need to be replaced, but, at the time, that was not possible. Valve replacement became practicable around thirty years ago, and that I am still among the living is owing to that; the improvement in available treatments led to prolonging my own life, as well of the lives of many others.

I had ample opportunity to learn about the effects of chronic or repetitive health events in patients and in my family. In a certain way, my personal experiences were less frightening than the fear I felt about the potential losses of other people. I never imagined being dead. If I thought about what being dead would mean, it was that being dead is losing everyone else who matters and having no one left. "The world isn't coming to an end" suggests that, if it were, you'd still be around to suffer the loss of all your hopes for the future.

I can think of a lot of ailments that were treatable but not curable. Heart failure, diabetes, asthma, duodenal ulcer, hypo- and hyperthyroidism, cancers, urinary obstruction, and many other ailments were common. There was no shortage of calls for treating them. All were progressive; they pretty much required, at least, medical follow-ups, but, usually, treatment or retreatment for life.

Urinary obstruction was among the conditions where the treatment was not a treatment at all: the elderly were treated by having sounds (a type of metal probe) of gradually increasing size inserted into the penis, to stretch the urethra, narrowed by prostatic hypertrophy, and allow the bladder to empty; but the effect was brief, sometimes ineffective, and sometimes the treatment caused trauma, leading to scarring and greater constriction. Luckily for me, we now have drugs that cause shrinkage of an enlarged prostate. Since Prozac appeared, we have SSRIs to use against depression. Although the drugs have undesirable effects on libido and erectile functioning, at least they allow one to pee in comfort and escape depression.

Then and now, people would arrive at hospital and undergo treatment, improve, go home, and, often, return with their asthma, heart failure, diabetic acidosis, complications of diabetes, or progression of pulmonary disease or cancer. The best one could hope for was a return to something like the preexisting state of health. Moreover, medical and surgical intervention could, and too often did, fail to ameliorate situations that one had tried to deal with. Every treatment has side effects, only occasional and only mildly annoying, but often unpleasant. In addition, hospitalization is demeaning and humiliating. Liberty and independence are severely curtailed. The patient is ruled by his illness, and often subject to what can seem to be the whims of the caretakers and the confusions of a large bureaucracy.

Choosing Psychiatry as My Residency

When it came time for me to decide among the choices of future career directions, there were a number of important considerations. I had deleted many selections from the menu, though several options were tempting. One was to drop out of medicine entirely and go into banking with my father. He had invited me to do this before I went to medical school. I had refused. This was partially because medicine was not only part of my family background, but also a worthy, humane social contribution. Medicine was an active field: discovery was constant, and physiology and pathophysiology were fascinating. I had worked on the border between autoimmune and microbiologic research at NYU, and although what I had worked on led nowhere, it remained an exciting area.

Weighing against the choice of remaining in medicine, I foresaw the inevitable transformation of practice that was already under way: more and more specialization and subspecialization, less and less room for individuality in the doctor-patient relationship as diagnosis and treatment became more routinized. Doctors were still admired and could make a reasonable living, and that was a plus, but it looked as though more and more ailments were going to be treated for longer and longer times and distributed among more specialties and subspecialties. That happened. Specialization reduced the number of puzzles of diagnosis and treatment the doctor had the opportunity to solve. There were more administrative burdens in dealing with payers and government oversight. I foresaw the coming contraction of independence for doctors, growth of group practices, increased income for the super specialists but less for the majority.

A second possible path to follow would have been to quit medicine and go into my father-in-law's perfume business. There was the likelihood of good money and of a life like the Poses's, of having a family business that might be passed on to children, with the fun of philanthropy and ,eventually, an independent life. I say "eventually" because working with Jack would have meant working under Jack, which would not have been easy. Also, Barbara thought Jack might take her in, and she would have been happy had he been able to do that. But he was unable to delegate responsibility to anyone, especially not to a woman. Even had he been willing, he would also have been taking her on; neither Jack, nor Lillian, nor Barbara were inclined to accommodate competitors.

It would have been impolitic for me to take a place Barbara wanted for herself; it rapidly became a rule that we never broke. I had my professional role and corner, and she had hers. I was more capable of keeping out of Barbara's way than she was of mine. I never learned much about food, though I developed a good palate and nose. I limited the use of my skills to tasting, and generally eschewed giving suggestions to Barbara. She, on the other hand, was quite willing to discuss technical matters relating to psychoanalysis. At one time, she considered going into medicine. I consulted with friends, who were high-ups at medical schools. Their advice was to tell her that, as she was in her early forties, it was too late. Given her constitutional impatience and impulsiveness, that was advice all to the good.

A third possibility was an academic career, which would have meant years more of study, and a Ph.D. or M.B.A. Ultimately, what

I experienced in terms of research dissuaded me. I hovered between medicine and psychiatry. I put off a definitive choice of academic medicine or clinical practice for a time, but I had to make a more immediate decision about what would come after the internship.

My Father—His Death

My father had suffered what was diagnosed as a minor cardiac infarct two or three years earlier (1957–58), but the diagnosis was uncertain. Some minor electrocardiographic indications were found at an incidental physical checkup. Later, this supposition seemed unlikely to have been correct. My father, the good man and patient, was told to lose weight, which he did. For the first time in my life, he could not realistically be called "*dickerle*."

Sometime after the initial infarct idea was floated, an episode of palpitation and shortness of breath occurred. I suggested that my father see Charles K. Friedberg, the Professor of Surgery at Mount Sinai in New York, who had written the "official" cardiology textbook, and had worked on direct-current cardioversion, which became the basic method for defibrillation. Friedberg started him on quinidine, a cardiotoxic drug that, at the time, was the main tool for controlling ventricular cardiac arrhythmias. Friedberg's method for producing cardioversion, electrical stimulation to restore normal cardiac rhythm in cases of arrhythmia, was not yet generally used. Hitting on chests and mouth-to mouth-breathing, plus, as a last resort, adrenalin injections into the heart, were what we had.

In the spring of 1959, when I was in intern, I received an anxious telephone call from my mother. My father was having a heart attack. I rode in the ambulance, holding his hand. He was evidently having a very rapid heartbeat and was white and terrified. He gripped my hand tightly and asked whether he was going to die, and would I help him?

Friedberg was away, and my father was admitted to Mount Sinai. I was with him, holding his hand, when he died, as the staff tried to regulate his heartbeat rhythm by injecting adrenaline into his heart. It failed. Autopsy found an essentially normal heart with a few small fibrous scars. He had not needed to lose weight.

My father lived sixty years, first as a semi-orphan child, then through four years of battles between the Austrian and Italian armies, between the ages of sixteen and twenty, during the First World War. He lived through depression, inflation, and political turmoil, and succeeded in banking. He lived through the early days after the Nazi invasion and managed to escape with my mother and their two children. He lived through the absence of his own father and the horror of leaving behind his mother and sister, who died in concentration camps. He lived through years of caring for a sick and deeply loved, dependent wife. In the twenty years that my family lived in New York before his death, he learned a new language and created a new life, and when he died left two highly educated and successful children behind, and enough money to support my mother in a simple but comfortable life. She never had to feel that she was a burden to her children. I am grateful for that. My father never turned to me for help until the end, when I could not help. As a child, I did not understand. Children learn more from experience than from words, Still, I think with more help, trust, and explanation, I would have understood more and been more prepared to deal with painful events. I regret having missed what I missed.

The Moment of Decision: The Man in the Clean, White Coat

I stayed with my medical career. I still had to decide what field to choose for my residency. Medicine, surgery, neurology, psychiatry, obstetrics, pediatrics, and gynecology were all possible. Neurology, pediatrics and gynecology were easy to eliminate. Neurology was out, except for the research possibilities, based on what I had identified at Queen Square. Pediatrics meant dealing with children and babies, and I realized that I needed to be able to communicate with my patients in words. Ob-Gyn was repetitive, messy, and I confess, a bit low in the prestige department.

What ended my lollygagging in making my choice of residency happened just in time. On the medicine internship rotation, I was working in the emergency room. A fifty-something year-old man was brought in with cardiac infarct symptoms. He had a characteristic infarct EKG, so we admitted him to the ward where I was scheduled to start work the next morning. He was also the father of one of the medical students; I knew her, but not well; but this was a short time after my father's cardiac death, so I was somewhat tender on the subject. The man was on the ward before I arrived, and he was evidently terrified, screaming, thrashing about trying to get out of bed, dislodging his IV. The nurses didn't know how to handle him. Neither did I, so I asked my resident what to do. "Get an emergency psych consult," he said.

Albert Einstein College of Medicine had a very forward-looking modern psychiatry program. One of the useful practices introduced at this new medical school was that psychiatry offered a strong liaison service, applying war psychiatry-learned techniques to problems encountered in general hospital medicine. Consulting on the wards was their mission. Other consultants would come, order this or that X-ray or blood test, or other procedure, make treatment suggestions, and leave; the psychiatrist, however, spent time with the patient and made an effort to instruct the house staff. The system was my first experience of the new order in psychiatry, a contrast with the scene in St. Louis.

That afternoon a man in a long white coat who was clean, well-dressed, and well-rested arrived. He took a chair to the lightly sedated patient's bed, pulled the curtain around, and I could hear the murmuring of conversation. After an hour, the curtain was opened, the consultant came over to me, took me back to the patient, told me to explain who I was, that I would see him at least twice a day, and would otherwise be available should he want me. The patient seemed quieter and somewhat reassured. The next day he accepted having his blood drawn, which he had refused the preceding day. The third morning he was much the same, still agitated and frightened, but not loud and crazy. That afternoon, the consultant arrived again, repeated the process of getting a chair, putting it by the bed, and drawing the curtain. Then he went to write in the patient's chart.

The patient was now calm, and the nurses were delighted. So, I, in my stained cotton jacket and bleary of eye, went to ask the elegant psychiatry resident what he had done. "I talked to him, I asked how he felt, how it felt when this was happening to him, what he thought this might mean to his life, how it would affect his family, and would he be able to work?" "And that is all you did?" "Yes, and I'll come back another time or two, and see how he fares. You know," he said, "we can treat people so that they become better and happier than they ever were before." With that stunning remark delivered, off he went, leaving me with a strong inclination to proceed in his general direction.

I concluded that psychiatry presented an unbeatable combination of attractive factors; it was a time when Freud's writings were of interest to artists, poets, filmmakers, writers, schools, corporations, and every sort of creative personality. Even at Barnes Hospital, with its un-Freudian psychiatry that was almost as dated as Harvard's mental health facilities, there was a faculty internist near my generation, David Graham, who was interested in psychosomatic medicine. His father was the celebrated Evarts Graham, who had performed the first lung resections, and thereby made it possible to prolong and sometimes to save the lives of lung cancer sufferers (given the right relatively slow growing cell type and an early discovery of the cancer); he had also been trying to discover the factors that allowed deer to regrow their bone antlers for years. He kept the animals he studied on the roof. That was surely a previous generation career.

Milton Rosenbaum and His Influence at Albert Einstein—The Stagecoach Club. My Introduction to the Mind

The newly created Albert Einstein College of Medicine of Yeshiva University (to give its lengthy title) used Jacobi Hospital, a part of Bronx Municipal Hospital Center, and staffed it as its teaching hospital. The first class to be graduated got their degrees in the year I joined the house staff. Milton Rosenbaum, previously a professor in Cincinnati, was the first Chair of Psychiatry; he hired an assortment of psychiatrists with different approaches to the mental. Teaching a mixture of approaches was modern in comparison with attitudes in the psychotherapy world where, then, different groups did not mix.

I applied for the residency at Albert Einstein and was accepted. The residency was a three-year program, with service on inpatient locked wards and in an outpatient treatment center, doing psychotherapy supervised by more senior people, with frequent meetings to discuss the contents of the therapy sessions that went on. In addition, there were weekly meetings of the whole department at which guests came from beyond the walls, who were experts in various diagnostic categories and espoused various approaches. They interviewed patients: schizophrenics, depressives, and those with other varieties of conditions, all of which were discussed by the faculty and house staff who were present at the interviews.

Milton Rosenbaum invited me to join his club, the "Stagecoach Club." It was a group of colleagues, who had served in the military during World War II. They came home at the end of the war, having trained as psychoanalysts before serving, or they finished training after discharge. After the war ended, these doctors came to occupy

RETURN TO NEW YORK — INTERNSHIP AND RESIDENCY

chairmanships of psychiatry in various institutions around the country; these included my department at Albert Einstein, and Cleveland, Cincinnati, Rochester, Pittsburgh, and others. These professors regarded themselves as pioneers; hence, the name "Stagecoach Club," and they got together at one of their home locations, rotating each year. They brought along star trainees, who presented work they were doing, or, even if they were not presenting work, could be introduced to their colleagues.

To reform academic psychiatry in a Freudian way was a large ambition. Bobby Kennedy visited our hospital with an eye to giving some funding for child psychiatric studies. Rosenbaum had been showing his group the facilities the morning before we were to leave for Pittsburgh to meet with the club.

A trio—Rosenbaum, Gerald Flamm, the administrator of the outpatient department, and I—sat in the plane, three abreast, with Milt in the window seat. He had a couple of martinis and began telling stories about his professional aspirations; he said that all he had wanted in life was to be a professor and live in a white house with a big lawn, where he and his students could walk and talk. Flamm giggled (also having had a bit to drink) and ribbed our boss, "Yes, Milt, you wanted to live in the White House!" We three, Milt, our Stagecoach ticket provider; Gerry Flamm, rewarded for his administrative services; and I, to represent the bright future the Chairman could show off, deplaned.

When we arrived at the motel, we settled in and then repaired to a conference room, which gradually filled with psychiatry department chairmen, who were enjoying drinking, and regaling their buddies with stories about their accomplishments over the preceding year. Most of the anecdotes were accounts about how many million miles they had flown on site visits, and how many millions of dollars they had authorized in awards for research and teaching. Although disappointed by the childlike competitiveness of the Stagecoach chairmen (I was snobbishly hoping for more refined patrons), I respected what they were trying to accomplish. I didn't admit it to myself then, but a weight was removed by the sight of their foibles.

One participant who interested me was Bertram Lewin, who was a visiting professor, a classical Freudian and sage at the New York Psychoanalytic Institute; he made a good impression on me. It was gratifying to be an intimate part of a community of interesting people, working on interesting questions. In contrast, the prospect of an academic career that required flying about, giving away grant money, did not appeal to me.

Kai Erikson, as young as I was, was one of the rising stars in the group. He was the son of Erik Erikson, who followed Freud in the interest in identity and the formation of groups. (Much of Freud's writings had to do with applied psychoanalysis, as, for instance, *Moses and Monotheism*). Kai presented a paper. He argued that groups construct ideas to differentiate their identities from those of other groups, which produces and maintains a sense of identity, by describing who—and what—they were not, as well as who they were. He cited political parties and religious sects as examples of social units and proposed the Salem Witch trials as one example. Such measures enhance the cohesion of the group, Erikson postulated. It occurred to me that competing professors, who represented competing institutions, were the same in thinking about what was different and better (or less good) about them and their institutions in a competitive world; yet, because they were capable of making relative rather than absolute distinctions, they were open-minded enough to accommodate differing views.

At a given time there usually are numerous possible ins and outs, and the groups of which we are members can change. As a Jew in Austria, after the annexation by Nazi Germany, there was one option as to in and out regarding Austria, and that was to get out. Though it was difficult to find somewhere else to go, there were more and less desirable destinations. In the interest of making an argument, as in a debate, one can shrink the options to two, and omit the presence of other rejected alternatives; but it is a rare thing to truly be faced with only two alternatives. In a war, usually two groups conflict. Each group considers the other group to be "bad," a population to be warded off or exiled, if not exterminated. The binary arrangement is unstable. As conditions change, arrangements rearrange.

Even a child of young age can imagine living in another family, with other parents. Should one or the other parent vanish, people who can become substitutes will often appear, and parents do remarry. My father, who lost his biological father, acquired a whole new family at an orphanage and again, later, by marriage. It struck me that this was true of me, as well as of other people. I needed to remind myself that I had to give up things; nothing is permanent, but everything is replaceable. Within every "out," there are almost always various possibilities. A fundamental attribute of people is the capacity to change and to adapt. The conclusion of Kai Erikson's argument: you are well-advised to expect impermanence in the inter- and intra-relations of groups. In particular, be aware of the tendency to idealize your group—and demonize others—if you want to thrive internally and externally.

The essence of diplomacy lies in having realistic, rational awareness and plasticity. Kai Erikson's contribution at the meeting was indebted to Freud's efforts to understand how individual psychology formed social organization. The attempt to conceive of a simple choice, either-or, as an example of group-think is a function of a grouping of individuals wanting community and establishing a basis for that feeling by reducing the complexities they face to a simple black or white. My career choice, and every other choice, would have been easier had there been fewer alternatives. I understood enough to realize, when I read Freud critically later on, that even he proposed simplistic theories at first, when he was young and eager. To an unusual degree, he was able to emend and complicate so that his student, Rosenbaum, no genius, knew well enough to pioneer a complex, catholic department.

My Introduction to Freud as a Resident; Maturation

Influenced by his contacts with Charcot in France, and stimulated by his discussions with Breuer in Vienna, Freud, always curious, turned from neurology (his first book was *On Aphasia*). He became interested in what was called hysteria. He began to listen to patients. Perhaps symptoms could be deciphered. As in interpreting a foreign language, some underlying meaning might be identified as expressed by seemingly unexplained symptoms. The term hysteria relates to a wandering uterus, but there was no evidence of physical pathology. I think he approached the symptoms as though they were a sort of sign language that could be translated into understandable words by listening to associations connected with them. He concluded that unconscious thinking influences behavior.

From the point of view of theoretical (often theatrical) attitudes, Freud's early ideas, including the seduction theory and that of abreaction, were generally discarded. More accepted was a theory that posited a maturational sequence of anatomical zones, the oral, the anal, and the genital, as dominant foci of excitation and sensual gratification. Each stage was thought to have particular forms of mental expression, which paralleled the evolution of the dominance of sensation in the organs during maturation, with fixation points, and possible back and forth movements, progressions and regressions, to and from one or another of those developmental stages. That is probably still taught, but as a historical footnote.

Freud's Topographic Theory of Thinking

Freud seemed to like threes. As to thinking, the topographic theory was an early descriptive theoretical proposal; it posited three levels of consciousness, the "conscious"—waking awareness, the "preconscious"—stored memories and ideas accessible to conscious thinking, and "unconscious"—ideas, theories and memories not directly available to consciousness. The last could leak past a mental barrier and appear in waking life, transformed into the form of symptoms—paraesthesias and paralyses, jokes, and slips of the tongues (parapraxes)—as well as in sleep, in the form of dreams.

A force called "repression" was supposed to force unwelcome wishes and associated thoughts out of consciousness; with that, away went the desires that caused the anxiety about anticipated possible dangerous acts. However, relegating desires to unconsciousness was conceived of as preventing gratification, thereby leading to neurosis; lifting repression, thereby making the unconscious conscious, was supposed to be curative. Bringing repressed desires to consciousness and inducing recovery of memories, recalling, reconsidering, and reworking conflicts with a more mature, less childish mind than that of the past, would allow the mind to modify the desires, once it recognized them, to make them harmless, and this would allow gratification (discharge of energies) to take place. It seems that this helps, particularly in working with post-traumatic states. Freud's early theory about the beneficial effects of making the unconscious conscious was stimulated mainly by the experience he had with patients when he used a hypnotic approach and, later, suggestion, to encourage them to reveal painful and anxious elements that had been kept out of consciousness. To rework, to juxtapose the past and the present, allows individuals to achieve Thomas Kuhn's proposed mechanism by which personal scientific revolution takes place.

Eventually, the accumulation of evidence shows the previous theory isn't productive, and at some point: a paradigm shift. Aha!

When I presented my first paper at a scientific meeting at my institute, as a student, I mentioned that there had been a correlation between forgetting and calm physiological measurements in the subjects of my experiment. My discussant spent several paragraphs chastising me for using the then-supplanted topographic theory in my suggestion that levels of consciousness might be involved in forgetting. In my mind, the forgetting seemed perhaps related to the forgetting of dreams, and the topographic theory might have had something to it. I was young and timorous, but my hero, Heinz Hartmann, read the paper a second time, and congratulated me. He said people criticized him, too; the basis of the negative comments often was that he brought up too many things and included peripheral matters that made his arguments too complicated, so I should persevere.

From listening to his patients' spontaneous, unedited trains of thought, associated with their symptoms and the elements of their dreams as told to him, as well as by examining his own dream associations, Freud came to believe that hysterical symptoms were reenacted suppressed memories of traumatic seductions by adults in childhood. He adopted a setting. He had patients lie on a couch with him behind in a chair, sometimes with a hand on the recumbent patient's forehead, suggesting that they say whatever they were thinking ("free association")—a state when the usual logical thinking of waking life is suspended. The strength of a hypothetical barrier that ordinarily prevents frightening, dangerous contents in the unconscious from surfacing was diminished. The result: memories of past trauma together with related painful feelings could appear. This was called "abreaction."

Later, that theory was supplanted. Freud's self-analysis revealed that unacceptable desires, masked and gratified, motivated his own dreams. What might seem to represent a suppressed memory of an event had been constructed under the influence of unconscious competitive and sexual desires. Freud found, for example, that he had demeaned and disparaged his father out of competitive desires. Dad was regarded as bad, by Freud, both because he was not a powerful protector and, also, a competitor. The Oedipus complex, in which the son kills the father and marries the mother, was an illustration using a literary example to represent unconscious desires. The theory was also applied to explain social conflicts and group antagonisms. The hostile and sexual wishes are attributed to others, making an innocent victim of oneself and justifying attacks on others. The initial theory, that the symptoms are a sort of reenactment of a traumatic experience, was too simple. One had to add the influences of the victim's motivation and state of physiological maturation as factors in the creation of the phenomena the outside observer sees and hears. The latter was illustrated by positing oral, anal, and, later, Oedipal stages.

Freud's Later Structural Theory: Id, Ego, Superego

The behavioral manifestations of "hysteria" could no longer be understood as a process for dealing with aftereffects of childhood seduction. Abreaction proved to be an unreliable effect. Even if the childhood trauma had occurred, since not everyone with similar trauma developed symptoms, the simple idea that trauma alone caused them is untenable. The "structural theory" came next. It added a number of factors that needed to be included in the menu of the way the mind's workings could be understood. Freud introduced another triad—three "structures." The id represented the biological forces that powered the instinctual drives. The ego was the executive arm of the tripartite structure—the seat of the processes whereby instinctual drives were modified, harmonized, gratified, delayed, or prohibited. The superego developed out of the ego and was populated by processes that influenced the ego so far as morality and ethical considerations were concerned. It represented the moral demands that came about during maturation and development of the person. The ego had the many faceted task of dealing with the id's instinctual drives, as well as with outer reality and moral imperatives. It had "defense mechanisms," ways of suppressing, modulating, and "sublimating" the urges the id fueled into socially acceptable gratifications. It established harmony among all the forces of needs, ideals, and anticipations. The structural theory persisted, despite the disadvantage that it encouraged mechanistic thinking; the structures were not structures at all, but functions. What are "functions"? The kidneys' function is excretion. The ego mobilized "defenses." What does this mean? When did each defense originate, and which defenses were pathological?

The Metapsychology of Anna Freud and Heinz Hartmann

By the sixties, the structural theory of the mind had been modified and incorporated into what was called "metapsychology." Here was another attempt to classify factors involved in mental life by Anna Freud and others, particularly Heinz Hartmann. Metapsychology was a yet more complicated way of looking at mental phenomena. It suggested ways of describing what went on in the mind at any point. Metapsychology proposed five modes by which to approach mental functioning: topographic, dynamic, genetic, adaptive, and economic. "Economic" is the amount of force involved in fueling impulses, defenses, and mental functions—changing intensities of instinctual drives, modes of gratification and management (also influenced by maturation). "Dynamic" refers to the interplay between opposing forces engaged in conflict (sexual, aggressive, defensive) and gratification, that is, between ego (the proposed group of functions subsuming defensive forces that are mobilized to restrict them) and instinctual forces (whose gratification would be dangerous). Anxiety signals that the conflict between impulse and defense is not successfully balancing those two tendencies. "Genetic" is the history of the development and evolution of the existing state of affairs, in the context of biologic maturation, which influences the evolution of impulse-defense balances, as well as the capacities to cope with environmentally sourced trauma, gratification and their sequelae. "Adaptive" is the relationship of the mind to outside reality, the mental organization in its functioning as an instrument for recognizing, accommodating to, and changing the real context. "Topographic" refers to the levels of consciousness.

The application of these different points of view (and each of the five constituents was complex as well) greatly increased the range of factors to be considered in any mental phenomenon. A variety of terms was put forth to describe how all the many factors involved in the mind at any moment come together, including "overdetermination," "multiple function," "and "compromise formation." It became the task of the analyst to include all five approaches in reaching an understanding of any particular mental phenomenon. In other words, as in any other field of medicine or science, the metapsychological model's descriptive approach continued the evolution from the simplistic to the ever more complex. Anna Freud and Heinz Hartmann were the two most important developers of the meta-psychological model. Hartmann's "Ego Psychology and The Problem of Adaptation" and his presentation of psychoanalysis as general psychology connected individual, group, and social psychology under one umbrella.

Brenner vs Hartmann

As had Freud, Hartmann wanted to arrive at an understanding of mentation in general. He hoped to prod psychoanalysis along to become a general psychology, not simply an approach to dysfunction on a medical model; he wanted to account for adaptation, which included creativity, invention, art, as well as psychopathology. He was not sympathetic to those, like Charles Brenner, who wanted to limit the branches of knowledge to be applied to a general theory. Brenner was a purist and minimalist; for him, studies of infants or of children were useless in understanding development. I never really came to understand why only verbal communication could provide usable evidence about inner life. Brenner gradually refined his theoretical stance so that everything was fitted into the idea of "compromise formation, to my mind," a terminological variant of what predecessors (Freud, Anna Freud, Waelder, and Hartmann) had called "over-determination," "metapsychology," or "ego psychology."

The gain from proposing the all-inclusive idea of compromise formation is that it focuses attention on the fact that a multitude combine. A "mental moment" is an act, thought, and feeling, and the coincident unconscious processes going on in the mind, a fugitive moment, in the constantly changing activity in billions or trillions of brain networks that might theoretically be identified. If one could understand what the trillions of neurons in the brain are doing from millisecond to millisecond, one might reach—what? If we limit our information to the verbal, we lose much of the information that is exchanged via non-verbal communication. If we eliminate attempts to discover what was learned in the preverbal era, maturational events influencing psychological development, how do we learn more about the origins of mentation? We are in the early stage of finding ways to study the mind and physical body. Beyond saying that there is no mind without a living body, we have to separate our efforts to discover and study parts of a whole from different points of view.

What Happened Next in Analysis—My Time

One wants to try to understand how analytic work helps the patient become more realistically adapted to life. The patient comes to analysis with ideas and expectations that date back, for practical purposes, to before birth. The baby needs to be fed, soothed, and cleaned, to sleep, but also to be awake. His capacity to communicate his needs, initially, is very limited. He can scream, thrash about, turn red, smile, and calm down. The caretaker needs to respond to these happenings as though they were signs to be interpreted so as to provide the needed. Gradually, the baby comes to recognize people, and to modify and complicate his communications, but it takes a great long time, and lots of pleasing, and, by contrast, lots of painful experiences that teach him he is not the center of the world. Rather, he is only the center of his world. As a basic fact, people are members of the animal kingdom, and quite self-centered as a consequence.

Psychophysiology is complex. The brain has a huge number of cells and a huger number of possible circuits but, still, to keep up with a rapidly changing environment, to which we need to adapt, is quite a job. The medical, scientific, political, and social areas of study have had to be subdivided. To encompass recent developments in our world is clearly beyond the grasp of the most brilliant Renaissance mind. A result has been more sharing of tasks through an expansion of experts to manage a multiplication of specialty areas of expertise. We need a way to put it all together. What Moyer said in 1954, that we were learning things most of which would be obsolete in the near future, turned out to be only partially correct. It is not that aspirin doesn't still do what it always did, but that we know so much more about how it interrelates with other factors. It's not a question of a thing replacing something else that doesn't work, but of coming from manual shift cars to computer-driven robot Mars explorers. And handling hackers, to boot.

In the 1960s, for the most part, physical, medical illnesses were named for the affected organs (colon, liver), mainly via compound words as organ plus pathogen (carcinoma of organ, sarcoma of organ, leukemia). As time passed and information became more extensive, more was included in diagnoses. An "itis," for organ plus inflammation (hepatitis) might grow to three and four words (viral hepatitis type A, B, or C). Apparent physical signs like "yellow jaundice" might not be used, but "renal colic" might be. Eponyms could be added to descriptors. (Waldenström's macroglobulinemia, for example—the eponym suggests that there are other macroglobulinemias). One can combine four or five elements, even if someone's name is not included by adding more details and a stage of progression, (pulmonary left upper lobe small cell carcinoma, stage 4). The elaboration of terminology reflects the great increases in medical knowledge that continue to take place. The complexity of classification is also reflected in words shortened to letters, like T.I.A. (now more subtly described according to etiology, as AI clot emboli, a subtype). Then we have CAT scans, MRIs, ADHD, PTSD, and other acronyms. The days when terms stating particular organs and simple causes, such as genes, germs, parasites, toxins, allergens, or trauma were able to provide enough information to communicate the important aspects of a particular ailment are no more. The elaboration of information given in diagnosis has paralleled the multiplication of specialties in the medical profession.

"Doctor" no longer covers the three main historic specialties, surgeons, general medical practitioners, and pediatricians. Now we have sub-specialists and sub-sub-specialists, surgeons and medical doctors who specialize in knowing and treating problems involving tissues from the brain down to the rectum, from the bones to the skin, from infancy to senescence. Often, surgical procedures vie or coincide with medical, and medical help is divided among generalists and specialists. I now have an infectious-disease specializing internist who referred me to a cardiologist, who referred me to a hematologist who discovered that I have a polycythemia and referred me to a to a sleep specialist, who made a diagnosis of sleep apnea and wrote me a prescription to take to an appliance source who provided me with a CPAP (Continuous Positive Air Pressure) machine. Then we need a collection of ancillary specialists who operate CAT Scanners, MRI machines, DNA analyses, and oodles more. Functionaries work with payers and make appointments. Nurses specialize. Office staffs include multiple assistants who take blood pressures, EKGs, and bloods, and assist with insurers. Both the "consumers" and "providers" fill out forms that are processed by distant readers and their machines. I had a cardiac arrhythmia which required an emergency room team, and an induced coma, and eventually, a cardiac surgeon who specialized in minimally invasive heart valve replacement, followed by rehab specialists, swallowing physiologists, a urologist and so on, without all of whose labor I would certainly have died. I was also offered the services of a psychiatrist who specialized in such traumas.

Mental health professionals are now also divided into a large number of specialties, subspecialties, and sub-sub-specialties. In the psychological domain, we moved from having alienists and neuro-psychiatrists to the current confusing mélange of available choices among psycho-pharmacologists, psychologists, counselors, and psychoanalysts of different schools, all offering to treat mental problems. This situation also reflects the accumulation of knowledge, the availability of various physical, physiological, and psychological approaches to treatment, and expanding definitions of what can be done to help with previously unrecognized or untreatable difficulties. The causes of ailments are multiple and interrelated. So are the ways in which the body responds to the unwelcome intrusion, physiologically as well as psychologically.

Compromise formation is not an answer to "how?" It is the beginning of an expanding search for answers.

Mort Reiser During My Residency

During my residency at Albert Einstein, we had a continuous case seminar, meaning that someone who was doing long-term psychotherapy reported what went on in the sessions; the participants and leader discussed what they thought was happening. The leader was Mort Reiser, a forty-something old professor, a psychoanalyst, and an advocate of the psychosomatic work then going on at the NIMH, where research groups were looking at the mind-brain (psyche-soma) from the psychological and physiological points of view concurrently. They were interested in what they might garner from observing the words, expressions, and behavior of experimental subject volunteers and monitoring their physiologic conditions at the same time. Blood pressure, skin resistance, pulse and respiratory rates, and the like were monitored and recorded. It was demonstrated that fearful states of mind and elevated blood pressure coincided. Stress was known to be followed by hormonal and emotional changes. Dreaming was another area of interest. REM cycles observed by electroencephalography were shown to be coincident with body relaxation, rapid eye movements, sexual arousal (erections), and visual imagery in dreams.

That excited me. To look upon the mind and brain as not separate, but the same thing looked at from separate points of view, settled the mind-brain question for me. I put the distinction to rest. I enlisted in the search for answers to "how?' in a small corner of the vast realm of the possibly useful, in the army of inquirers.

The Pötzl Study

An early student of pyche-soma questions was rediscovered at that time. This was Otto Pötzl (1877-1962), a prolific neurologist and a leader of the Vienna school of neurology. He studied under Richard von Krafft-Ebbing, and Julius Wagner-Jauregg, following the latter as professor and director of the Vienna Psychiatric-Neurological University Clinic (1928–1945). He wrote over two hundred papers on a variety of subjects, (including aphasia, the subject of Freud's first book). Pötzl and Freud knew each other. Pötzl was a member of the Vienna Psychoanalytic Association between 1917 and 1933. In 1917 he published a paper that presented data supporting the finding that rebus puzzles presented to subjects subliminally (below the threshold of conscious perception) could be solved unconsciously and that the solutions might appear in subsequent dreams. A rebus is a puzzle where the task is to combine pictured drawings of objects and words to present a composite meaning. In a confirmatory study, a momentary flash of light containing a subliminal rebus showing the word "tie" and a drawing of a knee was shown to a colleague of mine, at the time a college student volunteer subject in Chicago. She dreamed about a group of tiny people. The tie and knee had been combined to make tiny figures.

In the late fifties and early sixties, unconscious mental activity was a fashionable lab subject again. That unconscious factors influence conscious thought was a significant finding about how the mind works. Having rediscovered Pötzl, investigators combined the Pötzl technique with physiological measurement to bring in somatic connections as well. It seemed important to build on the Freudian notion that unconscious processing influences what we now regard as the evolutionarily more advanced cortex-influenced cognition. At the same time, the understanding of disease had proceeded to a point where the influence of mental states of arousal and experiencing could be shown to influence physiologic changes. The connection between mental perception and physiologic consequences, as well as between unconscious processes and conscious thought and behavior, could be studied. Behavior had to be examined from different points of view—psychological, biological and social. There was a great deal of interest in dreaming in relation to consciousness as well as to cognition.

I elected to undertake research with Mort Reiser. The study of psychosomatic ailments was proceeding with approaches guided by more appreciation that unexpected variables were parties in the mix of influencing factors. My idea was to diminish the number of variables in the Pötzl situation by eliminating the rebus in the light flash. Modern physiological instruments would still record measurements of ongoing somatic referents (GSR, pulse, and respiratory rates). Without the rebus, there would be only a flash of light and a request to the subject to generate a response. We assumed that would leave the relation to the experimenter and his task as the stimulus, another element we thought deserved attention.

The GSR (Galvanic Skin Resistance) is an important lie detector-indicator because it allows the investigator to compare physiological arousal responses to innocuous questions with responses to troublesome ones. To need to conceal a secret is to experience danger. The ongoing verbal lie communication is contradicted by the unvocalized fight or flight type emotional state. That is measurable by GSR (and other physiological) fluctuations. What if one presents a request, not a test? The experimenter simply asks for a reaction to a flash of light. That is more like the open-ended request that a prospective psychotherapy patient explain why she came to the consultant: "Start by telling me what's on your mind, whatever it might be." A person who comes to seek help has fears and secrets, as does anyone, but if there is an experienced danger, it is probably milder than it would be in an interrogation. (A physiological response similar to the variable responses to a lie detector would probably accompany turmoil in a therapy, but that represents an opportunity for the patient to examine an underlying problem; it is not an occasion for a sentencing.) The subject is not challenged or tested: the situation remains that of an experiment and an experimenter interacting with a subject in acquiring useful information.

Reiser and I used college bulletin boards to offer students a chance to participate in an ongoing psychophysiological study, for modest pay. The subject would arrive in the lab, sit in a chair facing a screen, and be told that he would watch the screen, see a series of brief flashes of light, then close his eyes and draw what he had seen on a piece of paper and describe it to the experimenter. He would be attached to some instruments that would record physiological changes. At the end of the series of flashes, he would tell the experimenter what he had drawn. Then he would get a look at his drawings, including any he might have forgotten, and tell any related thoughts that came to his mind. The arrangement did without the ink blot of a Rorschach, using the drawings of the subjects' spontaneous visual experiences as responses to be interpreted instead. An example was a Tom Seaver (a well-known pitcher) fastball flying out of the drawing paper toward the subject. The interpretation was that the experimental situation was one where the subject felt he was being thrown a fastball. Looking at the physiological measures, one saw that they, no surprise, showed activation (increased heart rate, etc.).

Reception of Our Work on the Pötzl Phenomenon

Heinz Hartmann read the resulting paper. Initially, he didn't say much, but the next morning he phoned me and said he liked the paper very much, it was quite original, and I should remember that he had often been criticized for wandering and making his arguments include too many asides. The best part of the reception of that paper was what Hartmann (another non-linear thinker) thought. That was a mild suggestion that I try a more direct approach in my reporting. I could have been clearer (and more punny) had I said that responses to the flash were more like screen memories—false or edited, reinterpreted recollections, masking other memories of deep emotional significance. The people created pictures, evoked from a simple flash on a screen, which represented events, frightening past happenings, that lay behind the screen, as a fast ball. The images represented future pain, presumably less traumatic than an earlier analogue and also possible to duck or maybe even hit back. And they were created in the context of successfully accomplishing an assigned task.

The good thing was that I had received a hearing. A bad aspect was that the paper didn't get published. At the time, Reiser was the editor of the *Journal of Psychosomatic Medicine*, and the president of the Psychosomatic Medicine Society, and felt it wouldn't be appropriate to publish his own work there. It was also not really neurological enough for a neurology journal, or psychoanalytic enough for a psychoanalytic journal. At any rate, the psychoanalytic world has become much more receptive to the information that is being produced by neuroscience and brain science than it was then, so this unpublished work is a source of pride to me now. But I was too timorous to assert myself when there seemed to be no suitable place to publish my work.

PSYCHOANALYSIS

Why Psychoanalysis? Back to My Inner World

I thought that psychoanalysis, which entailed psychoanalytic training following my residency, a schooling which would continue for some years, would be the route for me to follow. Psychopharmacology, which is now probably the main field in which psychiatrists can make a decent living, was only in its infancy at the time. Almost everyone who studied psychiatry then applied for psychoanalytic training. I say "almost," because there were institutions that held out and did not teach "dynamic" or "Freudian" psychology.

In fact, I needed analysis. Embarking upon it would benefit me by introducing me to a lengthy process enabling me to become healthier. During my residency, I was between the Devil and the deep blue sea: balancing my responsibilities as husband, doctor, and all-round mature adult while still hoping for the protective patronage of a mentor or other parental figure.

The Unconscious Pilot

Man lives with an unconscious pilot who insists on nudging here and there. Some are luckier than others in their pilot. I had questions. That a question comes out of left-field may relate to the limits of consciousness; consciousness seems to be constrained by the number of trains of thought that can be processed at one time. Unconsciously, a large number of processes go on concurrently; sometimes something pops up into consciousness—it can be clever or not so clever. Fearsome ideas can be imaginary, yet realistic, just as comforting ideas can be reassuring, but unrealistic. Dragons and Nazis are alike in being frightening; maybe Nazis glory in their feelings of being dragons—they can behave as dragons do, after all, spouting fire and smoke.

We invent things: if I have no memories of having experienced a particular new idea or object before, then I suppose that it was in my pilot/phenomenon and rose to my consciousness, or it just appeared from nothing. Or else I had forgotten it had been there before. I'll never know for sure, and it doesn't really matter. Some basic suppositions are formed before they can be evaluated rationally at all, but eventually they can be uncovered and reviewed. Sometimes, something seems really good to the one-track-at-a-time consciousness, even though the judgment says "unlikely to prove helpful."

We can apply our one-track conscious apparatus to tracing the trail left by the footprints of the congenial experience of a creative moment. As Einstein said, there is an external reality, independent of the presence of man; we can learn a lot about that reality. Freud gave us a way of approaching the inner, animal reality.

For the religious, study is unnecessary, even forbidden, because faith in revelation that comes from the incomprehensible creator is all that is needed. In the beginning was the Word.

Scientifically, looking for explanations, we have reached as far back as the big bang, but not the Word. We can be practical and leave metaphysics to metaphysicians. Meanwhile, we can attend to the expansion of knowledge of what can be studied.

An idea that had never come to my mind occurred to a rabbi, who passed it along to his audience at Temple Emanu-El, in New York, at Warren Manshel's funeral. Warren died of kidney cancer, two years after his wife Anita died of stomach cancer. Both were in their sixties, and were kind, generous, productive, wonderful people; the rabbi used these words in describing them, but then said that none of us can understand how, or why, such things happen. This proved, he insisted, the existence of God; the reasoning here appears to be, we cannot comprehend the whys and wherefores of our friends' deaths, and we cannot comprehend God. If only God can make a tree, he alone must have made everything else, including the incomprehensible; only God, himself incomprehensible, can comprehend the incomprehensible. Does there have to be a beginning and end of the universe? If the lifespan of a man is generalized, and becomes the model for the universe, then, "Yes." If not, then, "No." Meanwhile we can study.

My First Analysis: Milt Rosenbaum, Lou Robbins, & Edith Jacobson

My first attempt at psychoanalysis was a failure. Del Close of the Compass Players made a wonderful LP, in which he assumed the role of an analyst who maintained that analysis is always useful because "from every failure, we learn something."

In the early sixties, it was difficult to find an analyst with time enough to work with me. I knew that I would need a training analyst in order to become a psychoanalyst myself—psychoanalytic institutions appointed some of their members to teach, analyze, and supervise their students. It turned out that all the training analysts I knew of had long waiting lists, so I asked Milt Rosenbaum to recommend an analyst for me. He suggested Lew Robbins, who had recently moved from Topeka to take over the leadership of the psychiatric department at Hillside Hospital, Long Island. Having recently arrived, Robbins had time for new patients.

I commuted to Hillside Hospital for sessions. Several factors combined to make it difficult for me to be candid with him. I knew that, if all went well, and I stayed in New York as a student and was accepted at the New York Psychoanalytic Institute, I would change analysts. Second, after a few months of meeting with Robbins, I felt he and I did not connect. Third, Robbins developed an illness which kept him away for several months, and in the style of many analysts of the time, he gave me no information about what went on. He canceled our appointments. This activated—although I would not recognize it until a later analysis—my historic fear about being kept in the dark, as had happened in my family. That character trait was one of the reasons I needed help. Fourth, when he recommended Robbins, Milton Rosenbaum had told me that Robbins was likely to become president of the American Psychoanalytic Association, which would help my career. Careerism was not respectable, in my view.

When he returned to work, I was disappointed and angry. I closed up and distanced myself, and after a further few months, he told me I was "unanalyzable." This should have confirmed my impression that being with him was useless, but I took his opinion seriously. By then I had been accepted for training, and I felt like an impostor. If I was unanalyzable, I could not become an analyst. Another reason for having analysis.

Fortunately, I was healthy enough to ask for another opinion, and with help from Robi Bak (a soul brother, who taught at Einstein), I was able to schedule an appointment for a consultation with Edith Jacobson, a highly respected senior psychoanalyst, originally German. She was a pillar of the more humane European medical manner of psychoanalysts, in which normal social and professional relationships are observed. I explained how I had gone to Lew Robbins, at the recommendation of Milt Rosenbaum, and how he had recommended Robbins as a potential president of the American Psychoanalytic Association; I noted a displeased expression on Jacobson's face. I went on with the Lew Robbins story, and how he compounded my concern about his absence by giving no explanation of it. Then I told her I had had training admissions interviews before the "unanalyzable" diagnosis was delivered, and Robbins and I had parted and I didn't know what to do. Should I inform the Institute? Withdraw my application?

Jacobson tut-tutted a bit about Robbins' diagnosis, and asked me to tell her about myself. I had a totally different response to her than I had had to practically anyone else. I proceeded to tell my story—the war, emigration, my mother's bicycle accident, the rejection by most of my early teachers and classmates, and, finally, my mother's multiple sclerosis. At that point, Jacobson said, "That must have made a huge burden for you," and a bright "Eureka" flash went off in my head. Nobody had ever said anything like that to me in my life, and I had never dared think it myself; but, of course, my mother's illness had an enormous effect on me. My feeling had always been that my mother was a heroic victim, and I, the undeserving, somewhat disappointing beneficiary of her sacrifice—I caused her stretch marks, she wanted a girl, and all the rest.

The question arises, why did I not previously recognize the obvious truth which Edith Jacobson revealed to me? Why was her intervention even necessary? It was because I could not tolerate the reality that I did not have a strong mother; my mother's bicycle accident was a shock, partly because it aroused my awareness of her actual weakness. Partly, I was ashamed to be pleased, as a rival of Fritzl. I was entitled to as much attention as my brother was (I failed to consider age-appropriateness).

Oddly enough, the matter of entitlement came to be associated with a Heinz Hartmann idea. That was, the "Average Expectable Environment," a notion one could use to assess deviations from a conceivable norm. Who has a "right" that makes him "entitled" to live in an average acceptable environment, have average expectable parents, health, and so on? I could see how people could feel entitled to health care, or a functioning government, or property rights; but I could think of no way these things could be entitlements, particularly if we decided that everybody was entitled to an average expectable environment.

What is expectable? War? Disease? I was amazed that I had lived as long as I had, thinking that a person could actually be entitled to such things, without realizing how unrealistic I was. Bill of Rights indeed. Life, Liberty, and the Pursuit of Happiness? Liberty, Equality, Fraternity?

It ends up that that the "average expectable environment" is but a region on a curve, to which nobody is entitled: the unpleasant realization that one lives among others—*inter alia*—and is benefited by acknowledging the limitations of one's powers to influence one's environment. To do so requires a lot of experiences and a great deal of acceptance of one's capacities and limitations.

Beginning in my adolescence, I had consistently blamed my father for my family's financial plight at emigration. My father never gave any explanation, and Steinitz's later one jarred my belief that my family was my father's only interest and responsibility. He had to make choices, and one of them had to do with his responsibility to his clients and to his reputation.

"Shrinkage"

Psychoanalysts are lightly taunted by being called "shrinks," in analogy to headhunters who shrink their trophy heads. A less concrete analogy is that they are involved in shrinking narcissistic grandiosity in their client collaborators. Not that I forgive my father for his failure to talk to me. The news from Steinitz supported my realization that I had no entitlement to preferential treatment, even from my father. I wanted preferential treatment, to the extent that I felt a lack of it as if it were a "real" betrayal. I feel doomed to carry this feeling around with me, even though on a rational level, I know better. "Unforgivable" and "betrayal" are almost permanently joined together. I think that disappointment can be tolerated, and even accepted, relatively easily in comparison to the other feeling; I now think the betrayal is more likely to be, at least partly, unforgivable. The realization that talent doesn't come with rights to good teachers, or concert seats, I suppose I now define as shrinkage. Shrinkage is possible, and useful, though disagreeable. One advantage is that a shrunken capacity excuses a diminished responsibility. The shrinkage leaves the shrunken one a bit more freedom to feel comfortable about his limitations.

My Second Analysis, With Martin Stein

I accepted that I should attend the Institute. I had a good impression of the three people who had interviewed me. Martin Stein was one of them. I had been accepted for training, and he was another who didn't think I was unanalyzable, and my draft status was changed—one rejection that did not hurt. I began my second analysis—with Stein.

I responded to my conversation with Edith Jacobson with the comforting idea that a useful relationship with the analyst requires a sense of connection and, within limits, one wants the analyst to supply objectivity with empathy. I came to be more sensitive to the influence of the imponderable in connection with interrelationships. I also came to have more respect for my need for connection and for others' similar needs. My impression that talk therapy is a very incomplete name grew. Much more than talk is involved in any relationship, including that of analyst and analysand. You cannot conceal what you cannot conceal; Freud declared as much. My experience with Edith Jacobsen underlined the point. I soon knew that anonymity was not possible or desirable for anyone, including one's analyst. So it was with Dr. Stein.

I never had the feeling that Dr. Stein felt superior or inferior to me, or to anyone else; he could be critical, even disdainful of other people, but that did not mean that he felt superior. He was very self-assured, even Socratic. If Socrates really believed that the wise should be the teachers and leaders and ought to be listened to and studied but that, unfortunately, the followers were likely to object out of envy and resentment, that wisdom did not make him superior. Socrates, after all, took the poison, when a duly constituted jury had condemned him. Sometimes it is socially more reasonable to accept the death sentence (or to refrain from giving a true, tactless, and hurtful observation to a patient prematurely, just because you have understood some truth). Better yet, try to wait for the right moment to speak, when the patient is prepared.

The fact about me, as I came to understand it, was that I was never important and powerful enough to represent a serious threat to my analysts, or to my father. They were not so powerful as I wanted them to be; they didn't have the power to make me as important as I wanted to be, either. They were older and wiser, perhaps more—or less—gifted than I, and more or less fortunate in where and when they lived, but that did not make me or them superior; no more than, as a musician, Hildegard von Bingen was either inferior or superior to Mozart, who might have been better or worse than but not superior to Salieri. One is limited to the criterion of abler, or less able; to be powerful is a matter of circumstance. That must be the point of view of the analyst to the client.

Unfortunately, my father died young, at sixty, and I lost the opportunity to have a closer, less defensive and aggressive relationship with him. I waited too long; in retrospect that turns out to have been something I wish I could take back. We all would be better off if childish ideas about superiority and inferiority, and their relationship to power, diminished more as life passes; this not being the case, into the breach comes the sometimes attacked and unappreciated psychoanalyst. We hope the psychoanalyst knows that even when the patient's assessment of him is correct—that he is rigid, tired, mistaken, insensitive, too insistent or tactless—the patient is working with a transference (redirection of feelings and desires, especially those unconsciously retained from childhood onto a new person or thing—in this case the analyst), which affects his response to these manifestations of human frailty. Within limits, of course, we all have to come to expect—if with disappointment—a certain degree of frailty in ourselves, our teachers, and doctors. Generally, this may be so on a conscious or rational level, but remains unacceptable on an emotional level; the patient has to be patient with the analyst. Dr. Stein was clear in stating that I needed forbearance, not perfection.

In my thirties, I was not sure that I was an authentic person who had genuine feelings. I was still in my win-lose, superior-inferior, mode of feeling, and my affectionate aspect was squeezed to the side. For instance, my mother's health problems caused me much pain, but guilt was the major conscious source of it, not sympathy, or frustrated affection, which, then, was buried. I still, in the way of a child, took her frailty as a fault as well as a deprivation; this imbalance shifted with the passage of time and experience. At some point, I realized that my parents had a lot on their minds other than me, and quite a few of those were more important to them ("Aha"). Being the younger of two, I had to cope with the reality that I could be replaced. Still, every pain, from disappointment to disaster, arouses vindictiveness. If there is no better word than wisdom to describe what it is that permits me to feel less abandonment and betrayal and to have more sympathy and compassion than before, then let's call it wisdom. That was what I needed to develop, when I began with Stein.

I processed Stein's behavior with me, with him. He interviewed me and passed me on to admission to psychoanalytic training. I knew he had two daughters and no sons; Stein probably would have liked to have a son. Using that knowledge, and that he had admitted me and taken me as a patient, I theorized that he was looking for a son, and had therefore overlooked my lack of genuineness. As I was faking affection and interest, and was basically a greedy, self-seeking hypocrite, perhaps I was fooling him. After all, my first contact with an analyst left me with a diagnosis of unanalyzable. It is true that Jacobson's opinion was very much more benign, and that I had been evaluated by three experienced people and accepted. It took a long time for me to know how much guilt I carried around (that realization came later). Guilt demands punishment. I took the matter up with Stein very early in our work. His response was, "If what you think is so, (that he took me on because he wanted a son) it can be so, (he could want a son) and also transference" (I wanted him to adopt me because I felt I needed a father, mentor, patron because I felt weak, plus, it was also so that realistically, à la Rosenbaum, I had ulterior motives as well. (I wanted to enlist him as a practical supporter.) Another nail in the coffin of either-or thinking.

Psychoanalytic Studies and the Birth of Nicole

In 1962, my psychiatric training at the Bronx Municipal Hospital Center ended. I moved to the Albert Einstein College of Medicine's labs and I supervised the clinical work of some of my juniors. I began psychoanalytic studies at the New York Psychoanalytic Institute and my analysis with Martin Stein. I began a psychotherapy practice and welcomed a daughter to the world. My first meeting with Nicole was when I was shown her, held by a nurse who was combing her hair.

If it was something akin to love at first sight with Barbara, then it was the same with Nicole.

During the course of that year, Jack and Lillian invited Barbara and me to join them at a dinner at the Waldorf Astoria to raise money for the Democratic party. Before being seated, we joined a receiving line. I don't remember whether President Kennedy was there or not, but I do remember the handshake with the Vice-President, Lyndon Johnson; he managed to squeeze my hand twice in an instant, at the same time reaching for the next person and, I imagine, doing the same with him. I was easily impressed by the important figures there, and I relished being given the job of reserving a table at the Plaza Hotel's Oak Room for drinks after the event, with Mayor Robert Wagner and his wife, Phyllis. Barbara and I were well known to the headwaiter; we frequently had supper there after theater or musical events. We were on such good terms with the maître d', Mario, that when Barbara gave birth to Nicole, I went there for dinner with Brigitte, then Altman; and Mario fixed me with a cold Italian look and asked, meaningfully, with his eyes suspiciously fixed on my companion, "And where is Mrs. Kafka this evening?" Like the Italian Papa (and manager) he was, he sent some Champagne when I told him where Barbara was.

The General Status of Psychoanalysis From 1962 and Later on the Conservative Side; the Confluence of European and American Thought; Development of the DSM

When I was at medical school, Washington University had a chairman of psychiatry who was thought to be a psychoanalyst in the community, but whose training had consisted of spending part of a summer with Carl Jung in Switzerland. When he retired, his replacement's executive officer was a man who had trained in internal medicine, and never in a psychiatry program. The chairman himself was a pioneer of the effort to define diseases on the basis of behaviors which could be objectively noted and measured. Hysteria, for example, had, as one of the criteria for making the diagnosis, that the sufferer had undergone a number of unnecessary surgical operations. In a class of 85 medical students, two went into psychiatry, one as a hospital psychiatrist, and the other specializing in treating alcoholics. The DSM (Diagnostic and Statistical Manual) was his offspring. "Perversions" were included among the "diseases." The book was repeatedly updated and given the title DSM 1,2,3, et seq. Apparently, the DSM was an idea that appealed to insurers and doctors who needed to have well-defined diseases to treat.

St. Louis had three members of the American Psychoanalytic Association in residence; one lectured at the medical school, and another later became president of the Association. After my departure, a well-respected child analyst joined the group. Analysis was sparsely represented in other big cities.

Psychoanalysis remained heavily influenced by central European, especially Austrian, culture. Austria-Hungary was a polyglot mixture of regions, languages, religions, and customs; Vienna was a capital that attracted ambitious people from both the provinces and major cities of all those many regions; there was a culture of interchange of views and ideas. The factions in Vienna had their own newspapers, and they hung from hooks in the cafés, where anyone could sit and read them. Austrian history was filled with agreements, and disagreements, within and between the factions; there never was a simply binary division. *Kultur* was admired, and complexity accepted by a significant part, at least, of the intelligentsia. From a current perspective, Vienna looks like an early League of Nations, which collapsed when nationalism, the industrial revolution, and migration sundered the remaining feudal relics. As Beethoven and Brahms had become Austrian when they settled in Vienna, as Handel became British in London, and as Hitler became German, the talent and energy drifted to the greater powers. With the war, many left the small nations for the great ones. Thus, the United States became a home for talented psychoanalysts and physicists, but fifteen years after I left St. Louis, chairs of psychiatry departments still thought of themselves as pioneers. St. Louis was probably among the majority as to medical school opinion.

The American Psychoanalytic Association is a national organization, made up of local analytic societies, some of which, like New York, have training institutes. In my time, only MDs were accepted for training and allowed to become members, except that certain refugees who were not medical doctors, but had been trained by Freud and some of his early students and followers in Europe, were admitted. In Europe, Freud never restricted his following by requiring more than talent and interest.

Understandably, there were divisions among psychoanalysts. Many favored a rigorous orthodoxy, which included presenting themselves as objective observers and eschewing anything personal in their relationships with patients. They maintained that the analyst-patient pair can, and should, follow the model of surgeon and patient, or of two sitting next to a window of a train, of whom one describes the passing scene to his companion at the aisle who remains anonymous.

These analysts took Freud's 60-some-year-old recommendations to beginners as standards.

The less rigorous liberals were more likely to give themselves the freedom of action that Freud displayed in his actual clinical work. They were mostly Central Europeans who were more likely to treat patients and conduct themselves as people with the usual polite, well-mannered consideration of the professional for the patient and his troubles. They and American-trained colleagues formed a second group and, by and large, had identifiably different styles.

Some thought talk-therapy could cure "psychosomatic" diseases, such as asthma, duodenal ulcer, or ulcerative colitis. They were wrong: they were treating neuroses and character problems in people who lived with organ pathology. Duodenal ulcer, it turned out, is largely a bacterial disease, caused by a microbe that thrives in the presence of the unlikely environment of high acidity. A second factor, a congenital tendency toward high-acid gastric juice, plays a part.

Ulcerative colitis involves an autoimmune reaction. There were proponents of treating schizophrenia, manic-depression, depression, "perversions," and other ailments, for which there was little other effective help at the time, with psychotherapy or psychoanalysis. There were analysts who refused to treat patients who wanted to have medical or surgical and psychological treatment at the same time: this was supposed to "dilute the transference." There was also an effort to "cure" homosexuality.

All these were regarded by some as psychologically accessible diseases. In retrospect, these enthusiasts turned out to have been overreaching. Analysis can certainly help people cope with diseases, as with other burdens. Apparently physical ills have sources in genetic predispositions, as do psychoses and the cognitive deficits. We now know more about the effects of psychic trauma and that psychotherapy, as well as pharmacology, can help with its unwelcome effects. The general trend in science, and certainly in the biological sciences, is that every discovery leads to the conclusion that everything is more complex than we thought.

As a psychiatry resident physician, I learned some psychopharmacology, but not much. There were not many useful drugs at the time. Thorazine had serious harmful side effects (especially a Parkinson-like neurologic condition, Tardive Dyskinesia). We had electric shock treatment for severe depression, and insulin shock was also available. Prefrontal lobotomy, wet blankets, straitjackets, work therapy, and exercise were all in use. Why not psychotherapy at the same time?

What constitutes psychotherapy, and what constitutes psychoanalysis, has been argued for a long time. A definition would be that psychoanalysis is a psychotherapy where two people are involved, and the inner life of one is the focus while the other is a trained observer and commentator. The emotional interrelationships of the two, who it turns out cannot avoid having interrelationships, are central factors for both parties to identify and re-think. A crude comparison might be that analysis focuses more on feelings, dreams, and historical, developmental determinants of relationships. Psychotherapies can have a similar structure, but often the therapist plays a more educational part, and events and real current experiences are more important. De-conditioning to help with phobias, cognitive techniques, and support groups are examples. Psychotherapies can involve groups, such as families or people with related problems, such as alcoholism, phobias, or other social issues, where members can create an atmosphere, freely express their ideas and feelings, and share their responses to each other's presentations. This covers a range, from twelve-step programs, where the members of the group share their thoughts with each other without a professional interlocutor who focuses on them, through group and family therapy, where there is a person trained to facilitate and mediate discussion, and then there is a two person, more "classical" psychoanalysis, where two people work together, one as the protagonist who came for help, and the other as the helper.

That requires a re-self-education that teaches the protagonist to think about himself as an evolving being, a part of nature in the milieu of the changing world outside. A fundamental, hard-to-learn lesson is that whatever is considered has complex causes involving multiple interacting factors and complex effects. Some are innocuous, some profound, and others are dangerous. Learning, adapting to change, ending relationships and replacing them are possible throughout life. A person's every act expresses a choice among alternatives; whatever is chosen is at the expense of something else. It follows that, as beings who have many desires, any one wish will be in conflict with others, some of which are capable of being harmonized with others, and some that are not. My mother said, "*Mit ein Popo kann mann nicht auf zwei Sesseln zur zelben zeit sitsen.*" With one bottom one cannot sit on two chairs at the same time. That is not entirely accurate as most choices do not entirely eliminate every other. In that sense "compromise formation" is an optimistic term. At the same time, we are far from knowing what all the compromising factors are, how they interact, and what is excluded.

Psychoanalysis as Valid Science; The Oedipus Complex

My embrace of psychoanalysis was derided in some quarters; some of the psychiatrists at Einstein were of the opinion that analysis flattered the self-indulgent wishes of wealthy Park Avenue ladies who lunch. That part of this criticism indicated a misogynistic attitude that was not particularly rare. Occasional discussions revolved around the question, "Were there not more important things to do?" Important? Another immeasurable.

Sidney Hook was a philosophy professor. He participated in a discussion group that included Heinz Hartmann and Jacob Arlow, and the proceedings were published in *Partisan Review*. He maintained that to convincingly present something as scientific truth, you needed to give "Yes" answers to two questions: "Does the phenomenon to be understood appear in response to a particular cause, and can it be present in the absence of that cause?" He thought that since Freud proposed that the Oedipus complex is invariably present, it could not be accepted as a scientific explanation. If one cannot design an experiment where the phenomenon can only appear with the cause, and not if that cause is absent, i.e., if the cause is always present, then the proposition cannot be supported. When Hook discovered that I was a psychoanalyst, he taxed me with these questions, which he had raised with many analysts, including Arlow and Hartmann, about the Oedipus complex. Once we insisted that the Oedipus is universal and could not propose what the world could be in its absence, it failed as a valid theoretical idea.

I replied, with the question, "Sidney, I understand that you have a daughter and a son. Is that correct?"

"Yes, it is."

"How would you describe your relationship with your son?"

"Very good, but he's argumentative and hates to agree with me."

"And how about with your daughter?"

"Oh, we understand each other very well. We get along splendidly. She's a pleasure."

"And have you any friends who have noticed a similar difference with their kids?"

"As a matter of fact, often."

"Well, that's the Oedipus complex."

"Hmm. Nobody's ever put it that way before…"

I realized that what I had said was a smart-alecky simplification; on the other hand, his challenge was, in its way, also a smart-alecky simplification. I was original in my smart-alecky response; Sidney Hook respected the response he got to his challenge. Indeed, I could have described the conversation to him as reflecting an Oedipal relationship. My point is that in St. Louis and in New York at that time, in intellectual, psychiatric, and medical circles, psychoanalysis was often not highly valued and is still, as then, poorly understood.

More on the Oedipus Complex

"Oedipus complex" is a convenient simplification of a universal of the human's social condition. It is a label, not a definition, for inevitable and universal aspects of mental life; it is a metaphor, which subsumes many relationships. Freud started with a family triad. Boy child desires to possess mother and wants to be rid of the rival father à la Conrad

Sommer. Boy child wants to be receptive, to receive love from mother and father, and at the same time be active, and rid himself of one or the other parent. Any combination of three people, all with both receptive and active desires and sexual identities, is Oedipal. One can add siblings to the mix. We can divide the "Oedipal" crowd of *dramatis personae* to describe active, passive, assertive, submissive, aggressive, receptive, expressive, sexual, and other aspects of social interaction, and give subtitles to each of the combinations we extract from the mélange—as it exists in all its incomprehensible actuality—and create Oedipuses to our hearts' content. There is no unique Oedipus complex; relationships between men, women, and in groups, are fluctuating and complicated. That is one reason psychoanalyses last so long. A second reason is that you do need to know that it's hard to teach old circuits to re-form. A third common issue is that accepting ideas from other people as useful can be difficult, while "borrowing" them is easier. Understanding Oedipal impacts is easier with examples. As a child, Freud felt that his father humiliated him by being unmanly, stepping off a sidewalk into a street, and submitting to a Gentile who ordered the Jew out of the way. Years later, Freud proposed his seduction theory, which explained hysteria as a response to childhood seduction of little girls by fathers; this explanation was partly fueled by competitiveness and anger with his father. Before much time passed, he retracted that idea, having discovered that the seduction idea reflected his Oedipal competitive need to disparage his father.

My son, Michael, once insisted that when he was a child, I had very little to do with him; his evidence was that I spent most of my time in my office, that I did not discuss my work with him, except in general terms, and he was thereby excluded from my life. Naturally, that reminded me of my complaints against my own father; that I was an unwanted second child; he only gave in to my mother and then left me to her. He was a bad father because he felt obliged to do his fiduciary duties, to put his clients' interests ahead of his own family's; he was unmanly, and humbly deferential toward the Fould-Springers. On a trip to visit Washington D.C., my father caught me with a roll of Lifesaver mints, and responded with a humiliating and painful, angry, public slap in my face, because he had forbidden me to spend money on candy. In that instance he was not distant enough.

In an episode when, as a seven-year-old, I chased Peter Myron across a street, Miss Keenan, my second-grade teacher, was driving down the street, and that afternoon I received a merited lecture from her. I tried to lie my way out of being blamed and claimed that I was the one who was chased. I thought I was going to be punished for being aggressive, and I was embarrassed to realize that my teacher, whom I had painted as mainly punitive, was really more concerned that she might have run into me, than that I was being a bad boy. Of course, from the family point of view, at least in the instant of my father's slap, I was being punished for being defiant. My parents were rarely punitive; I was provocative and succeeded in getting my father to lose his temper. I was not simply a victim. Actually, I made much capital out of that for years after using it as an excuse for opposing or withholding behaviors.

The feeling of being excluded by an uncaring father had to be processed in some reassuring way. The stories about how lucky I was to have been brought into the world despite my father's one-child-only preference, as told by my mother, were seductive and easy to use, to justify me in my resentments and dad rationalizations. Like Sigmund Freud, I condemned my father, when convenient, as hostile and depriving toward me, but I also applied the criticism of hostile intrusiveness. He didn't deliver what I wanted, when I wanted it; he also meddled in my life. When I needed to, I treated my mother similarly. I didn't like performing for my parents and their guests at dinner parties. I could easily be unavailable or intrusive.

Naturally, as a small child, I didn't realize that adults were not put into the world to serve me; as a bigger child, I retained much of my earlier narcissism. I didn't know that it takes a long time for children to grow up and mature, and although my parents told me that it would happen, I failed to understand what that meant; I started to accept that unwelcome news when I realized that size made it so. Kids grew bigger—no effort, no agency, automatically, in time. Bigger people could row and steer boats; I was too small. I also realized that the larger people were not only bigger and stronger than I was but were also the source of food and care and of information, useful, useless, welcome, unwelcome. As time passed, I developed a new capacity—to tell time, and not only for days and nights. Having birthdays helped; a year was a long time. I accepted some of the more unwelcome aspects of what I eventually came to know as what is meant by "infantile" and later, "juvenile," and still later, "adult."

It's Not All About Me

Retrospectively, I am sure I was accepted as mature enough to be included in the family news much too late; I was not informed of my grandmother, Mami's death when I was in medical school, nor did I hear of Gusti's death at a later time. It took me a long time (and much psychoanalytic work) to realize that this method of childrearing had deleterious results for me. My parents had advertised it as for my benefit; but some of the benefits were theirs—keeping me around as a companion for my mother and avoiding potentially embarrassing revelations of inability to manage by confessing their weaknesses. In my father's case, he was the orphan who wanted to be part of a family but one competitor for his status (my elder brother) was enough. His negative feelings were about having a second child (my mother's), wanting a little girl, not another boy, and later, wanting a companion.

In other words, it turned out that my parents were humans, whose sole desire in life was not bringing up a healthy child. In fact, they both competed with me and, in subtle ways, abused me.

Awareness of the humanness of my parents came as an eye-opener during my Stein analysis, when the analyst and I discussed the question of the fee, its amount, and when it had to be paid. He demanded payment for his time, whether or not I showed up for the session. I held that giving notice in advance should allow me to not pay. He made it plain that he would agree to that only when he could use the hour for another consultation; he reminded me of the idea I had that I was entitled to good opera seats, as I was so gifted. Aha: neither the doctor nor my parents nor the performers were there just for me! They all had their own personal interests. People do not have children out of pure altruism; my parents were just reasonably normal, somewhat selfish people. The beneficial lesson: I was not responsible for the sad aspect of my case; farewell, a bit of guilt and a bit of inferiority complex. There's no cookbook recipe.

Thanks to analysis, I came to some degree of acceptance of the facts. I came to know my father's and brother's points of view were similar to mine, among other feelings about my existence, including affection, and amusement. At times they regarded me as a competing, and often burdensome, intruder—as I felt about them.

The Decision to Turn from Research to Interpersonal Psychiatric and Psychoanalytic Practice

When Mort Reiser told me that I would have to submit a grant proposal on my own to apply to the NIMH, the National Institute for Mental Health, for further funding, my response made it clear to both of us that I didn't really have the kind of focused need that good researchers have; I was better off teaching and treating people. I am sure that Mort had already come to that conclusion. I had asked his advice about what to write. He responded: "Take a look at what you've found, find a way to describe parts of it that you'd like to find out more about and what you expect to find through your research, and that is your proposal." I said that if I knew what I was expecting to find, I wouldn't need a grant; I wanted a grant to lead to results I wasn't expecting to find. Reiser responded that he completely understood my attitude, but that what he had told me was what needed to be done.

It didn't appeal very much, and I didn't continue my research career. I had finished my residency by then; we had presented a first paper at the annual Psychosomatic Society meetings. I continued to run the experiment for the larger follow-up paper. That was completed and presented at the New York Psychoanalytic Society. I remained curious about the interchanges between levels of consciousness—like reverie or hypnosis—not quite the tripartite divisions with barriers between at least the lower two and the uppermost level Freud posited. I thought of fluid mingling. However, I had made my choice. I made no grant proposal. I was going to be a member of the psychoanalytic club, not the Stagecoach Club. Mort Reiser and I remained close until his death, and I still feel close to his widow, my gifted professional colleague, Lynn Whisnant Reiser.

I decided that my professional life would center around interpersonal relationships and pursue either an academic or clinical focus. It turned out that that choice became unnecessary. I was able to teach as well as practice. Now I can see that one does not have to give up everything—only some things. Other things, one can do at the same time and still others, consecutively.

Psychoanalytic Training: Féria and Fafner, Among Others Empathy and Chemistry

In May 1962, an almost fully-fledged psychiatrist, I considered myself a professional and an adult. Barbara and I moved into the brownstone where she and I lived for 56 years until her death in 2018. I live there still. Barbara was pregnant, and I had been classified 1-A, liable to conscription, at the beginning of the year. Many colleagues were in the service or about to go. Shortly after we moved in, I was reclassified. I would not have to interrupt my nearly completed lab research or my domestic life; starting a psychotherapy practice would not be delayed. I began my private practice of psychiatry, while continuing to supervise psychotherapy students at Montefiore and pursuing my psychophysiological researches. I also began my formal training in psychoanalysis at the New York Psychoanalytic Institute. I learned from my teachers, my self-examination, my interchanges with colleagues both at formal meetings and study groups and in informal discussions, my reading, my patients and, after mid-July when our daughter was born, from the changed family dynamics. In June, I finished my psychiatric residency training and began my training analysis, as previously mentioned.

Of course, public life and private life are only partly separable. All of me went into my work, as all of me also lived my private life. The rules of games and the rules of life share a major element: constraints within elasticity. I think when one says, "a mature adult," it implies that this adult—unconscious internal pilot and all—"knows" about constraints. Hartmann's analytic postulate about human relations is that there is a somewhat elastic norm, "the average expectable environment." According to Hartmann, the constraints are modifiable.

One of the advantages of having worked at my academic job was knowing my colleagues' work. Amid all else that was going on, we had a group of analytically focused people at Montefiore; we read and discussed and invited outside people to talk about their work with us.

One discussion topic was ego psychology. In another project, we interviewed senior analysts who had been consulted to do second, and sometimes third, analyses in an attempt to see what could be discovered by reanalysis with a different analyst. A lot, it turned out. Robert Bak, Rudolph Loewenstein, Phyllis Greenacre, Victor Rosen, and Leo Stone were among the senior colleagues, and all of them eventually became friends.

CENTRAL EUROPEANS

My Friendship with the Reisers and Its Deeper Implications; Our Shared Love of Wagner

We Central Europeans are typically supposed to be cynical. I would say, ironic. That trait is concocted out of a pinch of negativism, a sip of hostility, a modicum of self-pity, and a bit of reality. My teachers and guardians pretended to more wisdom than they actually possessed. In my gullible, childhood weakness and consequent idealizations, I manufactured a vision of a secure future that failed to appear. I came to feel seduced and betrayed; adults were too weak to protect me, and too strong for me to influence, let alone to dominate. My outward expression of these myths (unbeknownst to me as a rational being) was aimed to hide, protect, and punish me for that aspect of me symbolized by greedy Fafner. Fafner embodied my secret lusts in relation an atmosphere fed by suggestions from my local culture through books, jokes, and history, all indigenous to my societal culture.

The unfortunate Fafner was, in fact, going to be cheated of his fee for building Valhalla for the gods; he never should have trusted them. He should have bargained and received advance payment. Therefore, he had to kidnap Freia, which threatened the gods with the fate of aging and dying, just as humans do. The gods had to give in by paying the ransom of the gold (and the associated magical treasures). Fafner got rid of his brother, Fasolt; this had to be hidden. "Peter Myron was the chaser," not I, I lied. I chased him and the teacher caught me. He was my friend but also my enemy.

Resemblance of Wotan to Milton Rosenbaum

The Wanderer (Wotan) was also bad, as well as good. Milton Rosenbaum was bad, too, as well as good. He presented himself as benevolent, a mild-mannered gentleman, walking around his white house, dispensing wisdom to his students—while exploiting them with low pay and demeaning tasks. I was wise to go off with Mort Reiser, and abandon Milt, who had seduced me by taking me to Pittsburgh, and then betrayed me by appointing one of my colleagues' chief residents, saying I deserved the job but the other fellow needed it more.

Years later, I read a book about Wagner and German philosophy. The Kafkas and the Reisers were good friends. We met often in Connecticut, where the Reisers lived, in Vermont, where we went in the summer, and, every year, in New York, at the time of the American Psychoanalytic winter meetings, to celebrate the Reisers' wedding anniversary. Over a bottle of wine at one of our celebratory dinners, I turned the conversation to the book I was reading about Wagner. I knew that Mort was working on a book about Wagner and the Ring cycle but made no connection between Mort's interest and mine. Mort had attended numerous productions of *The Ring of the Nibelungen* and wrote about it extensively. His book was never published; it was unfinished when he died. For us both, Wagner's masterwork displayed the myth and its ultimate destruction. So much for the happy endings, where tortoise defeats hare and outlasts grasshopper.

We two families were a pair in other ways. We bought a Portuguese Water Dog from the breeder from whom the Reisers had bought their Water Dog. (I think no one who lives with animals could imagine that we humans are not related to them as other sentient creatures. People who dislike dogs are suspect, as far as I am concerned.) Lynn Reiser, an excellent clinical psychoanalyst and teacher of analysis, is also a fine writer and illustrator of children's books. One of them is about the relationship between our two Portuguese Water Dogs.

Freud and I had a lot in common. He could have illustrated his findings about conflicted, ambivalently intertwined, entangled family relations with Wagner's work, alongside his examples of Hamlet, Oedipus, and his 1907 essay "Delusion and Dream in Jensen's *Gradiva*"—if Freud had had a musical side. He did take a walk with Mahler, discussed Mahler's passing potency problem with Alma, and reassured him. Alma, of course, became rather famous for her liaisons with other geniuses. Of personal interest to me is that I concealed the significance of the Fafner story, and the underlying incestuous conflicts, from myself—repeatedly, to the extent that I didn't realize that I had conflated the good side of my brother Fred and Mort Reiser to the degree I did (as I did with Warren Manshel), until just now, as I wrote this vignette.

Writing about the Reisers also made me think of my failure with Lew Robbins. "Why?" Answer: Something told me to examine the juxtaposition, Ernstl, Robbins, Reiser. Then, next, another realization came "as if out of nowhere." Despite all my prior training—in the form of "compare and contrast" essay writing in college courses, and in the use of differential diagnosis at medical school—at the time of my analysis with Dr. Robbins, I was unable to examine the treatment situation, reach the conclusion that I might be better off elsewhere, and leave, because I was afraid to be open with aspects of me. Fafner was indeed a projection of me, as well as an example that one should stay in one's cave.

I had steered Gordon Fair in a positive direction with respect to his crossword puzzle. I liked him. I had behaved in a way designed to steer Robbins in the other direction, to decide to terminate my analysis. I didn't like him. But more, wasn't there something fishy, ingenuous, about his somewhat ingratiating manner? And the cork target divided into "yes" and "no" sections with the darts sticking in them for decision-making. Wasn't that a screen? Robbins's absence from work, and his dimness about understanding me, was too much like my mother's illness and lack of psychological understanding to allow me to risk challenging Robbins's feelings. My inner pilot suspended my capacity to follow conscious paths to deal with practical choices. What was our passivity? Fafner should have stayed in his cave hiding? Ambition and greed? He ventured out and was slain. I was one who ventured out, into Robbins's cave, and he plunged the dart, the sword, into me. "You are unanalyzable." "Du bist ein dieb," said my mother.

She recognized me as a thief. She saw my inner Fafner. Fafner: my desired course destroyed. I found my way to Edith Jacobson, who disabused me of the burden of having to accept Robbins's view that I was the cause of the failure of our work together. She brought me out of my quandary back into the reality of waking life. The Institute accepted me, and later, when Robbins and I ran into each other, he was diffident and friendly, and so was I. I realized that I had a protective device—submissive behaviors, which came to me in early childhood—which was still available when confronted by a difficult situation later, even though a more rational approach might have been easier on me. Phobic withdrawal is a relatively extreme expression of diffidence or submissiveness. Both my parents valued diffidence, which they made clear was more necessary in the stratified familial and social Old World, where, presumably, I had taken it on for my use. It was less so in the New.

It is surprising—and not surprising—that neither Mort nor I, close as we were in our professional and personal relationships, realized how intimately connected and separated we were. This new appraisal of how important Mort (and some others) were in my life revised a construction I created previously. The effect of that construction was to keep a distance from strong feelings of affection; losses strengthened this tendency, demonstrations of dependability weakened it. Early childhood traumatic experiences had a stronger effect than later ones. The current construction allows me to have the warm feeling of missing Mort. I suppose that each example of how life has gone on, after some disaster has passed, lessens the need to try to preempt the future. It helps demonstrate how balance in conflicting desires can be achieved, relationships can last, and struggles can be managed, and so lessens the force of traumatic events. Grieving becomes more possible with every loss. Meaningful experiences of psychoanalysis, with a compatible and wise analyst, have been immensely reassuring.

For me, a benefit of writing an autobiography seems to be that the necessity to open old wounds and to recognize old "I survived," "It was just a bad dream," experiences, diminishes the fears of attachment; the process requires accepting the pain of reliving the suppressed feelings, consequent to disasters experienced, all along the way. I could write biographically (or historically) about Morton Reiser, but the absence of my personal feelings would be limiting; and it would deprive me of the possibility of rehashing and revisiting myself, wetly, with tears. I cry for the loss of Mort. Similarly, I revisit my familial relationships. My mother got over her disappointment in me. Edith Jacobson explained it to me. I am forgiven.

Our society has a judicial system that evolved out of a lengthy historical background. It seeks to adjudicate questions that arise out of disputes between people who have different points of view. We see that personal interests influence judgement, and that conflicts between interests need to be resolved by some means; in our society, the peaceable means are elections, negotiations, and courts. Judges, jurors, or arbitrators who have minimal personal interest in the outcome are assembled, to consider the evidence presented to them, in a situation when the state has an interest in resolving a civil or criminal dispute. We try to limit conflicts of interest, which can color the conclusions independent jurors would reach. Even so, the evidence the jurors depend on is what lawyers select to present and judges permit to be presented. The lawyer is there to make a case, and that defines what his viewpoint is supposed to be, and impacts how he makes his presentation.

The "chemistry," the "music," the "electricity" that is part of the connection between Reiser and Kafka, or juror and witness, or psychoanalyst and analysand is part of the communication between people. Facial expressions, bodily positions, tones of voice, shifting eyes convey meanings. Some gestures appear to be typical of a particular social status or environment. The bow, the way a person walks or talks with his hands, or shrugs, convey many things; sometimes a sign conveys something secret, as a football play, or fraternal recognition.

Part of the "music" between Mort and me was a shared response to Wagner. The "good," "constructive" relationship that ties people together, the positive placebo effect, positive transference, occurs when people who meet together trust each other. Mistrust fuels negative transference, the negative placebo. We might pay more attention to gathering more information about subjectivity, particularly as it appears in sensory "chemistry" between people.

As I look at myself, my sense of pleasurable surroundings, and agreeable people, is connected with early childhood. I like temperate climates, landscapes with hills and forests, freshwater lakes and rivers, and fields with butterflies; and I like (and associate with childhood) music, ceramics, oriental rugs, cars and trains, and the foods I ate as a child in Vienna, with a particular fondness for chocolate, chestnuts, and pastry, and duck made in the Czech style with crisp skin and lots of juicy sauce. In later life, I added cigarettes (which both parents smoked in moderation); bridge (which my parents played); paintings, drawings and watercolors, French food, wine, and many other pleasures, which came into my life with Barbara. Love of music can bring people together. Wagner's work has been studied for a long time. Responses to the question—how does his music affect the listener?—can range from "strongly" to "not at all." Mort and I were affected very strongly by the music and by the literary content. Wagner was a master of marrying the music and the words to each other, and he could convey mood and emotion as well.

The unconscious "music" we share in our interactions has made bonds between me and a few others. "Empathy" is probably the best term to describe wordless connection with another person. Art, poetry, music, love of nature were pleasures I shared with my parents. The historical backgrounds that led Robi Bak and me to feel like compatriots were that we were fellow Central European, upper middle-professional class descendants with a particular history. We had been through the disasters of Austro-Hungarian Jews, Bak and I never needed to discuss that, it was so obvious. Shared responses bind people to each other; take as examples, teams of athletes, units of soldiers, classmates at school, musicians in quartets, or orchestras, or surgical teams.

More on My Central European Legacy and Its Present-Day Resonance

In general, I find that the kind of things I grew up with, whether manners, music, or hard-to-describe body language, seem more natural to me than the tastes I acquired later in life. I find Asian music interesting, but it arouses no passions. Instead, it evokes a feeling of strangeness for which I imagine the proper word is "exotic." Jack Poses had strong attachments and vivid responses to his early language, Russian, and to Russian music, especially the folk music sung by choral groups. It was when they recognized each other's diction in English with its Russian overtones, that he and Mark Rothko fell into one another's arms, and happily carried on in Russian Motherland. Mother tongue and fatherland remind us of the connection to family, culture, childhood, our early connections.

I knew my family were in and of a certain place, whereas Yiddish speakers, as recent arrivals, and Wienerisch speakers, as members of a different class, were not part of our secular Jewish community in Vienna. I knew we were not part of the community in Jackson Heights. My in-laws made me realize that there were two tribes of secular Jews in New York—the ancients who were Sephardic, the more recently arrived Germans, and the still more recent arrivals from further East. I was a *Yekke*, classed with the fancy German Jews such as the Lehmans, the Kuhns, the Loebs, and the others who supported Mount Sinai Hospital, and belonged to the Harmonie Club. I was an oddity, and not a member of the more eastern Ashkenazi Jewish, Beth Israel group. Of course, I was harder to type, given that I was working at the Albert Einstein College of Medicine, named after a German, but supported by Eastern Jews, including the Poses family. The intra-tribal rivalries are apparent, but relatively polite. Unlike Mary Fould-Springer Wooster, who discarded the German language and became completely French and English, raising her children without connection to her prior culture, I never felt a serious urge to be estranged from my past.

History of Austria-Hungary

In the early nineteenth century, most of Western Europe was allied against Napoleon's France; in the later Bismarck time, the alliances came to be against Germany. Austria-Hungary lost the power it had previously enjoyed among the many small German states; Prussia defeated the Austrians in battle in 1866–67, and France in 1870.

Austria was encouraged to turn south to the Balkans, but the allies failed to support Austria-Hungary against Serbia in 1914; Germany stepped in. After 1918, "finis Austriae." My Central European milieu, heavily burdened by centuries of instability and wars, in the face of unsettled societal complexity with multiple languages and religions, finally ended with a German-speaking rump of seven million people out of 70 million, left over after the Treaty of Versailles. An example of cynical Austrian humor: I once asked my mother, what had been the aftereffects of the first War? and she said, "Well, good Hungarian salami became hard to find." Though it was her sole Graf Bobby-type joke, my mother's response to my question about Austrian history was typical of the attitude of both my parents. Serious questions were deflected with semi-pained, semi-humorous replies. My mother remembered her childhood salami and lived to eat it again in New York when my father brought some home to Jackson Heights from a Hungarian delicatessen on Second Avenue, run by refugees, Paprikas Weiss. She loved it. She was not one to lose hope.

The Status of Jewish Analyst Emigres in America

Depression, inflation, the assassination of a Chancellor, and the rise of Nazism led to Jewish migration from Austria, and this led to the problems migrations cause. In my case, as an extruded refugee, I felt confused and estranged. Many Americans were inhospitable. The State Department was quite unreceptive. The analyst refugees, though welcomed by many colleagues, were also envied and resented by others. They had been among the more prominent in the field, and they had help coming in, as did many well-known and well-connected individuals. It was both useful and practical to encourage them to move to various places across the country, where they could contribute as teachers, and also not disrupt referral patterns; they were sent to Boston,

Cincinnati, Chicago, and other urban centers. Several remained in New York. Arriving with provenances as members of Freud's circle, their writings lent them prestige; they started to teach students and joined in founding new training institutions.

Lore Reich Rubin, the daughter of Wilhelm Reich and Annie Reich, told a story about herself and her family's flight from Nazi Germany. They made several temporary stopovers before reaching New York; at each stop, they were met and were introduced to the local psychoanalytic community. Eventually, when someone asked little Lore where she came from, she replied, "The International Psychoanalytic Society (sic)."

In Perchtoldsdorf my brother Fritz read a book from his English class in Gymnasium, before the arrival of the Nazis. It told the story of a tribe of American Woodland Indians who abducted a settler child, and of his subsequent adaptation to the life of the Indians. When I could read myself, this tale made me feel relieved that I might be able to fit in eventually. The point of all this: the child's closed world is, in the main, the world of the family. Loss of a parent is serious, but countries and even parents can be replaced. There is always some place to go, some group to join, in the larger world that appears as the child grows and matures; and the effects of early setbacks can be mollified. Treating children often involves helping the parents, which helps the child. Maturation continues for quite a long time in the calendar of the young, and the lesson—that losses can be handled, and substitutes found—evades even adolescents, who often act as though a choice is a now-or-never-determining event. Your chosen college is treated as though it were the only college. Remnants of that sort of thinking remain long after adolescence. To be a white child among Indians, though, best be an older than five-and-a-half-year-old, and among Indians who want you to become one of them. It's also better to be one who has some alternatives. I think had I been older and wiser, or younger and more unformed, 1938 would not have been as damaging as it was.

ADULT LIFE—PASSIONS AND CHALLENGES

The Road Less Traveled? The Work of Writing; the Limits of Knowledge

By and large, my early adult guides were constructive in preparing me for later life, but in a Viennese environment. For life in America, less so. I was much on my own. I needed to rethink myself. That led me to a search for an understanding of who I was. I stumbled into a profession that had that very goal.

My psychoanalytic career, my analytic work with patients and with myself as patient, has changed me. The most telling, and most useful moments in the work—for the patient and the analyst alike—come when some idea from the inner mental life is exposed as a useless relic of the earlier life (when the mind was younger and feebler). For example: "Aha! I have a problem here. I don't understand; I seem to have difficulty accepting love and pleasure, with doing attractive things and enjoying them. What caused me to hinder my own way? What obstructed me? What a joy to have an idea, and not have to depend on somebody else, even a doting parent, to do my thinking for me." The conscious thoughts in a situation can be difficult to link together. The discovery of having lived by an obsolete childhood map leaves room for something new and better to replace it.

As a result of my involvement with analysis, adolescent questioning about whether volition, or something more like reflexive action, brought me to the point when the previous theories faded away, stopped seeming to me to be worth spending energy on. It was a turning point for me to conclude that it would avail me nothing to worry about the problem of whether free will, or animal spirits filtered through experiences, had brought about my becoming something different from what I had been. Or if a creator is responsible. Or whether, if everything is determined, is it by way of blend of nature and nurture, and in what proportions? Or are consciousness, and the idea of free will epiphenomena? If there were answers, they would be interesting, but useless. What an amazing thought: why worry about questions of agency, when one can experience the feeling of discovering something practical? The concern about who is the agent is a consequence of the childhood need to feel in some control over the repetition of trauma. Don't worry, be practical; go to medical school; follow the arts; have revelations; feel original. The question really is what happened to loosen the grip of the old and allow the acceptance of the new. How did I come to a more realistic understanding and lessen the strength of the past? How did I manage to discard either this or that limitation?

My father had a major influence in forcing me to accept complexity in politics and economics. No easy answers there. In 1965, the Dreyfus Corporation was one of the first mutual fund providers to go public. My friend, Howard Stein, was the CEO. He had a heart attack, and one of the early heart bypass operations, but not until he had led a dog-and-pony show over the country, selling the newly to-be-issued stock to institutions. The heart operation was difficult, and Howard had several blood transfusions, which caused a hepatitis C infection. In 1985, Howard was ill again, at the same time as I was going through a bad depression. Barbara and I went to dinner at the Steins and Howard and I felt close to each other. Howard suggested I change careers; he thought too much time at the same activity was not healthy, and that I was depressed because of my work.

At the time, Howard had a consultant named Stanley Druckenmiller who was an amazing investment student and manager. He told me he would get Druckenmiller and me together and ask Druckenmiller to take me on as an apprentice; the meeting took place, but Druckenmiller told us he would only take me on if I realized that it would be more than a full-time job. I mulled a bit, and the thought occurred to me that this was probably meant to be—it would have made my father happy had I done this with him before he died. I decided I couldn't give up my practice; it would have meant terminating my patients, and I knew that would be hard for them. Did I make the healthier choice? The Druckenmiller idea was the last time I made the decision not to follow my father. Whatever guilt I have about that, I have.

Druckenmiller went on to work with George Soros, then for himself, and became one of the most generous philanthropists ever; I think it would have been a lark, as I would have gotten a huge kick out of giving away money. (While I was chair of the board of the New York Chamber Symphony, I gave the orchestra my own retirement fund, which was a tidy amount, but I still couldn't raise enough money to keep the orchestra going; I was not in a profession where I could go to my clients.) But I'm not a bad investor myself, and Howard knew that when he put me on the board of one of his fund families. That gave me a good window on the whys and wherefores of how capitalism worked.

Beginning to Win at Poker—on Choice and Chance

Coinciding with the unregretted diminution of my hemming and hawing, and vacillating and worrying about deciding anything, I started winning at poker. Wishful thinking for a lucky draw seemed to become less dominant, and the capacity for dealing with complexity became greater—the therapeutic effect of psychoanalysis in a nutshell: terror and impotence might recur, but childhood is over forever. The era of greatest powerlessness is past. One is not so weak as to need to turn to luck. There is no magic. One can discover how the trick was done, and how one came to be deceived by an appearance.

Betting on the Odds of a Winning Hand

Poker involves betting on the odds of winning a hand containing a particular grouping of cards. The likelihood of winning is greater, the stronger one's hand; the possibilities are several, and the information is limited; but even in the long run, the one who has the better hand doesn't necessarily win. The one who keeps his weaker opponents in, and continuing to bet, and drives out the stronger hands held by competitors, increases the pot for the eventual winner. The player knows the odds and is affected by appearances, and what appears is affected by wishes and fears. It takes a certain head as well as a good hand.

In addition to weakening the power of wishful thinking, I became more practical. I spent less time and energy worrying about binary oppositions such as brain and mind, free will, and determinism, nature and nurture, and sickness and health. Those distinctions are rarely useful in assessing the odds in poker—or in life; if you wish to win, you need to control wishful thinking. The better method and, to me, what characterizes the scientific method, is to think in terms of possibilities. The underlying principle is that anything the person, patient, or analyst chooses to do has meaning; the person is continually evaluating a mass of prospects in the service of his conflicting intentions. Fears of losses can be overcome; tomorrow may well bring a useful discovery.

My analysis with Martin Stein was largely responsible for supporting me in a conviction about the usefulness of the foregoing. I had had a number of experiences that should have persuaded me that wishful thinking should be replaced by realism. My belief that I was entitled to good seats at the opera was derived from the childhood idea that it is unfair to be deprived of what others have, and somehow all will be supplied if you're good and wait for your turn. In childhood, impatient desire and need gradually morph and mingle with ideas, partly communicated by adults, defining fairness and entitlement.

The understanding that time, maturation, hard work, and luck are required requires time, maturation, hard work, and luck. In my case, a question from Martin Stein, "How do people get good seats for the opera?" finally crystallized that answer to the complaint," But it's unfair." The preamble to that point was long and the effect was late in coming, and still, often, weak.

1966 and Onward: Practicing Psychoanalysis and Finding Avocations in the Arts

In 1966, I finished formal psychoanalytic studies. I began to have a bit more free time in the late sixties and early seventies, and I was well regarded in the clubby world of the New York Psychoanalytic Society. At a party hosted by a psychoanalyst friend, Grete Froelicher, who was interested in music and in helping young musicians, Barbara and I met a couple who were both pianists, Jeaneane Dowis and Sam Lipman. Jeaneane was a piano coach, the assistant of the famous pedagogue, Rosina Lhevinne, whose students included Van Cliburn (with whom Jeaneane had been a student at Juilliard) and Misha Dichter. Sam had been a child prodigy who played with Pierre Monteux and the San Francisco orchestra at age eight and went on to a career of writing and publishing as well as concertizing. We met again in Aspen a few years later; Jeaneane and Sam were both teaching at the Aspen Music Festival one August, when Barbara and I were there for a two-week session of Psychoanalytic Studies at Aspen.

Psychoanalytic Studies at Aspen: Founders

This organization was one of two founded by Samuel A. Guttmann and Muriel Gardiner. Muriel Gardiner was an important, purposely anonymous, figure in the evolution of psychoanalysis. She never sought recognition for her contributions. Her short autobiographical book, *Code Name Mary*, covered the highlights of her role in saving lives during the period between wars, when she secretly travelled between Vienna and Prague to fetch Czech passports, which enabled threatened Austrians to escape the Nazis. She bought the house where Freud and his daughter lived in Hampstead, and, after Freud died, she sponsored the Freud Museum in it. She also financed the Freud Archives. All this was done privately, and the information shared only with friends. She went public only after Lillian Hellman stole her identity and wrote *Pentimento*, one chapter of which was made into the film, *Julia*, purporting to relate some of the events above with Hellman as the heroine. Muriel Gardiner said she asked many of the Socialist friends from the Vienna times (she was married to the head of the major Socialist party) whether there had been any other American woman at the time who had done what Hellman presented as her activities. They all assured her that she was the only one, and that encouraged her to write her book.

The first Aspen meeting mixed fifteen or sixteen young and older psychoanalysts, who met every day in order to discuss clinical and theoretical matters in a neutral environment. Both sponsors had summer homes in Aspen. They chose a group of leading, senior analysts to form a trial group to discuss clinical and theoretical questions. The members of the group found the discussions useful and the fishing, the music festival, and the hiking agreeable. The trial encouraged the founders, who decided to enlarge the organization by adding more groups with members again selected by the founders. The growth of psychoanalysis in the post-war years, and the consequent growth in numbers of analysts belonging to national and international groups, had lessened opportunities for intimate discussion among colleagues so these groups were attractive. Qualifications for inclusion were being able to listen as well as speak. This characteristic, plus having something interesting to say, could then be evaluated in the meetings at Aspen, where the founding group could interact with potential members of permanent new groups that were being set up for the second branch, the Center for the Advanced Study of Psychoanalysis (CAPS). These more permanent groups met at Princeton on three-day weekends in autumn and spring. I was extremely fortunate to be invited to Aspen and then to Princeton. It was a great privilege to be included among major, older generation figures and young colleagues. By the time I finally left, it had grown to sixteen groups. Being selective, it was not a democratic arrangement; I was one of the included. I remained a member of CAPS for many years, until I felt it necessary to give up weekends away from home. I also became a member of the board of the Sigmund Freud Archives, another Muriel Gardiner benevolence. A collection of papers and letters written to and from Freud, which was closed to the public, for reasons of confidentiality, at that time. It was housed at the Library of Congress and guided by Kurt Eisner. Later, I became secretary of the New York Psychoanalytic Society, then president, and an instructor and chair of committees. Later still, I gave up administration and teaching, with a conviction that it was time to make room for the younger people, many of whom had been my students.

I Reunite with Sam and Jeaneane and Take Up Piano Again

One consequence of my participation in the Aspen meetings was that it brought me back together with Jeaneane Dowis and Sam Lipman. Sam convinced me that I could resume work with the piano, even at age 40 (I thought that was too old for such an athletic activity after many years of absence). Jeaneane was an amazing teacher. She seemed to find muscles that moved fingers in ways my fingers had never moved before, and she brought me to a point where I imagined that, with enough time, I might be able to play anything. Unfortunately, I had to reconsider that. A passable version of Beethoven's *Sonata Opus 132* had taken me months to achieve, and, in one of Jeaneane's evenings, when her charges played in simulated recitals for each other, I had an attack of stage fright. I forgot where I was in the score; I had to stop and repeat a portion of the piece. That was a debacle and a wake-up call, which helped me to cut down on practice time, a thing greatly pleasing to Barbara and my children. My last hurrah as a pianist was when my son, Michael, asked me to play for his friends for his fortieth birthday (2004), which I did, to satisfying applause. The program had some Domenico Scarlatti, some Bach, and some Rachmaninov, but no Beethoven.

Gerard Schwarz; YMHA

My relationship with Jeaneane and Sam led to a friendship with Gerard Schwarz. The Young Men's Hebrew Association Chamber Symphony began in 1977 and played at the Lexington Avenue YMHA in New York. Gerard Schwarz was the music director and Omus Hirshbein was the general manager. The financing came from the YMHA, donors, and grants from New York State and the National Endowment for the Arts. Schwarz is a musical phenomenon. In 1977, he was thirty years old; he had already been the youngest New York Philharmonic first-chair trumpet player, performed with the American Brass Quintet, been music director of the Eliot Feld and Erick Hawkins Dance companies, and the Los Angeles Chamber Symphony. We became friends with Gerry, and his wife, the dancer Lillo Way, and his two small children; and even closer friends following their divorce and his marriage to Jody Greitzer (a flautist with whom I planned, but never got to play, the Poulenc flute sonata). Her father was first violist at the New York Philharmonic, and she and Gerry produced two talented children, a cellist son, Julian, and a daughter, Gabrielle, who became a Nieman Fellow and news editor. Gerry was teaching in Aspen. The orchestra had scheduled Eliot Carter's *Piano Concerto*, an incredibly difficult, complicated piece, with multiple concurrent time signatures and sudden changes; Igor Stravinsky, to whom Carter dedicated the work, dubbed it a masterwork, but wrote he had "trouble hearing everything that was happening in the score." In a 2004 article, Alex Ross noted, "If Stravinsky struggled what hope is there for the rest of us?" (Some years later, Sam Lipman spent two years working together with Jeaneane, who was aided by several metronomes, on the piano part, to prepare for a performance of the Concerto.) The young Gerry stepped in for an ailing conductor and, with two weeks of preparation, conducted the work successfully at the Aspen Festival.

"The Y," later the New York Chamber Symphony, lasted until 2002. The downturn started when "the Y," frustrated by Omus's management, by decreases in public funding, and having assumed the costs of an ever-enlarging roster of new cultural departments (poetry, painting, and political debates undertaken in an effort to expand its secular footprint) ousted the orchestra. The board of the orchestra was left with a small core of people who had significant fortunes, and a larger group of relatives of big givers to "the Y." Omus was a menace; while he had ideas and a sound fund of programming suggestions, he was bad about costs, which he ran up and then billed to the orchestra. A friend of mine from Harvard, John Rosenthal, who was the president of the Y's board at the time—having heard that Gerry had persuaded me to chair the orchestra's board with promises that he, Gerry, would stay around, and help raise money—warned me about Omus.

Omus claimed that new money was going to come, that Lincoln Center, or the musicians' unions, were going to give us price breaks, and that a few new board enlistees would provide enough money to fund everything. None of these happened. Gerry accepted a job as music director of the Seattle Symphony. Seattle had willing wealthy donors and great prospects, but when Gerry arrived there, he had a big job to do and a number of other irons in the fire: a summer festival here, another there, plus guest conducting. He came to have little time for New York, which had high costs and no supportive board: a psychoanalyst was hardly likely to have many wealthy friends. The orchestra paid its bills and went out of business; and my own personal retirement funds underwent significant shrinkage. Meanwhile, I had learned a few lessons; my idea was that classical and accessible contemporary music could attract audiences if ticket prices were low enough. A chamber orchestra, with forty or fifty musicians playing in an intimate hall, would be less costly to operate, and more acceptable, than a huge orchestra in a huge hall; I didn't know that a full small auditorium (we had many such) would supply not much more than half the running costs of even a small orchestra. On the other hand, I met, dined with, and heard a great number of fabulous, young musicians.

The Visual Arts: Forays into Museums

Over the years, I have had a good many interests, of which music was, and is, a very important one. In high school and college, I took part in a lot of extra-curricular activities. I made childhood trips to the museums, when I wasn't biking, roller skating, playing punch-ball or stickball in the wartime deserted street in front of our apartment building (gasoline was rationed, so there were few cars using the road). and I also had piano practice. Telling my parents that I was off to play with some friend, I actually went to museums in Manhattan. I particularly enjoyed the Museum of Modern Art, because of the movies shown there, but I also explored the permanent collection. I had a subscription seat of the Family Circle of the old Metropolitan Opera on Broadway during the war (1943–5).

Art Collecting with Barbara

Barbara and I shared most of our aesthetic preferences. She had a good deal of knowledge and taste. French art—what with her parents' Soutines, Utrillo, Dufy, and Buffet, and Jacques Guerin and his collections—was an example. I was delighted to learn from Barbara and her contacts and, after our marriage, we bought pictures from local St. Louis artists, as well as artists in New York. Collecting art was a joint activity with Barbara like everything else, save our different professions. Robert Motherwell, Helen Frankenthaler, Leo Castelli, André Emmerich, Kenneth Noland, Luca Samaras, Frank Stella, Barbara Rose, Henry Geldzahler, David Smith, Tony Caro, Wolf Kahn, and Emily Mason were all people we more than knew, but befriended.

Collecting British Drawings and Watercolors

In 1985, in England by myself (Barbara was consulting about food in Japan or Australia), I wandered about, in and out of galleries; I met a youngish man named Andrew Wyld, who dealt in British drawings and watercolors. Barbara and I had bought some Whistler lithographs and etchings (available for a few dollars in the late fifties and early sixties). I hung them on the walls in my office when I opened my practice. On this trip, meeting this interesting and friendly dealer, I began to concentrate on late eighteenth and early nineteenth century British works on paper. They were clearly the immediate product of the hand that made them, intimate, and not overpowering as some contemporary American art was. I was much taken with a number of the artists. Andrew was a scholar; he knew where the artists had lived, what they had made, who their patrons had been, the provenance of the work, what was authentic and what their condition was. Andrew's wife, Christie, is a paper restorer, as knowledgeable and warm as Andrew was. He died bravely of biliary duct cancer in 2011, at the age of sixty-two. He was an honorable man, and he and Christie were good friends to me; we sailed in Greece together, and we ate and laughed together.

Andrew was especially helpful when he introduced me to the work of Francis Danby, an Irish painter who migrated to Bristol from Wexford and then on to London. He failed to achieve membership in the Royal Academy in a year when he lost out to Constable. He had a scandalous affair with his housemaid, for whom he left his wife, and with whom he ran off to France. Andrew unearthed a number of his works and curated a marvelous Danby show at the Tate.

In my usual way, I appreciated the works I was able to buy and I also enjoyed learning about the artists. My collecting always had an ancillary purpose, to serve as a basis for study. I taught myself (as usual, from books) what I could about the technical aspects of painting in watercolors. I have little gift for drawing, but I do have a gift for appreciating; so, I bought Kolinsky (red sable) brushes, papers, and paints and experimented; I wanted to know what the brushes felt like, how the paints could be mingled, combined, and separated. I learned enough to be able to write occasional book reviews and comments, about eighteenth and nineteenth century British watercolorists, for a monthly newspaper called the *International Journal of Art*, of which the editor was my friend, Barbara Rose.

As a child, I wondered at my father's use of his pocket watch, and my mother's spring-powered train toy also piqued my curiosity. When I was in medical school, learning how the body worked, I began to wonder how clocks and watches worked. I read books and learned about escapements, the mechanisms that use cogs and levers to transfer energy from a spring to power the turning of hands. I bought a few different types of pocket watches and tinkered with them to get a bit of practical understanding of the works.

Photography

Another enthusiasm was, and is, photography. From childhood on, I watched my mother, an avid picture-taker, as she recorded vacations in Switzerland, Italy, and Austria—the last of which, in Milstadt, included me in various clothes and states of mind. Naturally, she kept photographic chronicles of me as a baby, and growing up, playing with my cousin Evi at my Uncle Gusti's house, and sitting with Fritzl, costumed in his soldier outfit, and later on with (the re-named) Fred. She photographed me in my high school marching band outfit, holding my oboe, and Fred in his U.S. Army uniform. In my teens I had my own camera, a silly Japanese made thing marked "Made in USA," (which I imagined was a fictional Japanese town); I have no memory of where this thing was acquired, but it hardly ever worked.

Later, I bought my own cameras, with money I earned as office boy in my father's office and from later jobs. At first, I took pictures of places I'd been and people I knew, which functioned as mementos, like any amateur. Gradually, my output became more individual. I began to use my odd ways of juxtaposing things: people pacing in airport waiting rooms, plants in unusual lighting, or streakers at a football game, running by an exhausted player slumped on a bench. I printed the photos at a downtown New York business, which rented dark rooms and the use of machines to professional and amateur photographers. For once, I had to take some courses to learn how to do that. I also learned how to use Photoshop, but I never tried go beyond cropping and playing with intensity, saturation, and light and dark. I worked in color, because color evokes movies, fashion and other advertising, or travel, while black-and-white automatically gives the viewer the sense that what they are looking at is art. To make color photographs unusual magnifies the difficulty of seeing differently as the photographer. I feel the same about "eye' in the visual arts as about "hand" in paintings and "tone" in music. When art strikes me as mechanical or formulaic, it bores. It fails to be art for me.

The Vermont and Garrison Houses—Vermont

When our children were old enough to sit up in a car, and I felt I was earning enough money to consider having a second house in the country, I began to discuss the idea with Barbara. Though we had been going to Westport fairly frequently on weekends, and Jack and Lillian were always glad to have us, Barbara was not happy there. Her parents were glad to have us stay and would have been glad to have us nearby; Had we been willing to buy a house near them, they would have been willing to repeat what had happened when we moved to New York, when they used Barbara's trust as collateral for a mortgage for the 92nd Street house, which we then paid off.

We didn't accept the offer. In the late 1960s, the government made it possible for a parent to give $35,000 to a child with no gift tax to be paid. My mother generously offered me and Fred each that amount. On one long weekend, in 1968, we drove to the Newfane Inn in Newfane, Vermont, together with another couple and their two children. A series of short articles in *Esquire* magazine by prominent people had told where they might spend a weekend. and John Kenneth Galbraith had written about the Newfane Inn in glowing terms. Ken owned a home in Townshend, a neighboring town and spent more than weekends there. However, he ate at the Newfane Inn frequently. There was an excellent French chef there. We took his advice and went, but it rained, so skiing and touring were out. However, we saw a sign in nearby Brattleboro next to a ramp leading to the Interstate, "Leon Tailleur, Real Estate (pronounced Taylor)."

I was amused; we stopped in, and Mister Tailleur/Taylor showed us a house in Newfane, up a dirt road to the top of a hill, five miles from the town. Newfane had a full-time population of 200 families, a Common, a Congregationalist church, a Grange, a Sheriff's Office with an attached jail, the Newfane Inn, a court house, an antique shop, a country grocery-wine-meat store, and a local curio-craft shop for tourists wanting to buy a shawl, a basket, or fudge. It was a charming example of Vermont eighteenth and nineteenth century villages, all white and simple, and the Shire Town.

The house he showed us sat on the hilltop, with a pleasant view over fields and hills. We were told there was a stream and ponds, covered with snow and therefore not visible down the slope to the south of the house. The road to it was plowed, but the snow around the house was so deep that our children could crawl up to the top of the garage roof and slide down.

The price for house, barns and eighty acres—"more or less"—was $55,500. I offered $50,000, but the offer was refused, and we returned to New York. In mid-April, the owner said, via Mr. Tailleur, that he would entertain an offer. I flew to Keene, an hour away from Newfane in New Hampshire, and drove to the house, still encircled by deep snow, and still highly desirable. The owner accepted an offer of $50,500 and we owned a weekend house.

Garrison

In 1999, I thought the stock market was bubbly, and I sold a good number of tech shares. We were in our sixties; I was no longer keen to drive long distances for weekends. The money had to go somewhere, and we decided to put it into a house, near New York. I promised not to campaign to go every weekend and to be responsible for the furnishing and the management. It helped that during the 1941–1945 war, Barbara's parents had rented a summer house, on a lake, near Ossining, in Westchester County; it was the house before the one in Westport and a happier time for the pre-teen Barbara. We put the new house into a trust with the children as beneficiaries, to take advantage of inheritance law (it was possible to create one house trust per parent that would pass ownership to a child as a gift after a set number of years. The gift would be valued at a discounted sum, depending on the length of time until ownership passed to the grantee. When ownership of the house passed on, there would be no tax to the recipients, as long as the donor was still alive.). We had made a similar gift of the Vermont house. It was a way to give our children a degree of independence before we died that Barbara's had not given her. They would own two houses to use or sell.

Barbara had wanted her perfect kitchen from the time we married, and an indoor swimming pool. I went on a solo search-trip after several months of our ranging through areas within one-and-a-half to one-and-three-quarters of an hour from New York, without success. At last, I saw three houses on the books of a local broker in Garrison. One was a 1900s Artisan house high up on a hill, with a fantastic view south to the Battery in Manhattan, lots of steps, and many cramped rooms with low ceilings. The second was a recently built spec house in a dark forest, on a lake enclosed by woods, that had been made virtually yesterday. The third was a 1970s house, which seemed to be of mixed Japanese-California design; it had a view across the Hudson and was up a dirt road at the end of a long dirt driveway which served three other houses, out of sight. It had huge glass windows and a wrap-around deck, and it stood on the edge of a precipice. Barbara, when she came and saw it, made the decision I expected her to make. We met the owner, he stated his price, and said, "no bargaining." We bought the house and six acres, four lining the drive up to the house, and the other two surrounding the house itself. To the east rose the hill on the side of which the house was perched, and Federal land around the Appalachian Trail. To the west was the Hudson river, and a small town; to the South were hills, and on the other side of the Hudson, Bear Mountain. Manhattan was an hour-and-a quarter down the Palisades Parkway.

Lee Balter

The man who sold us the house was Lee Balter, a tall, muscular man of my age. In 1999, when we met, he was an exercise devotee who had a gym in the house and jogged on the road. He also owned another building nearby, a 1900s folly, a Moorish castle on the top of a hill to the north, near Cold Spring, across the river from West Point. This building had stood empty, except for occasional visits by teen-age lovers (one of whom, we later learned, had lived in the neighborhood in his youth, before moving to Vermont, marrying, having children and running a realty business). Lee was renovating the castle, dividing it up into palatial condos, and selling them. In past days, he was a Wall Street trader and owned The Bird and Bottle, an eighteenth century inn and, during Barbara's childhood in the Ossining house, a first class, go-to restaurant; he also owned Tallix, a foundry in nearby Walden, which cast sculptures for artists, and buildings in Peekskill. He supports Dia: Beacon, the art museum in Beacon, a bit up the river; and is something of a ladies' man; and a gastronome. Lee, Barbara and I became friends just before we moved into his house, when he made dinner for us, and the inhabitants of the three other houses on the road, to introduce us, and say farewell to them.

Lee saw some photographs I had had framed, after we moved into his former house, and liked them. He offered to have more photos framed and to show them in one, large space of his newly usable castle. This was my first show. After that, my high school acting partner, Diane Kelder, then the curator of the New York City University Graduate Center gallery, gave me a show, as did three small Soho galleries, and the Brattleboro Museum and Art Center and Vermont Art Museum. People have told me my photos are beautiful, but gallerists tell me they are too classical and not "edgy" enough for their clients.

The Garrison house became another of my enthusiasms. Barbara and I needed to do work on the house. It was too close to the declivity that neighbored its site: the southwest corner was no more than five feet from a steep drop-off. The house was built on granite. One long side faced west toward the river; the east was built into the rising hill, which rose steeply from three hundred feet above sea level to six hundred feet. There was no place there for an in-ground swimming pool. The Hudson Highlands, our hills, were once part of the English Cotswolds; when the tectonic plates separated, they took the oldest hills in the current northern hemisphere with them to the west. The Hudson River flows south, cutting through the hills, dividing them into eastern and western. The lower Hudson is a fjord; tidal salt water reaches north as far as Poughkeepsie.

An indoor swimming pool would have to be dug into an excavation twenty feet deep and connected to the existing house, and it could not be placed anywhere except to the south of the house. The drive leading to the house came from the south and ended in a parking area between the house and a two-car garage on a flat place, also on the edge of the hill. I telephoned an acquaintance, the architect Richard Meier, who had done the interior of Barbara and Frank Stella's place thirty-five years before, when he had not yet become the famous Richard Meier he was in 1999. He suggested an architect called Tom Pritchard, whom we had known as the proprietor of our favorite New York florist. Educated at Harvard and Princeton, he was, at that time, designing houses and gardens for very rich clients, including the (later) notorious Bernie Madoff.

Tom Pritchard

Pritchard's plan solved all the problems. The original house had two floors; the top had floor-to-ceiling windows all around and was totally above ground. The bottom floor was built into the hillside; it had floor-to-ceiling windows facing the river, and the back rooms had small windows just below the ceilings. We blasted at the southern end of the house and used the boulders that were excavated to make a long rip-rap wall, parallel to the north-south side of the house, up to the level of the original lower floor, but further from the house than the original base. The pool went into the hole. Above rose a pool room that added to the lower floor of the house. Its roof was at the height of the entrance to the house and was paved to accommodate parked cars. Its rear wall, facing away from the river, leaned against the hill, preventing it from falling. The land at the base of the lower floor of the house was be expanded by filling in behind the rip-rap. The garage was removed. Meanwhile, Barbara designed her kitchen, which included sinks and stoves at a lower-than-standard height, to accommodate her size; she would no longer have to hoist her pots and pans up to the stovetop.

When the work was finished, we had a house with an office for Barbara, a bathroom connecting her office and our bedroom, a large kitchen, a very large dining-living room, and a deck at three sides on the upper floor. On the lower floor were two large bedrooms and one small one, a sauna (left over from the past, and rarely used by us), and a large room where I had a piano, a television, and lots of shelves filled with books, LPs, CDs, a good stereo system, a small bar with a refrigerator, and my desk and computer. I collected books about 20th century furniture and mixed a largely 1950s-60s bunch of specimens with an undertone of lounge chair and sofa comfort. As usual, the basis for my design choices, as well as for most of my other enthusiasms, was my mother's taste and her capacity for enjoyment in it. I inherited three of my mother's favorite pieces; all were simple, Bauhaus-y, carefully made in the Austrian Wiener Werkstätte style, using beautiful woods and modest designs; you saw their Biedermeier background. A cubical white cupboard hung on a wall, and when opened, it revealed drawers and shelves lined in polished grained-wood spaces meant for liquor bottles. There was a nest of brightly colored yellow, red, orange and blue enameled, individual ashtrays, and there were simple Bohemian tumblers and wine glasses, which my parents brought out in Jackson Heights for dinners or bridge games with friends. I have two other wooden pieces, a chair with Wiener Werkstätte covered cushions, and a rolling tea-cart.

My own eclectic-taste latter day version of that cozy Austrian time was Bauhaus-Danish-mid-century-Modern. As usual with my projects, I investigated and studied; I went to furniture shops and auctions, read books, and accumulated objects. At a psychoanalytic meeting in Denmark just before opening my office, I had bought Arne Jacobsen swan chairs for the waiting room, and teak tables. I now acquired Hans Wegner pieces: desk chairs, a desk, and wall storage shelves for Barbara's room. Her windows faced southwest to the river, and northeast toward the parking; the southwest side was screened by a bushy planting Barbara designed outside, plus some small Meyer lemon trees for her kitchen, which came inside during cold seasons. The bedroom had a bed, four Wegner armchairs around a Majolica-topped English table, and a small Wegner table that held an amplifier, and a small television. Barbara liked the English majolica pieces I found, for her a taste she shared with Leo Lerman, and his partner Gray Foy, who owned a large collection.

The Garrison house mélange of furniture included a Frank Gehry power table and four power chairs (which needed frequent applications of glue and small vises to keep the bands of bentwood together), Carlo Scarpa bookcases, Pierre Paulin red ribbon chairs, an Olivier Mourgue Djinn foam-filled sofa (like the ones used in *2001, A Space Odyssey*), three Gaetano Pesce chairs (made in 1969, packed into flat cartons, and self-inflating when taken out); a probable Jean Prouvé outdoor café table (nowhere published; but he was first to make such things out of cast iron, and it had to be rescued from rust), some Eames side tables (which I had admired at the Frankenthaler-Motherwell home), a Richard Meier coffee table and a bar stool (partly in honor of his referral of Tom Pritchard), and a Joe chair (Depas, D'Urbino and Lomazzi, 1966), a large chair on wheels, in the shape of a baseball fielder's glove, which I bought for my grandchildren to roll around on); and, of course, there were table silver, lamps, and pots and pans.

As usual, I was making yet another study collection-cum-esthetic experience. My mother's living room carpet in Vienna, the one she took up for my winter tricycling pleasure, was a Kermanshah, a Persian relatively formal object. I inherited it, and it lay in our New York bedroom, somewhat worn, but in its gentle, busy floral way, gratifying. We had bought the Garrison house after the collapse of the Russian empire (and the establishment of eBay), so there was an easily accessible supply of tribal rugs from the Caucasus, and from the Asian nomadic areas for sale. I suppose that, just as my father had been tempted to sell the Kermanshah to raise money before he found a job, people exiting from the Russian satellites were cashing in some of their possessions. I bought camel bags, grain sacks, embroidered textiles, as well as a variety of floor coverings, from a variety of places, and spread them about the Garrison house.

Barbara's freak accident; sale of the house in 2012

The trust ownership arrangement ended, but not before Barbara tumbled over the edge of the hill, in a freak accident, on a rainy, dark night, while walking our dog after dinner. We had erected protective hillocks next to the edge and had years of experience with the lay of the land, but she slipped and fell. This marked a turning point in her health and in our lives; the times we had had in Garrison, with only a few minor problems, were happy. I could drive there, play a quiet, solitary round of golf, exercise, and swim. When Barbara was otherwise engaged, I could read, listen to music, hike up the hill with Woof, our dog, to the Long Trail or to the top of Anthony's Nose, overlooking the Bear Mountain Bridge and Bear Mountain, and make a circle back home. We made friends and entertained and went to Dia:Beacon and the Storm King Art Center and sculpture park; there were comfortable restaurants nearby, and I had a garden to play with, to dig, and to plant with shrubs and fruit trees, and watch the seasons pass.

Neither of my children had any interest in keeping the house. They took some minor things when the trust ended in 2012. (Michael took the Joe chair.) I much regretted that almost everything in the house was sold; I am embarrassed to say that I felt a bit like King Lear.

Oaxaca and Folk Art

One of my other enthusiasms during the Garrison years was Mexican folk art. My introduction came from two sources, David Rockefeller and Arden Rothstein. Rockefeller had been in Oaxaca in the 1950s and seen the handicrafts artisans were making: wooden masks worn at festivals, woven cloths, rugs used domestically, pots for cooking, clay dishes, leather objects, and other useful things, art pottery and clay and wood figures. Rockefeller collected examples of these and encouraged the craftspeople to enlarge their repertoires. The new subjects included representations of real and fantasied animals, religious scenes, and a wide range of depictions of daily life in villages and the countryside.

Arden Rothstein, a friend and psychoanalytic colleague who spent vacations in Oaxaca in her adolescence, became fluent in Spanish and, as an adult, wrote a book about the work the artisans produce. She discussed the families that pass down the local techniques and the areas and specializations that characterize towns in the neighborhood around Oaxaca. The capital city of Oaxaca is known for its cooking, its colonial architecture, its university, its people, and the forty-odd local languages of groups descended from pre-Conquest inhabitants; local culture is made up of many cultures. Oaxaca, the state, of the Estadas that make up Mexico, is one of Mexico's poorest. There is but one growing season; the soil is dry and holds no rich mineral sources. The historical consequence was that the region attracted missionaries, but not looters intent on subjugating the inhabitants to labor for commercial reasons.

Arden, with other Oaxaca-lovers (including me), created Friends of Oaxacan Folk Art (FOFA) to publicize the local work, with teaching, prizes to recognize quality, and scholarships for children of the crafts families. Mexico City now has a museum of crafts well worth a visit; crafts have come to be a useful commercial commodity, and several Mexican cities hold craft fairs. I displayed both large (some as much as four feet high) small pieces in Garrison, and in New York—most of which I gave away to FOFA, which sold them at auction.

Not all my friends share my enthusiasm. During a conversation about style in art—among friends who were sharing their views, and guesses, about what was good, and might last, and what not, Barbara Rose declared her position—"*I* am style"—and was happy to hear that I had gotten rid of my "junk." I did keep a few pieces, including a wall-hanging about five feet square, covered with forty black clay skulls, surrounding a central square depicting a small skeleton crawling on a map of Oaxaca state. I don't generally favor political art, but this piece is quite powerful.

Oaxaca is a paradise for tourists, owing to its buildings, food, parks, and surrounding craft-producing villages. When the local teachers went on strike in 2006 (for the 25th consecutive year), they occupied the local Zócalo, the central park of the city. They erected tents to live in, and a stage from which to deliver harangues to show their students' families that they had not been forgotten. They addressed the crowds, waving Che Guevara banners and demanding recognition of their Popular Assembly of the Peoples of Oaxaca (APPO) as the local government of Oaxaca. The result was an economic disaster. Tourist activity plummeted. Shops did little business, hotels and restaurants closed, and I made a circuit of the craft towns commissioning work. I wanted to show the crafts-people that they had not been forgotten. Some months later I went back to pick up the pieces I had ordered and to pay for them. I took a room at the Camino Real, a luxury hotel housed in a 16th century monastery. After dinner, which I shared with a wedding party and a Mariachi band, I agreed to meet my driver for the next day's excursion and went to bed.

Just before I made this second trip, the Governor of the state ordered a helicopter to drop tear gas on the Zócalo. That led to panic. The orators urged the populace to remember a demonstration, years before, when a large protest in Mexico City had been broken up by the military, who killed dozens in the process. In this atmosphere, Oaxaca attracted representatives of native tribes, ecological enthusiasts, syndicalists, nihilists and other assorted leftists. They took over the University, the police stations, the firehouses and from time to time, they blocked the highway to the airport.

The morning after my arrival, Tino, the driver, and I had breakfast in a deserted hotel, and then we set out for the villages. In the afternoon, Tino received a radio-telephone call from his brother, who also worked in the family chauffeur-service business. An "event" had occurred at the hotel. The protesters had invaded the hotel, looking for Governor Ruiz, who was responsible for the tear gas, and who was rumored to be holding a meeting at the hotel. We returned to Oaxaca, and drove to the Camino Real, to find it deserted, and locked up. This was inconvenient: before leaving to do my rounds that morning, I had carefully put most of my cash, all but one credit card, and my passport, into the safe in my room. I spent the night on the outskirts, at an inn belonging to some of Tino's friends, who opened it for me. I had a pleasant dinner and felt glad that I had visited the very grateful families to whom I brought money and encouragement.

The following morning, I visited the American Consular Agent, a Texan who had taught English at the University for years. He represented U.S. interests only part-time; he told me not to worry about getting back in time to see my patients in two days. Homeland Security and the airlines were all aware of the situation, and after all, I was a native-born American citizen, was I not? No, I was not, I said; I was a citizen by virtue of the fact that, in 1945, my parents had received their citizenship papers; I, as their child, became a citizen by Derivative Citizenship. "Oh, then," said the Consular Agent, "no airline will fly you out without a passport. You'll have to take a bus, or find someone to rent you a car, though that might be tough, given that you have no passport. Go to the Embassy in Mexico City, spend the night in a hotel; the next day, you'll need to spend a day at the embassy to get a duplicate passport. Then you can go back and see your patients."

"Well," I thought, "our friend, and tenant in New York, Paolo Balardini, is the head of Unilever for the western hemisphere and will surely know what can be done." He spoke to a friend, the head of the chain of Camino Real hotels, then called back and said, "Don't worry, they're negotiating, and they'll probably settle it in a few days or a week. And maybe my friend can get the manager of the hotel on the phone and see if there's anything he can do." This sounded a bit chancy to me; fortunately, the hotel manager phoned me the next day, and in a timorous whisper, told me that if I went to the hotel, and knocked on one of the barricaded windows, he would let me in. I could enter my room to open the safe, pick up my bag, and pay my bill: but "only for the night you actually slept in the room" and he would hope to see me for another visit again soon.

I ran into the Consular Agent in the street and asked if he had any news about what had happened. He explained there had indeed been a rumor that Ruiz was having a meeting with some of his people in the hotel, so the demonstrators had broken in, and searched the place. They discovered some men with cameras, and two bodyguards, trying to sneak out of the hotel through a back door next to the laundry and tried to stop them. A bodyguard fired a pistol into the air. The bullet caromed and hit the arm of a demonstrator, whereupon everybody ran away except the manager, who stayed behind to lock up. "And what happened with the negotiations?" "Oh, they're still negotiating," the consul replied. "They're negotiating with themselves, the management, and employees, about when to reopen without risking any harm to the hotel employees, in case of another demonstration." "But what about the guests?" To this there was no response. Another series, though relatively few nights, of papers-necessary-but-not-at-hand dreams. The analogy to 1938 was clear.

My enthusiasms usually have a middling half-life. I also seem to suffer from my failures to ignite supportive, companionable enthusiasm among my children and friends—Barbara Rose was more explicit than some. Most of the acquaintances I approached to give money for the Chamber Symphony were not forthcoming, and one, who agreed to join the board and contribute, felt betrayed when the organization folded. When Michael grew up and left our house, he became lively in his expressions of resentment when I converted his room into an orchidarium. Howard Stein was an exception. He shared my orchid love. He contracted to have his New York apartment, and his Southampton house, festooned with flowering orchids, delivered and rotated with others as each dropped its blooms. My piano playing ebbed when I concluded that I had gone as far as I could reasonably musically expect, given my limited time to practice. I did feel some relief when I noticed a diminution of disapproving looks from my near and dear, as they passed by the now-silent piano.

Ongoing Evolution of My Family

My brother Fred married, and essentially became part of his wife's family, living with his in-laws, or near them, moving to Long Island as they did. He made a life quite different from mine. He and his sons' families live close to each other; Fred's daughter married, and she and her family live just far enough away from the others to have more separate lives. Fred's sons, a grandson, and a nephew work at the family business Fred inherited from his father-in-law.

Fred and I love each other, but have hardly ever socialized, never have had common friends; and our children, though not too far apart in age to share some similar amusements and interests, rarely see each other except for bar mitzvahs and weddings. We two brothers remember our time in Vienna-Perchtoldsdorf when we were much closer. I think Fred made a huge difference in my life; he was my best connection with the extra-familial world. A child is something like an invalid, in need of being informed about the world outside, and my sometime version of a newspaper was my brother. Eight years difference in age is a lot. We are different animals: he is quiet; I am sociable. I flirt and am funny and please people. Fred is not funny, has no jokes, is known to be a taciturn dinner guest, and people tend to respect him. I have seen him deep in conversation; at a party Fred met Frank Stella, and discovered that Frank is a painter, which led to a long conversation about paints. This was Fred's trade—paints, stabilizers, clays, colors; and those were Frank's tools.

These days, Fred is mostly confined to home. He has had several hospitalizations because of a fall and fracture, and bouts of pneumonia; he has had chronic leukemia for many years, which has now led to a complication, Waldenström's Macroglobulinemia. This affects the immune system, so that his resistance to infection is diminished. I visit him every month or so when I am in New York, and we have lunch, generously provided by my sister-in-law, Mindy, and spend an hour or two in comfortable talk. Otherwise, there are occasional phone calls that last a few minutes.

MEDICAL MISERIES

Barbara's Health: A Flashback to 1961

Here we need a flashback to 1961, to recount a little of Barbara's medical history. She went to Paris, and I planned to meet her a bit later in Stockholm, to join my mother on a visit to her Aunt Adi and cousin Anni. Barbara contracted viral encephalitis and spent a week-and-a-half at the American Hospital in Paris in a state of pain, alone and frightened. Barbara's mother, Lillian, and I rushed to Paris, and Lillian bought Barbara a get-well present, a bronze sculpture by the French sculptor, Germaine Richier; the subject, a nude, battered man, as though rising from ruins (presumably, the war) titled "l'Homme qui Marche" (the man who walks) was apropos for someone recovering from a trauma, especially in Barbara's case, an injured mind. Barbara recovered and decided it was time to have a child. I had been urging and she putting it off. Barbara soon became pregnant. Nicole was born in July 1962, and Michael in March 1964 (both uneventfully).

Early one morning in the early 1980s, Barbara awoke with severe abdominal pain and had to be taken by ambulance to Mt. Sinai Hospital. She had a retroperitoneal abscess. The cause—her OB had failed to check up on and replace her IUD with a fresh coil, as was recommended; Barbara had kept her regular appointments, but nobody, neither I, nor Barbara, nor our internist, nor the OB kept track of the time for a change. The OB immediately removed the coil when Barbara was admitted to hospital, and he and the internist, both stars of the Mt. Sinai teaching faculty, omitted the information that this had been a belated event from their notes in Barbara's chart, denied any lapse, and probably emended their office records. After ten or more chancy, frightening days of massive intravenous infusions of a variety of antibiotics, the infection began to diminish. My memory of time was never very exact but, in this case, Barbara spent months in bed at home in the maid's room, on antibiotics; our first lengthy period of separate bedrooms. Barbara was taken care of by the live-in house man, Alfonso.

My Novel

I occupied myself by writing a novel on one of those early MS-DOS computers, which turned out quantities of floppy discs. The subject was a young woman, who grew up in a Connecticut suburb, and moved to a very different community in New York's Soho. My friends who read this liked the first half, but not the second, which took place in Vermont—a fact which dates it to sometime after 1970, a few years after we bought our house there. Barbara recovered, and I abandoned the book. In retrospect, it was a fictionalized attempt at autobiography. It was another version of transformation—mine, by migration and physical injury; Barbara's, by disease (early childhood enteritis, recent encephalitis, and then betrayal by the doctors, resulting in a life-threatening infection).

MEDICAL MISERIES

Paul Desmond; Elaine's in the 1970s

Our friendship with Paul Desmond began when Ina Backman moved to New York. A college chum of Barbara's at Radcliffe, she had previously lived with her husband, Maco Stuart, in Houston where the Stuart family and its oil-holdings were based. Ina and Paul met when he was with the Dave Brubeck Quartet, on a gig in Houston. Ina was (and still is) gorgeous and intelligent. She had graduated from law school in Texas. When she divorced, she moved to New York. Ina was a great addition to the Kafka circle of friends. She introduced us to Paul, who became a close chum; Paul was at the height of his saxophone career at a time when modern jazz was still taking off.

A good deal has been written about Elaine's, about Elaine Kaufman, and about what the place meant to many people. Barbara and I felt welcome, assured of more than decent food (if one chose properly). and of interesting conversation, meeting people, table-hopping, and feeling part of a group of people worth befriending and spending time and making an emotional commitment with.

Besides Paul Desmond, regulars at Elaine's included Mike Stoller, the composer-musical and business side of the Leiber-Stoller partnership, and Jerry Leiber, the lyricist of "Hound Dog," "Blue Suede Shoes," "Is That all There Is," and "Love Potion Number Nine." Woody Allen also seemed to be at Elaine's, with a group of friends, every time Barbara and I went to dinner there—which was often. (He had Lafitte-Rothschild as his wine; and everyone felt he was entitled to it.) Among the many other creative types, journalists, and writers whom one ran into at Elaine's, I remember Emile de Antonio, a filmmaker who was particularly known for his film about Nixon, Billy Carter, Leo Lerman, the Condé Nast culture guru, Bob Motherwell, and A.E. Hotchner, who wrote a wonderful biography of Hemingway among other works (he was also a good poker player), David Halberstam, a friend of mine from Harvard

Crimson days, and Frederic Morton (ex-Fritz Mandelbaum), a fellow refugee who wrote best sellers about the Austrian Empire, Gay Talese, George Plimpton, and many others.

Paul used to come to dinner, which was really lunch or breakfast for him. He stayed up late, working or drinking, and chain-smoking Pall Malls, which killed him. Sometimes we met at Elaine's, sometimes at our house. He was very fond of ladies and squired quite a few; I was particularly impressed by Gloria Steinem. When he knew he was close to death, Paul invited us to have dinner with him at Elaine's in farewell and did so in a way that was dignified, without pathos or regret, as though we would meet somewhere again.

Barbara had another trauma in the early 70s. Though it seemed minor at the time, looking back forty-five years, it might just have been consequential. It was a head injury. We were having dinner at home with Paul and Jerry Leiber, who were exchanging jokes. This was a few years before Jerry moved to California and Paul died (in 1977, at age 52). Paul was able to face death with a sort of Roman *gravitas*, but Jerry Leiber was not able to control his mood swings; he could be the world's funniest companion, yet a threatening presence.

The conversation at dinner became more competitive, particularly on Jerry's part. I went to bed at about 11 PM, having to work the next day.

The next morning, Barbara told me that Jerry, on departing, had picked her up by the feet, held her upside down, and dropped her on her head. Jerry could be bizarre and violent when in an angry mood. Barbara had been egging both men on, and everyone had had too much to drink. The violence of Jerry's behavior brought to mind stories that one had heard about Jerry as a young man in California; Barbara should have known better than to provoke him. Maybe her later brain problems resulted from this injury.

My Heart Problems

An explanation of my father's death became evident when I myself had a diagnosis of a fairly rare congenital heart abnormality. My father had probably lived with a dominant genetic mutation, which causes a heart malformation, idiopathic cardiac hypertrophy and, frequently, sudden death owing to ventricular fibrillation or cardiac arrest, often in apparently healthy athletes. Studies eventually revealed that I had significant enlargement of my interventricular septum. It had been a missed diagnosis in my father's case, but it would have made no difference had the diagnosis been correct: there was no good treatment of the condition then.

Portuguese Water Dog, Stubbs, 1995

We bought a Portuguese Water Dog in 1995, with encouragement from Lynn and Mort Reiser who were delighted by their own. We named him Stubbs. (George Stubbs painted a wonderful portrait of an English Water Dog, and one entitled *Poodle in a Punt*, so though we couldn't afford a painted Stubbs, we could manage a living one.) As puppies ran about, sniffing to find a congenial spot to do their business, I ran with Stubbs. Then I fainted, sank to the ground, and revived with Stubbs tenderly licking my face. I thought that was a fine experience of bonding with my dog, but when the same thing recurred the following night, I called my doctor, Barry Hartman. He became quite involved; evidently, loss of consciousness while running with a puppy, after jumping out of bed during the night, is of significant concern.

None of the usual tests—blood, urine, EKG, echocardiogram *et al* showed anything unusual. The doctor and I decided I needed a stress echocardiogram with a radioactive isotope. I was panting on the treadmill when I heard someone, saying, "Stop, stop, his intracardiac blood pressure is 260 and the arterial is 80." Aha! Hypertrophic cardiomyopathy. But to me the really surprising thing was that cardiomyopathy is clearly shown by an echocardiogram. If only one looks at the state of the interventricular septum, one sees that it is unusually thickened. Dozens of echoes had been read earlier in my evaluation and during previous illnesses, and no one had noticed that my interventricular septum was quite abnormally thick. My father died of an arrhythmia and was autopsied. Did the pathologist who did the autopsy miss a thickened septum? Not unlikely. The condition that affected three generations of my family had been a diagnostic rarity, which had escaped the attention of the doctors.

New Technology: The Indwelling Defibrillator

Now, however, there is a treatment; technology has created the indwelling defibrillator, a small device buried under the skin of the chest. I now have one of these which regulates the rate of contractions of my heart, and, presumably, will shock the poor thing back into normal rhythm, should it have a tantrum. My son, Michael, has a DNA diagnosis of the condition.

A common complication of the underlying architecture of the heart is bacterial endocarditis. The thickening of the interventricular septum caused by the unruly proliferation of heart muscle distorts the architecture of the heart. It causes outflow blockage, increased intracardiac blood pressure, and abnormally shaped, incompetent mitral valves. That gives rise to mitral valve leakage and susceptibility to infection. Colonies of bacteria accumulate on the mitral valve and damage it, and pieces of endocardial bacterial colonies can break off and cause minor or major strokes. A hydrodynamic effect of cardiomyopathy is that, when the need for increased cardiac output causes elevation of the pulse rate, the tachycardia, in turn, lessens the time available for filling the ventricle, and concurrently brings about a decrease in the diameter of the aortic valve. The aortic exit from the left ventricle chamber is partly blocked. There is less blood flowing forward and more leaking backward, so shortness of breath appears with exertion, as in running, or climbing, especially at higher, less oxygenated altitudes. Those are symptoms my father had, and my son and I have. I could run like the wind, but only for a hundred yards or so. At Harvard, I was required to do remedial exercise when a health test showed I had an unusually high heart rate with moderate exercise. If I drank more than two—or a bit more—glasses of wine at La Caravelle, where we were regulars for wonderful dinners with the Manshels—thanks to the Thiokol coup—and I went down one flight of stairs to the toilets, I could sometimes barely make it back up, because of shortness of breath and nausea. I sometimes vomited because of sudden intense nausea. The doctors shrugged it off, when I asked about it at the time. My son, Michael, played football in high school, but could not play soccer which required more running.

My First Episode of Endocarditis, Vermont

My first episode of endocarditis struck on a weekend in Vermont with our friends the Abends. I made a self-diagnosis of fever of unknown origin, which often turned out to have endocarditis as its origin. A green streptococcus grew out of a diagnostic blood test. I was hospitalized at New York Hospital, where my daughter Nicole was a surgical resident. She assured me that the room she had found for me, the room where the Shah of Iran had stayed, was available at a reduced fee. I spent two weeks with an intravenous drip feeding me some heavy antibiotics around the clock. During that time, I had a Nurse Ratched who would come and wake me in the middle of the night, disconnect the IV, and leave it unplugged while she made phone calls while I, fever-delirious, imagined getting an air embolus. I went home in better shape than the Shah when he was discharged.

The course of recovery was followed by repeated echocardiograms, in and out of the hospital, which showed the progressive diminution and then disappearance of the bacterial colonies flapping about attached to my floppy, leaky, mitral valve. Nobody looked at the rest of the heart, an inspection that would probably have revealed the thickened, interventricular septum, responsible for the flapping mitral valve which then harbored the bacteria. Rare conditions are easily overlooked. Now, it is not so rare to discover this condition. Recent studies show approximately one case per 200 men and women.

Two More Episodes of Endocarditis

I suffered two more episodes of endocarditis, though I didn't have to stay in a hospital to be treated. For the first of these, I had the antibiotic infusions at home, continuing at the Hôtel du Cap in Antibes—another Manshel-Kafka watering hole, and much more agreeable. As a matter of record, the Hôtel du Cap was less expensive than the Shah's hospital room; we could see his widow, Soraya, lunching at a nearby table overlooking the Mediterranean—rather than the East River.

The third time I had endocarditis, before my home antibiotics, I spent a few days at New York Hospital (now known as New York-Presbyterian/Weill Cornell Medical Center) where I became a star patient, as various on-staff acquaintances and their students made their rounds, looking for petechiae under fingernails and in eye grounds, listening to my systolic mitral valve murmur (very loud), reading my echocardiogram, to see what they could of vegetations made by bacterial colonies attached to my valve, and totting up many of the signs and symptoms typical of my disease. I found the students enjoyable, and I enjoyed being a specimen, so I agreed to join the volunteer faculty. I led some seminars and supervised some residents, as clinical associate professor, which continued until there was a change of administration; Bob Michels became dean and was replaced as chair of psychiatry. With the new regime, the department shrank, dynamic psychiatry was downsized, and funding was more directed to drug research; I, as an alumnus of another training institution, yielded my place to graduates of the New York Hospital program.

Some important events, such as the medical circus I had experienced, might seem to be cause for resentment. But uncomfortable as they were, these experiences left me optimistic and gratified. I had survived. I had furthered the education of the medical students and of the house staff. These experiences and my hypertrophic cardiomyopathy diagnosis allowed me to resolve my prior feelings of athletic inadequacy. I took the whole business, distressing and frightening though it was, as evidence of medical progress. Good came from bad, teaching experience from trauma.

Three Episodes of Renal Calculi

I also had three episodes of renal calculi during the 1970s and 80s. The first was extremely painful. Dr Bob Seely prescribed Demerol (or perhaps it was morphine), lots of water, and filtering the urine to try to catch a passed stone. A small stone passed and, though it went to Seely for a lab exam, it got lost. During a second episode, five years later, Dr. Seely referred me to a urologist, who pelted me with tales about various colleagues and their stones and made a diagnosis of prostatitis, but no stones; he showed me a slide with lots of white pus cells. I told this to a friend, John Bussel, who had been a urologist in Poland before World War II (and was the husband of a psychoanalyst friend of mine); he reminded me that prostatitis is commonly associated with kidney stones.

I dismissed the urologist and found another; all the usual tests were done but no stone was found. Seely took pity on me because of the pain, so had Barbara inject me with opiates every six hours and dose me with Halcion for sleep. I became disoriented, was taken off the opiates, submitted to a great number of tests, was dosed with Halcion repeatedly, sometimes two or three times a night; until everyone realized I had become seriously depressed. I overheard a conversation about the possibility of some mysterious cancer and became more depressed; tricyclic antidepressants made me worse and were stopped after a couple of weeks.

Barbara, the children, Lillian Poses, and I went for a cruise on a rented yacht in Turkey. The presence of my family plus my mother-in-law was extremely helpful, but still I had lots of thoughts about how to commit suicide without making a mess. Looking down from a window in our hotel in Istanbul, I saw a man with a scraggly, underfed dancing bear on a chain, begging. I felt sorrowful for the bear and identified, in my crazy, depressed way with him. I seriously think that, had that window not been sealed, I might have jumped.

On returning from that trip, the urologist did a cystoscopy, decided I had cystitis, and started cephalexin; the pain lessened. After three months of persisting, off-and-on mysterious crampy pains, there came an equally mysterious quiescence. Five more years later, in England, at the restaurant Tante Claire, I had another onslaught of classic renal colic, complete with bloody urine, and was admitted to the London Hospital. A stone that had been in me all that time was on the move, having found its way to a ureter. It required a laser to break it into pieces, some of which passed and one of which was "blasted" back up to the right renal pelvis, where it remains to the present. I hope it rests peaceably for the remainder of my days. A stent was put into the ureter, and later removed, and I learned that there is a "dead man's" location, where stones can be hidden by bones; this had caused the diagnostic mystery five years before. In the wake of this competent (and successful) medical treatment, I had no depression until the next medical trauma, a cataract removal.

The cataract operation was an office procedure. Valium was the anesthetic, and I was awake enough to hear the conversation of two doctors. The actual operation was performed by a fellow or resident and a teacher, a woman I knew. The doctor who was supposed to do the job was not there. Unfortunately, post-operatively, an aurora around bright lights appeared. The next day, I telephoned the surgeon. I was told he was away on vacation but had coverage. I went to see the covering doctor, who examined the eye, and found the operation had been perfect. She did not explain the vision problem. When I went to see him upon his return and I asked him about it, I also said that I thought he had not behaved entirely correctly in failing to make it clear that a junior person in training would be doing the actual cutting. He flew into a rage, told me my operation was perfect, that he had done it himself, and that I was the type of patient who made him want to quit his practice. This was so strange and outrageous that I asked a friend, who was significant in the hospital administration, whether I might have imagined the whole thing. He replied, no, my experience was not infrequent. It was a teaching hospital, after all. The only hope of finding support for a complaint was the faint possibility that a naïve nurse or anesthesiologist had written the true names of the participants in the operative notes; an old hand would have named the people who were supposed to have been there. As for the aurora of light, that was caused by uncovering the sometimes encountered, but generally unmentioned, foveal degeneration of retinal atrophy.

Major Depression

Unfunnily enough, I had another depression, this one dealt with by increasing my daily dose of SSRI. It was by now abundantly clear to me that I had never overcome the response to the experience of fear and impotence when a trusted person betrays me, especially a doctor. I tolerate mistakes, but not when a doctor continues to work when ill, or is otherwise handicapped, usually with some rationalization. And lying and covering up?

Major depression is extremely painful. It feels very little like the ordinary feeling of being blue, which is more a listless, unhappy experience than major depression. There appears a feeling of dread, an absence of interest in what is going on in life. My sense of humor vanishes. I cannot make a joke, play with words, or experience anything funny. Every hope vanishes. I feel ugly and burdensome, and this becomes more and more severe. I become unreasonably fearful of disappointing people; the burden question becomes a suicidal preoccupation, which has to do with the fear of shocking or horrifying my family and friends, and the need for me to find a way of killing myself without making a mess and without causing people guilt.

The first such episode was marked by fear about going out of the house, where I might meet and disgust people I knew. I had a student who needed help with an application for permission to continue her training, and I felt absolutely incapable of putting pen to paper, or finger to keyboard; I had to telephone a colleague to ask him to take the responsibility for the student, but I could find no explanation for making the request. I was unable to bear looking at television, lest there might be bad news, such as reports about suffering people, and I could not tolerate movies showing anything of the dark side.

During a second depression, in New York, Barbara was away on a book-promotion trip, and I had arranged to take some friends from out-of-town to dinner. I was afraid of being unable to appear normal at dinner, as though that would have meant giving the guests as terrifying a feeling as the one I was experiencing at the time; I had to reassure myself that since there were going to be others there too, I might not be noticed. Cancelling would also be a terrible thing to inflict on the guests.

At the times I am describing, I knew that I was being crazy in having those thoughts, but at the same time, the pain and fear I was experiencing was so intense that I felt I might not remain able to tolerate it. Towards the end of one of these periods of agony, I realized it was passing only when I had what I took as being a funny thought: I would shoot myself, but I would do it wearing a mask so that no one would know who had done it.

Two More Serious Medical Situations

There have been three serious, near-death medical sagas. The first two happened to Barbara; the third to me. The first was Barbara's peritoneal infection. The second came in 1998.

Barbara began to have memory lapses, concentration problems, and balance difficulties, which gradually became more apparent. She would tire easily, leave the dinner table abruptly, often when we had guests who might be chatting away. She stopped writing, presumably because of difficulty organizing her ideas; this probably also had to do with remembering. She spent more and more of her time behind her computer screen, playing solitaire or bridge. Consultation with the chief of neurology at New York Hospital, a revered and honored man, brought no help or news; he told us that Barbara was bright, funny, and able, and though she had some brain shrinkage on a CAT scan, that was not uncommon at our age, and seemed to have no obvious effect. Barbara was more than willing to accept that opinion and resisted further investigation, saying it was just that she was tired and older, and intended to leave it at that.

I read up about this and found another possible diagnosis—normal pressure hydrocephalus. Cerebrospinal fluid (CSF) is secreted in the brain's interior caverns, the ventricles, circulated in and over the brain and spinal cord and reabsorbed. Sometimes, for unknown reasons, the balance between secretion and absorption changes, and reabsorption doesn't keep up with secretion. The brain is spongy and shrinks; Barbara's symptoms were suggestive of this condition. Gradually, Barbara got worse, her thinking became more problematic, and she began to tilt to the side at her desk.

Treatment for hydrocephalus became more effective with the development of a shunt that allows the cerebrospinal fluid to drain into the peritoneal cavity, where it can be absorbed with greater control than before, thanks to a new valve capable of responding to magnetic control from the outside. This means that the pressure can be adjusted with ease; if adjustments are needed, this can be done without the risks and discomfort of redoing the surgical implanting procedure.

A new chairman of neurosurgery who had experience in the use of the newer mechanical paraphernalia was hired at Cornell-New York Hospital. Philip Steig agreed to admit Barbara to the hospital for a few days, to take the modest but significant risk of reducing the cerebrospinal fluid pressure with a temporary drain, as a test of the idea that the CSF pressure, though normal, was not low enough. A release of some fluid might allow a useful amount of pressure to be released and the brain to recover a degree of capacity; the danger was that the brain might detach from the skull, causing bleeding and the need for further hazardous procedures.

In the event, Barbara made a remarkable improvement with the lowering of pressure. A shunt was emplaced. Over a period of some weeks, more fluid was released, and then a period of stable functioning followed. Barbara was able to complete two books, with the great help of Chris Styler, an associate for several years and a food expert and gifted writer as well. Barbara did not recover to the degree that she became the swift and creative thinker she had been, but she was much better. We were able to lead more normal lives, travel and enjoy ourselves, much as we had done in the past, until 2011.

One evening after a pleasant dinner at our house in Garrison, New York, Barbara took our then current dog (Virginia Woof) out for a walk. Woof returned alone, scratched at the door, and ran back and forth. I also ran about frantically looking for Barbara, first inside the house and then outside; my first thought was that the dog had run off, and Barbara had come home to wait for her return. But when I was unable to find her, I began to range farther away, and soon heard weak cries, of "Ernie, help, I can't move" coming from a steep drop over the edge of the property's precipitous hill. She had slipped and fallen over the edge to a sort of ledge, between fifteen and twenty feet below. I telephoned 911, and soon there arrived the sheriff, the state police, the emergency ambulance with the trauma emergency service, the EMTs, and the fire department. Barbara had to be lifted up on a stretcher, ferried down to the bottom of our hill, and helicoptered to Valhalla, the hospital with the closest trauma emergency facility.

She had seven broken thoracic vertebrae, two cervical, and six ribs, with some broken twice. I wanted to move her to Manhattan, given that the neurologist, neurosurgeon, and internist who knew her and had been her doctors, all worked at Cornell. There was a window of only a few hours when this could be done safely; fortunately, we were able to make arrangements for transport and hospitalization, though just barely in time. Barbara began to convulse in the emergency room at New York Hospital upon arrival and needed to have an intubation and ventilator; and then, the next day, a long operation to reconstruct her spine and fuse the vertebrae. There followed the period of recovery;

Barbara remained unable to breathe on her own for a few weeks, until the ribs healed to some extent and her chest pain lessened. Then she was transferred to a rehab ward, where she spent about ten days.

She was sent home, having fulfilled the criteria for discharge. She was deemed able to bathe with help, walk some distance, and go up and down stairs. She had several falls, walking to the bathroom, or around her bed. One of these led to a visit to the Mount Sinai emergency room, where she was stitched up, and there were one or two more when she bumped her head; ultimately, she slipped, fell down a flight of stairs, and broke her left humerus. It was as hard as ever to get Barbara to accept limits. That allowed her to be enormously creative. Sometimes she followed her impulses into danger.

Her fractured humerus meant emergency internal fixation—more screws and plates, and more anesthesia and hypoxia. The bone failed to heal; the surgeon had prescribed parathyroid hormone, but not calcium and Vitamin D supplements. The next orthopedist who took over Barbara's care a year later went over the records and discovered that Barbara had been discharged from the hospital with low levels of blood vitamin D and calcium. Therefore, the bone had not mended. There was no record of whether the original orthopedist had mentioned the blood tests; he insisted he had and blamed us. Barbara had to have a revision of the original surgery—more trauma, and anesthesia, added to everything that had already happened.

Unsurprisingly, with each event, she became more disabled. Barbara developed a collection of tics and trembles and scratched her head a lot, which led to an infection of the skin overlying the shunt on her skull, and so, for fear of the possibility that the infection might spread down the path of the shunt, the shunt was removed. Barbara was given an IV of an antibiotic, whose name I didn't recognize, and began to sleep most of the time. Nicole and I investigated the new antibiotic that Barbara had been given after the shunt was removed and learned that it contained a high volume of sodium, which caused excretion of potassium, which led to dangerously low potassium levels. This led to her sleeping so much, and we needed to persuade her doctors (who maintained this was a rare complication) to use another antibiotic.

All this happened in January of 2014, in Wellington, Florida, at the Palm Beach Polo and Country Club (the so-called winter horse center of North America) where we had rented a house to which we enticed Greg Parks, an old friend, our long-time Vermont house sitter and, later, very successful chef at the Four Columns Inn in Newfane, Vermont, to come with us to cook and generally help out. At the same time, I had a near-death episode from which I recovered. Barbara went downhill.

My Strokes and Cardiac Events

My own body had been developing a problem that led to my being admitted to the same hospital in Florida, at the same time as Barbara. A prelude in Vermont the preceding summer: we gave a dinner for various friends that included a new guest, who turned out to be argumentative; he and I got somewhat heated about politics and economics. The next morning when I got up, I could remember nothing about the preceding evening, so I took myself to the local hospital, but they could find no reason for this; they did a CAT scan but had no MRI equipment. On our return to New York, I went to my usual doctor and started a series of tests, which showed only my known cardiac hypertrophy and mitral valve abnormality. The problem of the memory loss was still unsolved. When December came around, this remained an open question; however, it was clear (MRI showed little spots of infarcts in my brain) that at least one shower of emboli, presumably originating in my heart, had occurred.

At New York Hospital I had more MRIs and a transesophageal echocardiogram, to look at a part of the heart that needed to be seen from the rear. Now there were two theories about the origin of the emboli; obviously, they came from the heart. There were two possibilities as to the cause: either a hidden endocarditis; or a clot in the left atrium, from which small pieces had broken off and gone to the brain. There was, however, no positive evidence to support either theory. A clot in the heart had never been encountered in my past, and there was no evidence of past transient auricular fibrillation which might have led to clotting in the heart not revealed in the transesophageal echocardiogram. Nor was there evidence of infection, or of the formation of bacterial vegetations, which might have broken off from my long-time damaged mitral valve. Unfortunately, only one of those two possibilities could be treated at a time. Anticoagulation, which would deal with the clot possibility, would also lead to lots of bleeding should a possible, though unseen, vegetation break off, and could become responsible for a new brain infarct.

Antibiotics could eliminate an infection, but would be no help should there be a clot. The decision was to give me antibiotics, because of the history of past endocarditis, and to use a monitor to see if any asymptomatic burst of atrial fibrillation occurred.

The Rarity of Barbara's and My Ailments

I go through these lengthy expositions about Barbara's and my medical problems because both of us seemed to have rarish ailments, which were undiagnosed, and led to interesting conditions (at least from the doctors' points of view), and difficult diagnostic and treatment decisions. My cardiac pathology was missed for years. Barbara's normal pressure hydrocephalus was neither normal pressure, nor was it diagnosed. Her retroperitoneal abscess would not have developed had not there been a rush to the use of intrauterine coils for the purpose of birth control. The investigations also point out the technical developments that were available, with regard to the mechanics of the shunt, and its valve, and the electronically sophisticated electro-cardiac possibilities. An EKG lead passed through the esophagus to examine the interior of the right atrium was unheard of when I was an intern fifty odd years ago. The diagnosis of stroke, and the sighting and locating of where a barrage of tiny emboli landed, would never have been discovered with the pre-digital visualization capacities of that time, either. The sort of stroke I had, when the more gross symptoms disappeared rather quickly, was labeled transient ischemic episode, and then nothing further was done. When the patient later experienced a more damaging stroke, not much could be done then either.

I left New York Hospital with some blood pressure medication and a monitor, another invention (it was able to broadcast an EKG that could send a message that something was going wrong) added to the diagnostic armamentarium, as well as the reassuring advice that if I did turn out to have auricular fibrillation, then anticoagulation would probably suffice to keep me alive for a good time: "One can live for years with AF." I was not given the name of a cardiologist, but that was no problem, as I already had contacts in Florida.

But then, only a couple of days later, I did have a transient AF; the antibiotic was stopped, the monitor removed, and the night before we flew off to West Palm Beach Airport, I had a definite persistent auricular fibrillation. I made an appointment with a cardiologist, who sent me home with a new medicine and another appointment a week later. One night, I awoke. I thought I was going to miss my appointment. I got up, took the car, backed into my neighbor's mailbox, drove to the appointment, waited an hour because I thought the appointment was earlier, drove around afterwards, set the GPS, arrived at home in time for dinner, and went to bed—all the time thinking it was an hour earlier than it was. A few normal days passed.

This behavior was revealed in retrospect; at the time, Greg, who was the normal person on the Wellington scene, knew I was acting peculiarly.

Three doctors whom I saw, an internist for referral to a cardiologist, and a second cardiologist whom I saw when the first was away and who medicated me, seemed to be unaware of the fact that when I was seeing them in their offices, it was under false pretenses. I was not quite there, but only not quite. This was similar to the experience I had with Barbara's doctors, when there was strong evidence that she was changing for the worse; our internist and neurologist were fooled by Barbara's near-normal behavior.

My Denial of Illness

Nor was I exempt from following along on the denialist bandwagon, for I readily accepted the idea, which Barbara also believed, that she was tired, overworked, possibly "coming down with a bug that had been going around," just getting older. I concurred that this was all there was to be said about her situation, and so it went on, until denial became impossible. If ever there was a demonstration of how intelligent people can be blind to unpleasant evidences about each other's and their own mental states and material being, Barbara's and mine were pathetic examples.

Having experienced all this, I also came to a new appreciation of the situation in Vienna in 1938; of course, the majority of the people didn't really accept the significance of what was happening. One sees this un-seeingness so often, with regard to health, stock market bubbles, the ludicrousness of politicians' claims, and on and on.

My Coma

One morning, I awoke five or six weeks later in a room in a hospital in Miami; I felt weak, but I was out of bed and could look at myself in a mirror. I seemed thin; I had lost forty pounds. Looking through a window, where I could see a small triangular grassy park, some trees, and a boulevard, I began to try to think how I could escape. Somewhat later, I woke again, and there was a young man asking how I felt; I realized I had a Foley catheter and an IV, but I could walk, slowly, and see a ward or two, other patients, and employees. This was either Albert Einstein or Mount Sinai Hospital in Miami; the names were all the same to me. (It was actually Mount Sinai.)

I believe my son Michael, and my daughter Nicole, appeared and disappeared. Perhaps I was hungry; I remember a dream in which I had received a pass to let me out of the hospital temporarily, and my two children and I were dining at a nearby restaurant which served local dishes that were Mexican. The next day, I thanked my children for the meal; however, I only thought I was speaking. In fact, having been on a ventilator for some weeks, I had such an injured larynx that I was unable to make understandable sounds, even in a whisper. I tried to print messages but, apparently, they were illegible. This may have taken place in another hospital which had a rehab division, near Delray or Boynton Beach which, at the time, I thought was "Boylston Beach."

There, my children informed me that Barbara and Greg Parks had found me unconscious on the floor of the bathroom in our rental at the Palm Beach Polo Club. I was ambulanced to a nearby hospital that had a trauma center; my rescuers were told I would probably be dead shortly, and the medics suggested that anyone for whom it might be important to see me should come immediately. My pulse was about 40, my blood pressure the same, but with a heart-assist balloon in my aorta, and whatever else, I lived on. A week later, as I was still alive, I was transferred to Miami where, another week later, having discovered that I had ninety percent occlusion of my right coronary artery, they stented it.

A week later, I was still alive and a vastly experienced cardiac surgeon, who had worked together with my New York cardiologist, made two small holes in my chest on the right, passed little instruments across to my heart, my lung on that side having been gotten out of the way by being deflated, and replaced my now useless mitral with a pig valve; he reconstructed the tricuspid on the right side, snipped off a bit of atrium on the left, and scarified the remainder of it. The result was a reconstructed heart, a prognosis that the repairs should last twelve to fifteen years (and could be repaired again then), and no atrial fibrillation. But I was to have a hideous, terrifying recovery, with lots of delirium, awful visions and horrible dreams, so that, in my saner moments, I was sure that I would never be able to go through such experiences again. I more than half wished I had died, so as not to be in danger of an encore. Dying had been easy; coming back to life proved to be very difficult.

Minor problems, which felt major at the time, included an indwelling urinary catheter; it had caused lots of irritation over the weeks when it had been in place and felt more like pain than annoyance. Then there was the skin reaction to the adhesive tape that failed to keep the rubber tube from moving around. A third matter was weakness; I could hardly get to the bathroom to defecate by myself without falling down. My lungs, having gotten very wet, especially the one that was collapsed on purpose to allow the surgeon room to maneuver, had to be dried out. This meant inhalants several times a day, which meant rousting me when I was asleep. Sleep was another issue: when I wasn't having terrifying dreams—which could probably be better described as delirious hallucinations, continuing into episodes of semi-waking delusions—there came nurses with machines to document vital signs.

Disgusting Soft Food; Unable to Speak; Post-Operative, Post-Traumatic State

The food was made up of various, semi-solid paps, which claimed to have fruit or vegetable flavors, but were disgustingly bad. Clearing the extra fluid from my body made me thirsty much of the time, but I was not permitted liquids and relied on occasional mouth moistening by bits of ice. Then there were tests to see if I was yet able to chew and swallow, which I failed for weeks. Neither my larynx nor my mouth and esophagus, nor my mind, seemed to operate properly. How much was due to removing whatever drugs had kept me comatose or why I was kept that way, I never knew.

I began by being able to make rasping voice sounds, then whispers, and finally words. I was largely disoriented. I gradually became more human, at least by day, though at night I was quite delusional for some time, and there were extensive journeys, being pushed in a wheelchair through endless corridors, to have physical therapy for the lower half; for the upper half, and speech therapy for my mouth and larynx. There was an occasional visit from a psychotherapist, who offered me an opportunity to talk, once I came to the point of speaking in comprehensible phrases. I wanted nothing so much as to be able to get out of bed, walk around, and escape from the infernal hospital.

My Delusional Roommate

A shred of normality was available to me—the realization that I was suffering from a post-operative, anoxic, opiated, post-traumatic state. My brief stay in the first step-down ward at New York Hospital (where I had been for a work-up of my strokes) included a roommate, a post-operative man, whose similar state to my own and later post-operative condition involved the delusion that his wife was running off with a bus driver. I remembered thinking this man should be told he was having a post-operative reaction which was going to go away and not merely that he was mistaken about his wife. I told myself this, and it helped.

DREAMS

Hallucinatory Dreams; Detailed Narratives

My nocturnal mental creations were truly hallucinatory, and persisted into my daytime thinking. There was my Gestapo luxurious private plane story. Then Gerard Schwartz came into the dream-picture, as a notorious roué in the 1930s, whose father had been a close friend of Hitler, as well as of Joan Fontaine (with whom Gerry was having an affair—she was also close to Hitler). Gerry knew that his father was trying to make a treaty for Hitler, with some country of the South, apparently a medieval country in the style of the movie *The Thief of Baghdad*—involving the assassination of the old king of *The Thousand and One Nights*—which was to supply the Nazis with luxuries unavailable in Austria. I upbraided Gerry for having failed to explain what was happening to the Allies; he became tearfully guilty at this accusation. (Guilt was very prominent in these experiences.) There was a hallucination about Lee Balter's Saturn-like dining room, from where we were teletransported to Vietnam, another site of depredation.

Dream of Benjamin Britten

In another dream story, I found, in a copy of a 1930s art magazine, an article with photographs of a gigantic siege cannon on a rail car, designed by the British composer Benjamin Britten and given to Hitler. My Britten, who somewhat resembled the Bruton Neville Chamberlain, had been a secret Nazi and needed to be exposed. I then found this cannon at a restorer's workshop in Tokyo and sent for Michael to photograph it. Britten made another connection with Hitler and my father's secret betrayer employee. *The Thief of Baghdad* had a cuddly sweet king, who was assassinated by a mechanical machine (read respirator and other hospital appliances).

Dream of My Hospital Ship

Later in recovery: I was on a hospital ship and could get up and move around. We stopped somewhere between Seattle and Alaska and were invited to dinner with some interesting people. I decided I should buy a hospital ship and travel north the following summer, touring, visiting, and helping the sick along the route with my ship. Michael was going to help me research this plan. I actually told Nicole, who stayed in Florida with me throughout this period, about this excellent idea, and she humored me by agreeing to do some research, an excellent sign of improvement.

Railroad Dream

Still later there was my dream of the railroad yard, where I sit up and see many other similar cars. Each one carries a dead person, and I wonder whether I am also dead. (I think the shuttling here and there was a replay of my daytime experience of being wheeled from one rehab appointment to another location for X-rays and back to my room, through long basement hallways.) In sleep, I was solving the question of what had happened to me during the preceding weeks of unconsciousness; the answer was, I had been dead; but now I was alive. How did I know? I woke up a little, and exercised a bit of wakefulness, sitting up, like someone waking from sleep, I looked around, and reached a realistic conclusion. Dead people don't sit up and look around, seeing only other dead people; life is not but a dream. Live people wake up from sleep, and one can wake up from a dream about being dead - and find oneself alive. This was the first real dream I had, which I knew was a dream I had actually awakened from, not reality; and I realized I was recovering. I had a series of dreams about living and being able to breathe underwater; but I was living as a captive. Those were early—still clearly post-traumatic.

Coherent Plots and Sequences

These dreams were coherent, though obviously improbable, stories with plots. They came in sequences from night to night, or skipping a day or a few days, like episodes of a cinema serial, and contained several characters out of my daily life. They overlapped into waking life—there were Nazi dreams, ship dreams, railroad dreams—travel was on my mind, evidently. My children, who visited regularly, were my contacts with the world (Barbara was either in the hospital herself or unable to travel); Michael served this purpose in my dreams. I combined post-traumatic memories of old times with experiences, recalled and repressed, of my recovery time.

The Dream-Subject of Captivity

Guilt, guilt, guilt. I remember these dreams still, and very vividly; normal dream images—composite figures, rebuses, word plays—did not figure; referents to recent experience abounded. Connections to childhood analogues were clear. Captivity was a frequent subject; for instance, I knew if I accepted that I was a prisoner, and didn't make a fuss, I would be released. Being underwater, but able to breathe, reproduced the ventilator, though I have no conscious memory of how it felt to be attached to one, as I was in an induced coma at the time; maybe the underwater was the ether of the distant past, more than the anesthesia of the recent past. I would be living with a sort of assistant, who cooked for me and made beds; this young man was a monkey but his fur felt like Nicole's Burmese cats. There were dream passes that allowed me out of the hospital for agreeable meals; one dream pass had me shopping, buying two dogs, and a house in New Jersey. In other words, there were representations from daily life that supported the feeling I had that when I was sleeping, I was really awake, and vice versa. That I can still remember so much, so clearly, now, almost five years later, strikes me as very unlike the usual situation, when so many memories, particularly of dreams, are so evanescent. Of course, I had become fairly comfortable with the return of childhood terrors, less frightening but still there.

The Purpose of Dreams

If one asks, "What inspired the dream in the first place?", one comes to another Freudian precept. Dreams are triggered by waking experiences that aroused guilt or other anxious feelings (Freud termed this the "day residue"). Freud wrote about seeing a botanical monograph which, through a long series of associations, he realized was related to guilt about a failed treatment he had employed with a friend. The friend was also a rival. The mistake, which contributed to the friend's death, was to recommend cocaine, a botanical. Seeing a copy of the botanical monograph revived Freud's guilt over his ambivalence, his competitiveness, his conflicted relationship with his friend, Fleischl von Marxow. When the friend died, Freud had dealt with the day's problem by putting it aside and turning his attention to another subject. It returned in a dream, where the problematic issue is represented as not yet resolved, but capable of resolution.

The toxicity of the problem is doubly diminished in the dream. The dream presents a situation as transferred into the future where it becomes potentially manageable, in the basket of things "I haven't gotten around to, but I can and will do." "And anyway, it's not real, it's just a dream." In the first place, the dream represents the task as yet to be accomplished. As an example, I dreamed that I had not yet completed my medical training and had no license, that I've been pretending to be a doctor. This goes back to my time as an intern, when I didn't know what I was doing, felt like an impostor, not really a doctor, and kept thinking my patients would denounce me as a fraud.

That dreams, jokes, errors, and memory-lapses could be influenced by and could satisfy unconscious wishes was, at Freud's time, a remarkable and original creative idea. It extended the view of dreams as vehicles of gratification by virtue of their capacity to represent unconscious wishes as satisfied. Nowadays, one might say that Freud projected outside his own unconscious internal conflicted, competing feelings and wishes, both competitive and affectionate. Freud's desires influenced his theory, for example, in such a way as to rationalize and justify his depreciating attitudes and his attachment to his father; rivalry, fear, and love led to, and frustrated, desires relating to his father.

He needed to depreciate his father, and to justify the put-down; he needed to deny his dependence on his father, and to assert his individuality against him. Freud's seduction theory diminished, and criminalized, the fathers of the preceding generation. That is not to say that there is no seduction, as seduction implies seeming to promise more than is delivered. As is usual in intimate relationships, a certain degree of seduction is exercised by the protagonists toward each other, and a certain degree of magnification is added by the recipient-victim. The child wants, expects, and feels entitled to more, and the parent likewise; invariably, tender desires are felt as ungratified and, to a degree, betrayed.

Freud was very disturbed by his father's telling him that many years before his son's birth, he had walked in the gutter on the orders of an anti-Semite, randomly encountered.

Ungratified love leads to disappointment and anger. Freud had dream images which related to this. In this instance, Freud wanted to entice his father to intimacy, and the father had similar inclinations in regard to the son; Freud's ambivalent relation to his father is the main issue—the anti-Semite is an occasion for Freud to focus feelings away from himself and onto his father.

However, the theory was not based solely on Freud's interpretations of his own psychic maneuvers; it was also based on interpretation of data provided by patients, who had their own reasons for describing their histories to Freud as they did. Fathers (or uncles or older brothers) can be seductive, but children can also be seductive; they can also feel betrayed by their beloved elders, when those elders are revealed to conduct more intimate connections among their own generational coevals. Envy and jealousy are also motives for vengeful behavior; episodes in literature, in classical Greek drama, in Shakespeare, in legend and myth, could also be seen as representing complicated, unconscious conflicts among wishes, fears, and guilt.

In my Oedipal state, the dragon was a polymorphous figure; it could, at the same time, represent my father, the enemy and greedy possessor of the treasure, with me as the hero Siegfried. But then, I was being the thief myself, a guilty patricide, eligible for retributive punishment myself; hence, the fear of the image of the dragon. Then the arrangement was revived in my adolescent state—of mingled love and hostility, self-assertion, a search for independence, of attachment, and a longing for freedoms. I demonized my father, but my hostility was overt, and my fear was hidden; now it is (in retrospect) expressed in examination dreams, and the phobia is replaced. (This became another publication.) My father was not the only one to serve as an "other," but he was the chief "other." Freud found that feelings in daily life, fed by hidden desires, influence thinking; thus, did I find that in myself. This aperçu meant that subjectivity was not influenced by experiences alone, but also by forbidden and unconscious wishes.

Return and Evolution of Post-Traumatic Dreams. Revelation: Intensity of My Irrational Guilt

Transferred to a rehab facility in Delray, I had a further period of having horrible dreams *qua* deliria—being tied down, imprisoned, chased by the Gestapo. It took me days to relinquish my waking beliefs that my dreams were waking experiences. I had a dream in which I was dead but could still hear a radio program to which dead people could subscribe, but only if they signed up within a day; I woke up, frightened, unable to remember the telephone number to call. In another I was at a dinner in a five-star hotel at the South Pole; the dining room was a passage built around a huge globe, which one could adjust so that one sat next to any point on earth; someone assigned us to Vietnam. I became terrified, and incredibly guilty, took off my clothes, jumped onto the globe, clutched it, wailing desperately: I had to atone for Vietnam. The next day, I implored my daughter to contact a friend whose father had been important in the state department during the Nixon administration, to persuade the man to apologize for Vietnam.

A partial interpretation: survivor guilt. I had survived the Second World and Vietnam wars (the first by being under-age, and the second by working on research relevant to lie detectors), survived my father's death as well as my own, now four times (three endocarditis and one cardiac near-arrest), without having deserved any of that. I had to make up for my sins before my final end; so, I must have thought I was on my deathbed during all of those weeks of unconsciousness.

Another example: I had discovered that Sotheby's was to have a sale of specimen trees growing in the Adirondacks since pre-revolutionary times; but now in need of care, as the descendants of the long line of settlers who had been maintaining the trees had died. I woke up, certain that I had a bill to pay for the trees; again, I desperately pleaded with my son to pay for the trees and keep them alive and told Michael that I had bought three trees by phone. These were not Bishop Berkeley's trees. They were my trees, ergo my life debts.

Santa Claus

I first heard of Santa Claus in school at the late age of six. Yet I believed in him, because my teacher said that good children receive presents from Santa Claus at Christmas time; and I assumed that Santa was probably a lot like Uncle Rudolf, except that he came for Christmas, not birthdays. When my parents received my news with incredulity and surprise that I could believe such nonsense, I felt humiliated (for having been fooled), and angry (because that meant no presents). This came from the same people who acted as though they knew everything or, at least, knew how I should behave and who refused to explain things when I asked. Children don't need hard evidence to believe in Santa Claus.

I Revisit My Theories About Life

Gradually, reluctantly, I emended my understanding of my experiences by revising my theories about life. Santa Claus came to be like a dream vision, and dreams came to be seen as unsubstantial: experiences to be sure, but experiences one could distinguish from experiences in waking life, at least after young childhood. Waking experience enters dreams, and dream life presents itself as waking experience. Dreams, hallucinations, deliria, fantasies, ego trips and drugged trips share similarities.

I concluded that there are some things I would never understand, and some things I would understand—and that this was true for everyone. No need to fret or stew or be mystical about it. What does it matter if what I experience as voluntary choice isn't? Life is full of acts that occur when there is no question of choice; when I walk down the sidewalk, I don't usually bump into other people. This is done without any effort on my part, a consequence of previous training of my brain, which now functions autonomously. I decide on the route I will take, based on an impression of how much traffic there will be; I make a choice, but that it is conscious doesn't mean that it will prove to have been the best route. When it becomes obvious that the way is blocked, I switch to an alternate route, and off I go. When I'm reasonably trusting about my unconscious thinking, interesting thoughts invariably pop out, without my having anticipated them; they probably originated in some unconscious process that takes place in the mind. If the issue is that some ancient theory out of childhood is doing the predicting, it might be editable.

Dreadful things actually happen; some of them happened to the adults in my life, and some happened to me. Unfortunately, traumas are real and, in earlier life, more potent in influencing the likelihood of anticipating similar events. Going on an exciting taxi ride to the country, being smothered with ether, and waking in a delirium were real. Riding in a Grottenbahn dragon into a dark tunnel was exciting, but what with skeletons leaping out, and screams and moans, it seemed analogous to being held down and asphyxiated and accounted for the appearance of waking fears, and night terrors, involving being immobilized and buried alive. The difficulty is that both benign information and trauma come from outside. Telling a miserable child that life is long and it takes time to grow up is fine, but the child may not have an inkling about time. Time and change have to be experienced.

Jonathan Swift elaborated in fiction much of what I describe of my experiences of myself. He wrote of "Gulliver," who also coexisted with little people and big people and experienced being tied down.

THE BEGINNING OF THE END

Barbara's Decline

Between mid-2014 and her death in June, 2018, Barbara declined, still gradually but more obviously. I had lost a large part of my Barbara, my wife, my friend, my rival, my lover, the extension of my mind, my traveling companion through the world, and through life, the one with whom I had learned and who had learned with me.

Tears come to my eyes as I write. My mood changed with Barbara's state of mind; if she seemed distressed, her face showed pain, and I couldn't help her. I would kiss her, rub her back, and buy her good things to eat. She knew me and loved me; she smiled when she saw me. I would tell her I was going out. She asked, "Where? I would explain, and an hour later when I left, she would ask again. "Where are you going?" People asked, "How is Barbara?" and I said, "Not much different than she has been." But how different she was from what she had been. It is a cliché to say, "One doesn't really know what one has until it is gone," but one doesn't know that until it happens. I never knew how much I loved my Barbara, and how much I would miss her when I lost her while she was still here and I was constantly reminded of our past together.

About a year and a half ago (2018), Barbara, her aide, and I went to a restaurant around the corner for dinner; Barbara walked with her walking frame. When it was time to go home, the aide said Barbara was too tired to walk home, and she would push her, seated on the walker, "No, no," I said, but the aide was too quick for me, put Barbara on the walker, pushed off into a bump on the sidewalk, where Barbara was pitched out, landed on her back and head; we had six hours in an emergency room, before we were allowed home. Why was I slow? Because the aide was the authority, the adult, and not to be contradicted. Could I have defied the authority of the aide more easily?

Towards the end, Barbara found it more difficult to communicate. Even during the years of her decline, she was able to feed herself, showed that she relished her food and drink, and could answer direct questions, though sometimes she was confined to a "yes' or "no." On the other hand, sometimes, suddenly, she seemed to pop back out. Once, she intervened in the dinner-table conversation to correct my spelling of some obscure technical term to do with roof building. If friends asked her whether she remembered some occasion or person, she'd reply with a single syllable but in a tone that made it clear she'd understood the question perfectly. And her "yes" was sometimes accompanied by a beatific smile of pleasure at the memory.

With her live-in caretaker, Angie, Barbara would join the party to go to the ballet with us and seemed to enjoy watching the performances. We always took her with us when dining out in a restaurant, and she was able to listen to the menu being read and completely capable of indicating what she wanted to order. Sometimes that would even be a steak—we'd usually share one—and though she could not cut it up for herself, she could use her fork to spear the pieces.

She knew her mind and appetite and would indicate clearly if, for example, she wanted dessert. At home, she always sat in her same place at the table, to my right. She responded to physical affection, with a sigh at having her neck or back rubbed. Thanks to Angie, and the other caretakers, Barbara was always immaculately dressed, coiffed, and made up. She came to want me to decide and share the food in which she had had such an interest. Angie had to feed her. She stopped taking wine at meals, and then even a glass of Champagne beforehand.

Barbara's Training Sessions with Susan Mask

In Palm Beach she had regular sessions with a genius personal trainer, Susan Mask (with whom I and the house guests also trained). With Susan, Barbara could do some surprising physical feats, including throwing and catching a largish ball. Susan finally got Barbara into the pool, which she adored. But by the time we got back to New York a few weeks later, in May, 2018, it was evident that Barbara was failing. She was having trouble swallowing, had lost her appetite, and was often too tired to get out of bed. On the 31st of May she showed signs of weakening still more; Nicole's professional opinion was that her mother might last another few days, but Barbara died in the early hours of June 1st. Though I was prepared—indeed, had been for years—I was shattered and rapidly sank into grief.

Some Jewish Cultural Practices at Our New York Home

There was, of course, no question of religious rites, but we did try to observe some Jewish cultural practices, and we received friends as guests at home in New York on the Wednesday. Michael and Jill had arranged for good wine and food from a good caterer. All the living generations were represented, with many friends of ours and our children, as well as those of our grandchildren. Several people observed the Jewish tradition of bringing food to the bereaved, and we ended up with about twenty surplus cakes.

Memorial Service

The memorial service on Friday was not a funeral (Barbara had been cremated days earlier), but an occasion, presided over by Nicole, for people to share their memories of Barbara. Speakers included Ann Bramson, her publisher and editor, Ina Backman (her Radcliffe friend, mentioned earlier), Corby Kummer, a fellow foodie, and Michael. Lunch after the service was at Sistina, one of the many restaurants Barbara had helped in her career. There was a misunderstanding about the reservation, and it was astonishing to see how they heroically provided lunch and excellent wine for sixty people they had not been expecting.

My State of Mind; Barbara's Obituaries Bothered Me

And me? Some of the time I was cross and tetchy. The obituaries were long and prominent, led by Matt Schudel's in the *Washington Post*, which was syndicated all over the U.S. and abroad as well. In the *New York Times* Sam Roberts wrote the obituary, and in the British national newspaper, *The Guardian*, Paul Levy (who, with his wife, Penny, made the trip to New York from Oxfordshire to support me) paid obituary tribute to his close friend. In short, much was written and much said. But I was bothered and annoyed. None of them really "got" Barbara, I thought. Except for Paul, none of them saw her as more than a figure in the food world—and even those failed to credit her with many of her accomplishments, ideas, and innovations, for some of which others had even been given (or had taken) the credit. Where was the account of her various business ventures, of her invention and marketing (though unsuccessful) of the electric whisk that eventually evolved into the stick blender? Where was the poetry? The dance? What about her "eye," that made her such a good friend to so many artists and led her to collect work of such merit? Where was asking for a Braque at age 13? The child prodigy with Massine and Ulanova? Sharing Fred Landesman's dreamy paintings with Alexander Iolas, who gave Fred a show that put him in the company of Magritte and Matta, when Surrealism was not widely known? Introduction of the microwave as a general cooking tool? Spokesperson for healthy artisan food? Why didn't the obituarists see the size and catholicity of her social circle, and the talent and distinction of her circle of good friends? Why couldn't they see how out of the ordinary, how special, how remarkable my Barbara was? How ahead of her time? (And how measureless my grief?)

My Anger and PTSD

I acknowledged that post-traumatic stress disorder genuinely existed after my cardiac crisis. I still had more than a smidgeon of it. Barbara's death was another great trauma. It was a good many days, and many deep troughs, before I could see the anger of my reaction, its similarity to the post-traumatic stress disorder, its connection with my dream-life, and with my guilt. Nag, nag, nag—my friends nagged me about my antidepressant medication. Why didn't I increase the dose a bit? Talk to another professional? Do something? Then, perhaps two weeks later, as I looked for my antidepressant pills, I realized with a shock, that they weren't there—and hadn't been on the shelf with my other pills for at least ten days. Had I knocked the bottle over into the wastepaper basket? Had I forgotten to renew the prescription? How could I have insisted, to my friends' and family's repeated questioning, that I was taking my meds? My grief, I was thunderstruck to have to acknowledge, had been expressed and compounded by the withdrawal symptoms of SSRIs. I was mentally furiously rending my clothes and eating ashes. As I write, I have misery.

June 19th, our 63rd Wedding Anniversary

Barbara on June 1, 2018. Our sixty-third wedding anniversary would have happened on June 19. Michael, Jill, Lily, Oliver and I had made plans to spend ten days in France, before Lily would return to start her first year at college and Oliver his last. It would probably have been our last vacation together. However, I had realized that Barbara was failing. She was hardly responsive.

There were many evenings at the dinner table when I had animated, if not fiery, disagreements with friends, then heatedness in discussions. I relished such moments, but whenever Barbara had said, "Quiet, Ernie," I tended to comply. Such moments had become rare and then not at all. She could hug and, barely, kiss, but not walk more than a few steps even with help from her ever present attendant, Angie. I cancelled my reservations, anticipating what might, and then did, happen. She woke from sleep, stopped breathing, and was dead.

I was utterly stunned. Barbara and I had experienced years of her decline. After 2007, when we toured Egypt, Syria, and Jordan, we continued to summer in Vermont and later winter in Florida. I had imagined that I had somewhat prepared for and accommodated to my oncoming loss, but that did not happen. Many friends consoled me, but I failed to be consoled. The best news I had from people who had lost some vital companion was that I would never quite get over it, but gradually I would feel better.

When a tree falls in the forest, does it make a noise if there's no one there to hear it? My most important tree fell, and I felt the crash.

FINIS

PART II – FURTHER PSYCHOANALYTIC REFLECTIONS

Subjectivity: The Power of Bedside Manner; Another Example of Subjectivity: Freud's Mythical Analyst, the Objective Man

Even the mighty Freud, and his students (I speak for myself here), have yet to deal convincingly with the professional subjectivity question. Only too often, we represent ourselves as having knowledge of politics, morals, or other uncertain areas of opinion, about which we claim to have special, objective knowledge. Early on, Freud proposed that the analyst can be objective, like a surgeon performing surgery; my experience with surgery does not support this argument. Another of Freud's analogies was to imagine a listener in a railway car, while his seatmate, next to the window, describes the passing scene. The listener can only report what he hears of what the neighbor sees, and that is subject, as is beauty, to "the eye of the beholder." Signs of subjectivity in the analyst were later regarded as "countertransferences" (irrational responses to the patient's reenergized instinctual forces and infantile transference in the analyst), some benign, others not. But, at bottom, countertransference was seen through a baleful eye. It is not realistic; it invades rational thought; it feeds subjectivity; it should be "analyzed out" by means of further analysis. This is unrealistic. The analyst cannot be entirely disinterested.

Subjectivity is an issue in the quest for reality. The sensory givens have permanent limits, beyond the problems of neurophysiological givens, and instinctual inherences. There is no "analyzing out" of countertransference or transference. Extending the sensorium by means of microscopes, telescopes, and computers helps. Perception is modified during maturation but objectivity remains limited; passions fueled by instinctual wishes never disappear. Conflicting desires may yield to compromise, but we can never have everything we desire, even when we try to, as in those old saws—"take things one day at a time" or "take a breath and count to ten." It would be nice to really know what's what.

"Disinterested" judges, even when appointed to lifetime terms, come to differing judgements. To acknowledge subjectivity is to understand, and believe, that we cannot really know reality. Wishes don't go away; desire is permanent; direct sensation is limited. The imperfections of our sensory apparati, and interpretations, are interposed between the forces that activate the sensorium, and the perceived experience. Having said that, we go on believing in free will, and even free lunch. Someone else will pay, and someone will decide; even the twelve good people (jurors) working together make questionable decisions, as do the nine Supreme Court justices. To the extent that we subjective creatures can be objective about reality—in our efforts to accommodate to it or manipulate it to our advantage—we differ from other organisms, who can only adapt to restricted environments, or else be extinguished by Darwinian chance. The subjectivity question has become a major issue in psychoanalysis during my time in the field. Thinking about how subjectivity can be approached more objectively is a prerequisite for a more accurate assessment of "reality."

Writing in ripe, mature age, early on in his *Autobiography*, Benjamin Franklin described how, during his adolescence in Philadelphia, he took up vegetarianism in (what I've been calling) a utopian frame of mind but soon gave it up. At eighteen, he was invited to a dinner at the home of a well-to-do-merchant, and noted, "Hitherto I had stuck to my resolution of not eating animal food, and on this occasion I consider'd, with my master Tryon, the taking every fish as a kind of unprovoked murder, since none of them had or ever could do us any injury that might justify the slaughter. All this seemed very reasonable. But I had formerly been a great lover of fish, and, when this came hot out of the frying-pan, it smelt admirably well. I balanc'd some time between principle and inclination, till I recollected that, when the fish were opened, I saw smaller fish taken out of their stomachs; then thought I, 'If you eat one another, I don't see why we mayn't eat you.' So I din'd upon cod very heartily, and continued to eat with other people, returning only now and then occasionally to a vegetable diet. So convenient a thing is it to be a reasonable creature, since it enables one to find or make a reason for everything one has a mind to do." It would be difficult to find a more telling example of how, as we mature, an ideal can be modified, guilt diminished, shrunken, together with youthful idealistic immodesty, and a desire satisfied. How much time it took me, alas, to eat my cod and like it. To discipline my thinking, to emend my perceptual distortions which I thought were partly responsible for my various miseries, to give up some of my presumptuousness allowed me freedom to be more objective.

Training in Psychoanalysis

The issue of training in psychoanalysis, from my personal experience as the subject of it (now we would say, "the consumer") and as the practitioner (now, "provider") can be divided into two general positions. One may be termed that of study emphasizing the rational capacities, where the aim is to enlarge the repertoire of factors that combine to produce change—in German, the *Naturwissenschaften*. I refer to the use of verbal language in concert with senses and operating *in extenso* via instruments, as the eye by the microscope, or the printed page by the Internet, or by mathematical constructions. Here we are concerned mainly with the physical sciences and with measurable factors—the body as machine, the mind as brain.

A second, in German, the *Geisteswissenschaften*, would include eye-training, in the sense of "an eye for art," or ear-training in relationship to relative pitch and musical sounds, or training in affect recognition, using posture, sound, facial expression of emotion; and social science, history, cultural anthropology, psychology, and the "soft" sciences. Here, an aim is to deal with perception. The brain as mind, the body as habitat. To the mind allotment, I want to add the unconscious aspects of thinking: unconscious influences on perception, the peculiar role of inspiration and esthetic-synesthetic experience, and sensorial inputs. In my former research problems, we tried to deal with the matter by adding examination of the substrate of thinking, the unconscious registration and processing in the mind, and the physiological undertone in the body. In contrast, I am now struggling with the question, what is creativity? What is originality? How can we cultivate these magical moments when we make new connections?

As students, most of us become reconciled to the idea that every cause has effects and that causes precedes effects in time, while not all temporal antecedents are causes: *post hoc* is not necessarily *propter hoc*. An antecedent may be a necessary predecessor, but it may need to have a milieu of a variety of ancillary factors (sufficient conditions) to produce a particular effect. Different effects may occur when the particular "cause," say, a gene, is activated in different circumstances. Concurrent events cannot be taken as one causing another. Not, at least, in complex organisms. A trainable reflex action should not be confused with, or taken as a model for, memory in a much more complex organism.

"Predisposition" and "trigger" concepts are often necessary even for simple organisms. That said, the inclination against complexity and pro simplification remains, no matter how much experience denies the validity of simple models.

The supposed incompatibility of psyche and soma, mind and brain, fight and flight, nature and nurture, arguments based on fallacies such as attributing adult qualities to immature organisms (e.g., ascribing complicated theories to babies) are all still discussed and argued, in the hope of unifying disparate approaches. Language is tendentious. Really, the *hoc* of the *post* should be a plural. So should the *post*.

I once accepted a dual approach. One was the psychological, which involves identifying the forces that interfere with objectivity; eventually, my interest in distortion in perception and thinking became a motive for entering the world of psychoanalytic self-study. The second was to think about how objective thinking can operate in a simpler, more focused, experimental ambience. Any situation that involves people inevitably activates interpersonal prejudices. While Galileo's Pisa discovery (that two objects fall with the same acceleration) involved inanimate objects, experimenting with people interacting involves action and reaction, and consequently, a continually changing state. One participant acts and then the other reacts. To follow the argument I outlined, that conscious and unconscious are entangled, is to suppose that the original Freudian theory, that the two are separated by a force, was incorrect. It would be an error to think of unconscious and conscious thinking as different and independent. They operate concurrently, overlap, and are interwoven together. But the idea is not incorrect. Just incomplete.

My two *ad rem* approaches disregarded the relativity attendant upon trying to differentiate between kinds of science. The German terms *Geisteswissenschaften* and the *Naturwissenschaften* fail to define two distinct sciences. It is certainly possible to contrast the mental and social with the inanimate, material worlds. The division "mind-brain" is a way of trying to simplify the subject of study, by reducing the complexity of the subject matter. When the brain can be treated as an organ, in the way that a liver may be, one can use the approaches of anatomy and physiology. The simplification of even the complex functioning of the organ doesn't deal with the ghost-in-the-machine problem. There is no mind in the absence of brain, nor can one study the brain mindlessly, that is, without subjectivity. While the brain would be part of the "*Natur*" and the mental would be part of the "*Geist*," the definitions are both right and incomplete. They lead and mislead.

In simplifying questions, we try to limit the problem of how the distorting mind distorts the studying; we pretend that the investigator of the psyche is objective, even though we know better. Interchanges between people cannot be free of the individualities of the participants. One of the most telling issues is the tendency to jump to simple conclusions. *Naturwissenschaft* and *Geisteswissenschaft,* like most things, are two ends of a more or less bell-shaped curve.

Examination of the vegetable and mineral parts of the natural world doesn't pose the problem which arises when a question is asked of another person, whose response causes a reframing of the question. When two animals are in a relationship, the situation is unstable. At one time, seemingly, the natural world could be studied using instruments that can be calibrated, a clock, say, that can be made to run at a specific speed, and be synchronized with a standard clock. The synchrony will remain synchronous; you can use the Internet to look up official US Time; as the time given is already synchronized with a clock that sets the standard for all other clocks, you can use that, and do so without synchronizing your own clock.

Then, Einstein discovered that clocks record different times, depending on how relatively quickly they are moving; this phenomenon is under further examination. Physics and mathematics, not introspection, are the tools for working on such matters; even so, measurable phenomena can be interpreted differently by different observers, and the observers don't know what unknown factors may be involved in the studies they are conducting. Relativity, Heisenberg, Bohr, upset the Newtonian apple cart. The Heisenberg Principle can be directly transposed to other contexts: if you can't know the position of the particle while you're measuring its velocity, because the measurement changes the measured, it's similar to when two or more people interact.

"Mind" is a concept, not a thing. Atoms used to be regarded as made up of matter, of "things," but no longer; mass and energy are interconvertible, time is no longer a constant; the speed of light is invariable, but not affected by the velocity of its source. Some particles are entangled in such a way that, though widely separated, an action performed on one can cause the other to undergo a change (what Einstein called "spooky action at a distance").

We design double-blind drug studies, in which neither the recipient nor the provider of the drug knows whether a particular subject receives the (we hope) useful active chemical, or the control, the (we think) inert one. This is supposed to eliminate the effect of allowing an enthusiastic happy doctor, who believes he is giving a good pill, to influence a suffering patient; by and large, the patient would get better just because he feels encouraged by an (often idealized) wise man. We know that people enlisted to be subjects respond to the experience of acquiring a relationship with outsiders who are very interested in their responses. Furthermore, subjects feel useful when they can provide useful information; most people like to please.

People get better when they have doctors whom they trust, with whom they feel comfortable, who they think understand them and want and are able to help. Teachers with positive, encouraging attitudes toward their students get better results than those with more negative attitudes. Parents who wish their children well, have a more positive attitude about learning, and enjoy learning together with their children are likely to have children who are interested in learning; after all, pleasing the parent, especially if the activity also pleases the child, is a good predictor of results. If the experimenter is enthusiastic for the patient's betterment, and thinks the drug being tested will help, the patient is likely to get better, even if only transiently. If neither the prescriber nor the subject knows what the subject is getting, it may not lessen whatever effect comes about, just by virtue of the fact that the subject is involved in a relationship with a doctor, who might be administering a useful drug. A good teacher who has a belief in some idea is likely to persuade the student to look on that idea favorably, whether the idea is right or wrong. This is the usual sense of the "placebo" effect. On the other hand, a sour relationship can have a destructive effect; parents are quite capable of inhibiting their children or worse. I know of no term that would describe a baneful effect, except "baneful."

At Queen Square, the Scot, Cameron, who had a mutually respectful relationship with his patient of the many lesions, probably had a significantly better effect on his patients than the browbeating, insulting St. Charles Elkington. Wouldn't it be interesting to be able to measure that difference, or to find out there is no difference? We could design an experiment, which measured the degree to which patients followed each of the two doctors' advice. Wouldn't such understanding help doctors and patients, psychoanalysts and psychoanalysands, to find good partnerships for their work together? One can, in any event, measure the placebo effect.

A frosty, unpleasant doctor, who dispenses an experimental drug, may have a negative placebo effect; his recipient may get worse, whether the actual drug is given or not. Therefore, large numbers of recipients have to be enlisted, enough so the studiers can conclude that the interpersonal effects will cancel out. Only then can the experimenters state that the placebo effects are not a factor that differs for the different groups, and that only the drug-no drug difference is responsible for the outcomes. Sadly, another researcher can come along and find that doing the same procedure doesn't end with the same outcome. Perhaps the diagnosis of the subjects was not identifying the same genetic factors (phenotype did not reflect genotype) so that though symptoms and lab findings might look the same, some other factors caused different drug responses.

Introducing Transference

In his interactions with patients, Freud often found that their attitudes toward the doctor seemed not to be consistent with the events and purposes which had brought them together. On the one hand, this gave the doctor the opportunity of tracing the patient's attitudes and feelings about the work and the relationship with the doctor to "real" experiences, which had occurred in the past, and were now transferred to the analyst, and repeated in accord with the patient's perceptions in the present. So long as the doctor did not behave, more than a smallish amount, as the patient's past objects had, the patient could be shown that his perceptions were actually misperceptions, related to past events, and to interpretations the patient had learned in the past. Now the past was identifiably past; the patient in the "now" had capacities he lacked in his earlier immature childhood years, which might lead to different understandings of relationships, along with the possibility he lacked as a child—to affect and change his environment. In the case of a too-much-reenacted intimacy, this weakened the force, and permanence, of the historically unsatisfactory non-resolution. On the other hand, if the relationship between the analyst and the patient became too real, too gratifying, then it would not allow the detachment individuals needed to achieve.

It is not hard to understand that the right balance between frustration and gratification in a treatment (or in parenting, teaching, etc.) is hard to establish. Too much frustration leads to feelings of disappointment, even of betrayal, anger, or depression, and to a patient who attacks the analysis, or flees it or too little results in a stalled analysis, with a dependent patient. The common situation is the repetition of similar relationships and failures.

Freud taught techniques to his students using analogies to illustrate what he thought, but he sometimes seemed not to realize that his thoughts were partly governed by his wishes. It is clear that, like everyone, on the most general level, he was looking for quick and easy solutions; hence his hopes for cure by hypnosis, by suggestion, by abreaction, using a simplistic general theory of neurosis as a response to seduction. Fortunately, Freud was capable of adapting new ideas. His early instructions were too unrealistic to be capable of achievement, and too mechanical and impersonal to accomplish a beneficial result. The analyst must participate and present a new, questioning experience for the patient. That is what fosters creativity.

Of course, Freud had a personality and a character, which could hardly be concealed. Patients who cannot tolerate the analyst's quiddities have to find another analyst they can put up with. If he tries to hide things, that is apparent; if he is oddly inclined, somehow the patient knows. If he is interested in a subject, he will react differently when the patient starts talking about that subject, rather than about something uninteresting to him. If he changes the subject, then the patient, at least, senses that that subject is one that the analyst thinks isn't leading anywhere useful, or the analyst is motivated by some other, perhaps personal, reason. If he asks a question, it shows he doesn't have some information about the subject the patient is discussing, or thinks the patient has reasons for leaving some aspect out. These are all examples of matters that patients bring up and are grist for the mill. If they don't bring up their ideas about the analyst directly, while indicating that something is omitted obliquely, he can ask why they haven't been mentioned or asked. Many of these realizations evolved in my head during my medical school internship and, later on, with experiences with patients and as one. The in-tune analyst also knows these things about himself and is in a position to take note, and to mention, what the patient fails to bring up.

The couch was supposed to have helped the treatment by diminishing the direct connection of patient and doctor, making it easier for the patient to think freely, and report without the distraction of seeing the doctor's expressions. For his part, the analyst was relieved of the effort to conceal his emotional responses. This reasonable sounding schematization, however, suffered from some defects.

What Makes a Good Therapist and Teacher

In trying to assess the utility of a psychotherapy, one should take the fit between the participants into account. Different patients have different attitudes about therapy, and toward particular therapists, and vice versa; unfortunately, the decision about referring cases is not easily explained. The predilections of each partner in the relationship between two people in the therapeutic arrangement play a large part in what develops between them. Two partners, the doctor and the client, interested in understanding the client's history and development, and capable of doing that, is the theoretical ideal.

My own opinion: experience is an important matter, not only of life, but also of the work. I had three analytic and two psychotherapy experiences as a patient, and I learned something from each of them. A large part of that was how important the therapist or analyst's empathic response and finesse was. This has a lot to do with the benefit of having similar "civilian" backgrounds, which lessens the amount of time taken up in educating the analyst, who needs to arrive at a good sense of the situations in which the patient evolved. In the case of a patient with a previous treatment encounter, it is important to know what the atmosphere had been and what had happened, both in assessing what was gained, and what was not. Having been in both situations, as "analyst" and as "patient," was of great consequence.

Craft and gift have a lot to do with whether the process works, and how well; practical experience of therapy on both sides of the couch is extremely beneficial. An institutional issue is that some analysts devote the major part of their time to doing analysis; others spend much of their time in teaching and administration at hospitals and medical schools; still others are largely involved in research. How much immersion in psychoanalytic clinical work, and writing and teaching about clinical work, using clinical examples, is best? How clinically experienced should the teachers of psychoanalysis be? No size fits all. What standards are appropriate for judging aspirants for positions of teaching and supervising the work of and analyzing candidates in psychoanalytic training? Those who are passed over feel, and are, excluded. Schisms were more frequent in the past than they are now, but that probably had to do with questions of supply and demand, as demand was greater than the supply in the past.

With regard to the parties who meet to create an analytic treatment partnership, they arrive with histories of impressions about reality, which resulted from perceptions (including idiosyncratic interpretations having to do with individual physiologies as well as previous experiences). The accuracy of the predictions based on analytic theories is limited by the boundaries of rational evaluation, the capacities of the sensoria, and the prehistory of the person seeking analysis. I can serve as an example: my experience with Edi Ehrlich and my parents around the adenoidectomy, even after years of maturation and development, and treatment of others and myself, left a residue of negative impressions having to do with my anticipations of the likely consequences of a repetition of the past. There were other bad experiences with doctors. I have also had good luck. I am suspicious but optimistic.

The performance of the consultant who soothed the difficult, traumatized patient at Albert Einstein's Jacobi Hospital was impressive, not because I was unaware of the fact that people influence each other, but because he seemed to know a method of producing a beneficial effect, quickly and easily. That was an "Aha" experience. Then another "Aha" came when I realized that the previous "Aha" came as though that very complex situation showed that a very simple action could "make a person better than he had been before he got sick." A Santa. A "miracle drug."

The explanation was rather more complicated than magical. The paranoid patient suffered from a traumatic upset of a kind that is not infrequent after heart crises, or operations, and generally resolves in time; the consultant helped the patient, but not to the extent he claimed. Rational discussion, understanding of statistical probabilities, cognitive learning, and sympathetic reassurance are all useful; good helpers radiate a feeling of concern, interest, competence, and understanding. The information they convey is useful, if the attitudes of the interlocutor are largely genuine, but sometimes also if he is a gifted psychopath, who can convey a sense of authenticity—such people exist. Unfortunately, everyone has experienced, in retrospect, ruptures of misplaced trust.

The Modification of Traumatic Effects

Victims of traumata are relieved by contact with helpful people but if the patient comes to feel repeatedly betrayed, what does he learn? Time is said to be the best healer, but it is only good times, not further traumata, that heal. The neural networks need to be rearranged; the prejudices, the relics of childhood learning experience, the lessons analogous to "once burned, twice shy"—are glued in by "sticky libido," two words for "we don't really have a lengthy, let alone a brief, explanation." If the forces that allow us to revise automatized behavior and perception are successful, then change is announced in consciousness and experienced as an "Aha" moment. It certainly helped me get into treatment to see this happen; but I needed many more "Ahas" to un-do, and re-do, some of the residues of the past.

"*Aha Erlebnis*," can be translated as "Aha experience," but I feel better with the German. *Erlebnis*, from the root, leben, "to live;" means something lived through. If you have just seen a marvelous piece in the theater and reviewed it saying *Das war ein Erlebnis*, then the experience was not just an experience, it was more significant than that. August Kekulé's dream of six snakes making a hexagon, which solved the problem of the structure of the benzene ring, was memorable. Fleming's insight at seeing his culture dish devoid of bacteria in the presence of the fungus contaminant, and to connect the fungus with the inhibition of bacterial multiplication, was an "Aha" moment. (Fleming *experienced* the sight of the Petri dish; but it was the *meaning* of what he saw that brought the "Aha" of recognition.) I always appreciate a gamut of terms. "Memorable." "Eloquent." The more sensory, the better.

A French contribution to psychoanalytic terminology is *"après coup,"* a retrospective reinterpretation of the meaning of earlier happenings, especially as to the effects of traumas. The "coup" can, as above, have been a belief, a seeming important realization, a conversion experience. Believers can be converts. Converts can re-convert. "Recoup?"

Strain Trauma

There are differences between acute or stress and chronic or strain traumas. I felt the acute traumas, like my mother's bicycle fall, as sudden, painful, and significant, and remember most of them. A sudden disaster is not easily forgotten. I took the chronic more as disagreeable (and more or less significant as they were more or less intense and less or more manageable) aspects of the state of affairs. They seemed "normal"; I didn't regard them as worth thinking about afterwards—except occasionally. There are incidents that are memorialized and others that are forgotten but lurk in the underground of the mind; they can only be deduced by their effects on the surface. Trauma varies in potency according to the maturity, mental development, and physiological condition (sleep, drugged, anoxic, etc.) of the subject who is affected by an experience. Some things cannot be tolerated; some don't seem worth bothering about. So far as immigrants were concerned, they were lucky to have escaped, and the nasty attitudes expressed to and about them were "just words." Immigration was an acute loss trauma. The difficulty of overcoming the stranger role was prolonged, felt as "normal"—a "strain."

Probably my connection to the German language reflects a feeling that I am not entirely American, because it was so difficult to enter and once here, so difficult to feel accepted. I think that my early experience that "Schmetterling" the word could represent so much must have been a huge "Aha Erlebnis." That it could be translated as "butterfly," with such a narrow definition was another "Aha," but not earthshaking enough to be an Erlebnis.

Cinematic and Other American Myths About Psychoanalysis; A Paean to Progress

In the 50s and 60s, Hollywood discovered Freud, but as presented in movies. It included the early Freudian idea—that recovery of repressed traumatic experiences, allowing them to become conscious, would cure neurosis. Freud himself had emended his early ideas about abreaction as cure, and childhood seduction as cause. His capacity to do so was one of his rarest. Later critics were less able to revise than he. Freud's thinking was not stagnant; however, its practitioners were presented so in the cinema.

Ongoing objections to psychoanalysis are still written. Like movie ideas of Freud and analysis, they often misunderstand and misrepresent. Psychoanalysis is false, useless, and destructive. It is for the relatively spoiled, healthy few who have the interest, time, and money to pursue it. It misallocates resources. It has an intimidating effect, destroys creativity, encourages submissiveness, releases antisocial behaviors, or is a pseudo-religion, promulgated by pseudoscientists. It lacks an experimental basis and proposes that anecdotes can be regarded as evidence—a few case histories here and there do not amount to proof. Psychoanalysis, in general, and the Oedipus complex, in particular, are misogynistic, misanthropic, and disrespectful of faith and spirituality. As far as the Oedipus complex is concerned, that is reductive as well.

At the time when I began my training, these concerns had much more foundation than they do now. Many psychoanalysts and psychiatrists, then, regarded homosexuality as perverse and criminal or as a disease. Not any of those simplifying attempts at classification gave useful information as to cause or the process of development. To question that was shocking. Many proponents of psychoanalytic ideas acted as though their ideas were derived from natural science, which they were not—another shock to early adherents. Furthermore, the idea that one could successfully cure either psychiatric conditions like depression, manic depression, or schizophrenia, or so-called psychosomatic illnesses, like ulcers, asthma, or colitis with talking treatment soon proved to be wrong, wishful thinking.

The gurus who claimed that some form of talk therapy could cure schizophrenia and somatic ailments—or who claimed that their discoveries about pathogenesis showed that parenting or social constraints caused them—suggested solutions ranging from foster placement to psychotherapy. It isn't so simple. Intervention sometimes

PART II – FURTHER PSYCHOANALYTIC REFLECTIONS

favors simplistic, better yet, also inexpensive ideas, as though the brain-mind were relatively invulnerable to inherited distortions. Autism, Asperger's, and dyslexia were not recognized as having neurological, congenital, as well as societal determinants, which influence perception and expression, and require special and costly educational methods to help. The neurologic factors underlying cognitive deficits not only went unrecognized, but the children who had such troubles were often regarded as stubborn, negativistic, or stupid. When I was an intern, if no diagnosis could be arrived at, the patient was described as "having a high porcelain titer," as in "a crock of shit." In earlier times, probably witchcraft was blamed.

In the sixties, one reason why psychoanalysis was attempted, and encouraged, for some conditions was that no other treatment was available. We had drugs for schizophrenia, the Promazines. They came with harmful side effects, particularly Parkinsonian neurological complications. The antidepressants, imipramine and iproniazid, were not very effective. Electroshock was useful in fewer cases than then thought; for mania, lithium or other "mood stabilizers" were not yet in use and electro-shock was resorted to more often than it is now. Prefrontal lobotomy was an abominable intervention. Medical and surgical treatments for ulcer or colitis had benefits, together with complications. They have much improved. Patients had to adapt to painful illnesses and were denied psychological help for dealing with them; we were near the beginning of offering psychiatric consultations in hospitals. It was no wonder that patients, families and doctors often turned to folk-medicine remedies. The overselling of psychiatric, psychoanalytic therapy, billing it as curative, not as part of the armamentarium, was harmful because it promised much and delivered much less. A psychoanalytically-oriented teaching that medical intervention ruined the usefulness of psychoanalysis by diminishing the patient's motivation for examining himself wreaked harm.

There were, however, areas where talk therapy proved useful. With few satisfactory approaches to mitigating sufferings, the numbers of applicants for training in psychotherapy on Freudian lines increased. Treating PTSD (previously regarded as malingering), as well as postoperative deliria and disaster effects, turned out to be highly successful, and became employed as a matter of course. Major institutions that had previously taught how to institutionalize patients, treat them with fresh air and exercise, and control them with padded cells, straitjackets, and wet blankets, recruited psychoanalysts to head departments. Psychotherapy was taught and practiced at out-patient clinics. Sadly, inexpensive therapy was expensive for the hospitals, and psychiatric training turned from the clinic to pharmacology. Psychiatrists now often make a living by prescribing drugs and use part of that income to support therapy or analysis practices. In my day, some of us subsidized poorer patients with higher fees that we could charge the richer.

An important trend was the acceptance of the importance of studying child-in-family interactions with longitudinal studies, which clarified some frequent, major maturational and developmental influences, often harmful, and generally challenging. Cognitive and intellectual deficits, chronic illnesses, hostile parental attitudes, parental conflicts, mental disease and addiction often complicate development. Recognizing psychological factors has influenced the teaching and practice of social workers, teachers, healthcare, and child care workers, as well as of medical doctors, psychiatrists and psychologists. The advice that some things in life must be borne is not very helpful when now something better is out there. Territoriality and doctrinal controversy, among and between different professional approaches, and sniping by one group at another inevitably happens, but coercing people out of their troubles, using carrots and sticks alone, should be more a thing of the past.

PART II – FURTHER PSYCHOANALYTIC REFLECTIONS

Exchange of Ideas and Theories Among Different Schools of Psychoanalytic Thought: A New Flexibility

Among the many beneficent changes of approach during my professional lifetime was the acceptance of the idea that attention deficit, hyperactivity, dyslexia, and several other cognitive deficits are genetically transmitted physiological conditions, not hysterical or behavioral disorders. They affect behavior that may disrupt a class, but the child is not unusually stupid, obstinate, or aggressive. I was disruptive in fourth grade but not stupid. I was bored and resentful at being held back; I was probably a victim of discrimination as a refugee and certainly traumatized by the disruption of my life. I had the treatable condition of boredom and resentment at being held back by the school authorities and that had to do with the America-First sentiment at a time of economic depression. It had a lasting impact as another blow to my optimism about respecting people in positions of authority who don't exercise it in a constructive way. I had a behavior problem, not a cognition problem. However, the way I was treated because I was foreign and unwanted led me to an understanding of how such a status can wound.

Why are there still those who deride or deprecate Freud's standing in intellectual history? He is still criticized over what he thought, or what he is supposed to have meant or done, at different times in a long career that ended with his death in 1939. Often, those who followed Freud and modified or changed his ideas are either unknown or assumed to have continued slavishly to promulgate his sexist imaginings among credulous followers. People still ask, "Are you a Freudian?" Freud's successors at other schools are still known as Jungian, or Reichian, or Sullivanian or Horneyan, or Kohutian or Kleinian, or something else, but the founders of those groups aren't targets as Freud is. It is as though no evolution or development has been accomplished by Freud's followers with or after him. To be a Freudian is often regarded as to be a relic of ancient times. In truth, differentiating theories among the various schools and professional psychoanalytic associations have diminished. Each group has accepted therapeutic approaches based on the findings of the others. That is yet another advance.

That has also happened within the International Psychoanalytic Association, the group that Freud founded. This was originally a small group. On vacation in Maine, and at a meeting in Vienna, schmoozing with those who were among the pioneers, Jeanne Lampl de Groot, Bak, Dora Hartmann, among others, I heard nostalgic memories about the old days when there were only sixty in attendance. I have no nostalgia for my professional younger days, so far as knowledge is concerned, but I do greatly mourn the loss of the pioneers I knew who were responsible for much of the progress in the field at large before and after I arrived on the scene. The International meeting now attracts a few thousand every other year, and one hears opinions and findings from all over the world. It includes many students of once-upon-a-time schismatic teachers whose ideas have been assimilated into the formerly "official" circles as some of the "official" views have gone away.

Evolution of Theories of Early Childhood Development From the 1950s to the Present

Overall, Freud's fundamental findings about mentation and motivation have seeped into the current culture. They were included in the ideas of earlier split-off groups as well. Arguments had to do with what words were used or what idea was overemphasized, under-emphasized, or rejected. It often seemed that when someone presented a perception, or a good idea, he or she made it a central point. Terms that attempted to encompass the complexity of the mind included "Overdetermination," "Metapsychology," "Multiple Determinants," "Harmonization,"

"Compromise Formation," all of which convey the realization that there are many forces at play in mental life, as well as that no one has come up with a perfect word that summarizes it all.

Suppositions about babyhood are criticized on the grounds that neuronal development, language availability, memory, cognitive development, and thinking in general cannot have been available to the developing infant or young child; nor can non-verbal expressions be counted on to allow reliable interpretations by adult observers. Yet, clearly, brain development begins before birth, and mental development at some early time as well. If much goes on in later development, so too must it be so at earlier, preverbal states. Few, now, would maintain the contrary or that we can afford the luxury of ignoring current, related investigations in adjacent fields.

I made an experiment using my grandson, Oliver, as a subject, starting at age one-and-a-half, as he was making progress in using words. He could say "yes" and "no" to food he liked or didn't like; mac and cheese were favorites, and he was definitely developing a taste for caviar. I thought he was precocious, but, as a grandfather, I overestimated his capacity for self-observation. When he was two-years-old, I asked him what it was like before he could talk; he looked at me with an incredulous expression. (I should probably not have imputed incredulity to a two-year old. Puzzlement would have been more apt,) Somewhat later, when I posed the same question, he looked more puzzled to me and less incredulous, but he didn't remember having been asked about this before. I remembered him as he had been preverbally, and he had certainly made his needs and feelings plain enough, so that one could intercede with fresh nappies, food, and cuddling. But Oliver remembered nothing of his preverbal time.

Anna Freud and Melanie Klein differed about what small children were capable of doing with regard to organizing ideas. Klein wrote a book in which a child played with boats and seemed to have trouble removing some submarines from a harbor. She interpreted this as representing an idea about his parents' sexual activity. She told the boy that he thought his father was having difficulty with withdrawing his penis during coitus. Lacan and Kohut both founded schools of thought about early development, which reflected highly ingenious thinking, but little evidence. Imputing adult ideas to small children might well be seen as a variant of what Ruskin termed the "pathetic fallacy," but discarding nonverbal communication as an event linking adults, adults and babies and toddlers together, seems to me equally inept.

How to conceptualize (rather than invent) how mentality evolves in early development in the absence of memories from the preverbal time I do not know. I have not been satisfied with ideas that colleagues have floated, for instance, the Kleinian belief that the preverbal child harbors fantasies, with content in a "paranoid-schizoid" or later, a "depressive" stage or "position." This is proposed to precede the point where the child has the capacity to understand the connections between objects and verbs, that is, with cause and effect. Or there is a view that infants acquire a sense of themselves, via the caretakers' reactions to the child's behavior: the child reaches a conception of himself through perceiving how the caretaker experiences him. If taken literally, that would mean that Klein's submarine representing a penis would have brought about a quite marvelous notion of anatomy. I myself observe that I frequently misinterpret what others make of me, as when I feel misunderstood, and there is more going on than I perceive.

I think that in my five-year-old head, I had enough information and sufficient mental capacity to allow me to form simple ideas about meanings and purposes, which were buzzing about when I constructed my dragon phobia. I can see the analogies between my creative thinking then and my subsequent, more subtle and complex social anxiety, examination, and more to the point, performance anxiety, and, more primitively—and closer to Fafner and Siegfried—fear and anger toward policemen stopping me for speeding, poor doctors, and a batch of other sorts of social interchanges. Unlike some other analysts, I don't think I am entitled to rely entirely on a reconstruction of the prehistory of the creative process before the age of five, which proposes an explanation of the causes that led to my phobia. I do assume, though, that my mother's bicycle and my ether experience had aftereffects, which last to the present day, and incorporate my experiences of that early time—all this suddenly sprang up out of some things.

A complicated construction includes a basis of root-foundation-like (trees, again) impressions from a period of unconscious pre-mind. Piaget wanted to know at what age a child could know that similar volumes of liquids attained different heights depending on the diameters of the receptacles. When is the brain mature enough to be mindful in the sense that it can invent complicated theories of cause and effect? I could do it before age five. It looks as though there had to be quite a bit of unconscious organization of fragments to allow me to create a phobia.

My proposal: the earliest memory is sensory memory. The infant responds to sensations long before he responds to words; infants respond rapidly to experiences, and learned responses quickly appear. There is no reason to think that sensory memory does not continue to operate throughout life—call it "muscle memory" if you will, though I think that is a misnomer. Muscles have no memory; nervous systems do. They grow, change, and strengthen in synapses, with experiences.

Eric Kandel showed that the training process could be duplicated with a primitive organism, the sea snail, *Aplysia*. *Aplysia* has about a thousand neurons, and they are large. The dendrites that extend into the intersynaptic space are plain to observe under a microscope. We knew that nerve cells have axons, which transmit excitation electrically to synapses where chemical neurotransmitters cross the synapse. Incoming impulses connect afferent, sensory neurons, and efferent, muscle innervating neurons, across an intersynaptic space. The intraneural conduction becomes inter-neural conduction. Kandel showed that dendrites multiply, and "potentiation" occurs as a food stimulus-and-response becomes established: the involved nerves grow more nerve endings at the synapse. Kandel won a Nobel Prize. The simple relationships between stimulus and response are analogous to reflex events, and Kandel proposed that the term "memory" could be applied to the process of enhancing communication between cells. It seems a great distance from a reflex to a phobia, but why not entertain the leap?

In higher organisms you could label this "Pavlovian" training if you like; perhaps it is better to call it the basis underpinning the development of object choice, taste, esthetic response, or whatever needs to be described by analogy to another sensation. There are innumerable examples of this: "Sweet as sugar," "salty as seawater," "dry as dust," "heavy as lead,"" light as a feather," "blind as a bat," and metaphor extends this to "Juliet is the sun." "The moral of the story is," "people who live in glass houses shouldn't throw stones," and "the early bird catches the worm"—a long story is summed up in a few words, which evoke common sensory experiences. I don't have a contribution about how to study what comes just after *Aplysia*. The jump from snail to sentience is wide.

In the psychoanalytic retrospectoscope such a multitude of events and experiences influences the construction of a personality, and even of a characteristic of a personality, as to make a comprehensive understanding impossible. If one problem is complexity, another is ignorance about the effects of matters before the arrival of language and consciousness—a second unanswered question. A third is the psyche-soma question: what happens when and where and how in the brain and how is that connected?

PART II – FURTHER PSYCHOANALYTIC REFLECTIONS

How Does Thinking Become More Realistic?

There are forces that produce aversion to recognizing realities. There are also limiting factors as to what the brain can do. In just those situations that are ambiguous and threatening, when clear thinking would be most useful, one tends to err either in the direction of ignoring or magnifying danger signals, or in the direction of drawing erroneously simple conclusions, in the course of grasping at straws. For Europeans, the conscious or unconscious choices that resulted in denying and minimizing danger signals and following simplistic thinking about how to deal with them turned out to be dire, both in the settlements of World War I and in the events that led to World War II.

Whether it comes to nations or individuals, there are too many variables to make it possible to isolate a seemingly crucial event, say the assassination of Franz Ferdinand, and predict what a state's, or a person's, response will be. The more one studies such a question, the more variables will be uncovered, the more chains of associations and connections, neurological or mental, will be elicited. My response to the effects of the spasms in the world of my past was to become more focused on these questions: "What happened, how did it come about, why did the elites behave as they did? How can I avoid acting on impulse, irrationally, and how can I help other people to be more realistic?" One route to reality is the scientific method, useful insofar as it is possible to design simple situations in which subjectivity is minimized and small findings appear; the second approach is the psychoanalytic, which deals with the emotional bases for decision-making. These are strongly influenced by automatic assessments arising under the influence of what the analysts call instinctual drives, and what we can regard as the mind's operations, outside of a conscious sense of volition. That means, subjectivity (which begins to be formed before logical capacity to think arises) underlies the purportedly rational examination of external reality.

Therefore, subjectivity, the internal reality, is studied in order to learn how it leads to distortion of the understanding of the external reality, while also distorting the thinking of the investigator.

The Significance of REM Sleep

An idea that was pretty widespread, and not new to me, in the sixties, was that emotions influence physiological conditions, as well as vice versa. The "fight or flight" response has become a clichéd idea that was proposed as a description of responses to arousal in 1915. In my time, in the sixties, Fisher and Dement and others studied what came to be called the REM Periods, the rapid eye movement periods that occur together with visual dreaming at typical intervals of normal sleep in humans and other animals. Electroencephalographic recordings display changes in brain wave activation during the REM Periods. Waking a sleeping subject during or just after REMs allowed experimenters to learn what subjects had dreamt, and it turned out that there are periods of verbal non-REM dreaming, as well as the visual REM dreams. Watching REM and non-REM dreaming, and measuring physiologic activity happening at the same time, allowed one to observe brain functioning and mind functioning, using the natural science and the psychoanalytic approach simultaneously. The brain surgeon Wilder Penfield talked with his patients as he was stimulating their brains, and so he was able to follow their experiences. When particular loci were electrically stimulated, particular sensations, emotional feelings, thoughts, and body movements followed. Penfield's method combined observation of the brain, as material organ, and the mind, as concept, functioning concurrently.

PART II – FURTHER PSYCHOANALYTIC REFLECTIONS

My Writings on the Psychological Effects of Cognitive Weaknesses

In addition to the unpublished piece about the work I did with Mort Reiser between 1961 and 1966, I wrote another, partly about a patient who, embarrassed, revealed that he needed someone to write his checks because his handwriting was so bad, and who sometimes got on the wrong subway train, one that was going in the opposite direction to where he wanted to go. I saw another who was ashamed about being mechanically maladept and who tried to deny to himself that anything was wrong, but with little success. Socially, he found it hard to take advice or to accept that he had special difficulties in some areas. A third patient felt like a faker, when he memorized pages of a textbook to quote in exams and felt he did not really understand what he was quoting. There were, I thought, an unusual number of tales of that sort, and no papers about the effects such defects had in many people's lives.

This led to the tack that I took in such cases. I regarded the shame and low self-esteem, and the efforts to conceal a minor cognitive weakness, as symptomatic; I led the patients to consider the possibility that it might be useful to regard the cognitive defects in the same light as they would have done when they had the flu, or diabetes, or trauma, or any other blow of fate. These narcissistically disappointing events had been none of their doing. Of course, the idea of "none of my doing" is invariably disagreeable. At an extreme, the wishful insistence of the afflicted that they were entitled to be given relief and, at another, the guilt of those who claimed their affliction minor and wished to provide relief for a beloved person (or one disliked, or regarded with strongly ambivalent feelings) doomed to die from some deadly, incurable disease, seemed to me to necessitate exploring the effects of these focal defects in cognition. They had to do with competitive problems, as I had with my brother and father when

I was a child, unable to row a boat, stop a car, speak English, or do a hundred things that might have made me feel less inept. The inadequacy of the "It's unfair" but "Be good and wait your turn" route was a long overdue recognition. My low self-esteem issues allowed me to understand the painful experience of those with cognitive deficits, who had often been treated as though they were dumb or obstinate. Shame, and compensatory behaviors which served to deny culpability, or the narcissistic wounds resulting from feelings of impotence, are not funny, as I realized when I mocked Mort Reiser.

Aging and Ill Analysts

In my role as teacher and supervisor of aspiring psychiatrists and psychoanalysts, I was in the position of trying, sometimes successfully, to help extract students from treatments with ill, sometimes even demented, analysts. This was a painful situation; the analyst was too ill to be capable of working well, or to realize that he should stop. Robi Bak's joke, very characteristic of his Hungarian cynical realism, was, "Psychoanalysis is such a wonderful profession. You can keep on working as long as you're capable of sitting in a chair, and saying 'Gaga, Gaga'." I was very determined that I would not become a "Gaganalyst," and I stopped taking new patients at the age of seventy.

Bak was, in general, correct; few doctors retire in time. Many continue to do what they consider to be work. Often forgetfulness or bad decisions are ignored with the rationalization that great experience begets great wisdom, which more than compensates for defects in memory or judgement. Rarely is serious damage done. The patients are aware of the situation but cannot allow themselves to suffer the guilt of feeling they have abandoned someone who has been so helpfully disposed to them during their lives. That is probably more true when it comes to subtle mental changes.

Rarely is working with an aged or ill analyst useful. At lunch with an acquaintance, with whom I was involved in a public charitable effort, we were talking about raising money and about how to help the organization along. My companion began to talk about some feeling of distance he experienced with his wife. They were spending too much time apart, and it seemed to him that she was the cool one. He went on and asked me if I was aware of the fact that he had been in analysis. I had not known this. "Yes, I was seeing Dr. X. Things were going along, though slowly. Then he had a stroke, and then, when he came back to work, he seemed somewhat confused and forgetful. Did you know him?" I knew of him and said so. "Then," my acquaintance went on, "I realized that I had had a problem with my father. He died when I was thirteen. We had never been close and about that time, he had a stroke and died. When Dr. X. had his stroke, I realized I had never had the chance to show him how much I appreciated what he had done for me. That was when I began to feel better, really, I think because I felt I was helping to take care of the analyst, something I had not been able to do with my father." I may have been wrong, but that lunch struck me as something of a session.

Unfortunately, when age or illness causes a diminution in an analyst's capacity to "get" his patient, the analysis effectively ends. No further understanding and relearning can be gained by the patient. The reasonable plan, in such cases, is to continue the analysis with a competent person. This friend never had the chance to really address the relationship with his father or to learn to understand a number of reasons for leaving the analysis, such as to escape.

The Freud Archives

During my early psychiatric residency, I had a phone call from Kurt Eissler. Harry Freud must have talked to him about me and told him my family knew Sigmund Freud, and that I might have met him. I thought it odd that he wanted to make an appointment to interview me about Freud. I told him I might have sat on Freud's lap once or twice, but I had no personal memories about him. Eissler replied, "We know that, once one gets started talking about something, things come to mind." Eissler ran the Sigmund Freud Archives, a large collection of notes, papers, and patient records, which Freud left to Anna upon his death. Some of Freud's followers wanted to further his findings. They were carrying out his wishes after his death. Probably that had some relation to wishes to thank and repay their earlier fathers and teachers and thereby escape indebtedness. As an ambition, giving back to the community which has given us life and learning is useful to giver and recipient. Anna Freud came to New York, and gave a packed standing room audience a lecture at the Academy of Medicine, for which she sent me an invitation labeled "Amicus Familiae"—which Kurt Eissler noticed.

I suspect that Eissler was a bit disappointed in my free associations. He still invited me to be on the board of the Sigmund Freud Archives. That allowed me to observe some peculiar behavior, particularly on the part of Jeffrey Masson, who created a furor by using some information from sealed material in the Freud Archives in Washington and publishing it.

Clubs and Divisions in the Analytic Community

Martin Stein, my second analyst, was a convinced psychoanalyst, strongly motivated to preserve his métier, which meant working with patients and teaching students. As chair of the American Psychoanalytic Association Board of Professional Standards at that time, he was important in setting criteria for training as well as ethical standards. He had to deal with difficult situations; he was the censor. Two of his good friends married former patients, which meant they were likely to lose their positions in the administrative hierarchy and as teachers. Stein was going to be one of the arbiters, so it must have been a question of protecting or abandoning his friends. The New York Psychoanalytic Society of the sixties was conservative; the historic attitude in Europe had no objections to people having training wherever they were able to get it, so long as they were intellectually and emotionally suited for the field. There were, and still are, endless arguments about what the criteria, if any, for accepting students should be. The

American system, which originated in the days after Freud made his trip to lecture at Clark College in Worcester, Massachusetts, was led by physicians; they ran the mental hospitals and psychiatric facilities attached to medical schools and, therefore, also had responsibility for inpatients. Training that was done via apprenticeship required that there be a supply of material; if the material one worked with was a patient, then teaching required a supply of patients. This meant medical schools and referrals, which led to an arrangement whereby MDs ran the field.

In Europe, that was not the case. People were trained who were interested, and they came from non-medical as well as from medical backgrounds. Leading examples were Ernst Kris, an art historian, and Robert Waelder, a physicist. Unfortunately, the early years of the profession were times when there were many shenanigans between patients and therapists. Sexual and financial situations then, and in the time I am writing about, were not uncommon. Hence, there were efforts to oversee and filter out the misbehavers.

What was then called "convoying" was involved in psychoanalytic politics. Would-be leaders would convoy followers, protecting them, and fostering their careers; if they chose well, there would be no problem, since the more successful would be recognized. Sometimes, nepotism was too evident. This was so in the New York group, when spouses of eminent members were given courses to teach or otherwise welcomed to the faculty while others, who thought themselves, and sometimes were, more qualified, were passed over.

There was a second area of competition. This was between the immigrants who had fled the Nazis - many of whom had been prominent as writers and teachers and as students of the pioneers, and who, indeed, were outstanding thinkers and scholars—and the native-born. Some of the native analysts saw themselves as undervalued in comparison to the newcomers; there often seemed to be two parties: the direct student descendants of Freud, including some American natives, and the comparatively less revolutionary or privileged. Stein was among the first group and Milton Rosenbaum (my Einstein chairman), the second.

It was not clear to me at the time that Rosenbaum's attitude was responsible for his rejection when he wanted to join the New York group; politics was supposed to be kept out of work with patients. Analysts were supposed to avoid any hint of favoring or disfavoring their patients; but cliques had formed often in the psychoanalytic world, and they were usually formed by acolytes of a particular, charismatic analyst who wanted to lead a group. Rosenbaum was clearly one of those, but this attitude was clearly harmful to good work with patients.

A third issue was—what I thought unprofessional—prejudice against women in the field. This was more evident among the Americans than among the Europeans, though both American and European women were important clinicians and writers. Whisperings and mutterings were that the women were too supportive, or even seductive, or were capable of making up data. I was unusual in trying to resist the temptation to adopt rigid rules.

There was a certain camaraderie in some quarters, not less among the Europeans than elsewhere; this was less damaging than out-and-out guru-following. Groups formed to protect principles, by excluding those that were thought not likely to follow them, with some notable exceptions: people who had major affiliations with medical schools, or did formal research work rather than chiefly clinical work directly with patients were more likely to be excluded than were the more historically traditional analysts. Another basis for excluding people was the MD versus non-MD argument: Americans were more likely to hold to the idea that MDs were the only ones sufficiently prepared to train as analysts, while many Europeans had come from other fields, like Kris, Waelder, or Anna Freud ("my son Anna," as Sigmund, now labeled a Victorian misogynist, put it). Charles Fisher and Morton Reiser straddled whatever lines there were; Fisher was a full-time researcher at Mount Sinai, and was doing dream research, a seemingly promising approach to the mind-brain questions of the time. Reiser, who was a professor at Einstein, and head of the labs that did longitudinal studies, physiological work, and eventually became chairman of psychiatry at Yale, was considered a part-timer so far as practice was concerned, as were other professors and chairs. Some analysts felt that those who didn't concentrate on clinical work were not "real" psychoanalysts. I had no position on these disagreements, though I could appreciate some of the arguments made by the differing sides.

A pro-MD argument was that medical school gave the students an opportunity to become clearer about what could be achieved in helping people. Limitations could be experienced; the doctor would have had experience in dealing with the painfulness of illness and could learn how to comfort patients and their families and to resist becoming personally entangled with patients.

PhDs or social workers were presumed to be unlikely to have much experience along those lines. Before I was an intern, and certainly during my internship, I had ample opportunity to see MDs at work, and they were certainly not uniformly humane, or objective, about dealing with their patients; to be able to care for other people reasonably and humanely seemed to me not easily correlated to educational tracks. The Europeans, with whom I felt comfortable, were mostly better able to act like polite human beings with their patients than the Americans, who seemed more puritanical.

Lillian Ross wrote a series of short stories à clef for the *New Yorker*, featuring characters obviously from the NYPSI, renamed Blauberman and Selboat Selzer, among others. Janet Malcolm wrote *Psychoanalysis, the Impossible Profession* (1981) in which differing approaches to the work were represented by the humane and human Leo Stone; rigorous distance was attributed to Charles Brenner. I think that the conceptual distance between Brenner and Stone was real, but the distance between him and a child analyst like Berta Bornstein was greater. Child analysts were not considered real analysts by some "orthodox" analysts, who regarded normal human behavior of adults with children, which involved playing with them, and talking with them, as un-analytic; as an analyst, you listened and sometimes gave or made interpretations. Furthermore, you avoided contact with your adult patients in social situations, and also had as little as possible to do with their relatives and friends. (The Hartmanns had no hesitation about inviting Barbara and me to parties in the country and the Steins as well.) The analysis of a child necessarily includes contact with the parents, and often with other family members, as well as discussions with those important in the child's life, about what went on at home. Family members could be referred for help with their problems as well. But a strict analyst would not give any form of practical help to a patient, and that included suggesting another analyst for a patient's friend or analyzing two friends at the same time.

It was pretty plain to me that one had to treat children, particularly, and adolescents, also, as different from adults; young children don't do as well with words as older people usually do, so play therapy was invented, in which ideas are shown by way of interaction while playing.

Groups are good; toys and dolls and diverse games are good; moralistic horror stories are not good. People who think child analysis may be useful but isn't "real" (i.e. strictly verbal) analysis, are wrong; it is useful and real, and, anyway, adult analysis isn't strictly verbal.

Students had to be analyzed by analysts approved to be training analysts, and if they became students while already in treatment with a training analyst, even one from another recognized institute, the student had to switch to one of ours. Still today, this procedure survives.

Those without a medical degree were barred from membership in the American (though not the International) society, as well as from training in the affiliate institutes of the American society.

It was possible to find training in institutes not affiliated with the American Psychoanalytic Society, and Sullivanian, Horneyan, Jungian, Reichian (and other schools) happily accepted applications. People who had not taken a medical degree found there were plenty of opportunities to train at many institutes; furthermore, there were no general standards of what psychoanalysis is.

The fact that the efforts to maintain these rules gave way to moderation as time passed leads me to trust that common sense can soothe professional rivalry. To better understand human behavior is the basic aim and has gone on over millennia. Freud's contributions took place over years; he often edited, added, and elided; and so did the heirs to his work. I was interested in what other groups were doing, and others' ideas certainly affected my own; it gradually became a more general practice for the varying groups to poach each other's work. My impression was that the more ways of thinking about anything that were available to be applied, the better. I came to think that the most useful comment to make to a person who was insistent about a particular idea about what had caused something, especially a simple, easily understood cause and effect idea, was to ask, in one way or another, what reasons someone else might have for reaching a different conclusion.

People want simple answers, but interesting questions are complex. There is a pleasure in complexity, as well as frustration. That there are a multitude of factors which determine a particular act or mental condition, is inconvenient. A listing of factors, without which we should have arrived at a different situation, at any moment, is beyond counting; Caesar could write a treatise about *how* he conquered Gaul, but not convincingly *why* he could conquer Gaul. The initial, single New York society and training institute shrank when two groups left and formed new organizations. The Downstate and Columbia groups were both founded by figures who found reasons to leave the parent group and to take their supporters with them. The field was growing. Sometimes analysts had dual appointments; at one time, New York had between thirty-five and forty "institutes" offering training to psychiatrists, psychologists, clergy, social workers, or family therapists. I was invited once to give a paper by one of these groups and found two colleagues ready to discourse on "love"; I am now ashamed to report that I accepted. An audience of several hundred attended; the venue was the Performing Arts High School auditorium. At the end of the meeting, I answered one member of the audience who posed a question about something I'd said, evidently unclearly; but how could I have answered clearly? In return, I asked what was the history of the group that hosted the conference. "Oh," she said, "it was founded by Dr. So-and-So. He had started another group but gave it to his then wife, and when he remarried, his new wife wanted her own institute so he founded this one for her." I could have cried, or I could have said, "That's love."

Consciousness

Who came up with the idea that there is something unique about conscious thinking? Freud. Is thinking discontinuous? Conscious or unconscious? It is not only that early childhood development of brain-mind takes place in an environment which adults cannot remember. Infants distinguish between faces; they have expressions and behaviors. Caretakers respond as though these are useful signals and reflect needs they can satisfy, like food, or burping, or cleaning, or warming or cooling. We presume that the behavior of the parents teaches the offspring what can be done with what they are emitting; their needs may or may not bring responses, which the parents recognize as having satisfied the child, depending on how the child responds—by going to sleep, gurgling happily, and so on. Parents learn through their interactions with their babies, as the babies learn through their interactions with the ambience. Then things get more complicated, ultimately so complicated that we are left with "compromise" as the description. Maturation comes along

Is there a particular role here for consciousness? There is much of the implicit, and the interpretative nonverbal, on the part of all concerned, as there is much that is implicit and interpretative in perception throughout life. This brings up again the subject of subjectivity, which, in psychoanalytic-ese, is called transference and countertransference; in drug research, placebo; in hypnotist-language, suggestion and suggestibility; and in my language, intra- and inter-relatedness of conscious and unconscious memory and learning.

Everything that enters into the relationship between experimenter and subject, or analyst and patient, teacher and student, parent and child, and anyone with anyone else, is the same in that the consciously experienced intention to convey a particular meaning is evinced by words, pauses, seeming changes of subject (otherwise known as "associations"), tones of voice, volume, facial expressions, laughter, and body movements. Response depends on the receiver. A conversation is something like a walk in the park where, while avoiding running into other people and via various inspections and impressions of passersby, one is stimulated and creates impressions and ideas. Subjectivity is stimulated and exercised galore. We are not "aware" of most of this—with "aware" seeming to mean conscious, "unaware" unknowing.

New ideas occur in sleep—e.g. Kekule's solution to the shape of the benzene molecule in his dream of six snakes all joined mouth-to-tail—and in transient, musing, waking states; the muses were supposed to be the bringers of inspiration. To the question, "When do you have time to think?" Einstein supposedly answered, "I think all the time." Others say, "My ideas sometimes come when I'm shaving," "or "going for a walk," or "at a concert," or "driving the car." I was popular with artists during the fifties in New York, when some experimented with drugs; ashrams, poets, writers, or Reichian Orgone boxes. One, supposedly original, idea was that anything was art that was deemed "art" by the artist, and hopefully accepted as art by critics and buyers. All this ferment was there in my environment, together with changes in science and the physical and human environment. At that time, I was thinking like the Surrealist artists, and their contemporary followers. Dream images, drugs that changed states of consciousness such as psilocybin and LSD, were used by painters, musicians, and other artists in an experimental way, in attempts to expand the contribution of unconscious processes to their work. I used No-Doz to stay awake while studying in college, and ritalin later on. Freud had run into problems recommending cocaine, which he used himself and thought mentally helpful.

Ideas and how they happen, and what conditions might help one to experience creative ideas, have been questions for eons. One thing, though, is evident: ideas spring from minds and appear in all sorts of situations, and in words—but not only words: visions, or mathematical equations, or musical constructions, or physical movements, or expressions, or sounds. This has seemed obvious to me for as long as I can remember; perhaps the need to change languages as a child made me more aware of the fact that there were many means of communication, many languages. The discovery that I had an unusual gift, that I could know what notes came from the piano, and name them before I could read or write (though I had, of course, to have mastered the names of the letters of the alphabet) probably contributed to my understanding that language was not just strings of words. I read *Doctor Dolittle*, fascinated by his ability to speak to the animals, never once wondering whether they spoke in anything but Animal; I never imagined that they used German or English: I could see that animals could communicate with each other, using sounds or musical notes; why not with us? I didn't even know about whale sounds or pheromones.

I knew that babies and adults communicated with each other, and that one thing adults could offer preverbal children is words to describe what the children were signaling, such as hunger, or fatigue, or fear. What they could not put into words were tastes, as in "how do apples taste?" This could only be communicated by analogy, by naming another taste. You could say, "Apples taste something like pears. Snake tastes something like chicken." Fear is an indescribable physical feeling; perhaps children learn the words for fear when they wake up from a dream and are told they had a scary dream, and also that dreams are not "real," unlike other scary experiences, such as "Remember when you got lost that time in the store and didn't know where I was?"

The significance of subjectivity has often been in the background in writings and teachings about psychodynamics. Early in my psychoanalytic training, the importance of trauma was frequently overlooked, and the power of unconscious fantasy overemphasized. It seemed to me, after a time, that though blessed with the benefit of hindsight over many years of Freudian evolution—with its changes in emphasis about the meanings of observed behavior—the importance of the subjectivity of the analyst was still underestimated. For example, we were taught that patients invariably harbored unconscious processes that underlay their transferences, but analysts' countertransferences were neurotic responses to the patients' transferences—counterparts, really, unconscious (conflicted and therefore irrational) responses to the patients' transferences. Supposedly, the well-analyzed analyst could recognize his distortions of reality when influenced by the patients' neurotic conflicts and could compensate for those distorted responses by virtue of going back into analysis to "analyze out" his neurotically influenced relationship to a patient. Analysts who behaved unethically were advised to go back into analysis to better work out their countertransferences; this view was probably related to the idea that the analyst could be objective, to the degree that his own irrationality could be "analyzed out."

More Martin Stein; Unobjectionable Transference

My training analyst, Martin Stein, published a paper that argued against Freud's idea that there was such a thing as an "unobjectionable transference." One example was the choice of profession; for example, the choice of the profession of psychoanalysts had generally been assumed to be unobjectionable; wanting to help people is a good thing, with nothing symptomatic about this. There was quite a brouhaha over Hartmann's idea that there was a "conflict-free ego sphere." Hartmann supposed this idea would be understood as referring to something relative, not absolute; ultimately, thanks largely to Charles Brenner, it became a generally agreed upon conclusion, that no psychological element could be conflict-free. There came to be no such thing as "analyzing out."

Another wishful notion that flatters the analyst's desire to feel objective is that analysts need not have had experiences such as deaths and illnesses of important people in their lives, or marriage, or having children, to be able to understand what people go through in relation to such common events. There are things which have to be explained in terms of analogies, because they are sensations not ideas. Such ideas go back to Freud's heuristic examples, which posit that, in their professional acts, analysts can function as objective persons with special knowledge, like the surgeon or railroad car companion, or like the parent teaching that what feels real in sleep is actually a dream. In other words, the listener's contact to the passing landscape is the edited interpretation by the reporter. What does the listener do with the material he hears? He gives the reporter an interpretation; this model supports the implication that the analyst is an outsider, totally dependent on the observer's report.

In the surgical example, the patient presents an anatomy which the surgeon has to dissect in order to preserve the normal, while removing the pathological. The surgical patient doesn't give his impression; he contributes a description of the history of his complaints and allows his body to be examined by a variety of instruments. The doctor consults his mental library of possibilities, as taken from books and personal experience. His studies throughout his professional life have made it possible for the surgeon to find objective signs, make a diagnosis, imagine how the anatomy might look, isolate the pathologic parts, drape the body, create a surgical field, anesthetize the patient, cut and sew, and, later, give a prognosis and order aftercare. The surgeon can remain more or less removed from personal investment in a relationship with a patient; an analyst cannot. Key words here are "more or less." After the analytic work with someone stops, this is construed as a pause; the patient can come back or proceed on his own, armed with more realistic thinking.

When it comes to the psychoanalytic hour, we need to think in terms that will allow inclusion of the atmosphere as a part of what needs to be examined. One could propose that a positive atmosphere is supported by the rational element of mental functioning, by making judgments based on a capacity for reasonable evaluation of a situation; but also, it requires a confluence of subjective perception between two people who perceive in a similar way. In this case, two individuals are able to shift between dream-like, symbolic and wider-awake-like states, when the fantasy and real can be opposed. Preconceptions about women or men, such as my mother and uncle had, were the natural order of things in their lives. This is less true in the present, though it was still important when I began to be trained. One aspect of a relationship is seemingly rational agreements, say, when two people agree to remain as wide awake as possible, talking to each other, and sharing ideas on a limited subject as a better way to come to a resolution of a problem than a "debate" designed to train people to practice logic. Therapy is better viewed as something more free-form: "Brainstorming."

My Experiences as Analysand

Listening to myself talk to Dr. Stein, my second analyst, I knew that at the very same time I was talking, I was hearing what I was saying. Sometimes I felt surprised at what I had said; usually, I was able to go back and work out the connections that gave rise to the verbal language I was using to communicate with the analyst. But other work was going on in my mind that affected what I was saying. As I write, I monitor what I am writing; I recognize if I have come to an "Aha" (or an "Uh oh"). Writing or analyzing or listening to music or doing math problems is not a one-track process; there is stuff going on in the mind that is not registered, and other stuff that is. Somehow the flow is interrupted, or a parallel flow develops, and attention is focused on what has occurred.

I sometimes felt as though being psychoanalyzed was a kind of examination. I was aware of editing, choosing between words and subjects, and more or less aware of being intent on making an impression, or multiple impressions, on my analyst. Sometimes I talked on and on, knowing that at some point I, or my colleague, the analyst, would make a comment; a subtext of any such comment would be—it was implicit in the process—that we had been listening, as well as having ideas about what was being said. We could switch from conscious theme, to underlying purposes, supplementary and alternate meanings, and aspects implicit in what I said—and capable of becoming overt—one at a time. I was aided in that, in point of fact, at that time I had already had training and many hours of listening in what was labelled "free-floating attention."

Examination Dreams

Freud wrote about universal dreams, of which one was the examination dream, an anxiety dream in which you face a situation for which you are unprepared. To me, seeing an analyst once meant that I needed to present myself as an educable and gifted aspirant, in order to become a successful member of the psychoanalytic profession. It also meant to me (at the time) that I had to reveal what I would prefer to conceal: my greed, piggishness, selfishness, and destructiveness in the face of frustration, and my vengefulness in the face of slights and humiliations, real or imagined. This attitude, when I became aware of it, I did not bring up as an issue in my analysis; I also knew that I wanted to be interesting to myself as well as to the analyst. "Say whatever is in your mind" is impossible, and gives an impression that thinking is narrow. Thinking is symbolic in the same way as dream images or poetic images are symbolic; many meanings are condensed, in words as in images, as they are produced.

I had an interest in discussing my inclination to try to manipulate my analyst with him, but I also had fear. My referral to my first analyst raised questions about the trustworthiness of analysts; after all, both analyst number one and Milton Rosenbaum failed to meet my standards of what an analyst should represent professionally. I could not reveal things which could have meant raising a question about my honesty, my reliability as an aspirant, my ethical strength, or my feeling that I could be one of those who might exploit patients. In a land of back-and-forth referrals, cliques, and institutional shenanigans, I feared for myself;

and that was merely on one of several levels: guilt and self-esteem were even more significant issues. I had certainly not attained Satori, or even modest philosophical tranquility; a more realistic and less guilty self-image was eventually achieved—with lots more shrinking. Given my experience with analyst number one—whom I freely criticized to his face, and who fired me on the basis of his impression that I was unanalyzable—saying whatever might come to mind was a matter to be tested out, not one to be freely accepted.

This all leads to my continuing guilt and anxiety about pretending to be a good boy but being a faker. Martin Stein, for his part, did not raise questions about my ambition to become an analyst; though I talked about how I thought becoming a doctor had come about, the unattractive aspects of becoming a doctor didn't seem to come up much. This subject arose more in private retrospection and in my next analysis. Stein, presumably, regarded that as part of the "unobjectionable transference"; curiously enough, Stein was aware of the fact that correct judgments might be consonant with subjectively influenced perceptions, i.e., that I might be correct that he, Stein, wanted a son, but also that I was hoping for a father, not just a colleague who would recognize me as a good successor in our shared field. "Just because something is transferred, doesn't invalidate it as part of a conclusion about reality," he said to me, when I was maintaining it had to be one or the other. Another "Aha" for me and another nail in the coffin of either or, together with another block to being good, not bad. I got to become both a good boy and a faker; sometimes to lie is okay, not to mention that holding back information is not necessarily bad. I still have a residue of behaving as though being good will be rewarded but, at the same time, I know that human rights are decided by human communities and written down as laws. Socrates' death was unfair but lawful; ergo, laws are not necessarily fair. Who decides what's fair? Children and their parents.

Stein responded to his disappointment about his friends' questionable behavior with former patients by becoming part of a group of people who studied successful graduate psychoanalytic students. They came up with a conclusion—following clues about professional motivation in the analysands—which showed that if their career interests seemed unobjectionable or unconflicted, pursuing the histories of those resolutions should still be examined - because they weren't unconflicted after all. I suppose he came to realize he had left out well-disguised secrets in his work. He did the wise thing in researching the problem, publishing his results and changing his ideas and usages; he availed himself of the psychoanalytic attitude, that there are always other ways of thinking about a conflict, problem, or issue, which might be more useful.

"Honeymoon" Period of Analysis

In the early days of a treatment, especially if the patient is naïve, and feels (as I did with Edith Jacobson) that for the first time in his life he may have found an adult who is interested in him, wants to understand and help, and is not making judgments, he becomes readier to give the method and the therapist a chance. Let's call this a positive placebo effect, in jargon, the "honeymoon period" of the early months of the analysis—positive transference. Sometimes one finds a patient who arrives having had four or five previous therapeutic failures, but claims he knows this time will be different, because you come highly recommended as a therapist; probably, there will be another failure. The patient may well be out for revenge—for who knows what?—so watch out for negative transference, negative placebo effect. Sometimes the MD therapist is so mistrusted that treatments fail, until the patient finds his way to a Ph.D. psychologist, or another type—a Jungian, perhaps or a therapist from some other school; anything but an MD. The more likely result is another failed treatment. I, relatively traumatized, by earlier and by more recent events, was a "difficult patient." I had needed one analysis where the analyst, the referring man (and I) all failed; one, my training analysis, where I got to the point of being moderately trustful, with Stein; and one where I profited greatly, with Edward Kronold.

My Analysis with Edward Kronold

As I have noted, Freud famously wrote that certain elements of transference are "unobjectionable," not necessary to analyze. Hartmann wrote about a (relatively) conflict-free ego sphere; and others described the positive, hopeful, respectful feelings of the patient about analysis and the analyst, as "positive transference," and regarded it as a necessary foundation for the patient's involvement in the analytic work. (Greenacre and some others assumed that a significantly positive experience with babyhood caretakers is a necessary prerequisite; Kohut thought an analytic experience that replicated and replaced the missing experience could serve.)

Aspects of my analytic relationship with Martin Stein, and my favorite post-Stein analyst, Edward Kronold, soon gave me the insight that looking for a conflict-free ego sphere is a waste of time. The notion of a conflict-free ego sphere implied that the choice of profession might have been conflict-free. My experience in analysis demonstrated that was not so.

Without question, Edward Kronold (1899–1993) helped me the most. His name was shortened from Kronengold; he arrived in Vienna from his native Ukraine at the age of 19 to study with Freud. (He was co-author of only one paper, written with Richard Sterba.) He became one of the very few analysts' re-analysts. Robi Bak recommended me to Kronold, and Kronold to me; his fee was $35 an hour. (Stein's had been $25.) Kronold was in his seventies when I knew him as my analyst in the 1970s.

He had been one of the first generation of young enthusiasts in Freud's circle of students. His waiting room had a piano in it, a Blüthner with 1920's neoclassical fluted legs, which just happened to be identical to the piano we had in Vienna and brought to New York. My mother had practiced on it almost every day, and I from the age of five, until I went off to college at seventeen; that piano had a soft warm tone, and a light action, which made it ideal for pre-Liszt, that is, pre-dramatic, romantic, exhibitionistic music. Kronold was generally regarded as devoted, excellent and clinically gifted.

Beyond the information that I gleaned about Kronold from the piano in the waiting room, there were other clues in his demeanor, like a published photo of Kronold with friends with familiar faces (Richard Sterba wrote an autobiography with photographs of members of the group, including Kronold and his attractive wife). Kronold knew how to laugh and smile in his chair behind the couch, and I knew when he was smiling, because he'd lean forward—as one does at performances, when one wants somehow to approach the stage, appreciatively.

Once, I talked about my feelings of uncertainty about having as productive a life as others of my family, and I repeated a story Irene Ehrlich, the wife of the adenoidectomist, had told about my great-grandfather Hecht's funeral. She claimed that Hecht was such a great man in Vienna that there was a parade in his honor down the Ringstrasse for his funeral. Kronold cleared his throat and said, "You know, only the Kaiser ever had a funeral procession on the Ringstrasse." There was something about that remark, which was such a minor revelation in itself, that impressed me with the realization of how childish my reverence for the elders was, and how mature I now was, as a colleague of this wise old fellow.

Another experience with Kronold underlined the egalitarian quality he exuded—that he was one of a useful group, not to be idealized, but not to be undervalued. Kronold was respectful, but not awed by, Freud and the other pioneers; he possessed self-respect, but not immodesty. One day I brought him a recording that had been made of the Vienna Philharmonic playing Mahler's Fourth Symphony in 1938. A crew had come from England to record the event, which everyone knew was one of the last performances that orchestra, as then constituted, would give. It was certainly the last Mahler concert, as Austria was about to be invaded, and the many Jewish players in that orchestra, including several people in my family's circle, faced a dangerous future. Bruno Walter, a friend and exponent of Mahler, led a grand and touching performance. The end of Austria was at hand, and the feeling of the end of an era, as sentimental as it sounds, was emphasized by the technically poor sound conveyed by the scraped-together recording equipment. I knew that my mother and father had been there to hear it.

Kronold thanked me and remarked, "I was there too." This meant, we survived, we're still here, that's past. Hardly an interpretation in the strict sense; but the meaning to me was that the idealized parents were never real, and now, evidently, not to be retrieved and that it was a crushing blow to all of us. Tears come to my eyes as I write this, tears of grief over the loss of Kronold, of my piano, of my parents, of my Austrian childhood.

It was not easy to feel "objectified" (to use a modern word) with someone like Kronold, as it had been, first with Robbins, later with Stein, both of whom were not quite comfortable. Kronold brought the view that a doctor may treat a patient with respect and tact, without fear of overstepping boundaries or becoming too intimate.

PART II – FURTHER PSYCHOANALYTIC REFLECTIONS

Robi Bak in My Analysis with Ed Kronold

One of my "Aha" experiences was that Ed Kronold opened a session just as I was lying down on his couch by asking me why I was angry with him. I was a bit taken aback by that question, as I had no conscious feelings of anger, nor did I remember anything that might have irritated me during the previous day's session. Indeed, I had no memory of what we had been talking about then.

I thought for a moment, and then I remembered talking about how annoyed I was with Walter Stewart. Stewart had been a friend, somewhat in the manner of a pet dog following his master, of Robi Bak. (Bak, as previously noted, was a good friend to Barbara and me, starting in my time at Einstein. An analyst with an aura, he was a connoisseur, a scholar of Renaissance Italy and collector of Maiolica and medieval ivories, a ladies' man, a sneaky politician not fearful of making enemies in the European-American internal analytic wars, an outstanding teacher, a fisherman, a cigar smoking Hungarian duelist, and a wit. He was brave. He had his first heart attack in his early forties and several afterwards and died in his sixties.)

Robi Bak had appointed Walter Stewart his executor, though in life he had not always treated Stewart respectfully. He made it clear that he understood his follower's attitude toward him to be fawning, ingratiating, with a not quite manly quality. However, Bak saw to it that Stewart would follow him in teaching a course on the subject of sexual variations, which included homosexuality, at a time when homosexuality was regarded as a serious disorder. Sensitive responses to others were thought to be limited by this "disease." A form of narcissism, it disqualified the person who had that orientation from becoming a psychoanalyst in some psychiatric circles. Without empathy, how could one understand one's patient? Bak was empathic about the social and personal problems of the "perverse," but he did see a bit of cowardice in the seeming lack of self-knowledge, or in the concealment that was involved in staying in the closet or, from the outside, in ignoring the behavioral signs.

As executor, Stewart had the task of selling what remained of Bak's collections. Bak had previously sold his more important pieces when he gave up his practice, to spend the time with his woman friend who had cancer. The two had left for Europe to spend the time remaining for each of them in a pleasant way, and Bak had organized a catalog for Parke Bernet, with provenances and descriptions of the Maiolica he was selling. When the couple had to return to New York, Bak began to see patients again, but the treatments he conducted were not formal in the classic sense: he had a blind man, a cripple in a wheelchair, and a few others who needed to be treated in a personalized fashion, and he began to buy and collect again.

After Bak's death, Stewart consigned his important collections to a second-class auction house, and when I went to the sale, I was shocked at the ignorance of the auctioneers about the pieces they were handling. I told Dr. Kronold that I could have done a better job as executor. Kronold replied, quite accurately, that I wanted to be the executor of Robi's narcissism. He referred to Robi's fierce ability to ignore hazards, whether in dueling with swords, or colleagues, or with his heart disease.

I understood the comment he made. It was an "Aha," and that was about my resentment about losing my friend, and my rivalry with Robi's other friend. Evidently, this insight was not altogether pleasant. I still wondered about how my analyst had known I was angry with him. He told me, "When you came into the office, before you lay down, you had your hands in your pockets. No well brought-up Viennese boy, from a family like yours, would ever enter his doctor's office with his hands in his pockets—except to show contempt."

My jealousy about Robi's friend was also in evidence on an earlier occasion, when I commented that I found funny the image of the little

Mort Reiser, on the couch of the large Bak—actually a masked criticism of Reiser. Dr. Kronold said, "But Mort Reiser has a very big brain." So, my "Aha" interpretation is, "Here is another iteration of my life without father: I had a big brother, now represented by Mort, on the couch with big Robi as the father. I was on Kronold's couch, lamenting having been passed over for Stewart. Kronold was pointing out that making fun of Reiser was similar to deprecating Stewart. I was reliving something out of my past as a child. and I had no need to feel small.

Berta Bornstein and Child Analysis

At about the same period when I saw Kronold, I thought that working with children and adolescents—thereby witnessing early developmental stages—would enhance my ability to analyze anyone. I was interested, too, in longitudinal studies of babies and children being conducted at Yale, Einstein, and many other schools. These studies, pioneered by psychoanalytic thinkers such as Anna Freud, Margaret Mahler, Sybil Escalona, and various others, were common. They observed the development of children in play in the presence of families.

I had an eight-year old child patient, with Berta Bornstein (1899 Cracow–1971, Maine) as one of my supervisors. Everyone knew her as "Bertl" and loved her. Extensive files, including her correspondence with child and adolescent analyst specialists and many other important figures in this field at the time and other papers repose in the Library of Congress. Bertl, like Jacobson and Kronold, represented an ideal for me: a person with commitment to the highest standards of work, which included a directness—whole, humane, and hospitable—which was also mannerly, respectful, and unobtrusive.

Bertl had an aged cocker spaniel, who would come and visit in the waiting room, holding one ear in her mouth; the first few times I came for my supervision, I patted the dog and took her wet ear out of her mouth, whereupon she immediately shook her head, caught the ear, and comfortably continued with it in her mouth. Unlike the tranquil dog and the tranquil Bertl, who also seemed unruffled, my little boy patient couldn't sit still, didn't want to come to appointments, was constantly excited—running around my office, pulling books from shelves and making a mess—or else glumly sitting in a chair, refusing to speak.

Bertl told me a story about a boy of similar age. He was quite talkative when he started coming, and she thought the work was going well, until one day the child arrived and didn't say a word—and then Bertl told him that she couldn't understand why such an intelligent and helpful person, as this boy was, who seemed to get along with her so well, didn't want to talk to her. The child finally, timorously, said that he had done a bad thing and he was sure that if she knew what it was, she would have nothing more to do with him. Finally, following still more reassurance, he told his secret; he had stolen a magazine from the waiting room. "Oh," she told him, "I'll tell you what I think; I think—what might have led such an honest and decent boy to do such a thing?" "What led to it" became a frequent question in my repertoire with my patients, but I had no success in opening a door to greater communication with this boy. I could see that he was highly stimulated, and I knew what led to it, but I failed to persuade his mother to behave less seductively, to stop showering with him, taking him into bed with her—particularly in recent weeks, after she and the boy's father separated. Suggesting that less stimulation might help seemed to have no effect; nor did hazarding to the boy the idea that his sad look might have something to do with losing his father.

Bertl had yet another story about simultaneously setting a child at ease and calling attention to a fear. In a consultation with a shy little boy, she suggested: "You think I look like an old witch." This was said in such a way as to make it clear that, appearance aside, if she was a witch, she was a good witch; the child smiled, sighed, was relieved, and the work went on. Bertl had been able to use the occasion to show that she was unlikely to feel sensitive about her appearance and, probably, other things as well. Fortunately, I learned the lesson that one needed to help frightened children (and adults) feel less frightened and fearful. Unfortunately, I did not find a way to do that with my young patient.

Though I had at different times in childhood a "normal," "un-normal" or "unusually difficult" development, I still classed my evolution as "unusual." It would have been better for me to have had more socialization with other young children. It was pretty plain to me that one had to treat children, particularly, and adolescents, also, as different from adults; young children don't do as well with words as older people usually do, so play therapy was invented, in which ideas are shown by way of interaction while playing. Groups are good; toys and dolls and diverse games are good; moralistic horror stories are not good. People who think child analysis may be useful but isn't "real" (i.e. strictly verbal) analysis, are wrong. Child analysis *is* useful and real, and anyway, adult analysis isn't strictly verbal.

"Basic Trust" and Evolution

In the early part of my career, a theory was that an underlying positive transference (usually thought to derive from a good-enough early relationship with a caretaker) is a necessary prerequisite for a successful relationship between analyst and analysand. This did not preclude the likelihood that later events might upset the psychoanalytic office apple cart. "Basic trust" would tide one over the shoals of disappointment.

I recently attended an intimate meeting of good analyst friends in Paris. The talk was wide-ranging; and one question was, how would we all have treated the question of whether or not to bring up a matter, which seemed significant, but had not been brought up by a patient? An example: a punctilious patient who missed one or two meetings but offered no explanation. In the main, the French were firm in saying they would wait until the patient brought it up herself. The rationale was, if she were ready to discuss it, she would raise it. My alternative might be to say something like, "I noted that you missed an appointment and haven't said anything about it." That would leave open the question of, why not be explicit? The French evidently thought that the patient should not feel directed; it's up to the patient to introduce a topic. On the other side, one could say, "Certainly, the patient might feel directed, but one could then discuss it in terms of the idea that she is presenting something by her behavior, which is already a communication."

The French had a *rule* for such occasions, whereas Kronold, Jacobson, and Bornstein had "touch," the appropriate sound among a passage of sounds for each note.

For me, any act is a part of a performance that transmits "touch." The touch makes the music—*le ton fait la musique*. To have a good touch means you can produce the sound of each tone, so that what is played gives not only the correct pitch, but also the timing, loudness, and duration, as part of a flow of sound, which reveals the essence of what the performer, as agent of the composer, feels. It is uniquely itself and spontaneously of the moment. It gives every live performance a unique life; a live performance differs from a recorded one. Similarly, waiting is a response to a late patient, but what it represents in the interaction is unclear, or less clear, than the patient's mentioning that she hadn't felt well, or overslept, or whatever reason or excuse is proffered. I came to believe that schemata, maps, and recipes are valuable, but insufficient. To be original and creative requires being able to act on impulse, to be relatively free of restraint, to trust one's unconscious processes; one can almost always reconstruct how an idea had come to mind, after the fact of having expressed it, trusting the patient and oneself to find an answer.

When I was applying for psychoanalytic training, there was a joke idea that was not all that funny—it was a joke about jokes.

PART II – FURTHER PSYCHOANALYTIC REFLECTIONS

Certain interviewers were said to ask applicants to tell a joke and then purportedly based their opinions of the applicant's capacity to use analytic training on whether the joke was Oedipal, anal, or oral. Judgements were held to be based on strict ideas about each type. Regression to the oral stage was much touted as an explanation of schizophrenia, for instance. I was pretty sure that jokes were pretty inclusive of a multitude of sources and meanings; but lots of people took the idea of stages of development literally. Still, such a possibility probably inhibited me in my second analysis, with Martin Stein, such that I did not bring up certain concerns. He, like the French, did not introduce them.

A sign of my immaturity that I came to weigh during that analysis came through my recognizing my avoidance of feeling mature enough to contemplate the idea that I was responsible for other people—for Barbara, my children, patients, and our dog, principally. That came a bit after my recognition that I was pathetically concerned about having someone take care of me, not in the maternal sense but in the paternal. For example, the chair of Medicine at Einstein lived near us on Park Avenue in Manhattan, and when I passed near his building, I hoped we would meet and form a relationship which would help me progress in my career, but more, constitute a parent-child, patron-acolyte opportunity. My father was an orphan who had responsibility thrust upon him, without having had the experience of family from which to grow up. I wanted to leave authority to someone else. Let them be blamed. It's better to feel hurt than ashamed and/or guilty. Nonetheless, I never talked with Stein about how that problem influenced my behavior.

Issues unaddressed had been significant, previously, in my failed treatment with Robbins. When I consulted Edith Jacobson, a pillar of the European analytic model (she defied the rigid attitude of having no extra-analytic contact with patients by actually talking to me and by asking to meet the fiancée of a friend of mine who was a patient of hers), it was she who raised some. She snorted at the idea that I was unanalyzable and suggested that my mother's multiple sclerosis must have made problems for me, at which, Eureka, I realized it wasn't my fault that I couldn't work with Robbins; I couldn't work with him, but partly that was because I couldn't discuss my problems with him.

With Stein there were experiences that helped me a good deal, such as when he helped me to realize that being gifted didn't automatically lead to being preferred. Often enough, it led to being envied and disliked. When Hershel Baker tried to recruit me to the Harvard English department, I was restrained by the mistaken idea that this solution was too easy, too self-indulgent, and insufficiently a service; it would not gratify my mother for one thing. My previous possibility, music, was not practical—it was too "girly" to be a pianist; I had no decent training owing to my family's financial circumstances. I was overawed by my mother's devotion to the idea of Horowitz as genius, which had early convinced me that I could never measure up. (The final obstacle was that my fingers got thicker as I grew older and were too hard to fit between black keys, when using straighter Russian finger-holding technique than the curled-finger manner of my mother's Austrian style.)

This all led to my half-thunderstruck understanding that my parents had their own reasons for making children, not all of them helpful to me and some outright negative. Vladimir Horowitz did not succeed through talent alone; I was no Horowitz, but I never had the circumstances that might have enabled me to become one. Currying favor with possible benefactors doesn't necessarily work. Having talent isn't necessarily only a good thing; it brings envy of and by others, for one thing. I suppose most, if not all, children believe that their family environment presents a norm for the rest of life; the culture in which I grew up, with its frightening children's storybooks, and its parental attitudes of secrecy, contributed to the belatedness of my understanding of some of the realities of life. It made me significantly more passive than necessary.

I owed it to my parents to be what they wanted, which happened to be more passive than I wanted to be. My father, the orphan, and my mother, a seductive somewhat too clingy female, and sick to boot.

The construction of a warm relationship requires a sense of connection (and room to work, too). Barbara had a real knack for being both protégée and worker bee in relationships, with Jacques Guérin, Joe Baum, Leo Lerman, Jim Beard, and others; I envied her more than was reasonable. Actually, she paid for her talent by giving her sponsors too good a financial deal. We both worked more out of interest and pleasure on projects than most people do, and we both tended to avoid commercial bargaining (though less so as time went on). We were like one of my more successful patients, a man who was CEO of a succession of major companies, who began to make better deals for himself during his analysis (a frequent effect). As for me, I started winning at poker.

How Far Can Analysis Take Us?

Adults have disadvantages. They have stored away obsolete, now useless, or even counter-productive adaptations, often achieved at an important cost. Established people have investments in established ideas. Why study to learn what will soon be replaced? The answer—to discover where the theory fails to apply. The more receptive young are lacking in experience, and so, more able to doubt. From a Darwinian point of view, it might be that it is a good thing to have generational changes every twenty-five years or so and, thereby, have a goodly number of people in their most productive years around all the time. Parents think they know. Youth discovers what the elders have not noticed. Eventually, Kuhn's paradigm shift occurs. So too in psychology, previously honored "facts" become more provisional and less useful.

Brenner and others argued that nothing is conflict-free; there will always be conflicting wishes about anything. Every solution, no matter how satisfactory, constitutes a compromise and, by definition, represents a limited success. It cannot eliminate conflict, as gratification of one desire privileges it, at the expense of other desires, and we want to have things every-which-way—and immediately; waiting one's turn is not ideal.

Psychoanalytic therapy requires some freedom from acute stresses, and also, some general calm. Being a rapidly changing child or adolescent, or facing grief, disease, or the like, makes a time-consuming re-education more or less unpracticable. The successful treatment necessarily brings about moderation: of grand desires, utopian ideals, and egotistical wishes for fanciful Vulcan, Spockian logical control.

I have recounted something of what analysis allowed me to rework. That included problems about my rivalry with my father which I expressed in relation to our financially impoverished emigration and very nastily, too. Then I multiplied my attacks upon him on the basis that he imperiously deprived me of participation in his world by excluding me from it; that was probably a more important impoverishment. He had a more intimate closeness with Fred, another objection I had, and with my mother—still more impoverishment. I had a Freud-like issue with my father; I sneered at (what I claimed was) my father's servile attitude toward the Springers. Of course, I knew little about growing up in an orphanage, spending four years of adolescence on a war front, and coming back to a destroyed country; besides, I avoided realizing what I knew. That left me guilty. I tried to make up for it by being patient and affectionate with other people, which never dissolved my guilt or lessened my disappointment at having missed out with my father. My childhood facts failed to explain or support all of my theory.

In addition to this egotistical stance—e.g., "I am the center of *this* world" (not simply the center of "my world"), there was a lot of frightening reality for me to deal with, as well as my Oedipal conflicts. From a rational point of view, most of this could not be laid at my father's feet. But, if one (mis)uses the capacity to reverse figure and ground and looks at all this not from an "either-or" point of view, one sees that it all came out quite well. Bad things happened to my father, and he overcame them; bad things happened to me, and when I became able to accept them, I had many good years. With respect to the heart issue, advances in surgical technology mean I'm still alive; not many would have predicted that minimally invasive cardiac surgery would save me, or that fracking (those two have in common piercing surfaces with long tubes and manipulating far-distant areas) would make us free from Mideast oil.

One thing that is left out in making projections about the future is unexpected creative ingenuity. Thanks to the former Vice-President, Dick Cheney, it now seems more familiar to cite dangers (known, unknowns we know, and unknown unknowns). On the other hand, good things, unexpected good things, and hoped-for good things, can also happen. Possibly, evolution has left us with a bit more fear of potential hazards than is actually useful. Have times changed for the better during my time? I think a resounding "Yes" is in order; perhaps it might be possible to achieve increasingly appropriate judgment and lessening impatience.

I have lived through three "major" depressions, three episodes of endocarditis, one near-death cardiac arrest, and one near-drowning. Except for the near-drowning, which resulted from going into the sea in Puerto Rico and encountering a strong current which left me almost exhausted before I got back to the beach and crawled out—all these other events might well have killed me had I lived in the previous generation. Technology, drugs, and psychotherapy got me over the same situations which had led to the deaths of my father, my uncle, and probably, my grandfather, Gottlieb, who died of the consequences of rheumatic heart disease. Predicting these happenings, mastering "unknown unknowns," was impossible. Past disasters repeat. Future successes eventuate.

Transforming my orientation towards the idea—it's my world and I'm the center of it—into, I'm the center of my world, which I can improve but not rule over—is an example of my personal shrinkage. I am freer and more optimistic than I was before. It was a sad conclusion for me to realize that Horowitz probably had more talent and motivation than I; he didn't have magical powers. Horowitz lived one street north of us and walked his dog, and I walked our dog. One day, we met dog-walking, and I told him how grateful I was to have been able to hear many of his performances. I also asked how much he practiced? He replied that he used to practice but didn't any longer; he merely spent four or five hours every day playing the piano.

I changed, partly with the help of psychoanalysis, and also psychoanalysis changed. In 1959, when I began my residency, psychiatry was a medical specialty and that meant it dealt with diseases. Historically, mental diseases were of the brain, the model being medical, and medical diseases were diseases of the soma, of organs. American psychoanalysis was fragmented; so-called neuropsychiatrists or alienists staffed mental hospitals which often followed traditional practices—fresh air, exercise, and physical activities, as well as giving the few (and often toxic) drugs then available—in circumstances of confinement. There were a variety of schools, the most important led by followers of Harry Stack Sullivan, Karen Horney, Wilhelm Reich, Theodor Reik, C.G.Jung, and Alfred Adler who were themselves trained by followers of Freud, who had set out to found their own schools.

PART II – FURTHER PSYCHOANALYTIC REFLECTIONS

The Biopsychosocial Approach, Intersubjectivity, and Creativity

Our recent progress would have been right up Freud's alley. It is well known that Freud looked forward to a convergence of parallel avenues of explanation, the mental and the physiological. He didn't have a problem about not reconciling the abstraction, "mind" and the material "brain," nor of separating nature and nurture. However, he did not stick with simple constructions like "seduction" or "abreaction" as explanations when it became apparent that they were insufficient. Left versus right may be useful at times; it may even be derived from the observation that we have two arms, legs, eyes, and so on; but there are more sides to a discussion than two. Fight or flight sounds good, but fight *and* flight are aspects of the same situation; the responses to threat include fight and flight, but are hardly limited to them. Freud's problem, as any teacher's, was in contextualizing and describing complex systems.

Reiser suggested the term "biopsychosocial," indicating three approaches to be used to define the origins and development of mental functioning. Relations with other people and with societal institutions have psychological and social effects. Yet, if one starts from focuses on disposition, development, maturation, and triggers, one soon falls upon complicated problems of genetic inheritance, biological life changes, complicated interweavings of experiential type, and symbolically complicated threatening events, of brief and long duration. My depressions would be explained on a predisposition level, by genetic inheritance—the bio part—Uncle Gusti, and also great-uncle Rudolph Stern's son, Robert, killed themselves. The complicated involvements with doctors and diseases, which my mother, father, and I experienced, would be classed as contextual causes with psychological ramifications. If "a" led to "b" led to "c" led to "d," that would seem a manageable line of thought; unfortunately, they all exist at the same time, and interact; all are changed by the interaction. We cannot do without making categories, but we must remain able to interconnect them and make subcategories as we make medical specialties and subspecialties.

Questions arise as more knowledge points to more possible factors. New words have to be invented and old words acquire new meanings; words accumulate more and different meanings and usages ("transference" is an example), so every discussion should (but doesn't) begin with agreed definitions. This is a burden in itself. A significant current task is to try to go beyond nature and nurture and go on to inspiration.

"Intersubjectivity" has become a catchword for what goes on between people and, given the observation that words are not the only way we influence each other, we might try to give more attention to how other forms of communication work. Years ago, the American Association for the Advancement of Science had a large meeting in New York; one of many interesting contributions used extremely slow-motion movies to examine minute changes in facial expressions and body movements. This approach has now reached the internet, where one series called *Lie to Me* presents detective episodes that involve crimes and problems, which Dr. Leitman, the body language-expression researcher, deals with by evaluating the meaning of expressions, facial and postural. Usually the subject is unaware of the fact that he is giving himself away or exonerating himself; Leitman is a walking Lie Detector, who is always right. Another such series features a woman whose perceptions are invariably correct and are based on some sort of intuition. I think "intuition" is probably akin to the popular uses of "electricity," or "chemistry"—words that conceal ignorance. I believe that "unconscious thinking," "subjectivity," "intersubjectivity," "unconscious communication," or "brainstorming" are better terms in considering the problem of understanding what enables people to bind or separate, to integrate and innovate.

In playing the piano myself, my technique was never even second-class, but the ear, the musicality, was there. I never had one interpretation; there was a different interpretation, a different way I wanted to hear, each time. (Robert Motherwell would go to the studio, turn on the music, and paint a big picture—or several little ones. Picasso did the same, and he also painted over what he had just done; so instead of inventing variations on a theme, he made his variations one on top of another.)

As for "intersubjectivity," I have come to think of the interrelation between people in terms of "the Word" plus "the Rest," the latter encompassing all sensations, including emotions. The Word is extremely important, and some words are stronger than others; they convey literal meaning, and the more sensory parts of experience. They evoke taste (like chicken), skin sensation (such as foggy, dewy, smooth, rough, cold, warm, hard, soft), auditory experience (loud, soft, rasping, shrill), visual experience (bright, dull, near, far, colored, black, white, figure, ground), or anatomical feelings (weight, dizziness, nausea, spasm, stretch, relaxation, faint, sleepy). These words convey subjective judgments; the best one can do is invent scales for questions like, "On a scale of one to ten, how much pain would you say you're having now?"—the response reflects subjective experience. (As the patient knows pain medication will be provided in response to a reported number of probably seven or more, the desire for an opioid might influence the patient's judgment.)

Subjectivity necessarily results in ambiguity of verbal communication. More or less specificity and harmony or disharmony (what goes together with what) in relation to quality, intensity, interrelation with the ambiance, etc., is always an issue for performers. In this, they approach the intercommunication world of mystery: "chemistry," "electricity," "homey," "strange," "eerie," "sympatico," where definition is non-specific. This is the world of gesture, expression, tone, myth, instinct, hypnosis, placebo, or shareable affective states such as anxiety, depression, and sympathy, which are still more distant from the measurable, definable noun or verb. Perhaps this is closer to the animal mentality, to the life of the dog or lion, where the recognition of a fellow member of the species extends to recognizing specific individuals, allowing for family, herd, and social organization, as well as a sense of hierarchy, danger, or fear.

With regard to the analogy of human life and social organization and animal life, one can point out similarities and, clearly, differences. For me, the most important difference is that the human does more than survive and multiply—the human creates.

INDEX

Abduction from The Seraglio, The (opera), 191
Abend, Sander ("Sandy"), 288f, 291f, 403
abreaction, 322, 323
Ackerman, Loren, 172
adenoidectomy, Ernest's, 35, 36, 39, 49, 59, 60, 213, 448
    dreams related to, 35, 39, 113 (*see also under* dreams of Ernest Kafka)
    ether anaesthesia for, 35–36, 60, 94 (*see also* ether anaesthesia)
    revival of adenoidectomy trauma, 94
Adirondacks, 100
aging and ill analysts, 464–65
Aisenstein, Marilia, 288f
Albert Einstein/Bronx Municipal house staff (1960), 276f
Albert Einstein College of Medicine, 133, 301
    Milt Rosenbaum's influence at, 316–17
    psychiatric residency at, 302–4, 316, 330, 335, 348, 350, 356, 357, 465–66, 496

    choosing psychiatry, 310–15
    introduction to Freud, 320
    psychiatry program, 314
    See also Jacobi Hospital
alcohol use, 131, 206, 298, 403
Allen, Woody, 399
Altman, Bernhard (Cecil's father), 192, 193
Altman, Brigitte de Vallée, 257, 296
    and Barbara Kafka competing at cooking, 257, 295
    Cecil Altman and, 192, 257, 296
    Ernest and, 192, 257, 295, 297, 345
    leaving Germany for France, 195–96
    marriages and affairs, 192, 296, 297
    Brigitte Altman and, 192, 257, 295, 296
    story about his Onkel (Uncle) Fritz, 192–94
American Hospital in Paris, 397
American in Paris, An (Gershwin), 197, 198
American Psychoanalytic Association

("the American"), 346, 347, 471
amyotrophic lateral sclerosis (ALS), 230–31
anaesthesia. *See* ether anaesthesia
analysts. *See* psychoanalysts
analyzability, 338, 339, 341, 344, 362, 480, 492
"analyzing out" (transference and countertransference), 437–38, 476
animal experiments, 162–65
"Anschleichen" (game), 31–32
anti-Semitism, 19, 132, 206, 215. *See also* Holocaust; Jews: discrimination against
antidepressants, 104, 309, 406, 435, 453, 495
Aplysia (sea slugs), 459
arrhythmia, 312–13, 329
art, 198, 246, 249–50, 474
    Barbara Kafka and, 141, 204, 246, 257, 300–301
        art collecting with Barbara, 379–80
    Barbara Rose and, 252, 381, 391
    collecting British drawings and watercolors, 379–81
    David Smith and, 251–52
    Ernest and, 99, 365, 379–82, 391–92
    Henry Geldzahler and, 251–53
    high, 73, 204
    Oaxaca and folk art, 390–91
    political, 391–92
    style in, 391
    Vogue and, 300–301
art historians, 72
art museums, 154, 157, 252, 378–79, 385, 386
art song, 73
artists, 209, 246, 247, 249, 250, 255, 474
    Barbara Kafka and, 246, 379, 434
    Ernest and, 75, 246, 249–50, 255, 379–80, 474
    Henry Geldzahler and, 252
arts
    finding avocations in the, 373–74
    visual, 379 (*see also* art)
Aspen, Colorado, 374–77
Aspen Music Festival, 374, 377
Aspetuck River, 126–27, 186
    swimming in, 137, 211
Athens, Greece
    travels to, 238–39
atrial fibrillation (AF), 414, 415
attention deficit hyperactivity disorder (ADHD), 201
Austria
    banks, 21–24
    family uninformed that and how they would leave, 41–42
    family's fear of being trapped in, 41–42
    history, 11, 12, 14
    international politics in 1938 and end of Austrian state, 26–27
    Jews in, 11–14, 23, 24, 27, 29, 41, 52, 140, 145–46, 175, 318 (*see also* specific topics)
    memories and relics of life in, 17–21
    Nazi invasion of, 21, 38–39
    travels to, 238
Austro-Hungarian Jews, 27–29, 194, 365
Austria-Hungary, 40–41, 346

INDEX

history, 346, 366–67
Austrian Civil War, 49
autobiography, 2
autoimmune disease, 224
autopsy, 171
 first participation in an, 169–71
average expectable environment, 340, 357

Bak, Robi, 142, 338, 358, 365, 456, 464, 485–86
 Barbara Kafka and, 142, 485
 death, 485, 486
 Ed Kronold recommended by, 482
 in Ernest's analysis with Ed Kronold, 485–87
 Walter Stewart and, 485–87
Baker, Herschel, 114
Balter, Lee, 385–86
banks
 in Austria, 21–24
 See also under Kafka, Adolf: employment
bar mitzvah, 93–94
Bard College, 112
Barnes Hospital, 148, 152, 154, 159–60, 215
 farewell to, 240
 psychiatry department, 315
 working at, 156
Bartlett, Whiting, 118
Beacon Hill, the haunt of, 113
bedside manner, the power of, 172, 437–39
beer barons, 156, 216
behavioral psychology, 106
Bello (Mami's dog), 213
Berg, Paul, 162
biography, 1

biopsychosocial approach, 497
Bismarck, Otto von, 14
Bloom, Claire, 229
body relative direction. *See* left–right confusion
border crossings, 195–96
Bornstein, Berta "Bertl," 470, 487–89
Boston, 109, 112, 113, 199. *See also* Harvard University
Bradish, Gaynor, 114, 119, 273f
brain–mind division. *See* mind–brain division
Brenner, Charles, 326, 470, 476, 493–94
Brill, A. A., 132
Britten, Benjamin, 422
Bronx Municipal Hospital Center, 276f
 psychiatric training at, 344
 See also Jacobi Hospital
Bussel, John, 405

Cam, Helen Maud, 114, 115
Cameron, Dr., 234–35, 237–38, 444
 empathy and humanity towards a badly damaged patient, 235
cardiac arrhythmia, 312–13, 329
cardiologists, 164, 415–18
cardiology, 312, 314, 413–16. *See also* endocarditis
cardiomyopathy, hypertrophic, 82, 402–3, 405
cardiovascular disease
 Adolf Kafka's, 82, 100, 312–13, 401–2
 Ernest Kafka's, 401–5, 414, 428, 495
 See also endocarditis
Caro, Anthony "Tony," 246, 254–55, 379

Center for the Advanced Study of
    Psychoanalysis (CAPS), 282f,
    375
cerebrospinal fluid (CSF), 410
Chamber symphony, New York, 394
Chaucer, Geoffrey, 118
chemistry, 91, 106, 108, 119, 154,
    160–62
Chevy (dog), 210–12, 274f
child analysis, 7–8, 470–71, 487–89
childhood development, early
    evolution of theories of, 456–60
    See also development
children, 177
Church, Frank, 245
cigarettes, 209, 364–65
cigars, Jack Poses and, 131–33, 239
clannishness, 227. See also tribalism
Clark, Mark, 256
Clinical Pathological Conferences
    (CPCs), 171–72
cocaine, Freud and, 78, 425, 474
cognitive deficits, 84, 200–204, 453
    Ernest on, 202
    writings on the psychological
        effects of, 463–64
collectivization of groups, 216. See
    also nationalism; tribalism
Commanderie de Bordeaux, 298–99
communication through words and
    non-verbal means, 74–75
communism, 86, 97. See also
    McCarthy, Joseph
compromise formation, 326, 329,
    350
Condé Nast
    Barbara Kafka's career at, 142,
        300–301
    Leo Lerman and, 142, 300–301
conflict-free ego sphere, 476, 482,
    493–94
consciousness, 472–76. See also
    topographic theory of the mind
constraints, 357
Cori, Carl and Gerty (professors of
    biochemistry), 154, 161–62
Count Bobby. See Graf Bobby
countertransference, 437–38, 473,
    475–76
creativity
    biopsychosocial approach,
        intersubjectivity, and, 497–
        500
    new interests in, 5–7
    See also art
crossword puzzles, 151
Crystal Palace on Olive Street, 117,
    208–10
Cuisine et Vins de France (magazine),
    297–98
currency, 99–100

Dana, Richard Henry, 1–2
Danby, Francis, 380
Darden, Severn "Sevvy" Teacle, III,
    112, 113
day residue (dreams), 424
de Waal, Edmund, 193
Debs, Eugene, 136
defibrillator, indwelling, 402
Delray, Florida, 427
Dennery, Phillipe, 295
depression, 149–50, 239, 249, 250
    Ernest's, 25, 48, 98, 104, 107,
        148–50, 179, 206, 250, 309,
        435
    major depressions, 232, 239,
        371, 406–9, 495, 497
    treatment, 104, 309, 348, 406,
        435, 453, 495

INDEX

Desmond, Paul, 76, 77, 275f, 399, 400
Detur Prize, 119, 152
development
    maturation and, 320, 323, 325, 326, 368
    See also childhood development
developmental deficits, Kohut on, 482
Dia:Beacon, 385, 390
diagnosis, 171–72, 202, 231, 236, 237, 328, 329, 346
    learning patience in, 167–68
    See also autopsy
Diagnostic and Statistical Manual of Mental Disorders (*DSM*), 346
    development of, 346
dickerle, 67, 312
Doctor Dolittle (Lofting), 475
doctors, 328
    anger and disapproval towards doctors who work past their viable years, 232–34
    anger at incompetent and dishonest, 175–78
    illness in, 173
dog walking, 99
dogs, 210–14, 261f, 263f, 361
    behavior in dogs and humans that goes beyond reflexive, 79–80
    history of Sterns and Poses's families' love and attitude toward, 213–14
    Portuguese Water Dogs, 280f, 361, 401
    Virginia Woof, 390, 411
D'Orsay perfume business, 125, 128, 132, 133, 184, 210, 311
D'Orsay perfumes, 183

Dowis, Jeaneane, 373, 374, 376, 377
dragon phobia, formation of, 43–48, 427, 458
dragon-train, 34
dragons, 430
    Nazis compared with, 336
    Siegfried and, 43–44, 48
dream images, 424, 474, 479
dream interpretation, 39
dream research, 469
dreams, 43, 330, 332
    August Kekulé's dream of six snakes, 450, 474
    contrasted with real life, 422–23
    Ernest and, 39 (*see also* dreams of Ernest Kafka)
    examination, 39, 170, 427, 479
    fear and anxiety, 239, 475, 479
    forgetting, 322
    of Freud, 46, 47, 322, 426
    Freud on, 46, 322, 424, 479
    Freud's topographic theory and, 321, 322
    hallucinatory, 421
    purpose, 424–27
    REM and non-REM, 330, 462
    return and evolution of post-traumatic, 427–28
dreams of Ernest Kafka, 170, 394, 417, 423
    anxiety dreams, 239
    coherent plots and sequences in, 423
    dream of Benjamin Britten, 422
    dream of hospital ship, 422
    the dream-subject of captivity, 424
    dreaming in German, 146
    Nazi dreams, 423, 427
    nightmares/bad dreams, 39, 46,

104, 419, 421, 435
  related to ether anaesthesia, 35, 39, 113
  railroad dreams, 422–23
  related to adenoidectomy, 35, 39, 113
  and theories about life, 429
Druckenmiller, Stanley, 371
drug use, recreational, 77, 150–51. *See also* alcohol use
drugs, pharmacological, 453. *See also* antidepressants; specific drugs
Dunster House, 111, 151
  Barbara Poses's visits to, 181, 183
  Christmas plays, 123, 183
dyslexia, 84, 453, 455

Eames, Charles, 155
Eden Roc, 190
ego psychology, 325–26. *See also* Hartmann, Heinz
Ehrlich, Edi, 59, 60, 94, 113, 174, 177, 448
  Ernest's dislike of how Ehrlich practiced medicine, 60
Ehrlich, Irene, 483
Ehrlich, Paul, 59–61, 113
Ehrlich, Reni, 59, 60
Einstein, Albert, 336, 442–43, 474
Elaine's Restaurant, 78, 155, 209, 399, 400
electroconvulsive therapy (ECT), 453
Elkington, John St. Clare, 234, 236, 237, 444
emigration. *See* immigration
empathy and humanity towards a badly damaged patient, 235
Encounter (magazine), 226
Encyclopædia Britannica, Inc.

  Barbara Kafka at, 229
endocarditis, 308, 414
  bacterial, 402–5, 414
  first episode (in Vermont), 403–4
  two more episodes, 404–5
Erikson, Kai, 318, 319
Ernest Kafka exhibition, 289f
ether anaesthesia, 196
  for adenoidectomy, 35–36, 60, 94 (*see also* adenoidectomy)
  aftereffects, 60, 459
  dreams related to, 35, 39, 113
  for tonsillectomy, 94
  trauma of, 35–36, 39

Fair, Master Gordon, 151, 152, 214, 362
fairy tales
  terror and psychological realism of, 43–46
  See also Siegfried
Farrar, Straus and Giroux, 187
Fechheimer, Margaret ("Maggie"), 121
Fieser, Louis, 119
"first, do no harm," 163, 165
Fisher, Charles, 469
Flamm, Gerald "Gerry," 317
Flushing, Queens, 61
Flushing Meadow Park, 62–63
folk art, 390–91
Foreign Policy magazine, 245
Fould-Springer, Baron, 147–48
  and the Kaiser, 147–48
Fould-Springer, Eugène Charles Joachim, 143, 146–47
  Marie ("Mary") Fould-Springer Wooster and, 57, 146–47
Fould-Springer, Hélène ("Bubbles"), 144

INDEX

Fould-Springer family, 147–48
    Adolf Kafka and, 353
France, 22, 148, 190, 195, 196, 295, 298, 366, 380
    economy and currency, 100
    Emile Stern and, 20
    Ernest in, 191, 195, 196, 298, 436
    Eugène Fould and, 146
    history, 366
    mobilettes in, 149
    World War I and, 22
    World War II and, 49, 145, 242
    See also Paris
Frankel, Chuck, 143, 273f
Frankenthaler, Helen, 246, 248, 251, 255
    Barbara Kafka and, 248, 379
    Ernest and, 248, 255, 379
    events hosted by, 228, 248, 249, 255
    family, 248–49
    photographs of, 281f, 285f
Franklin, Benjamin, 438–39
Franz Joseph I of Austria (Kaiser), 16, 29, 30, 146–48, 307
Frasers, 126–27
free association, 322
French art, 126, 379
French government, 146, 298
French language, 16, 52, 69, 146, 190, 366
French people, 156–57, 195, 196, 216, 295, 299
French psychoanalysis, 450, 490, 491
French Riviera, 189
French wine, 297–300, 365
Freud, Alexander (Sigmund's brother), 17
Freud, Anna (Sigmund's daughter), 324–26, 457, 466, 469
Freud, Harry (Alexander's son), 86, 303, 465–66
    Adolf Kafka and, 86, 101
    Hitler and, 86
Freud, Sigmund, 14, 319–20, 360, 374, 426–27, 437, 456, 466
    Anna Freud and, 469
    as clinician, 347
    cocaine and, 78, 425, 474
    correspondence, 376
    criticisms of, 455
    development of psychoanalysis, 2
    on dreams, 46, 322, 424, 479
    dreams of, 46, 47, 322, 426
    Edward Kronold and, 482, 483
    Ernest and
        might have met, 466
        similarities between, 353, 361, 494
    Ernest's introduction to Freud as a resident, 320
    father issues, 47, 323, 352, 353, 425–26, 494
    Fleischl von Marxow and, 425
    followers/successors, 455–56
    Heinz Hartmann and, 175
    how his desires influenced his theory, 425
    on incorporation, 13
    Kai Erikson and, 318, 319
    listening and, 70
    and the mythical analyst, 437
    Otto Pötzl and, 331
    personality, 446
    photograph of, 277f
    on psychoanalytic technique, 170, 347, 437
    psychoanalytic training and, 347

self-analysis, 46–47, 322–23
structural theory, 323–24
theoretical challenges, 497
topographic theory of the mind, 321–25
on transference, 445, 446, 476, 482
triads in the theories of, 321–24, 351, 356
writings, 318, 361, 471
    botanical monograph, 424–25
See also seduction theory
Freud Archives. *See* Sigmund Freud Archives
Friedberg, Charles K., 312, 313
Friedman, Albert Barron, 118–19
Friends of Oaxacan Folk Art (FOFA), 391
Fritz (great-uncle/Oma's brother), 16, 19, 29, 45, 120, 145
Froelicher, Grete, 373

Galbraith, John Kenneth ("Ken"), 383
galvanic skin resistance (GSR), 332
Gardiner, Muriel, 374, 375
Garrison (New York), house in, 155, 382–86, 389–91, 411
    2012 sale of, 390
Gaydosh, Jill (daughter-in-law), 249, 287f, 433, 436
Geldzahler, Henry, 251–54
    father, 252–53
    homosexuality, 253
gendarmerie, 194
German language
    influence of German sentence structure on Ernest's English writing, 139–40
    loss of, 67
    upon emigration, 25
German words
    abiding resonance of, 65, 66
    onomatopoeic quality (for Ernest) of, 67
Gershwin, George, 197, 198
Gersuny, Fritzi (Kafka), 175
Gersuny, Otto, 175, 178
    "Bauchreden" with, 175–76
    as role model, 174, 177
Gestapo, 21
    dreams about, 421, 427
gifted children, 82–83
Goldstein, Libby, 64
Golschmann, Vladimir, 157
Gottschalk, Alex, 160
government(s)
    Adolf Kafka and, 88–89
    personal identity and, 85–86
gradualism, 116
    examples of the power of, 117
Graf Bobby jokes, 75–76, 367
Graham, David, 315
Graham, Evarts, 315–16
grapes, 299–300
Graves family, 100–101
Greece, travels to, 238–39
Greenacre, Phyllis, 358, 482
Greenberg, Jay, 292f
Grottenbahn, 34, 46, 191, 430
GSR (galvanic skin resistance), 332
Guérin, Jacques, 141
    Barbara Kafka and, 141, 379, 493
    friendship with, 255
Guidotti, Guido, 112
Guttmann, Samuel A., 374

Haas, Barbara, 297, 300

INDEX

Haas, Bob, 297–300
Halberstam, David, 109, 273f, 399–400
Hammerschlag, Nellie, 18, 53–54
Hardwick, Elizabeth
  amusing acquaintanceship with, 228–29
Hartmann, Barry, 401
Hartmann, Heinz, 175, 322, 333, 340, 350, 357
  on average expectable environment, 340, 357
  Barbara Kafka and, 142, 470
  Charles Brenner and, 325–26, 476
  on conflict-free ego sphere, 476, 482
  Ernest and, 178, 322, 333
  funeral, 175
  metapsychology, 324–25
  photograph of, 275f
  publications, 322, 325
Harvard Crimson, The (newspaper), 104, 108–9, 121
Harvard Medical School, 151–52
Harvard University, 217, 304, 403
  on to, 103–5
  in 1950s, 104–7
  Barbara Kafka and, 181, 205
  Beacon Hill contrasted with, 113
  demographics of
    encountering better educated students, 107–8
    white and smart students, 105–7
  Final Clubs, 215
  friends from, 192, 242, 378, 399–400
  graduation from, 242
  professors, 114–19, 142 (*see also* specific professors)
  revisiting Harvard in 1983, 121
  roommates at, 60, 104–5
  second year at, 110–11
  senior year at, 149–51
  Warren Manshel at, 242
health workers, 222–23
heart disease. *See* cardiovascular disease
Hecht, Oma Clara/Klara ("Omah") (great-grandmother/Mami's mother), 13, 14, 31
  death, 14, 20
  photographs of, 258f, 262f
Hecht, Opa Alexander "Opah" (great-grandfather/Mami's father), 13–15
  characterizations of, 13, 483
  death, 14, 20, 483
  Ernest and, 14
  funeral, 483
  life history, 14
  overview, 13, 14
  photograph of, 258f
  at Waisenhaus, 15, 145
Hecht family, 15, 27, 29, 259f
Hellman, Lillian, 374
high art, 73, 204
  vs. popular art, 204
Hillside Hospital, 338
  reasons for commuting to, 338
Hirsch, John, 111, 113, 181, 182, 187, 273f
Hirtz (baker), 17, 31
Hitler, Adolf, 45, 93, 144
  Benjamin Britten and, 422
  Gerard Schwartz and, 421
  Harry Freud and, 86
  Jews and, 22, 28, 29, 215
  Mussolini and, 26, 38, 49

Vienna and, 21, 22, 38–39
Hockney, David, 252
Holocaust, 22–24, 145, 194
   relatives who died in, 20
   See also Hitler, Adolf
homosexuality, 118–19, 253
   psychoanalysis, psychiatry, and, 348, 452, 485
   See also Bradish, Gaynor
Hook, Sidney, 350–51
Hopf, Hans, 156
Horowitz, Vladimir, 99, 492
   Ernest and, 98–99, 492, 496
Hospital for Nervous and Mental Diseases (in Queen Square), 225, 314, 444
   after, 238–39
   artistry of simple procedures at, 236
   contrast between Elkington and Cameron at, 234–35, 237–38, 444
   neurology treatment taken over by surgeons and internists, 236–37
   socializing, manners, behavior, or the professional approach, 230–31
   teaching at, 231
hospital life, lessons from, 219–20
hospital setting, challenges to the healthy in a, 220
Hotchner, A. E. ("Hotch"), 155, 399
Hotel Bisson in Paris, 197–98
Hotel du Cap d'Antibes, 190
Hudson River, 384–86
Hungary. *See* Austria-Hungary
Huntington, Samuel "Sam," 228, 245
hydrocephalus, 410–11

hysterectomy, 168–69
hysteria, 320, 346
   seduction theory and, 46–47, 322, 323, 352

id, ego, and superego, 323–24
idiopathic thrombocytopenic purpura, 164
immigration, 72–73, 215, 451, 468
   anti-immigrant sentiment, 66, 215
   to United States, 18, 42, 127
   Jewish jokes post-emigration, 138–39
   and loss of people, things, and German language, 25–26
   and status of Jewish analyst emigres, 367–68
   See also migrations; specific topics
implantable cardioverter-defibrillator (ICD). *See* defibrillator
incorporation, 13
inter alia, 340
International Psychoanalytical Association, 368, 456
intern–patient interviews, 305–6
interpersonal psychiatry and psychoanalytic practice, 4–6
   decision to turn from research to, 355–56
intersubjectivity, 497–99
investment, 371. *See also* Thiokol

Jackson Heights, Queens, 61–62, 69, 85, 112, 175, 213
   community in, 366
   Ernest's parents in, 367, 388
   Fritz Kafka in, 25

INDEX

Hanni Kafka in, 18, 62
residences in, 61, 99, 367
settling in, 28, 61
summers in, 62
Jackson Heights Kindergarten, 85
Jacobi Hospital, 301, 316, 449
   Ernest's internship at, 447, 453, 469
      beginning of, 225, 241, 301–2, 469
      and the effect of chronic and repetitive health problems in patients, 308–10
      life on the wards, 302–4
      rotations, 302–3, 314
Jacobson, Edith, 338–39, 362, 363, 481, 487, 490, 491–92
   consultation with, 338–39, 341, 344, 362, 491–92
   and Ernest's analyzability, 339, 344, 362, 492
Jansky, Jeanette, 84
Japan, 95, 255–56
Jewish analyst emigres in America, status of, 367–68
Jewish cultural practices, 134–35, 433
Jewish Japanese, 256
Jewish jokes, 87, 305
   post-emigration, 138–39
Jewishness
   Barbara Kafka and, 134
   Jack and Lillian Poses's different sort of, 134–35
   See also Judaism
Jews, 52, 86, 119, 145, 366
   and the aristocracy, 56, 86
   assimilated, 29, 56
   in Austria, 11–14, 23, 24, 29, 41, 52, 140, 145–46, 175, 318
   Austria-Hungarian, 27–29, 194, 365
   discrimination against, 23, 24, 62, 127, 215 (*see also* anti-Semitism)
   French, 145
   German, 132
   Hitler and, 22, 28, 29, 215
   names, 27, 29, 52, 62, 306
   Russian, 127, 131–32
   shtetl, 138, 140
   See also Holocaust; Waisenhaus
Johns, Jasper, 252
Johnson, Lyndon B., 345
jokes
   are funnier to people with shared backgrounds, 75–78
   See also Jewish jokes
Judaism, 15, 86. *See also* Jewishness

Kafka, Adolf/Adolph (father), 14–17, 20, 28, 29, 62, 67–68, 224, 225, 495
   on America, 85
   in army, 15, 29, 71
   birth, 16–17
   characterizations of, 20, 67–68
   childhood of, 313, 319, 354, 491, 494
      childhood friends, 71
      Santa Claus and, 428
   Clara Hecht and, 258f
   daily life, 30
   death, 22, 240, 297, 312–14, 342–43, 402, 428, 495
   employment, 16, 25, 64, 65, 389, 422
      in banking, 15, 21, 22, 64, 88, 93, 99, 224, 310, 313, 340, 352–53

511

secret betrayer employee, 422
Ernest and, 59, 96, 99, 297, 355
Ernest working for, 310, 381
Ernest's birth and, 60
Ernest's conversations with, 38–39, 88–90, 93
Ernest's relationship with, 22–24, 32, 60, 61, 67–68, 82, 185, 252, 313, 340–43, 352–54, 370, 371, 427, 463–64, 466, 494
Ernest's tutorials with, 245–46
family and relatives, 16, 20, 137, 313, 319, 354
siblings, 16, 17, 20
fatherhood, 28, 60, 61, 206, 352–54
finances, 22–24, 61, 63–65, 88–89, 96, 185, 224, 297, 313, 340, 352–53, 389
and the Fould-Springers, 353
friendships, 71, 99, 142
Fritz Kafka (son) and, 34
government and, 88–90
Hanni Kafka (wife) and, 15, 28, 40, 60, 67, 68, 313, 352
residences, 21, 22, 61 (see also Jackson Heights)
Harry Freud and, 101
health problems, 401, 403
heart attacks, 312–13
heart problems, 82, 100, 401–2
Judaism and, 93
legacy, 313
life history, 14–15, 313
music and, 82, 96
names, 28, 65, 67, 85
Nazism, the Holocaust, and, 21–24, 38–39, 86, 196, 224, 313, 422

personality, 22, 64, 67–68, 71, 78, 100, 224, 352–54
photographs of, 258f, 260f, 271f, 273f
on politics, 38–39, 45, 85, 88–89
and the Springers, 494
travel, 32
at Waisenhaus, 14–15, 59, 71
Kafka, Barbara Joan Poses (wife)
Albert Barron Friedman and, 118
ballet and, 139, 183, 432
Bob Motherwell and, 248, 257, 297–98
car accident, 194, 200
childhood, 139, 213, 384
amid anti-Semitic social snobs, 206
cognitive issues, 200–204
dementia, 305–6
cooking, 192, 257, 295, 298, 301
competing with Barbara, 257, 295
dancing, 183
death of, 433
Ernest's anger and PTSD, 435
memorial service, 434
obituaries, 434–35
dress, 137, 186, 433
education, 139
at Radcliffe College, 123, 124, 131, 140–41, 204
uninteresting Ph.D. studies at Washington University, 184, 187, 203–6
employment, 187, 206, 493
as editor of *Cuisine et Vins de*

INDEX

France, 297–98
  at Encyclopædia Britannica, Inc., 229
  at *Mademoiselle*, 300, 301
Ernest and
  63rd wedding anniversary (June 1, 2018), 436
  Europe with and without Barbara (1953), 142–44
  first meeting, 123
  going to St. Louis, 200
  home and social life, 304
  reuniting, 181–86
Ernest's competition with Debbie Stern for Barbara's attention, 148
Ernest's marriage to, 206, 207
  honeymoon, 146, 187–88, 197–200, 307
  married life in St. Louis, 208–10
  wedding, 185, 186–87, 208, 240, 271f, 307
Ernest's relationship with, 184, 204–7
  Barbara's support for Ernest, 25
  breakup at Harvard, 205
  effect of Ernest's grudges and guilt on, 197
  Ernest's envy of Barbara, 493
finances, 129, 130, 207–8, 243, 382
freak accident, 390
health problems, 203–4, 206, 409–10, 412–14
  decline, 431–33
  fractures, 412
  medical history, 397–98
  peritoneal infection/retroperitoneal abscess, 397–98, 409, 410, 414
  rarity of her ailments, 414–16
Jack Poses (father) and, 297, 311
Jacques Guérin and, 141, 379, 493
Jewishness and, 134
learning to drive, 201
Lillian Poses (mother) and, 406
Margaret Fechheimer and, 121
mental functioning, 201–2, 409–10
  ADHD, 201
  left–right confusion, 124, 200, 201
motherhood, 206, 207, 357
as natural philanthropist, 129–30
need to know, 202–3
oddities/eccentricities, 124–25
party for Hanni Kafka's 70th birthday, 23
perfumes, 182, 183
personality, 129, 182, 183, 186, 204–6, 493
photographs of, 266f, 272f, 273f, 285f, 286f
physical appearance, 123, 433
  posterior, 123
presents/gifts received, 182, 185, 243, 249, 257, 307, 397
relatives and family background, 127–28, 135, 136, 138
  half-sister, 131
residences, 182
restaurants and, 296, 298, 432, 434
Ronnie (childhood dog), 213
surgery, 416

swimming pools and, 384, 433
theft of her engagement ring,
  189–90
training sessions with Susan
  Mask, 433
trauma, 397–98, 400
travel, 307–8
Vogue and, 300–301
wine and, 247, 296, 297–98,
  433
writings, 203, 205
See also specific topics
Kafka, Camilla (aunt), 16–17
Kafka, Ernest
  ("Ernie"/"Ernstl"/"Bubi")
alcohol use, 298, 403
analyzability, 338, 339, 341,
  344, 362, 480, 492
anti-Ehrlich file, 60
arrival in United States, 59
Barbara and (*see under* Kafka,
  Barbara)
birth, 28, 60, 61, 352, 353
Central European legacy and
  its present-day resonance,
  365–66
character, 97
childhood, 74–75, 90–91, 177,
  204, 352–54, 463–64 (*see
  also under* Kafka, Hanna)
  attending church, 48
  in Vienna (1932–1938),
    11–13
childhood medical models,
  174–75
childhood strategies for becoming
  an American, 88–89
clothes, 103, 315
defense stamps and Victory
  gardens, 89
dramatic performances, 109
drug use, 150–51
education, 108–11 (*see also*
  medical schooling: of Ernest
  Kafka; specific educational
  institutions; specific schools)
  changing majors, 108
  in chemistry, 91, 106, 108,
    119, 154, 161
  class valedictorian, 96, 103
  in English history, 108,
    114–16
  grades earned, 114
  in history, 108, 109, 114–16
  history of Ernest's motivation
    toward medicine, 173–74
  in literature, 108, 114,
    117–18
  premedical, 106–7
  transfer to "middle school,"
    91–93
emotional life, 204, 205 (*see also*
  depression)
  attraction to girls, 97
  greed for recognition and
    joining a group, 82–83
  grudges, 197
  guilt, 197, 427–28
  resentment about being
    left out and uninformed,
    33–34, 40
  sexuality, 97, 253
employment, 310
  first jobs, 99–100
  working for Adolf Kafka
    (father), 310, 381
enthusiasms shared with family,
  32–33
exploring subjects from different
  angles, 84

family and other stories told to him before he could read and write, 80
family background (1932–1938), 13–17
fatherhood, 206, 207
finances, 90, 184, 207–8, 243, 245–46, 297, 355, 371, 382
  investments (*see* Thiokol)
health problems, 416–18, 428, 495 (*see also* adenoidectomy)
  cardiac events and strokes, 413–14
  cardiac problems, 401–5, 414, 428, 495 (*see also* endocarditis)
  cataract surgery, 407
  coma, 416–18, 428
  denial of, 416
  dislocated arm from skiing injury, 110–11
  fevers, 188, 403–4
  insomnia, 27, 104, 179, 239
  paratyphoid fever, 188
  rarity of his ailments, 414–16
  renal calculi (kidney stones), 405–7
hospitalization
  delusional roommate, 419–20
  disgusting soft food; unable to speak; postoperative, post-traumatic state, 419
introduction to the mind, 316–19
issues with knowing powerful and/or influential people, 229
journey to United States, 58
learning English, 65–67 (*see also* German words)
learning to drive, 101–2
loss and abiding resonance of German words, 65–67 (*see also* German words)
loss of people, things, and the German language upon emigration, 26
maturation, 11–12, 97, 177, 227, 353–54, 448, 491 (*see also* maturation)
musical ability, 474–75 (*see also* music; piano playing)
nanny, 47–48
  betrayal of, 47–48
nicknames, 28, 61
oddities/eccentricities, 124–25
personal analyses
  first (training) analysis with Lew Robbins, 338, 339, 361–62, 479, 484, 491, 492
  second (training) analysis with Martin Stein, 341–44, 355, 357, 373, 466, 478, 480, 482–84, 491, 492
  third analysis with Ed Kronold, 46, 482–87
personality, 74–75, 90, 204–6
photographs of, 262f–65f, 273f, 281f, 285f, 286f, 291f, 294f
political events in the life of, 115–16
presents/gifts received, 17, 18–19, 42–43, 119, 185, 207–8, 243, 247–50, 307, 382, 428
  toy dining car, 35, 37
prizes and honors, 96, 103, 116, 119, 150, 152
reasons for becoming analyst, 39

reception of his work on Pötzl
  phenomenon, 333–34
residences, 52, 208 (*see also*
  Dunster House; Garrison;
  Jackson Heights; Newfane;
  Perchtoldsdorf; Vermont)
  Morty & Klaus apartment on
    Beacon Hill, 113
  New York apartment (130 E.
    67th St.), 64–65, 241, 245
  New York brownstone (92nd
    Street), 257, 297, 307, 357
  St. Louis apartment (326 N.
    Euclid Ave.), 208
  Vienna apartment, 17,
    30–31
reuniting with Jeanene Dowis
  and Sam Lipman, 376
revisiting his theories about life,
  429–30
singing, 109
skiing, 110–11
smoking, 132 (*see also* cigarettes;
  cigars)
suicidality, 406
swimming, 60, 111, 187, 297, 390
  learning to swim, 62–63, 110
tendency to "digress," 84
trauma (*see under* trauma)
turn from research to
  interpersonal psychiatry
  and psychoanalytic practice,
  355–56
writings, 39, 139–40, 333–34,
  356
  on ALS, 230–31
  controversial "squib," 108–10
  novel, 398
  on the psychological effects
    of cognitive weaknesses,
    463–64
  See also specific topics
Kafka, Franz, 27
Kafka, Frederick ("Fred"/"Freddie"/
  "Fritz"/"Fritzl") Max (brother),
  32, 33, 54, 355, 395–96
  in army, 28, 34, 68, 91–92, 95,
    143, 223, 242, 381
  bicycle (riding), 36, 48, 51, 54–55
  clothes/dress, 34, 64, 78, 381
  discussing politics in Vienna
    with, 48–49
  education, 23, 49, 65, 68, 91,
    95, 103, 106–7, 242, 368
  employment, 63, 79, 395
  Ernest and, 33–35, 107, 355,
    361, 395
    bedroom shared by, 28
    Ernest's birth and, 28
    Ernest's relationship with, 33,
      55, 56, 395, 396
    envy and rivalry, 31, 33, 34,
      36, 37, 40, 48, 55, 56, 60,
      64, 78–81, 107, 120, 339,
      354, 463–64
    Fritzl's importance to Ernest,
      33
  family, 224, 395
  family business inherited by, 395
  father (Adolf Kafka) and, 30, 31,
    34, 38, 55, 81, 82, 354, 494
  finances, 224, 242, 382
  illness, 396
  marriage to Mildred Joachim,
    95, 395
  Mort Reiser and, 361
  mother (Hanni Kafka) and, 28,
    31, 36–38, 40, 48, 55, 81,
    339, 381, 382
  names, 16, 28, 61, 79, 381

INDEX

Perchtoldsdorf and, 16, 23, 31–33, 78, 81, 368, 395
photographs and, 17, 21, 381
photographs of, 261f, 262f
post-war life, 224
residences and travels, 16, 17, 25, 28, 33, 48, 61, 395
toy train, 32–33, 35–36, 55, 78

Kafka, Hanna ("Hanni") Stern (mother), 15, 34, 35–36, 44, 46, 60, 214, 339, 367, 388, 492, 493
Ani Stern and, 19
belongings brought to America, 17
bicycle accident, 339
emotions aroused by, 37–38
envy of Fred and, 36–37
Ernest's head injury and, 38, 39
childhood, 15
death, 22, 175
delight in the film *Snow White*, 53
dogs and, 213, 214
dress, 18, 19
employment (*see also under* piano playing)
cake-baking enterprise, 63–65
Ernest and, 17, 20, 35–37, 43, 63, 64, 81, 182–83, 198, 339, 343, 352–54, 367, 382
Ernest's nanny and, 47–48
Ernest's piano instruction from, 81
Ernest's relationship with, 20–21, 25, 28, 37, 47–48, 60, 78, 82, 177, 178, 353, 354–55, 363, 493
Ernest disciplined by Hanni, 90
Hanni clinging to Ernest, 97, 493
expressions used by, 66, 67, 350, 362
family and relatives, 15, 19–20, 24–25, 115
friends, 19, 53
games and, 78, 81
hobbies and leisure activities, 32, 53
as housewife, 16, 53
baking, 16, 17, 31, 53, 65
illness, 100, 343 (*see also under* multiple sclerosis)
motherhood, 28, 60, 352
music and, 198 (*see also under* piano playing)
personality, 78, 81, 213, 493
photographs of, 259f–62f, 271f, 273f
physical body, 18, 213
reading books to Ernest, 44, 45
70th birthday party, 23
trains, travel, and, 32
visiting Sweden, 19
See also specific topics

Kafka, Hermann Chaim (Franz's father), 27
Kafka, Jill Gaydosh (daughter-in-law). *See* Gaydosh, Jill
Kafka, Lily, 287f, 436
Kafka, Michael (son), 249, 299, 390, 394–95, 403, 433–34, 436
birth, 249, 257, 397
childhood, 352, 376
Ernest and, 352, 376, 394–95, 417, 422, 423, 428, 436
illness, 402
marriage to Jill Gaydosh, 249
photographs of, 280f, 281f,

517

285f, 287f, 291f
Kafka, Mildred ("Mindy") Joachim (sister-in-law/Fred's wife), 95, 289f, 395, 396
Kafka, Nicole (daughter), 121, 257, 390, 424
   Barbara Kafka and, 257, 412–13, 433, 434
   birth, 207, 344–45, 357, 397
   Ernest and, 344–45, 403, 417, 422, 428
   photographs of, 278f, 282f, 285f, 291f
Kafka, Oliver (grandson), 287f, 457
Kafka, Sophie Dub (paternal grandmother), 16, 20
Kafka family, 16
   names and the, 27–30
   ongoing evolution of, 395–96
   photograph of, 267f
   traditional roles in, 33–34
   See also specific topics
Kaiser (Franz Joseph I of Austria), 16, 29, 30, 146–48, 307
Kandel, Eric, 459
Kanemitsu, Matsumi, 255–57
Kaplan, Jack, 242
Katz, Philip, 306
Kekulé, August
   dream of six snakes, 450, 474
Kennedy, John F. ("Jack"), 244
Kennedy, Robert F. ("Bobby"), 317
Kermanshah rug, 17, 31, 64–65, 389
Kirkman, James, 279f
Klein, Melanie, 457–58
knowledge, the limits of, 370
Kristol, Irving, 225–26, 228
   Warren Manshel and, 225, 226
Kronold, Edward, 483–87, 490
   as analyst, 482–83, 485
   Ernest's analysis with, 46, 482–87
   life history, 482, 483
   music and, 483
   personality, 483–85
Kulicke, Bob, 130, 246–47

La Paulée de Paris, 298
Lake Placid, 95, 100–101
Landesman, Fran, 208, 209
Landesman, Fred, 208–10, 435
Landesman, Jay, 208, 209
language, 29, 72–73, 139–40. *See also* dyslexia; specific languages
Lansner, Kermit, 75
Lawrence, H. Sherwood (Jerry), 224–25
"lay analysis" (psychoanalysis by non-MDs), 469, 471
left–right confusion, 124, 200, 201
Leiber, Jerry, 255
Lerman, Leo, 142, 242, 389, 399
   Barbara Kafka and, 300, 388–89, 493
Levee, John, 198–99
Levy, Paul, 293f, 434
Lewin, Bertram, 318
Lie to Me (TV series), 498
Lipman, Sam, 373–74, 376, 377
Loeb, Dr., 3–4
London, 148, 149, 225, 227, 229–30, 238. *See also* Hospital for Nervous and Mental Diseases
Lou Gehrig disease, 230–31
LSD (lysergic acid diethylamide), 77

Maas, Arthur, 116
Mademoiselle (magazine), Barbara working at, 300, 301
Manshel, Anita Coleman, 135, 228, 243, 337, 403

Manshel, Ernest, 120
Manshel, Warren Demian, 120, 135, 225, 228, 244, 403
   background and early life, 120, 242
   death, 337
   Irving Kristol and, 225, 226
   personality, 120–21, 243
   professional accomplishments and positions held by, 226, 242, 245
   relationships, 120, 243
      friendship with Ernest, 120, 245, 361
   on spirituality and metaphysics, 337
   stock market advice, 243, 245
Mask, Susan, 433
maturation, 168, 353, 357, 373, 438–39, 473
   development and, 320, 323, 325, 326, 368
   Ernest's, 11–12, 97, 177, 227, 353–54, 448, 491
   lifting repression and, 321
   perception, objectivity, and, 438
   and the structural theory, 324
Mayer F. M., 64, 65, 99
McCarthy, Joseph, 86, 119
medical decision-making
   making one choice eliminates other possibilities, 165–66
   Sophie's Choices, 164–65
medical profession, perils of the, 305–8
medical school, 165, 166, 467, 469
   Ivy League schools, 107, 119, 151–52
   See also specific schools
medical schooling
   of Ernest Kafka, 176–78, 183, 222, 223, 310, 381 (*see also* Albert Einstein College of Medicine; Hospital for Nervous and Mental Diseases; Washington University School of Medicine)
   applying to school, 107, 151–52
   Barbara Kafka and, 181, 184, 187, 204
   confronting and learning about the unknown, 222–24
   evolution of pharmacology; study of physiology, 162
   experiments on live animals, 162–63
   graduation, 225
   history of Ernest's motivation toward medicine, 173–74
   internship, 447
   learning/knowledge gained, 164, 222
   learning patience in diagnosis, 167–68
   learning tact and kindness towards patients, 166–67
   summer work at NYU lab with Jerry Lawrence, 224–25, 237, 310
   uncertainty about becoming a doctor, 178
   fascination with anatomy study, 160–61
   psychiatry and, 467
   required for psychoanalytic training, 469 (*see also* "lay analysis")

"Medical Student's Disease," 166–67
mental moment, 326
metapsychology of Anna Freud and Heinz Hartmann, 324–26
Michels, Robert "Bob," 292f, 405
migrations
    early huge global, 216–17
    See also immigration
mind, 442, 443
mind–brain division, 441–42
mind–brain questions, 330, 442
Modern Art, Museum of, 93, 379
Mon Amour Lodge, 100–101
Moore, Carl V., 158, 159
    radiated dedication, simplicity, focus, and honesty, 159
Morton, Frederick, 400
Motherwell, Mrs., 251
Motherwell, Robert "Bob," 247–50
    art and, 249–50, 257, 499
    Barbara Kafka and, 248, 249, 257, 297–98
    cars and, 247, 248
    death, 249, 254
    Ernest and, 246–51, 253, 379, 399
    family, 248–49, 254
    photograph of, 281f
    poker evenings, 246–47
    publications, 250
    TV interview, 250
Moyer, Carl, 159–60, 169, 223–24, 327
multiple sclerosis (MS), 198, 224, 231
    of Hanni Kafka, 22, 36–37, 40, 65, 92, 95, 97, 143, 159, 198, 224
        Ernest and, 95, 106, 177, 224, 492

    family's lack of awareness of, 36–37, 40
    See also under Kafka, Hanna
Museum of Modern Art, 93, 379
music, 73, 96, 98–99, 373–74
    composers, 30, 198
    Ernest and, 484
    Ernest's heart, heredity, and, 80–82
    the unique timelessness of, 73–74
    See also piano playing
Mussolini, Benito, 26, 38
    Hitler and, 26, 38, 49

names, the meaning of, 78–79
National Institute for Mental Health (NIMH), 355
nationalism, 41, 86, 87
Nazi experiments compared with animal experiments, 164–65
Nazi invasion of Austria, 21, 38–39
Nazism, 11. *See also* Hitler, Adolf; Holocaust; World War II
neurodiversity, 202–3. *See also* cognitive deficits
neutrality. *See* objectivity
New York
    artistic circles in, 241–43
    return to, 241–43
New York Chamber Symphony, 371, 377
New York Hospital–Cornell Medical Center, 403–5, 409–15, 419–20
New York Philharmonic, 377
New York Psychoanalytic Institute, 318, 338, 339, 347, 472
    beginning training at, 344, 357
    decision to attend, 341
    Ernest accepted at, 338, 362

Ernest presenting paper at, 322
New York Psychoanalytic Society, 347, 356, 373, 376, 467, 472
positions held in, 376
New York Psychoanalytic Society & Institute (NYPSI), 470
Newfane (Vermont), house in, 383, 384
Newfane Inn, 382, 383
Newman, Paul, 155
Newtown High School, 95
successes at, 96, 103, 108
Newtown X-ray, The (student newspaper), 98
writing reviews for, 98
Noland, Kenneth "Ken," 246–47, 253–54, 379
normal pressure hydrocephalus, 410–11
North Conway, New Hampshire, 110

Oakley, Joseph Carter, 104–5
Oaxaca, Mexico, 390–93
objectivity, 437–38
Oedipal conflicts, 38, 42, 48, 232, 351–52
Ernest's, 48, 351, 427, 494
Freud's, 48, 323, 352
Oedipus complex, 323, 351–52
criticism of, 350–52, 452
Freud on, 48, 350, 351–52
oenophilia, 297–98
Office of Price Administration, 90
Opportunity Class, 91
boon of the, 91
orchestras. *See* New York Chamber Symphony; New York Philharmonic; St. Louis Philharmonic; Vienna Philharmonic

overdetermination, 325, 326
Owen, David, 116–17

Palm Beach, Florida, 433
Palm Beach Polo and Country Club, 413, 417
Paris, 20, 139, 141–46, 182, 196
analysts in, 489
Barbara Kafka in, 141, 142, 148, 298, 397
Ernest in, 52–54, 143–44, 148, 198, 397, 489
Hotel Bisson in, 197–98
Jacques Guérin and, 141–42
last sunny days of relative innocence in, 52
Mary Wooster in, 143, 198
Nellie Hammerschlag in, 18, 53–54
residences in, 52, 141
Ritz Hotel in, 57, 139
terror at the film *Snow White* in, 53
Parks, Greg, 413, 415, 417
Passau, Germany, 194, 196
Pavlov's dog, 79–80
Perchtoldsdorf, 16, 19, 25, 31–33, 68, 69, 141
Fritz Kafka and, 16, 23, 31–33, 78, 81, 368, 395
memories of, 395
residences in, 15, 23, 78, 81, 213
summers with Mami and Tatti in, 80–81
Perry, Herman (Jack Poses's brother), 127, 129
personal life and professional life connection of, 1–3
See also private life and public life
Pesetskis, 127. *See also* Poses, Jack

Phi Beta Pi, 159, 160
photography, 381–82
piano playing, 81
    Ernest's, 63, 66, 69, 72, 81, 82, 90, 92, 163, 376, 379, 499
    Ernest's piano lessons and instruction, 81, 92, 99, 194
    Hanni Kafka's, 33, 37, 53, 64, 80, 82, 92, 483
    Hanni Kafka's piano teaching, 63, 65, 81
pianos, Ernest's, 17, 51, 61, 62, 64, 208, 388, 395, 483, 484
placebo effect, 172, 237, 364, 444–45, 481
Pledge of Allegiance used to create a politico-cultural community, 89–90
poetry, 150, 203, 365
    of Barbara Kafka, 203, 205
poker, 493
    beginning to win at, 372
    betting on the odds of a winning hand, 372–73
poker evenings, 246–47, 249
poker game, downtown, 255
Poses, Barbara (wife). *See* Kafka, Barbara Joan Poses
Poses, Jack (Barbara Kafka's father), 127–32, 141, 206, 239, 240, 311
    alcohol use, 131, 206
    Barbara and, 130–31, 182, 184–86, 207–8, 243, 297, 308, 311
        companionship, 133
        Jack's maternal role, 134
    Barbara taught to drive by, 201
    Barbara's thwarted ambition to work for, 129
    Chevy (dog) and, 210
    childhood, 128, 206, 239
    cigars and, 131–33, 239
    education, 128
    employment, 128, 208
        D'Orsay perfume business, 125, 128, 132, 133, 184, 210, 311
    Ernest and, 131, 132, 184–86, 201, 207–8, 210, 243, 297, 311
    arm wrestling, 131–32
    family and relatives, 130, 132, 134–35, 206
        three "Jacks" in one generation of Pesetski siblings, 127–28
    finances, 128–30, 133, 184, 208, 243, 297, 311
    languages spoken, 135, 140, 254, 365–66
    left–right confusion, 124, 200
    Lillian Poses and, 155
        Barbara and, 139, 183, 207–8, 213
        different sort of Jewishness, 134–35
        Ernest and, 132, 210, 366
        family gatherings, 132, 174, 211, 225, 239, 240, 345, 382
        finances, 129, 207–8, 311, 345, 366
    lifestyle, 127, 129, 133
    marriage/relationship, 130, 131, 134, 186, 206
    parties and entertaining, 126, 131, 174, 254
    residences, 125–26, 182 (*see also under* Westport)
    vacations, 238–39

INDEX

Mark Rothko and, 254, 366
other daughter, 131
personality, 128–32, 186, 201, 208, 311
photographs of, 272f, 273f, 279f
positions held by, 131–32, 253
relations with women, 130–31
    extramarital relations, 131
relationship with mother, 130
Russian culture and, 365–66
Russian language and, 135, 140, 254, 365–66
Poses, Lillian Shapiro (Barbara Kafka's mother), 135, 136, 183, 206, 241
  Barbara and, 127, 133, 134, 137–38, 182, 207–8, 397, 406
  Barbara's ambivalence about, 137
  childhood, 134, 206
  dislike of house-pet animals, 213–14
  education, 135
  Ernest and, 135, 207–8, 366, 406
  and Ernest and Barbara's wedding, 186
  family and relatives, 134–37, 206
  finances, 207–8, 366
  personality, 127, 131, 134, 137–38, 183, 186, 213, 311
  photographs of, 272f, 273f
  professional and political work, 133
    law career, 133–36
  and the Roosevelts, 136, 137
  vacations, 406
  in Washington, DC, 133
  See also under Poses, Jack
Poses Foundation at Brandeis, 133

Poses Newman Preserve, 155
post-traumatic dreams, return and evolution of, 427–28
post-traumatic memories, 78, 423
post-traumatic states, 196, 321
  postoperative, 419
  See also trauma
post-traumatic stress disorder (PTSD), 196, 435, 454
  Ernest's anger and, 435
  See also trauma
Potofsky, Jack, 136, 186
Pötzl, Otto, 330–31
Pötzl study, 330–31, 333–34
present and not-present, the, 74, 78
Price Administration, Office of, 90
Pritchard, Tom, 387, 389
private life and public life, 357. *See also* personal life and professional life
Propper de Callejón, Eduardo, 144, 145
Propper de Callejón, Hélène ("Bubbles"), 144
"provider," meanings of, 220–22
psychiatric writing, homogenization of, 5–7
psychiatry
  biological, 453 (*see also* antidepressants)
  psychoanalysis and, 4–7, 315, 317 (*see also* psychoanalytic training)
  See also specific topics
psychoanalysis, 4–7, 335, 470–71
  cinematic and other American myths about, 451–54
  clubs and divisions in psychoanalytic community, 466–72

contrasted with psychotherapy, 348–49
defined, 348–49
general status from 1962 and later on the conservative side, 345–49
has become part of the general culture, 5–6
"honeymoon" period, 481
scope and limitations, 493–96
as a valid science, 350–51
See also specific topics
psychoanalysts, 12–13
aging and ill, 464–65
objectivity vs. subjectivity, 437
psychoanalytic institutes, 5, 338, 347, 368, 471, 472. *See also* New York Psychoanalytic Institute; psychoanalytic training
psychoanalytic schools of thought, flexibility and exchange of ideas and theories among, 455–56
Psychoanalytic Studies at Aspen, 374–76
founders, 374–76
psychoanalytic terminology, 324–26, 456–57
psychoanalytic training, 344, 357–58, 439–45, 466, 467, 471
for non-MDs ("lay analysis"), 469, 471
positions on, 439
prevalence, 335
what makes a good therapist and teacher, 447–49
See also psychoanalytic institutes; training analysis and training analysts
psychophysiology, 327–34
psychosexual development and maturation, 320
psychosomatic disease, 332, 347–48, 452
psychotherapy
contrasted with psychoanalysis, 348–49
what makes a good therapist, 447–49
See also specific topics
public life and private life, 357. *See also* personal life and professional life
Public School (P.S.) 148, Ernest's transfer to, 91–93
Public School (P.S.) 149, 28, 89–91, 111
initiation into a new tribe at, 86–88
Jews and, 28, 90

Queen Square, London. *See* Hospital for Nervous and Mental Diseases
Queensboro Corporation Development, 62

racial segregation and discrimination, 215
Radcliffe College, 121
Barbara Kafka at, 123, 124, 131, 140–41, 204
rats, killing, 163
Reichenbach, François, 182
Reichenbach, Phillipe, 182
Reiser, Lynn Whisnant, 356, 361, 401
Reiser, Morton "Mort," 283f, 357, 361, 401, 487
on biopsychosocial approach, 497
Ernest and, 332, 333, 355, 356, 359–61

during Ernest's residency at
    Albert Einstein, 330
mocking and criticism of, 464,
    486–87
positions held by, 330, 334
research, 330, 332, 333, 463,
    469
relativity, theory of, 442–43. *See also*
    Einstein, Albert
religion, 86. *See also* Judaism
REM sleep, the significance of, 330,
    462
Richards, Arlene, 292f
Richards, Arnold "Arnie," 292f
Ritz Hotel, Paris, 57, 139
Robbins, Lew, 338, 339, 362, 484
    Ernest's analysis with, 338, 339,
        361–62, 480, 484, 491, 492
    and Ernest's analyzability, 338,
        339, 344, 362, 480
    recommended by Milt
        Rosenbaum, 338, 339, 480
Roberts, Sam, 434
Rollins, Hyder, 117
Ronnie (Barbara's childhood dog),
    213
Roosevelt, Eleanor, 137, 139
    Lillian Poses's admiration of, 137
Roosevelt administration, 133, 136
Rose, Barbara, 251, 255, 278f, 394
    art and, 252, 381, 391
Rosenbaum, Milton "Milt," 316,
    320, 468, 480
    Ernest and, 316, 317, 338, 344,
        480
    influence at Albert Einstein,
        316–17
    Lew Robbins recommended by,
        338, 339, 480
    resemblance of Wotan to, 360

Stagecoach Club, 316–17
Rosenberg, Anna, 133, 241
Rosenberg, Julius, 241
Rosenthal, John, 378
Ross, Lillian, 470
Roth, Philip, 229
Rothko, Mark, 253–54
    death, 254
    family, 254
    Jack Poses and, 254, 366
    Russian language and, 254, 366
Royaumont, 54–57, 143–44
Rubin, Lore Reich, 368

Santa Claus, 428
schizophrenia, 8
Schoenberg, Arnold, 92, 191, 194
Schratt, Katherine ("Schratti"), 147
Schwarz, Gerard, 376, 377, 421
sea slugs, 459
seduction theory, 46–47, 322, 352,
    426, 451
    Freud's abandonment of the,
        46–47, 323, 352, 451
    hysteria and the, 46–47, 322,
        323, 352
Seely, Bob, 405, 406
selective serotonin reuptake
    inhibitors (SSRIs), 104, 309,
    435
Sella, M., 190
Shakespeare films, 98
Shapiro, Beth (Barbara's cousin/
    Lillian Poses's niece), 136
Shapiro, Dora (Lillian Poses's
    mother), 126, 134, 137, 273f
Shapiro, J. Irwin (Barbara's uncle/
    Lillian Poses's brother), 134, 135
Shapiro, Joe (Barbara's cousin/Lillian
    Poses's nephew), 136

Shapiro, Lillian. *See* Poses, Lillian Shapiro
"shrinkage," 340–41
shtetl Jews and shtetl life, 138, 140
Siegfried (opera by Wagner), 43–44
    characters in, 43–45, 48, 156, 170, 359–60, 427, 458–59
    See also Wagner, Richard
Sigmund Freud Archives, 374, 465–66
Skinner, B. F., 106
smoking. *See* cigarettes; cigars
Sniders, Edward, 296
Snow White and the Seven Dwarfs (film)
    Ernest's terror at, 53
    Hanni Kafka's delight in, 53
Socrates, 342
Sokolov, Ray, 290f
Sonya (Jack Poses's oldest half-sister, who helped raise him), 135
Spender, Stephen, 226
Springer, Gustav von, 14, 15, 42, 54
    Eugène Fould-Springer and, 146–47
    Marie ("Mary") Fould-Springer (daughter) and, 42, 57, 146–47
    titles and, 146
    Waisenhaus and, 14, 145
Springer, Marie ("Mitzi"). *See* Wooster, Marie-Cecile ("Mary"/"Mitzi"/"Frau Baronin") Fould-Springer
Springer family, 54, 56, 57
    Adolf Kafka and, 494
    Ernest and, 57, 145
    Kafka family and, 41–42, 56
    political acumen and influence during World War II, 145–48

SSRIs (selective serotonin reuptake inhibitors), 104, 309, 435
St. Louis, Missouri, 153–57, 217
    Crystal Palace on Olive Street, 117, 208–10
    lessons from a border city, 214–16
    moving to, 200, 242
    See also Washington University School of Medicine
St. Louis Philharmonic, 157
Stagecoach Club, 316–17
Steig, Philip, 410
Stein, Howard, 293f, 370–71, 395
Stein, Martin, 373, 466–68, 470, 481
    children, 344
    Ernest's training analysis with, 341–44, 355, 357, 373, 466, 478, 480, 482–84, 491, 492
    personality, 342, 344
    photograph of, 293f
    positions held by, 466
    on "unobjectionable transference," 476, 480
Steinberg, Saul, 125, 128
Steinem, Gloria, 77, 400
Steinitz, Mr. (Adolf Kafka's banking partner), 23, 340, 341
Stella, Frank, 252, 255, 379, 387, 395–96
Stern, Adi (great-aunt), 19, 25, 51, 397
Stern, Ani (Hanni's cousin/Rudolph's daughter), 19, 24–25
Stern, Debbie, 148
Stern, Emile (maternal great-uncle/ Gottlieb's brother), 20
Stern, Evie/Evi-Ruth (cousin), 15, 21, 31, 51, 52, 174–75, 264f, 381

Ernest's relationship with, 15,
    20, 25
  migration to Palestine, 24
Stern, Gottlieb "Tatti" (maternal
    grandfather/Hanni's father), 16,
    20, 24, 25, 174, 495
  as (model) doctor, 16, 20, 174,
    175, 177
  alpine walking and climbing,
    82, 110
  in army, 16, 29
  death, 20, 25, 28, 42, 495
  descriptions of, 175
  Emile Stern and, 20
  Ernest and, 25, 31, 80, 110,
    174, 175, 178
  family, 15
  Hanni Stern Kafka (daughter)
    and, 40, 82, 175
  life history, 20
  photographs of, 19, 261f
  protecting the Sterns, 42, 51, 52
  Zionism, 24, 145
Stern, Gustav ("Gusti"/"Gustl")
    (uncle/Hanni's brother), 15, 18,
    32, 54, 59, 82, 497
  Ernest and, 31, 110, 174
  family, 15, 52
  Hanni's multiple sclerosis (MS)
    and, 40
  Judaism and, 52
  lifestyle, 33
  Lise Stern and, 15, 18
    divorce, 174, 175
  names and, 52, 54
  Naomi (daughter) and, 52, 174
  Otto Gersuny and, 175
  Palestine and, 20, 24, 51, 52
  personality, 177
  photographs of, 19, 259f, 261f
  as physician, 15, 33, 174, 175,
    177
  residences, 174, 381
  suicide, 174, 240, 354
  swimming pool, 18, 25, 31, 69
  travel, 20, 24, 32, 33, 51
Stern, Lise (aunt), 18, 24, 31, 51,
    174, 175
Stern, Margaret ("Mami") Hecht
    (maternal grandmother), 13, 15,
    25, 29, 42, 78, 81, 137, 273f
  death, 240, 354
  dogs, 213, 261f
  Ernest and, 28, 63, 142, 175,
    240
  finances, 142
  immigration to New York, 25,
    28
  as pianist, 15, 33
  residences, 15–16, 28, 213
  Tatti Stern and, 175
  World War I and, 29
Stern, Naomi (Gusti's daughter), 52,
    174
Stern, Robert (Hanni's cousin/
    Rudolph's son), 19, 25, 497
Stern, Rudolph "Rudi" (great-uncle/
    Tati's brother), 18, 19, 25, 29,
    42, 497
  Ernest and, 18–20, 25, 42–43,
    51, 120, 428
Stern family, 15, 24–25, 27, 42, 259f
Steuermann, Eduard, 194
  piano lessons from, 99
Stewart, Walter, 485–87
Stillman Infirmary, 111
Stone, Leo, 358, 470
strain trauma/chronic trauma, 34–
    35, 450–51
  vs. acute trauma/stress trauma,

527

35, 450–51
structural theory, Freud's, 323–24
Stubbs (Portuguese Water Dog), 280f, 361, 401
subjectivity, 437–39, 499. *See also* intersubjectivity
Swift, Jonathan, 430
swimming pools, 384, 386
    Barbara Kafka and, 384, 433
    Gusti Stern's pool, 18, 25, 31, 69
    See also Kafka, Ernest: swimming
Switzerland, escaping over the border to, 51–52, 195–96

Tablas Creek, 299–300
talents and their consequences, 82–83
Tennessee Valley Authority (TVA), 116
theater, 93, 98, 109
    private, 191
thinking
    how it becomes more realistic, 461–62
    See also cognitive deficits
Thiokol, investing in, 243–45, 298, 403
Thomas, Lew, 224–25
Thomas, Y. Gregory, 298–99
thrombocytopenia, 164
Tino (driver), 392–93
    brother, 392–93
tonsillectomy, 35, 94, 104
topographic theory of the mind, Freud's, 321–25
training analysis and training analysts, 233, 337–39, 357, 471. *See also under* Kafka, Ernest: personal analyses
transference, 343, 344, 445–47, 475
    countertransference and, 437–38, 473, 475–76
    Freud on, 445, 446, 476, 482
    negative, 364, 481–82
    positive, 364, 481, 482, 489
    "unobjectionable," 476, 480, 482
Traubel, Helen, 155, 156
trauma, 168, 239, 363, 370, 429, 430, 449
    dealing actively vs. passively with, 40
    experienced by Ernest, 11, 39, 40, 196, 329, 405, 407, 419, 450–51
        1950s insomnia and nightmares as a result of 1938, 104 (*see also under* dreams of Ernest Kafka)
        first big trauma (*see* adenoidectomy; ether anaesthesia)
    psychoanalysis and, 321–23, 475, 482 (*see also* seduction theory)
    treatment, 321–23, 329, 348, 454, 482
    See also strain trauma/chronic trauma
traumatic "day residue," 39
traumatic dreams, 39. *See also* dreams of Ernest Kafka
traumatic effects
    of illness, 219
    of immigration, 451
    of medical treatment, 309, 407, 419, 449 (*see also* adenoidectomy; ether anaesthesia)
    modification of, 449–50

traumatic memories, 78, 423
tribalism, 41, 84, 86, 215, 216, 227.
  See also nationalism
trust, basic
  and evolution, 489–93
Tzappert, Terci, 21

unconscious. *See* topographic theory
  of the mind
unconscious pilot, 336–37
University of Music and Performing
  Arts Vienna (Vienna
  Conservatory), 15, 16, 33

Vallée, Brigitte de. *See* Altman,
  Brigitte de Vallée
Vallée, Patrice de, 295
Vermont, 90, 398
  first episode of endocarditis
    while in, 403–4
  summers in, 297, 360, 413, 436
  See also Newfane
Vienna, Austria
  apartment and neighborhood,
    17, 30–31
  Hitler and, 21, 22, 38
  so familiar yet strange, 191–92
Vienna Conservatory (University
  of Music and Performing Arts
  Vienna), 15, 16, 33
Vienna Philharmonic, 15–17, 484
vineyards, 298–300
Virginia Woof (dog), 390, 411
Vogue (magazine), 300–301

Wagner, Richard, 365
  Ernest and the Reisers' love of,
    359–60, 364, 365
  See also Siegfried
Wagner, Robert "Bob" (New York
  mayor), 186, 345
Waisenhaus (orphanage), 14–15, 59,
  71, 113, 142
  Adolf Kafka's experiences at, 59,
    71, 145
  Gustav von Springer and, 14,
    145
  Opah Hecht (great-grandfather)
    at, 15, 145
Washington University School of
  Medicine, 152, 154, 157, 158,
  301–2
  autopsies, 169–71
  Barbara Kafka enrolled in
    English department, 184,
    187, 203–6
  Carl Moore at, 158–59
  demographics of students, 215
  Ernest's acceptance at, 149, 151
  frightening experiences at,
    168–69
  graduation from, 240
  learning patience in diagnosis,
    167–68
Washington University School of
  Medicine faculty, 154–55, 158–
  59, 161–62, 345–46. *See also*
  doctors; medical school; medical
  schooling: of Ernest Kafka
Weiss, Adolf, 21, 23
Westport, Connecticut, 132, 155
  Poses's weekend house in,
    126–27, 132, 133, 137, 141,
    155, 185, 201, 211, 307–8,
    382, 384
Whiting, Barlett, 118, 124
Wienerisch jokes, 75–76
wine, 297–98, 433
wineries, 299–300
Wolteger, Fritzi Kafka, 69

Wolteger, Oscar, 69, 99
women and psychoanalysis, 468
Wood, W. Barry, 158–59
Woof (dog), 390, 411
Wooster, Francis ("Frank") George Leyland, 42, 57, 143
Wooster, Liliane (Mary's daughter), 143
Wooster, Marie-Cecile ("Mary"/"Mitzi"/"Frau Baronin") Fould-Springer, 143, 144, 147, 193, 307, 366
  Barbara Kafka and, 146, 307
  family background, 15, 42, 54, 57, 146, 148 (*see also* Fould-Springer family)
  marriage to Eugène Fould, 57, 143, 146
  marriage to Frank Wooster, 15, 25, 42, 57, 143
  overview, 57
  photograph of, 268f
  relatives of Ernest protected by, 14, 25
  Royaumont and, 54, 143–44
  and the Sterns, 51
  visiting, 54, 143, 146, 198

work and love. *See* personal life and professional life
World War I, 18, 20, 26, 29, 115, 140
  Adolf Kafka and, 22
  Ernest and, 93, 115
  films about, 93
  Fritz Kafka and, 55
  Mami Stern and, 16
World War II, 115, 144, 244, 316
  adapting to America during, 86–88
  Edward Snider in, 296
  France and, 49, 145, 242
  Nazi invasion of Austria, 21, 38–39
  political acumen and influence of the Springers during, 145–48
"Wound-Dresser, The" (Whitman), 219
Wurstelprater, 34, 191
Wyld, Andrew, 379, 380
Wyld, Christie, 380

Yamasaki, Minoru, 153
Young Men's Hebrew Association (YMHA/"the Y"), 376, 377

www.ingramcontent.com/pod-product-compliance
Lightning Source LLC
Chambersburg PA
CBHW071948110526
44592CB00012B/1031